D1034154

Critical Essays on Vladimir Nabokov

Critical Essays on Vladimir Nabokov

Phyllis A. Roth

G. K. Hall & Co. • Boston, Massachusetts

Library of Congress Cataloging in Publication Data
Main entry under title:
Critical essays on Vladimir Nabokov.
(Critical essays on American literature)
Annotated bibliography of Nabokov criticism,
by B.L. Clark: p. 222
Includes index.
1. Nabokov, Vladimir Vladimirovich, 1899–1977—
Criticism and interpretation—Addresses, essays, lectures.
I. Roth, Phyllis A. II. Series.
PS3527.1A5Z67 1984 813'.54 83-18671
ISBN 0-8161-8678-2

CRITICAL ESSAYS ON AMERICAN LITERATURE

This series seeks to anthologize the most important criticism on a wide variety of topics and writers in American literature. Our readers will find in various volumes not only a generous selection of reprinted articles and reviews but original essays, bibliographies, manuscript sections, and other materials brought to public attention for the first time. Phyllis Roth's volume on Vladimir Nabokov is a welcome addition to our list in that it is the most comprehensive collection of criticism ever published on this important writer. Among the twenty-nine essays are three early comments translated from Russian for this volume, an essay by Claude Mouchard translated from French, and reprinted essays by John Updike, Diana Butler, and Simon Karlinsky, among others. There is also a revised review by Joyce Carol Oates and original articles by Carl Eichelberger, Roger B. Salomon, D. Barton Johnson, Ellen Pifer, and Beverly Lyon Clark. In addition, Professor Roth has written an extensive introduction that surveys the history of scholarship on Nabokov. We are confident that this collection will make a permanent and significant contribution to American literary study.

James Nagel, General Editor

Northeastern University

For Tom

CONTENTS

INTRODUCTION

When Jackson R. Bryer and Thomas J. Bergin, Jr. produced their "Vladimir Nabokov's Critical Reputation in English: A Note and a Checklist" for the Spring 1967 issue of *Wisconsin Studies in Contemporary Literature*,[1] they observed that "the single most notable—and deplorable—characteristic of Nabokov criticism is the disproportionate amount of attention devoted to *Lolita* and the resultant lack of serious comment on the other fiction, poetry, and translations." Moreover, in their view, "most of the serious and incisive commentary has appeared in the form of book reviews. . . . There is a great dearth of worthwhile critical essays. . . . Nabokov simply has not yet been 'discovered' by the critical quarterlies. . . ." Fortunately, this assessment is no longer accurate. In the ten years between the appearance of the checklist and Nabokov's death at the age of seventy-seven, Nabokov completed three novels in English, in addition to the five already published, the "Englishing" of the three remaining Russian novels previously untranslated, as well as several other major works; in the sixteen years since 1967, a major body of Nabokov criticism and scholarship has emerged, including—in addition to reviews of each new publication—over twenty book-length studies devoted exclusively to Nabokov, and at least as many more that focus on Nabokov among others, more than sixty dissertations, many devoted exclusively to Nabokov, several collections of essays on Nabokov, including special issues of critical journals, and scores of essays in English alone on Nabokov's fiction.

Vladimir Nabokov's biography is unlike that of any other American author. Born in Russia in 1899, forced by the Revolution to flee his homeland in 1919, exiled in England, Germany, and France from the land of the language in which he first wrote—though he spoke English fluently from childhood—Nabokov wrote nine novels in Russian before being compelled again to emigrate. Having already written his first novel in English, *The Real Life of Sebastian Knight*, Nabokov came to write in America in 1940 at the age of forty-one and spent subsequent years becoming an American writer.[2] He is, then, both a Russian and an American writer, the two dimensions now inseparable in his fiction.[3] In addition to the nine Russian novels, now all translated into English, as well as a score of other languages, and eight novels written in English, Nabokov published collections of short stories and poems; a number of important translations, including translations of Lewis Carroll's *Alice in Wonderland* (1923) and his own *Lolita* into Russian, and the ferociously controversial "literal" translation into English of Pushkin's *Eugene Onegin*; letters and interviews; reviews and critical essays; dramas and scenarios, including his screenplay of *Lolita*; and, most recently, the three volumes of lectures on literature Nabokov prepared for his classes at Wellesley, Harvard, and Cornell, magnificently edited by Fredson Bowers.

Although Nabokov's works have not always received sympathetic treatment, increasingly they have enjoyed deserved critical acclaim. Even the earliest reviewers and critics in English applauded the awesome descriptive powers, precision of language, startling imagery, and lexical play that comprise his "stylistic signature."[4] However, the history of Nabokov criticism is marked by passionate disagreement and profound discomfort, a measure in part at least of Nabokov's unique talents and disposition. As Carl Proffer observes, "Few writers require more of their audience . . . [an ideal reader who] would be a literary scholar trained and widely read in several European languages, a Sherlock Holmes, a first-rate poet, and the possessor of an eidetic memory."[5] Indeed, those critics who first approached his earliest novels written in English confronted basic reading problems despite, or often because of, the dazzling play of language and detail, as well as the extended and parodic treatment of other fictions within his novels. Most significantly for both the comprehension of individual novels and for the development of thinking about Nabokov's art in general, some critics' discomfort has derived from their reading of the author's presence as an especially antagonistic and arrogant absence: that is, Nabokov's deliberate exposure of his narrative artifice, his foregrounding of technique, in combination with a narrational detachment from his characters' pain and, frequently, madness, has been read as a failure of humanity. More, this detachment, or coolness, is often read as arrogance toward his readers and described as a lack of morality or human sympathy in his works. Attempting to invest the works with a more human presence, some critics compounded their difficulties by identifying Nabokov with his characters and reading the fiction as autobiography. Moreover, crucial difficulties—and opportunities—for interpretation are created by the "polylingual matrix"[6] of the writing: not only is Nabokov's language highly allusive, the allusions entail the lexicons and literatures of several languages and often generate (realistic) anxiety on the part of critics. Additional sources of readers' discomfort are readily enumerated: Nabokov's strictures about how to read, typically prefacing each novel like a shark-infested castle moat; the scope of Nabokov's knowledge and the corresponding allusiveness of the fiction, not only to literature, but also to science—in particular, of course, lepidopterology; and the brilliance of his manipulation of narration, one talent about which critics have been in increasing agreement.

Additional problems derive from the current unsatisfactory state of bibliographic data. The most comprehensive primary bibliography to date is Andrew Field's *Nabokov: A Bibliography*,[7] superceding the one appearing in his *Nabokov: His Life in Art*[8] and a 1963 compilation, revised in 1964, by Nabokov's German translator, Dieter E. Zimmer. However, Field's dating of a number of Nabokov's writings during the émigré period has been challenged by Michael Juliar who promises a corrected and updated bibliography to be published possibly as early as 1984.[9] Field's bibliography has been emended in issues of the *Vladimir Nabokov Research Newsletter*, edited by Stephen Jan Parker, which also has published additional bibliographic items made available by Véra Nabokov, as well as a complete list of Nabokoviana in containers in the Library of Congress.

Despite these difficulties, since the 1960s Nabokov's readers have begun to learn the lessons he taught his students, with the result that the relationships between author and characters, between a central theme of art and the deranged if poetic visions of his lunatics and lovers, between Nabokov and a number of literary traditions, and even between Nabokov as aesthete and Nabokov as humanist,[10] are far more clearly and sensitively defined now than they were at the end of the 1960s when Bryer and Bergin observed that Nabokov scholarship did not afford a measure of Nabokov's achievement or reputation. Vladimir Nabokov is now widely recognized as one of the finest and most influential writers of the twentieth century.

Critical response to Nabokov's writing during the thirty years preceding 1955, when *Lolita* was first published in Paris, can be divided into two groups: that of the émigré communities in Berlin and Paris and that of the earliest reactions of Anglo-American critics to Nabokov's first works in English. Throughout *Nabokov: His Life in Art*, Andrew Field provides summaries of émigré reaction to the early publications, including the first translations of sections of several reviews. Additionally, two scholarly essays provide English readers access to the émigré communities' reactions to V. Sirin, Nabokov's major *nom de plume*,[11] describing the publishing history of the early novels and stories and annotating a substantial number of the reviews published in the émigré journals in which most of Sirin's novels were first serialized: Ludmila A. Foster's "Nabokov in Russian Émigré Criticism" and Marina T. Naumann's "Nabokov as Viewed by Fellow Émigrés."[12]

Additionally, several of the most important émigré reviews of Sirin are now available in English translations. Appearing in the present volume for the first time, in translations by Marina Naumann, are a 1926 review of *Mary* by Mikhail Osorgin; a 1927 review of Nabokov's story

"Terror" by Iulii Isaevich Aikhenval'd; and a 1929 review of the collection of stories, *The Return of Chorb*, by A. Savel'ev. These reviews are among the first responses to Nabokov, written prior to his becoming well-known in émigré circles; as such, they are of special historical interest. More, each suggests a view of the work of Sirin to which American critics have come, but only after a far greater exposure to Nabokov's art than that afforded his first reviewers. Osorgin applauds the "absence of all political tendentiousness," what Nabokov called "topical trash"; Aikhenval'd recognizes the tension depicted in Sirin's work between the temptation of the imagination and the necessity for acknowledging reality. Emphasizing Sirin's joyous, even pious, appreciation of life, Savel'ev discusses the relation established between nature's tricks and those of art; the "special ways" the past and "Russia penetrate his pages"; and the by now famous "mocking smile" which Savel'ev believes to be necessary to Sirin's artistic vision. All three critics applaud Sirin's sharp eye and precise verbal evocation of detail. Two additional émigré reviews are reprinted here: Andrew Field's versions[13] of Nikolay Andreyev's stunning survey review of the early Nabokov novels and Vladimir Weidle's brief but important reading of Sirin's central theme. Several other translations of early reviews have been published in recent years, the most significant and influential of which is that of Vladislav Khodasevich's "On Sirin,"[14] the 1937 review which anticipated by at least twenty-five years the best of Nabokov criticism written in English.

The émigré reviews of Sirin bear some fascinating correspondences to later American reviews, confirming the existence both of a number of characteristic reader responses and of themes, techniques, and problems in Nabokov's work from the beginning of his career. As the Foster and Naumann essays make clear, émigré readers responded as passionately—and with as much disagreement—as American readers were to do twenty and thirty years later. Moreover, the subjects of discussion were very much the same: for example, the significance of memory and the experience of exile; the question of Nabokov's literary progenitors; and the sensuous detail and technical mastery of the fiction but what many saw as the spiritual emptiness of the plot. Most fruitfully, several émigré critics argued that the artist is the central figure in Sirin's fiction and, as Vladimir Weidle perceived it, that the plot derives from the conflict between the artist's creations and the recalcitrant material of "reality." Khodasevich elaborates this view, providing an analysis of the form of Nabokov's work that has become a cornerstone of Nabokov criticism: for Khodasevich, Sirin's "brilliance . . . catches everyone's eye . . . because Sirin not only does not mask, does not hide his devices . . . but . . . places them in full view like a magician who, having amazed his audience, reveals on the very spot the laboratory of his miracles."[15] In Khodasevich's view, all Nabokov's heroes are artists in disguise, and Khodasevich himself brilliantly anticipated—in 1937—the direction Nabokov's fiction would take, concluding his review with the prediction "that Sirin, who has at his disposal a wide range of caustic observations, will some day give himself rein and favor us with a merciless satiric portrayal of a writer."[16]

Two other émigré critics, writing twenty years after Khodasevich, represent other important and recurrent views about Nabokov's art. In "The Double Life of Russian Literature," Gleb Struve distinguishes between two lines of Russian literature which resulted from the 1917–20 Revolution—Soviet Literature written inside the U.S.S.R. and émigré literature—and traces their development through the ensuing decades. Further distinguishing between two generations of émigré writers, he argues that "The most original . . . was Vladimir Nabokov . . . [about whom] the majority [of critics] agreed . . . that they had to do with a writer of great originality, completely outside the Russian tradition, without any literary ancestry at all."[17] On the other hand, in his "Vladimir Nabokov," Georgij Adamovich treats Nabokov harshly, condemning the lack of what he calls a "soul" in either characters, narrators, or, most important, Nabokov himself.[18] While all major perspectives on Nabokov afforded by members of the émigré community have engendered further study and debate, perhaps none has been so wrongheaded and so tenacious as the accusation of aestheticism leveled by Adamovich and many others after him. For example, a *TLS* reviewer was to maintain in 1961 that "there is no writer in English today who in sheer literary talent is Mr. Nabokov's superior; more, that it would be hard to name his peer. If he is not what is termed a 'great' writer, it is for moral reasons: Mr. Nabokov does not take people seriously enough."[19] And Philip Rahv "recognizes in Nabokov something like a phobic fear [sic] of all critical techniques not strictly literary in reference . . . the radically one-sided approach of an extreme aesthete-modernist who takes the literary act to be a phenomenon solely 'of language and not of ideas.' "[20]

However, the most fruitful and persuasive interpretations of Nabokov's art have been written by those who are able to account for, indeed, to synthesize, the "aethetic" dimension—the games, the allusions, the boisterous verbal wit, the narrative self-consciousness and reflexivity—with Nabokov's humanism. For example, in his review of *King, Queen, Knave*, Alfred Appel argues:

> Some readers . . . may feel that works that are in part about themselves are limited in range and significance, too special, too hermetic. But the creative process is fundamental; perhaps nothing is *more* personal by implication and hence more relevant than fictions concerning fiction; identity, after all, is a kind of artistic construct, however imperfect the created product. If the artist does indeed embody in himself and formulate in his work the fears and needs and desires of the race, then a story about his mastery of form, his triumph in art is but a heightened emblem of all of our own efforts to confront, order, and structure the chaos of life, and to endure, if not master, the demons within and around us.[21]

As artist and lepidopterist, Nabokov delighted in the various metamorphoses undergone by his works. In his foreword to the 1966 revised edition of *Speak, Memory: An Autobiography Revisited*, he observes gleefully: "This re-Englishing of a Russian re-version of what had been an English re-telling of Russian memories in the first place, proved to be a diabolical task, but some consolation was given me by the thought that such multiple metamorphosis, familiar to butterflies, had not been tried by any human before."[22] In addition to the metamorphoses undergone by several other of Nabokov's works, the history of critical response, in at least two languages, to Sirin/Nabokov reveals an analogous metamorphosis, since Nabokov began the "re-versions" of his Russian novels while writing his novels in English: whereas the Russian critics read the first nine novels in chronological order, many English-reading critics have read both these novels and several of those written in English counterclockwise, so to speak, a trick on time Nabokov doubtless appreciated.

There were, however, a few English and American readers who reviewed Nabokov's first novels. Those interested in tracing the history of response to Nabokov from this period have available to them several bibliographies of secondary material. The 1967 checklist by Bryer and Bergin, with its particularly extensive listings of newspaper and journal reviews, should be supplemented by those in the annual volumes of the *Book Review Digest*, as well as in other compendia of reviews.[23] The most substantial compilation and annotation of critical response to Nabokov, primarily though not exclusively in English, is Samuel Schuman's *Vladimir Nabokov: A Reference Guide.*[24] Schuman's bibliography includes, in his words, casual citations, news stories, reviews, studies of individual works, studies of specific themes, as well as general studies. Entries are listed chronologically, up to and including a partial listing for 1977, with lucid and succinct annotations, obviating the necessity of providing such a compilation in the present volume.

As Schuman indicates, probably the earlist discussion of Sirin in the United States appears in an essay by Albert Parry in the July 1933 issue of the *American Mercury.* Entitled "Belles Lettres Among the Russian Émigrés," Parry's essay contains what now seem highly ironic assertions, such as his claim that "There are no Joseph Conrads among [the younger émigrés]," and that "it is best for them to write in their own language, and not risk excursions into the French, German, and English"; nonetheless, Parry is to be credited with a very early recognition of the importance of Russian émigré writing and for his argument that Sirin, Aldanov, and Berberova "bear watching and deserve translation."[25]

The first of Nabokov's novels translated into English were *Despair*[26] and *Camera Obscura.*[27] I have located no reviews in English of the early edition of *Despair*, but *Laughter in the Dark* (Nabokov's title for his 1938 translation of *Camera Obscura*) did garner some response. Writing for the *New Yorker*, Clifton Fadiman introduces the novel dramatically as "A first-rate thriller with clever psychological trimmings and an atmosphere combining Chekhovian lassitude with surrealist degeneracy. . . ."[28] *Saturday Review*'s Samuel Nock sounds several notes later to become major chords in American criticism, saying that "Looking at his characters, all foolish or bad, with ironical detachment, but without cynicism, [Nabokov] presents them and their idiocies with grace and urbanity . . . without getting himself involved at all."[29] And Harold Strauss's review, the first to be published in the *New York Times* as far as I can determine, makes an accusation which has been perennially leveled at Nabokov: "*Laughter in the Dark* is a deft performance which cannot be called more than deft only because Mr. Nabokoff has no real sympathy for any of his characters."[30]

Several years after the initial English appearances of *Laughter*, Nabokov entered the "third arc"[31] of his existence, emigrating to the United States in 1940 and publishing his first novel written in English, *The Real Life of Sebastian Knight* (1941). The pre-*Lolita* response to Nabokov reveals an audience rather unprepared to come to terms in any great detail with Nabokov's themes and compositional strategies. However, the enormously divergent opinions articulated in these early reviews are those which recur with each newly published Nabokov novel, representing passionate disputes never dispelled by enhanced sophistication. For example, Walter Allen observes of *Sebastian Knight*, "one is merely left, as with Pirandello, thinking, 'It's all done with mirrors,' and with the feeling of depression that technical virtuosity unaccompanied by adequate content so often induces."[32] Equally proleptic of later though quite different response is a review by Kay Boyle, one of the first of many novelists to write about Nabokov. Boyle finds *Sebastian Knight* to be "told with a brilliancy, a delicacy and a grave and exquisitely venomous humor which make it a delight to read."[33]

Nabokov's study *Nikolai Gogol* was first published in 1944. Not widely reviewed, the attention it did receive was positive, Babette Deutsch remarking clairvoyantly on a "sharply individual" approach to the subject which would "attract [students] by its remoteness from the chalk-dusty atmosphere of the lecture halls."[34] It is *de rigeur* these days to concur with Bernard Guilbert Guernay, one of Gogol's translators, that "Nabokov may be said to have created his own Gogol, adding one more to his phantasmal gallery of 'strange creatures.' . . ."[35] And, all reviewers at the time agreed that the most obvious and distorting, if characteristic, way in which Nabokov did this was to deny Gogol "his academic accretions as 'realist,' and 'social satirist,' as 'the Russian Dickens. . . .' "[36] Only Edmund Wilson accedes to Nabokov's view that, if Gogol is a realist, he is "a long way . . . from the familiar Russian realism . . . [rather, he] is primarily a poet."[37]

Nabokov's second novel in English and the first he wrote in America, *Bend Sinister* (1947),[38] has received some important critical attention recently, primarily focusing on the narrator as "an anthropomorphic deity impersonated by me," as Nabokov describes himself in his introduction, and on the relation between the political and aesthetic themes of the novel,[39] most explicitly articulated here and in *Invitation to a Beheading*. While the early reviews of *Bend Sinister* are understandably not as sophisticated as later treatments, they do reflect a considerable advance in the recognition of Nabokov's special talents, developing comparisons of his art to that of Joyce, Kafka (inaugurating a long-standing debate about the possible influence of Kafka on Nabokov), Gogol, and Flaubert. More fully appreciative of Nabokov's language than most other early readers, a *Time* reviewer calls the novel "a lip-smacking over the flavors of English prose to rouse the tired syntax in 10,000 editorials, . . . rapid, brilliantly metaphorical, daintily savage and smooth." More, while others find the treatment of Krug callous, this reviewer recognizes that "The secret of *Bend Sinister*'s effect is that it places side by side, heightened by the selectivity of an adept and angry writer, the most moronic abominations of totalitarianism and the finest lights of the secular European mind. . . . When the Ekwilist State triumphs, murdering innocence, Nabokov's style is still playful, but it takes on a Swiftian intensity. . . ."[40]

When Nabokov published the first stage of his much metamorphosed autobiography, entitled *Conclusive Evidence—A Memoir* (1951),[41] reviewers were quick to observe resemblances between Nabokov and Proust, agreeing too that there is no bitterness in Nabokov's portrayal of his lost childhood, that "No other Russian writer has recreated [that world] in all its magic and all its perversities as has Vladimir Nabokov."[42] Moreover, they found the strength of the memoir in its poetry. For Marc Slonim *Conclusive Evidence* "has no unity of plot or narration; it presents episodes, characters and scenery in a succession of kaleidoscopic flashes, and the unity it does achieve is that of a poetic whole."[43]

In the following year, Nabokov's Russian novel *Dar* (*The Gift*) was first published in its entirety, but it was only reviewed by American critics when Nabokov published the English translation in 1963; by then Nabokov had become well-known indeed, for by then the stories in *Pnin* published in the *New Yorker* had been collected and expanded into a novel first published by Doubleday in 1957, and by then *Lolita* had burst on American shores having first created a furor in France and England.

Alone among Nabokov protagonists, Pnin engaged the wholehearted sympathy of the reviewers. As a result, unfortunately, some were lulled into complacency not only about the structure of the novel—about its texture—but also about the overall effect and, especially, about the narration,[44] Granville Hicks sounding a battle cry when he describes the novel as "a series of loosely related episodes."[45] An important exception is Victor Lange whose review in the *New Republic* suggests to readers that the novel is more than a padded version of the several chapters previously published, that Nabokov's vision of the particular object or incident defies facile generalizations, that "the resonance of this world is immeasurably extended and enhanced by the discrete yet delicious strategy by which Mr. Nabokov, through a gradually more implicated narrator, reports on Pnin."[46]

The first reviews of *Lolita* in the United States were primarily preoccupied with three issues: its publishing history and difficulties; the question of pornography;[47] and the question of whether critics (the others, of course) could separate their evaluation of the novel from their outrage at its being considered pornography.[48] Subsequent to these responses were those whose aim was to determine what the novel was really about. Harry Levin is often quoted as having said that the novel is "a symbol of the aging European intellectual coming to America, falling in love with it but finding it, sadly, a little immature." Others, on the contrary, have found it to be about young America seducing old Europe. Equally allegorically, Elizabeth Janeway argues that Nabokov "is writing about all lust."[49] In his now famous essay, Lionel Trilling argues the opposite, that *Lolita* is not about sex or lust, but about the passion love described by Denis de Rougement (see Beverly Clark's discussion of Trilling in the present volume). John Hollander contends that "*Lolita*, if it is anything '*really*,' is the record of Mr. Nabokov's love affair with the romantic novel . . . ,"[50] in response to which Nabokov commented that "The substitution 'English language' for 'romantic novel' would make this elegant formula more correct."[51]

Clearly, critical response to *Lolita* shares the dominant characteristic of Nabokov criticism as a whole: its extremes. Orville Prescott argues that "There are two equally serious reasons why it isn't worth any adult reader's attention. The first is that it is dull, dull in a pretentious, florid and archly fatuous fashion. The second is that it is repulsive."[52] Others, however, find in *Lolita* that "Scene after scene that might be tedious or unpleasant becomes under [Nabokov's] conjuring hand uproariously funny."[53] Despite the wide divergence of opinion, the initial responses to *Lolita*'s appearance in the U.S. set the critical stage for a much larger role for Nabokov than he previously enjoyed. While it may have seemed at the time that *Lolita* made Nabokov only notorious, in fact, from this point on the reviews of Nabokov's publications increased in number, length, and sensitivity and, albeit gradually, scholarly journals began to afford critics space to consider Nabokov's fiction at length. Moreover, the recognition achieved by *Lolita* prompted the first of several special issues of journals devoted to Nabokov: the March 12, 1959, issue (Vol. 4, No. 5) of *Geste*, published in England at the University of Leeds. Only twenty pages in all, containing brief discussions of *Speak, Memory* and *Pnin* and four short pieces on *Lolita*, the issue is noteworthy for its recognition of Nabokov as a major literary figure.

Reprinted in 1960, *The Real Life of Sebastian Knight* enjoyed a post-*Lolita* rediscovery, though some reviewers saw its only interest "as a retrospective companion-piece to *Lolita*."[54] However, others, often also considering *Invitation to a Beheading* published the year before, reveal a more serious and sophisticated attitude toward Nabokov's achievements, indeed, a fully committed attempt to explain the secret life of the novels.[55] One reviewer observes of *Invitation*, for example, "what brings it off is the familiar Nabokov mixture of exactly visualized everyday detail—every hair on the hare—filtered through a nightmare fantasy that is indeed earned on every page."[56] And John Wain's sensitive review in the *New Republic* marks a point in Nabokov's publishing history in English when critics felt able to attempt general assessments of the corpus. Wain makes one of the earliest observations of the significance of memory and of the hatred of tyranny in Nabokov's work and draws some provocative distinctions: "I don't . . . want to present a picture of Nabokov as a mere aesthetic trifler. He may not be very interested in opinions, but a strong set of attitudes is clearly visible in his work, and the fatiguing, cloying flavor of his books is due more to an over-elaborate surface than to an inner emptiness."[57]

Bend Sinister, published originally in New York in 1947, was reissued in England in 1960. The responses of a small number of British reviewers indicate the way in which the morality—or lack of it—of Nabokov's art is often perceived. Malcolm Bradbury calls the novel "a moral fable told in an amoral voice," objecting to the "rhetorical zest" with which Nabokov treats Krug's tragedy.[58] Providing the most thoroughgoing rejection of Nabokov I have read, W. L. Webb laments "the contemplation of sadism and violence" in both *Lolita* and *Bend Sinister* and asserts that, "The violence, perverseness, and relentless exhibitionism of the style are as radically anti-art as the interests on which it feeds are anti-life."[59] But Frank Kermode directly confronts the alienation Nabokov forces on his reader and, employing an extended and extremely effective comparison between Laurence Sterne and Nabokov, illustrates the "rigorous subordination of all these stunts and rhetorical exercises to the shape of the whole."[60]

Viewed by some as Nabokov's—or Kinbote's—revenge on readers of *Lolita*, *Pale Fire* (1962) generated fewer responses but no less heated a debate than did *Lolita*. Dwight Macdonald "sensed a perverse bravado, as if the author, with a superior smile, is saying to the large reading public that read *Lolita*: 'So you think I'm a manufacturer of best-sellers? Try *this* on your pianola!' "[61] Macdonald is responding in part to Mary McCarthy's now famous and widely read review; both Macdonald and Frank Kermode[62] appreciate McCarthy's illumination of the text; however, they adamantly oppose her description of *Pale Fire* as "a creation of perfect beauty, symmetry, strangeness, originality and moral truth"; from them comes the by now familiar "complaint against cleverness . . . when it becomes disconnected from meaning, when the virtuoso becomes so proficient at his instrument that his delight in showing off its qualities goes beyond the artistic purpose technique is supposed to serve."[63] Another important critic who shares this view of *Pale Fire* is George Steiner who, while seeing in its "secret core" the "lament for language lost" that he elaborates in his *Extraterritorial*,[64] finally finds the novel "a pedantic witticism spun out at great length and solemnity."[65] All readers do agree about the novel's difficulty, however, as described by Donald Malcolm in his excellent review in the *New Yorker*.[66]

The next of Nabokov's novels to appear was *The Gift* (1963), a translation of the Russian *Dar*,[67] a long, dense, highly allusive novel explicitly tracing the growth of an artist in exile from the land of his language. Now widely recognized to be one of the more important of Nabokov's fictional works—probably the most important of his Russian novels—and seen as highly autobiographical, *The Gift* is so Russian in its context and allusions, though concerned with the place and role of the émigré writer, that it has received less critical attention than it deserves. Nonetheless, the initial reception accorded *The Gift* resembles that received by most of Nabokov's fiction, with reviews by Hilary Corke and Donald Malcolm being the only ones worth returning to now.[68]

In 1964, Nabokov published both the first version of his translation of *Eugene Onegin* with its huge commentary and the English translation of his third Russian novel, *The Defense* (called *The Luzhin Defense* in its *New Yorker* serialization). The *Onegin* touched off an explosive critical war—still being waged by Dimitri Nabokov—about the nature of translation and about *Onegin*'s previous translations, Nabokov himself sounding the call to arms in a review assaulting the Walter Arndt translation published just prior to his own. Shortly thereafter, Edmund Wilson escalated the battle with an attack on Nabokov's literal translation (see Beverly Clark's discussion of Nabokov and Wilson) and numerous others took up arms. While the arguments and history of this episode in Nabokov's career are of considerable scholarly interest, they have been discussed elsewhere: in particular, Andrew Field has devoted the better part of a chapter in *Nabokov: His Life in Art* to defining the terms of the debate, and both the Schuman and the Bryer and Bergin bibliographies list most of the participants in the combat.

Field sagely begins his review of *The Defense* with a comparison to *Pnin*, and several critics found Luzhin to be Nabokov's most likeable character after the endearing professor.[69] While others found the novel boring, the characters cardboard and sterile, there is more critical consensus about the achievements of this novel than has been evident so far. In fact, with this novel, several reviewers "rediscovered" Khodasevich's argument that Nabokov's heroes are all artists, albeit usually in disguise, a key which unlocked a number of essential doors to Nabokov's art. Malcolm Bradbury, for example, speculates that "*The Defense* is not only about the deprivation of order and meaning, but the aesthetic sources in which meaning and order can be, however dangerously, recovered."[70]

Two reviews of *The Defense* deserve special attention. John Updike's "Grandmaster Nabokov," the first in a series of brilliant review-appreciations of Nabokov Updike was to write through the years, is the most widely read review of the novel. Observing that Nabokov "writes prose the only way it should be written—that is, ecstatically,"[71] Updike takes on those critics who claim that Nabokov's art is all and only " 'virtuosity,' as if he is a verbal magician working with stuffed rabbits and hats nobody could wear. . . ." Updike agrees rather with those who find that the great success of the novel is in its characterization, especially its delineation of Luzhin's childhood and the juxtaposition of that childhood to his "chess-sodden adulthood [which] islands the childhood . . . so that, superimposed upon the grown figures, it operates as a kind of heart, as an abruptly doused light reddens the subsequent darkness."[72] In an equally important review, Robert M. Adams writes of *The Defense* in the context of Nabokov's Russian novels as a group, analyzing the relationships between the protagonists and the author of the novels, and between style and humanity in Nabokov's art.[73]

Soglyadataj, variously published (in Russian) as a novel in 1930, as a novella in a collection with the same title in 1938, and in its English incarnation as *The Eye* in 1965, has received less attention than any other of Nabokov's novels. Despite Nabokov's reputation by the time of its translation—and despite its initial publication in *Playboy*—so that a number of newspapers around the country did briefly review it, it was not widely read or appreciated[74] and, in fact, remains Nabokov's most obscure novel.

In 1966, Nabokov published *Despair*, a second and revised translation of the Russian *Otchayanie*, and the revised version of his memoir, now titled *Speak, Memory—An Autobiography Revisited. Nabokov: His Life in Art* includes a revision of Field's long review of *Despair*[75] which remains one of the richest readings the novel has received, including a brief history of the doppelgänger motif and an analysis of its uses here. As with *Despair*, the revision of Nabokov's memoirs generated more interest and received a considerably larger audience than the earlier incarnation,[76] critics unanimously applauding its stylistic beauty and evocativeness. For John Updike, "Nabokov has never written English better than in these reminiscences; never since has he written so sweetly. With tender precision and copious wit, exploiting a vocabulary and a sensibility enriched by the methodical pursuit of lepidoptera, inspired by an atheist's faith in the magic of simile and the sacredness of lost time, Nabokov makes of his past a brilliant ikon—bejeweled, perspectiveless, untouchable."[77] However, only Alfred Appel suggested at the time[78] that close analysis of *Speak, Memory* reveals a careful—and artful—structure; only V. S. Pritchett perceived what the memoir may have meant for Nabokov himself, arguing that "for the exile, the man with the Nansen passport, to establish the past is an imperative";[79] few have suggested substantive connections between the memoir and the fiction.[80]

Published in 1968, *King, Queen, Knave*, originally Nabokov's second Russian novel, was widely acclaimed despite the familiar critical disagreement between those who find the book's virtues in its narrative strategy and lexical play, laying bare the artifice of fiction, and those who find it heartless.[81] Some wisely see in it the parody of literary conventions or formulas which Nabokov continued to exploit. Denis Donoghue, for instance, points out that the parody subverts "the procedures of the Love Story (*Anna Karenina*), the Psychological Story (*Madame Bovary*), the Murder Story (any one) and the Bedroom Comedy (any one)."[82]

While it is the case that Nabokov's American readers, in increasing numbers by the time *King, Queen, Knave* was published, had learned to read his fiction with skill and sensitivity, the publication in 1969 of the monumental *Ada* sent many reeling. (A *TLS* reviewer described *Ada* as "clearly the author's Waterloo: it is less clear whether he figures as Wellington or Napoleon.")[83] Several major elements of the novel are responsible for the pained reaction even among some of Nabokov's most devoted American critics: the fusion of the Russian with the American author, much as in the novel Russia and America become Amerussia, thereby requiring, as Simon Karlinsky demonstrates in "Nabokov's Russian Games,"[84] considerable background in Russian literature, as well as European; the linguistic exuberances, even excesses, which constitute the text; the ambiguity of Van Veen as the novel's nasty and lewd though evidently not mad "hero" and primary narrator; and the presence of Van's long, philosophical treatise on "The Texture of Time." However, despite these extraordinary difficulties, *Ada* touched off an avalanche of critical attention, the best review written by Robert Alter, one of Nabokov's finest readers. Alter's analysis of Nabokov's use of Marvell's "The Garden" is especially brilliant, demonstrating the connections between what might seem to be joking and passing references and the thematic center of the novel: "the interinvolvement of art and pleasure transcending time."[85] With one or two exceptions, *Ada* is typically and rightly read as both more quintessentially—or excessively—Nabokovian than *Lolita* or *Pale Fire*: with these two earlier novels, however, *Ada* is likely to stand as constituting the supreme "triptych of bottomless light" that is Nabokov's art.

The first post-*Lolita* critical essays began to appear in the late 1950s with Leslie Fiedler's early recognition of Nabokov as belonging to an Anglo-American literary tradition. In one of a series of essays published in the *New Leader* in 1958, Fiedler says of *Lolita*, "In a single work, Richardson, Dickens and Henry James are controverted, all customary symbols for the encounter of innocence and experience stood on their heads. Nowhere are the myths of sentimentality more amusing and convincingly parodied. . . ." Indeed, Fiedler suggests that *Lolita* was banned not for pornography but for apostasy: "It is the final blasphemy against the cult of the child"; more, that "it is the naive child . . . the American who corrupts the sophisticated adult. . . . [It is the child who is] rapist, murderer, seducer."[86] In his preface to excerpts from *Lolita* published in the *Anchor Review 2* (1957), F. W. Dupee argues, unlike Fiedler, that Humbert's sensibility is the center of the novel and that "of course [Humbert] did betray [Lolita] unspeakably. It did not constitute any justification of Humbert that she was his willing mistress at first and already knew the ropes."[87] Several years later, Denis de Rougement offered another approach. In "New Metamorphoses of Tristan" in his *Love Declared: Essays on the Myths of Love*, de Rougement defines passion as "that form of love which refuses the immediate, avoids dealing with what is near, and if necessary invents distance in order to realize and exalt itself more completely,"[88] and applies this definition to Humbert's nympholepsy. Given his definition of passion, de Rougement is able to explain the apparently dual focus in *Lolita* on the girl and on American popular culture: "this ambiguity . . . expresses and irresistibly translates the fundamental ambiguity of passion, antisocial by definition, hence linked to the social milieu by a permanent strife without which it would not exist. . . ."[89]

Despite these different approaches, almost a decade after its first publication, critics had failed to interpret *Lolita* in a convincing way from within the framework of Nabokov's work, rather than by means of an extrinsic system, such as the myths of passion-love or of childhood innocence. However, in 1960, an essay appeared which enabled readers to appreciate a motif which pervades all of Nabokov's fiction; cited throughout Appel's notes in *The Annotated Lolita*, Diana Butler's "Lolita Lepidoptera"[90] has not been readily available; it is published here for the first time since its original appearance. And, in 1964 two essays were published which signaled a new comprehension of the Nabokovian text and had important implications for all Nabokov scholarship. In "*Lolita*: Parody and the Pursuit of Beauty," G. D. Josipovici develops the line of analysis begun by Khodasevich: the central character is a type of artist, the journey of the hero provides a lesson in discovering the gap between the real world and the imagined and in learning the limits of one's art. Moreover, "the memoir, like Proust's *A la recherche du temps perdu*, spirals in upon itself being at once the history of how it came to be written and the outcome of that history, at once the problem and the solution, at once the quest and the goal. For the goal is the quest transmuted into language."[91] In "Vladimir Nabokov's Great Spiral of Being,"[92] L. L. Lee goes beyond Josipovici to offer an explication of what might be called Nabokov's philosophy—of time and timelessness, form and subject in art. Using Nabokov's image of the spiral to reveal the structure of time and plotting with particular attention to *Pale Fire*, Lee explains that Nabokov includes his own experiences in his fiction not autobiographically but dramatically, portraying the drama of imagination transforming memory to create timelessness.

Another of Nabokov's most intelligent critics during these years was R. H. W. Dillard, whose "Not Text, But Texture" provides clear and succinct readings of a number of the novels. Also echoing Khodasevich and Weidle, Dillard argues that "The central figure of Nabokov's novels is the artist, the man of sensitivity and imagination. Hero and dragon alike dream the creative dream and either shape that dream into immutable art or are destroyed by it in a mutable world. . . ."[93] Dillard's description immediately brings *Pale Fire* to mind and, also in 1966, Jay Arnold Levine published an essay on "The Design of *A Tale of a Tub* (with a Digression on a Mad Modern Critic)." The "Digression" is an important discussion of *Pale Fire* whose "deliberate details and . . . essential spirit and manner [constitute] a bright after-glow of Pope and Swift,"[94] even a "neoclassical" sensibility characterized by "rage for structural order, for symmetry, for the literary tradition, and for the craft of writing."[95] Also available in the 1960s was Simon Karlinsky's superb discussion[96] of both the structure and the literary criticism in *The Gift* (*Dar*), demonstrating the range of Nabokov's erudition and the precision, not only of his use of language and detail, but—less frequently observed—of elaborate and meticulously planned large structures.

In 1964, the second special journal number devoted to Nabokov appeared, this time in France. Intended to offer readers an introduction to Nabokov, this issue of *L'Arc* (24 [Spring 1964]) includes, in addition to translations of a fragment of *Pale Fire* and the story "Cloud, Castle, Lake," brief scholarly pieces[97] and a detailed primary bibliography.

The first books on Nabokov began to appear in 1966 with Page Stegner's *Escape into Aesthetics*. While this study has the virtue of a healthy irreverence for some of Nabokov's more outrageous pronouncements, it is both thin (much of the analysis of individual novels is, in fact, plot summary) and confused: on the one hand, Nabokov's fiction is an "escape into aesthetics, into art and the creation of beauty through language,"[98] aesthetics being "a virtual religion for Nabokov";[99] on the other, the games of the novels have what Stegner calls "philosophical application." Stegner deserves notice, and did in fact receive gratitude from other critics at the time, for attempting the first book-length examination of the novels with which most readers were familiar. However, the weaknesses of his book became even more glaringly evident in the light of Andrew Field's splendid and rich *Nabokov: His Life in Art* which appeared the following year. In speaking of art and madness in Nabokov's stories and novels, Field provides an apposite distinction to contrast with Stegner when he says of the son in "Signs and Symbols": "His desire (he has attempted to commit suicide several times already) is 'to tear a hole in his world and escape'; the real artist can draw a hole in the world and return unharmed and exhilarated."[100] For Field, Nabokov's fiction portrays characters ranged along a spectrum from delusion to inspiration, Kinbote to Shade perhaps, but in Field's reading, unlike Stegner's, Nabokov always depicts the globe of mortality, "reality" to the extent to which we can know it, encompassing the colored spiral of artistic creativity.

Field's book sets a high scholarly standard: rightly claiming it to be the first study of the oeuvre, Field explores in considerable detail Nabokov's work in all genres and in both Russian and English, arguing for the interrelation of techniques and themes throughout the corpus. With this work, Nabokov criticism achieves maturity, for Field provides a full measure of Nabokov's accomplishments and demonstrates throughout the oeuvre the presence of Nabokov's most insistent concerns: art, the artist, and madness; death; exile and reconstructed youth; the relation of fictional characters to their author.

Also in 1967 a special issue on Nabokov of *Wisconsin Studies in Contemporary Literature*, the first major collection of Nabokov criticism, was published and then reprinted, with the addition of two essays, as *Nabokov: The Man and His World.* Explicitly or implicitly, the essays in the volume elaborate the discussion of art and "reality" as Nabokov's major subjects; taken together, these essays reflect the extent to which Nabokov's art mirrors other art, his fiction mirrors his nonfiction, and his characters reflect each other. Especially noteworthy among them are those by Clarence Brown and John O. Lyons—on Nabokov, Pushkin, and *Pale Fire*—Charles Nicol's important discussion of *The Real Life of Sebastian Knight*, and Alfred Appel's seminal study of parody in Nabokov's art.

Carl R. Proffer's *Keys to Lolita*, which provides some of the same assistance as Appel's *The Annotated Lolita* to those undertaking painstaking readings of the novel, was the most important publication of 1968; it is still in many ways the best introduction to reading Nabokov and to some of the special effects of the prose. With no desire to be exhaustive, Proffer familiarizes the reader with the uses of literary allusion, with the complex system of cross-references underlying the identification of Quilty, and with several of the more striking features of Nabokov's style, focusing on "the sound of his prose, a few characteristic rhetorical figures, and some aspects of the imagery,"[101] the last leading the way in one of the most fascinating and illuminating directions taken by subsequent criticism.

The late 1960s can be usefully described as a period dominated by critical efforts to grasp a vision underlying all the novels. By the beginning of the 1970s, many readers were able to locate in each new or newly translated work that appeared the central concerns discussed at length in *Nabokov: His Life in Art* and *Nabokov: The Man and His Work*. From this period on, Nabokov scholarship developed in two major directions. Broadening their base for interpretation, and providing an arena in which to evaluate Nabokov's contribution to contemporary fiction, many critics were increasingly concerned with the issue of artifice, with contemporary developments seemingly antagonistic to the tradition of literary realism—an issue that became more compelling and complicated as the Nabokov canon lengthened at both ends; simultaneously, others focused more narrowly and thoroughly on individual novels, on the tensions between their narrators and their author, between art and life (or "that other VN, Visible Nature," as Nabokov puts it), and on a language and style which enhances both the palpable texture and the artifice of the fiction.

In "A Russian Preface for Nabokov's Beheading," Julian Moynahan asserts that "Nabokov is a towering figure among modern American novelists. . . . He has shown an entire generation of American writers how to seize reality in its often outrageous and fantastic variety and mystery, and to express their vision of things in boldly imaginative new forms."[102] And, in *The Novel Now: A Guide to Contemporary Fiction*, Anthony Burgess argues that despite Nabokov's frequent "preciousness, . . . he is a major force in the contemporary novel, and an example of the manner in which an alien culture . . . and what we may go on calling the European sensibility, are able to fertilize a tradition in danger of inanition through looking inwards and feeding on itself."[103] The idea of a tradition suffering from inanition, or "exhausted" as it is more often described now, and the argument that Nabokov plays a major role in the development of "post-modernist" fiction, represent widespread views most clearly articulated at the time in John Barth's seminal essay on "The Literature of Exhaustion." While Barth focuses on Borges, he defines the concept of exhaustion in ways that contribute to an understanding of Nabokov as well. In passing references Barth places Nabokov in the context of the best of contemporary fiction in its recognition that "certain forms . . . [or] certain possibilities"[104] are used up. What is not exhausted, and can never be in fact, is the possibility of rewriting one's precursors (to paraphrase Borges), an "intellectually serious" idea in Barth's view and one which he finds in Nabokov's *Eugene Onegin*. Indeed, this is one of the "ideas" of Nabokov's fiction as well and, as Barth say of Borges, "he confronts an intellectual dead end and employs it against itself to accomplish new human work."[105] Such considerations of Nabokov's place in a tradition, and the nature of the tradition itself, become increasingly important through the 1970s and into the 1980s.

Two volumes of considerable significance were published in 1970. Intended primarily, but not exclusively, as an introduction and reader's guide to *Lolita*, Alfred Appel's *The Annotated Lolita* is essential reading not only for its explication of puns, allusions, cross-references, parodies, and other games, but for Appel's analysis of the uses to which these strategies are put. (See Beverly Clark's bibliography.) The Winter 1970 volume of *TriQuarterly*, a festscrift "for Vladimir Nabokov on his seventieth birthday," appeared also in hardcover edition as *Nabokov: Criticism, Reminiscences, Translations, and Tributes* edited by Appel and Charles Newman.[106] The single most important contribution is the translation of Khodasevich's 1937 "On Sirin," but the volume also includes a translation of P. M. Bitsilli's 1936 "The Revival of Allegory," one of a number of émigré essays concerned with literary influence. And, related to the issue of influence, George Steiner contends in the same volume: "I have no hesitation in arguing that [the] poly-linguistic matrix [in Nabokov] is the determining fact of [his] life and art. . . . To be specific: the multilingual, cross-linguistic situation is both the matter and form of Nabokov's work (the two are, no doubt, inseparable and *Pale Fire* is the parable of their fusion.)"[107] For Steiner, all Nabokov's novels dramatize "complex erotic relations between speaker and speech" and resound with "laments" for his loss of Russian.[108]

The festscrift also includes excellent essays on individual novels, noteworthy among which is Robert Alter's superb discussion of mirrors, metaphysics, and morality in *Invitation to a Beheading*. Alter explores the novel in the context of Nabokov's reputation for "mere technical virtuosity" and for an "imagination [which] whirl[s] all social, political, and psychological materials into a circumscribed inner concern with art and the artist. . . ."[109] For Alter, there is a crucial connection between the primary theme of art and the subordination of politics, indeed a demonstration of "the essential, inexorable antagonism between totalitarianism and authentic art."[110] In his analysis of this antagonism, Alter exemplifies the richest, most intelligent of readings now achieved by the best of Nabokov's American critics: "Execution is the central rite of Cincinnatus's world, . . . because that world, in all its institutional arrangements and daily social relations, is explicitly contrived to numb, cloud, cripple, and finally extirpate individual consciousness. It therefore must remain a relentlessly incredible world from the viewpoint of any genuinely human consciousness. . . ."[111]

In 1970 Nabokov himself celebrated his seventieth birthday with the publication in English of his first novel. Although *Mary* provides a startling contrast to the linguistic labyrinth of *Ada*, it also reveals the continuity among the novels. As Gillian Tindall remarks, *Mary* represents Nabokov's "first whistled attempts at a grand orchestral theme. . . ."[112] Appropriately, the publication in English of Nabokov's first novel was followed rapidly by the publication of his seventh English novel, *Transparent Things* (1972). More widely reviewed than *Mary*, it was often treated far less kindly.[113] *Glory* (published originally as *Podvig* in 1931–32) also appeared in 1972, completing the translations of his Russian novels into English. Described as "a glorious novel—better than *Pnin*—with which to make converts" to Nabokov, *Glory* shares with *Speak, Memory*, according to J. D. O'Hara, "some of Nabokov's most pleasant qualities: quiet humor; sensuous absorption in moments of stopped time; evocations of childhood's dreamy experiences (snow, train rides, toys); and sympathetically funny descriptions of adolescence with its joint onslaughts of puberty and poshlost'."[114]

In 1974, Nabokov published his last novel, *Look at the Harlequins!*. Focusing on reviews of these four novels published in the 1970s, one observes that while many readers found a repellent coldness and cruelty in the later novels in contrast to the early and "sunny" works being translated and published in alternation, the last novels provided much more fertile soil for debate and interpretation.[115] This suggests not so much that criticism thrives on complaint (in fact, the best reviews are typically those which admire Nabokov's strategies), but that the last novels are richer, more "mature" than the early works, providing the reader of the oeuvre with a perspective on the development of Nabokov's art. This development concerns not so much the central theme with which Nabokov was preoccupied, for that has remained the same—"mirrors for immortality," to appropriate a phrase from Robert Alter[116]—but the increasingly complex rendering of that theme and the multiplicity of perspectives achieved through the accretion of its fictional renderings.

In the 1970s the rate of publication of criticism and scholarship on Nabokov accelerated so rapidly that, for the first time, it became difficult to keep up with the new material. In addition to dozens of articles, quite a number of them excellent, two collections of essays, and several general studies of fiction including chapters on Nabokov, fourteen books devoted entirely to Nabokov were published between 1971 and 1979. Studies of the fiction in general, typically with an emphasis on the novels written originally in English, include Douglas Fowler's *Reading Nabokov* (1974),[117] Donald Morton's volume in the Modern Literature Monograph Series (1974),[118] L. L. Lee's volume in the Twayne American Author Series (1976),[119] H. Grabes' *Fictitious Biographies: Vladimir Nabokov's English Novels* (1977),[120] and G. M. Hyde's *Vladimir Nabokov: America's Russian Novelist* (1977).[121] Other studies focus more narrowly and fully on individual aspects of Nabokov's art, such as Julia Bader's *Crystal Land: Artifice in Nabokov's English Novels* (1972; see Beverly Clark's bibliography for a discussion of Bader). In his delightful *Nabokov's Dark Cinema* (1974),[122] Alfred Appel demonstrates that film imagery and techniques and allusions to film permeate Nabokov's fiction and analyzes the ways in which Nabokov employed one medium to enrich the strategies of another.

Other critics focus on the style and imagery of the fiction, such as William Woodin Rowe in his unfortunate *Nabokov's Deceptive World* (1971)[123] and Jessie Thomas Lokrantz in *The Underside of the Weave: Some Stylistic Devices Used by Nabokov* (1973).[124] Two of the most important books published in the 1970s take still other approaches. Jane Grayson's *Nabokov Translated: A Comparison of Nabokov's Russian and English Prose* (1977) is the only thoroughgoing treatment of this major subject discussed previously only in short articles focusing on individual translations.[125] (See Beverly Clark's bibliography.) Bobbie Ann Mason's *Nabokov's Garden: A Guide to "Ada"* (1974) analyzes in detail the novel's natural imagery, what Mason astutely describes as "art imitat[ing] nature mimicking art"[126] (including the not-so-natural Veen family tree), Mason clear-sightedly demonstrating the nature of the relationships between Van and Ada, Terra and Antiterra, character and author. Provocative reading, Mason's study is one of the richest considerations of the divergent uses to which Nabokov and his characters put art.

In 1977 Andrew Field published his disappointing *Nabokov: His Life in Part*,[127] intended as the biographical counterpart to his splendid *Nabokov: His Life in Art*, but in no way equal to the achievement of the earlier volume. Most fortunately, Brian Boyd, with the cooperation of Véra Nabokov, has undertaken a biography that promises to be a hallmark in Nabokov studies; however, we will have to wait a few more years for its publication.

The most important of the general studies of fiction which include discussion of Nabokov[128] is Robert Alter's "Nabokov's Game of Worlds" in his *Partial Magic* (1975), a major contribution to the enterprise of placing Nabokov within a literary tradition. Tracing a "self-conscious tradition" in the history of the novel, beginning with Cervantes and ending with Nabokov and some of his contemporaries, Alter defines "a self-conscious novel . . . [as one] that systematically flaunts its own condition of artifice and . . . by so doing probes into the problematic relationship between real-seeming artifice and reality"[129]—thus, a "philosophic novel."[130] Arguing that Nabokov not only belongs to this tradition but "has been more self-conscious about his novelistic self-consciousness than any of his predecessors or imitators, more sharply focused on a continuing critical recapitulation of a whole literary tradition,"[131] Alter not only provides a way of reading all of Nabokov's novels, but also discovers an effective means for distinguishing between the more and less successful novels: "the constructed fictional world . . . [must be allowed] sufficient vitality to give the dialectic between fiction and 'reality' the vigorous to-and-fro energy which it requires."[132] Moving back and forth between individual metaphors or passages and the structured theme of the whole of *Pale Fire*, Alter both demonstrates the ways in which the novel employs the strategies of the self-conscious tradition, and dramatizes the dialectic of the constructed world and the self-conscious fiction.

Two collections of essays on Nabokov were published during these years. The aptly titled *A Book of Things about Vladimir Nabokov* (1974), edited by Carl R. Proffer,[133] which includes seven pieces originally published in a 1972 issue of *Russian Literature TriQuarterly* as well as another fourteen essays or items, contains Ludmila Foster's essay on émigré critical reaction to Nabokov, Proffer's "Glossary of Allusions to Russian Literature" in *Ada*, and an excellent essay by D. Barton Johnson, "Synthesia, Polychromatism, and Nabokov." Developing a persuasive hypothesis about the way in which Nabokov's memory actually functions, Johnson also provides a model for critics attempting to relate the art to the life. At the end of the decade, *Modern Fiction Studies* devoted one of its issues to Nabokov scholarship, including another superb study by Johnson, "Nabokov as a Man of Letters: The Alphabetic Motif in His Work." Here, Johnson describes Nabokov's unique "stylistic signature . . . [characterized by] the integration of theme, plot, and motif . . ."[134] and demonstrates that, most recently, the best of Nabokov criticism is able to use the definition of Nabokov's central theme, developed independently by Khodasevich and Weidle and American critics of the 1960s, as a basis for fully comprehending both the relationship of art to reality in the novels and the specific stylistic and linguistic techniques through which that relationship is articulated, revealing along the way the extra richness afforded Nabokov's bilingual critics.[135]

Of the many articles published individually in journals during the 1970s, quite a few stand out as especially provocative or fruitful in attempting to resolve critical problems or to initiate new directions for study. Several focus on the reinterpretation of a single text. Charles Nicol's "Pnin's History"[136] is intended to lay to rest forever the misapprehension of *Pnin* as a series of fragments, a basically simple book—"*Pnin* is as complicated as a pet snake," Nicol says. In exploring the changes in Pnin's character, the Cinderella theme of the novel, Nicol demonstrates both its unity and the complexity of its narration. In "Form and Meaning in Nabokov's *The Real Life of Sebastian Knight*: An Example of Elegaic Romance,"[137] K. A. Bruffee proposes a radical rereading of the novel as one of a class including, among others, *Pale Fire*, *Moby Dick*, *Remembrance of Things Past*, and *Heart of Darkness*. Bruffee's analysis dispels many of the confusions generated by prior interpretations of *Sebastian Knight*. In an important essay which focuses on the critical reactions *Lolita* first engendered, Donald Rackin suggests that "Trilling, Green, and many other readers committed to aesthetic considerations . . . are so attracted by the Humbert whom Humbert creates with his delighted readers' collusion that his persuasiveness and charm finally wipe out all of his crimes."[138] However, Rackin argues, this is another trap for the reader, creating for those who succumb to Humbert's charms a "moral quandary at the end" to which even Humbert is superior: "unlike the esthetes and intellectuals who have identified with him, become his doubles, and finally forgiven or justified his horrendous acts, Humbert ends by proclaiming his damnation."[139] In "Humbert Humbert *Through the Looking-Glass*," the best of several articles on Nabokov's use of Lewis Carroll, Elizabeth Prioleau argues that an exploration of the parallels between *Through the Looking-Glass* and *Lolita* substantiates the view that "Humbert the protagonist of the 'confession' pierces the mirror only to arrive at imprisonment; Humbert the author writes from the nether side of the mirror only to come to self-bafflement and entombment. The trap is double-locked."[140] Also starting from the reaction of previous critics to Humbert's charms, Nomi Tamir-Ghez's "The Art of

Persuasion in Nabokov's *Lolita*,"[141] the best esssay written on the rhetoric of Humbert and *Lolita*, details "the specific devices" of the novel's art of persuasion and convincingly demonstrates—by formulating elegant and important distinctions between the two audiences Humbert addressses and the two Humberts doing the addressing—that Nabokov systematically subverts Humbert's persuasiveness.

In "The Scientific Art of Nabokov's *Pale Fire*," Timothy Flower reminds readers of the fact that "Nabokov combines scientific allusions and characteristics with literary ones because his most basic themes and methods describe relationships between art and nature, not just between art and art."[142] Flower is thus able to explain the differing senses of reality achieved by various parts of Kinbote's commentary; moreover, his argument reinforces Alter's conclusion that Nabokov's narrative strategy is based upon a dialectical tension between artifice and mimesis. Essays suggesting other new approaches include Phyllis Roth's "The Psychology of the Double in Nabokov's *Pale Fire*,"[143] which attempts to demonstrate that Nabokov employs and parodies the psychoanalytic explanation (à la Otto Rank) of the doppelgänger "as a springboard" for his repeated demonstration that he and his characters are not to be identified with each other, that "resemblances are but the shadows of differences." Employing the analysis of voice and narration developed by Gérard Genette to sort out the narrative complexities of *Sebastian Knight*, Shlomith Rimmon's "Problems of Voice in Vladimir Nabokov's *The Real Life of Sebastian Knight*"[144] distinguishes among the many levels of the text, thereby exposing the deliberate interpenetrations of narrative levels Nabokov devises to portray the ambiguity of "reality." Rimmon's analysis can serve as a model for reading other of Nabokov's most intricate narratives as well. Another fine essay establishes from a different perspective the same need to retain distinctions in Nabokov's art. In " 'The Viewer and the View'; Chance and Choice in *Pale Fire*," David Walker maintains that "The novel's two parts, like life and art, are necessary and complementary mirrors, but it is impossible to identify one as the primary object and the other as its mirror."[145] And in "Proust, Nabokov, and *Ada*,"[146] J. E. Rivers provides the most thoroughgoing examination to date of both parallels and differences between Nabokov and the author to whom he is perhaps most often compared, and a model for any critic whose concern is with questions of literary traditions and influence.

Still other critics are concerned with language, languages, and stylistic devices in Nabokov and their essays provide readers with assistance in attending carefully to the most basic constituents of what is unique and essential in Nabokov's art. In addition to the work of D. Barton Johnson,[147] the following essays are well worth studying: John F. Fleischauer's "Simultaneity in Nabokov's Prose Style"[148] which explores the relationships between Nabokov's views on time and space and his imagery and syntax; Antonina Gove's excellent study of "Multilingualism and Ranges of Tone in Nabokov's *Bend Sinister*";[149] "Nabokov and the Verbal Mode of the Grotesque," in which Ralph A. Ciancio explicitly connects the lexical play of the novels with the concerns of "realistic" fiction—"As the demonic is built into the fabric of all that exists, so it is built into words, phrases, and sentences, which is where the connection between the phenomenal world and Nabokov's epiphenomenal world takes root";[150] and Gabriel Lanyi's "On Narrative Transitions in Nabokov's Prose"[151] explores an element of Nabokov's style not previously isolated for study and identifies a significant Nabokovian device which dislocates the reader in time and space and collocates events, persons, and motifs constituting the patterned texture of the novels.

Four final works from this period can usefully be considered together. By the late 1970s, the issue of Nabokov as aesthete or humanist, of his art as reflexive or mimetic, was firmly established as the major issue in the criticism. In "On Human Freedom and Inhuman Art: Nabokov," Ellen Pifer reminds us of the terms of that debate when she argues that it is precisely Nabokov's laying bare of the artifice of his fictions—that which is, in part at least, the basis for describing him as a "mere aesthete"—which should make evident that Nabokov does not confuse the games of the text, and his authority over his characters, with an arrogant despotism over real people, specifically his readers. Indeed, throughout his career Nabokov has created and condemned—in what Pifer describes as a "lucid indictment of the aesthete's confusion of values"[152]—characters who do to others that of which some of Nabokov's critics would accuse him. As Pifer says, "With regard to the prerogatives of art, Nabokov exhibits greater detachment and moral rigor than many of his own interpreters."[153]

Similarly, Dabney Stuart's *Nabokov: The Dimensions of Parody* is an attempt to bridge the games of the novels and "higher regions of emotion."[154] For Stuart, at the heart of Nabokov's art is the "implication . . . that, since any fiction is a parody of life, the best fiction, or the fiction that is most consciously itself, is the fiction that acknowledges as completely as it can be made to do its own parodic nature."[155] Stuart argues that "what is parodied turns out to be not so much a literary form used by other writers as more basic assumptions about perception and its relationship to so-called factual reality. . . ."[156]

Such readings as these, which can be described as efforts to bring Nabokov's art within the fold of the tradition of "realism," though with important qualifications, are opposed by a reformulated and updated articulation of the position which has always held that Nabokov's art is not mimetic. In "Nabokov's Performative Writing," Maurice Couturier celebrates the achievement of the *nouveau roman* in which, unlike traditional or "realistic" fiction, the referent of the text is not a reality external to it but the artifice constructed by the text. Nabokov's fiction is performative because "the writing designates no other reality than the novel itself."[157] Nabokov's novels do not have a function; rather, they have an "impact": in telling us "about nothing except [their] own making—that is except the author's art . . . they afford us much pleasure . . . by allowing us . . . direct participation as readers in the making or activating of the works of art."[158] Despite the distinction Couturier attempts to make here between "function" and "impact," the conclusion of his analysis actually recalls Stuart's argument; finally, the artist is always engaged in making meaning and meaning is always determined by reference to something external to the text even if that something is not a naive belief in an objective reality but the reader's act of reading itself. The fact that these self-consciously opposed arguments can be sustained, however, testifies to a richness in the novels themselves which is best done justice to by Robert Alter's argument in "Mimesis and the Motive for Fiction" that even the most self-consciously artificial of fictional works entails an "intermittent" use of language as referential. Using Nabokov's *Transparent Things* as one example, Alter contends that even "Hugh/You, this Person, the focus of certain contractual assumptions between writer and reader around which a narrative can be constructed. . . . is given convincing mimetic specificity. . . ."[159] Most important, "the narrator, through his constant attentiveness to the ways in which the mind transforms what it contemplates, involves us in the life of consciousness, and in the epistemological anxieties of the life of consciousness, which is our most immediate human reality."[160] What seems to be the case, then, is that the two sides of the critical debate about Nabokov as aesthete or humanist are distinct by virtue of which element of Nabokov's fictional strategy they choose to privilege, not by virtue, as Alter shows, of a radical and absolute separation from the "realistic" tradition in Nabokov's artistic enterprise.

Two publications early in the 1980s articulate this position more fully and are, moreover, especially significant in that they attest to both some degree of critical consensus and a wide audience for Nabokov and Nabokov scholarship. Ellen Pifer's *Nabokov and the Novel* (1980) develops in fullest and most lucid detail the argument that Nabokov is indeed a humanist, that the emphasis on artifice in the criticism has skewed "the question of realism" in such a way that readers have been unable to perceive the ethical concerns of the novels. The first article on Nabokov to appear in *PMLA*, Dale Peterson's "Nabokov's *Invitation*: Literature as Execution" (1981), takes a similar approach, Peterson arguing that "Nabokov's notoriously composed fictions exemplify an honest solution to the problem of perpetuating a humanist and ethical literature once we have seen through the conventions of nineteenth-century narrative realism."[161] Both Pifer and Peterson are considered more fully by Beverly Clark. Several essays in *Vladimir Nabokov: His Life, His Work, His World/A Tribute* (1980), edited by Peter Quennell,[162] also contribute to the discussion of Nabokov as aesthete or humanist, but the volume is most noteworthy for the wonderful reminiscences by Hannah Green, Alfred

Appel, and, especially, for Dmitri Nabokov's "On Revisiting Father's Room."

As Nabokov and Nabokov criticism reached a wider audience, more and more critics became concerned with Nabokov's place and role in "post-modernist" literature.[163] Most originally and usefully, in *Victims—Textual Strategies in Recent American Fiction* (1981), Paul Bruss traces epistemological shifts in painting and sculpture, music and fiction, finding in each medium "developments which have, since 1860, transformed the nature of Western art: (1) the artist's assumption of impersonality, (2) the artist's desertion of context, and (3) the artist's shifting of responsibility for his work to his audience."[164] Employing John Shade's distinction between text and texture, Bruss argues that the three writers he discusses—Nabokov, Barthelme, and Kozinski—are "victimized by the textual insufficiency that attaches to the modernist awareness of the intricacies of perception and language."[165] In the face of this victimization, these writers explore and celebrate "not text but texture," in which "gaming serves as the crucial ground of human experience." Thus, as is the case with earlier discussions of contemporary fiction and of the role of games in Nabokov's fiction,[166] for Bruss the play of Nabokov's textures is serious indeed. Unlike several others, however, Bruss provides not only a history and context for the epistemological dimensions of Nabokov's art, but also several stunning readings of individual textures, especially those of *Pnin*, *Transparent Things*, and *Look at the Harlequins!*. More problematic, his discussions of *Lolita*, *Pale Fire*, and *Ada* will nonetheless inspire fruitful disagreement.

A final book to focus on Nabokov's fictional games and their seriousness is David Packman's *Vladimir Nabokov: The Structure of Literary Desire* (1982), the most extended treatment to date of Nabokov's reflexivity and an attempt to create a dialogue between *Lolita*, *Pale Fire*, and *Ada* and contemporary theories of narrative. Packman argues that Nabokov's game entails not only the depiction of the artist but also the "thematization" of "the role of the reader as well."[167] That is, the novels Packman explores parodically dramatize an analogue of the reader reading and, particularly, of the reader desiring a full and complete meaning. Thus, in *Lolita*, Humbert's cryptogrammic paper chase, in which Humbert attempts to read the referent out from behind the linguistic signs, is the parodic double of the reader's desire to read representational certainty into the text. More, since Humbert's quest is a parody of detective fiction, a genre based on the final consummation of clue and truth, and since Nabokov's parody frustrates the desire for that final consummation, the novel is doubly reflexive and "the reader's desire for full meaning is travestied."[168] Although Packman can explain Humbert's nympholepsy, Kinbote's attempted appropriation of Shade's poem, and Van's desire for incest as analogues of the reader's desire for meaning, and as demonstrations of the reflexivity of the Nabokovian text, he does not confront the question of why the desire of these characters takes the specific forms and objects it does, nor the very human, mimetic dimension of the novels. Nonetheless, as an exploration of narrative artifice and its effect on the reader, Packman's study is well worth reading.

Having speculated earlier about ghosts and the ghostly in *Transparent Things*,[169] in 1981 William Woodin Rowe published an extended treatment of this theme, aptly entitled *Nabokov's Spectral Dimension*,[170] which he perceives, often on the basis of tenuous evidence, as a ubiquitous element in the novels. Short, and at that rather repetitious, Rowe's book nonetheless suggests an important and almost totally unrecognized theme in Nabokov's art. Also published in 1981, Brian Boyd's essay on "Nabokov's Philosophical World"[171] provides a far more persuasive discussion of the existence in Nabokov's world of a dimension beyond human consciousness and human conceptions of time and space. Not widely known, Boyd's essay is, moreover, the best and fullest analysis of a philosophy to which most others have merely alluded previously. Also concerned with the world beyond that which is perceived by human consciousness, Lucy Maddox, in *Nabokov's Novels in English* (1983),[172] focuses on the "novel-as-commentary," the first-person narrations of characters obsessed with determining—or creating—the final meaning of existence and, most often, doomed to failure. The virtue of Maddox's approach is its emphasis on the human (and erotic) reality of the characters' obsessions; however, this emphasis exists in uneasy relation to the dimension of artifice, leading Maddox to conclude that novels such as *The Real Life of Sebastian Knight* and *Bend Sinister* are ineffective when it is they, among others, which are ultimately most revealing about the dialectic of "reality" and artifice in Nabokov's art.

A final volume published to date, *Nabokov's Fifth Arc: Nabokov and Others on His Life's Work*, edited by J. E. Rivers and Charles Nicol, is a collection of essays, translations and notes, almost all previously unpublished, intended to "review [Nabokov's] career as a whole and to appreciate its sweep, its variety, and its inclusiveness."[173] In assembling the collection, the editors identified and included examples of the major critical issues and lines of argument in the scholarship, and provided, for the first time in a collection on Nabokov, a sense of the development of his concerns and strategies. Individual essays enhance that sense, such as Beverly Lyon Clark's analysis of Nabokov's translation of *Alice in Wonderland* into Russian (1923)[174] and William C. Carroll's analysis of *Despair's* allusiveness.[175] Several essays in the volume address at length questions or issues which have been previously treated only in passing, or not at all, such as Margaret Byrd Boegeman's consideration of Kafka's supposed influence on Nabokov,[176] and Phyllis Roth's heretical call for a psychoanalytic study of Nabokov's art and exploration of *Speak, Memory* as an expression of Nabokov's personal need for the freedom from pain, loss, and death afforded by artistic control.[177] Other essays contribute to previous criticism, such as Julian W. Connolly's "*Pnin*: The Wonder of Recurrence and Transformation," with *Ada* receiving the greatest amount of attention: in Charles Nicol's blunt and persuasive analysis of Van's utter unreliability in "Ada or Disorder"; and in the lengthy "Notes to Vivian Darkbloom's Notes to *Ada*" by editor Rivers and William Walker. The volume also offers readers a republication of Nabokov's "Notes to *Ada* by Vivian Darkbloom," appearing before only in the British paperback edition put out by Penguin; and the first translation into English of Nabokov's "Postscript to the Russian Edition" of *Lolita*, prefaced by a brief but informative note by the translator, Earl D. Sampson.

While most of Nabokov scholarship to date focuses on the novels, the major part of the canon, there is however a significant body of material in other genres. However, with the exception of Simon Karlinsky's "Illusion, Reality, and Parody in Nabokov's Plays,"[178] almost nothing has been written of Nabokov's plays and scenarios. What has been written concerning the poems, and there are a number of reviews, places the poetry very much in the frame drawn by the prose fiction. Indeed, it is the novels which most likely justify the reprinting and reviewing of the poetry. Howard Nemerov, for example, claims "that Nabokov's poems written in English are in large part deft and neat and not much more, some of them not far from cute. . . ."[179] However, a *TLS* reviewer says that the poems "reveal more than one aspect of Mr. Nabokov's genius,"[180] and goes on to argue that the "human sympathy," which others claim to be missing in the fiction, is present in the poems. Anthony Hecht argues, on the other hand, that "In every case [Nabokov] stands at a polite remove from experience, and even when he deals with violence or madness or the grotesque it is always with a flawless social poise."[181] Most enthusiastically, M. J. Bruccoli catalogs the poems as "major items in the Nabokov canon . . . splendid."[182] The fullest discussions of Nabokov's poetry appear in F. W. Dupee's excellent "The Prose and Poetry of it All," in *The King of the Cats*, and Field's *Nabokov: His Life in Art.*

Over the course of his life, Nabokov published nine collections of his short stories, in some cases with considerable overlap among the contents. In his last collection, *Details of a Sunset and Other Stories* (1976), which he describes as "the last batch of my Russian stories meriting to be Englished," he includes in the foreword a useful list of all the stories translated into English since the 1950s. Of course, Nabokov also wrote stories in English, including several of those most widely read and discussed. Reviews of the stories point to the same areas of concern and debate appearing in the criticism of the novels.[183] Far more substantial than any of the reviews, though, are the small number of essays on a few of the individual stories, four in particular having received substantive attention: "That in Aleppo Once . . . ,"[184] "The Vane Sisters,"[185] "A Guide to Berlin,"[186] and "Signs and Symbols."[187] The two most important works for consideration of Nabokov's stories are Field's *Nabokov: His Life in Art* and the only full-length study devoted to the stories, Marina Turkevich Naumann's *Blue Evenings in Berlin: Nabokov's Short Stories of the 1920's.*[188]

Clearly, Nabokov's poems, plays, and stories deserve fuller consideration than they have received, and one can hope that the promised appearance of Dmitri Nabokov's translations of poems and plays will elicit serious response. Additionally, much more remains to be said about the novels, as attested to by the recent excellent examinations of pre-*Lolita* works such as *Despair*, *Invitation to a Beheading*, and *Bend Sinister*, by the many questions remaining about *Lolita* itself, and by the essays appearing here for the first time. Carl Eichelberger's "Gaming in the Lexical Playfields of Nabokov's *Pale Fire*" demonstrates the value of approaching Kinbote and Shade, not as characters in some realistic sense, but as distinct loci of lexical games which simultaneously constitute a single narrative line. Roger D. Salomon's reading of "*The Gift*: Nabokov's Portrait of the Artist," together with Simon Karlinsky's work, should enable English-reading critics to approach that important novel with a greater sense of confidence; Salomon argues that the theme of art and the artist, explicitly rendered in Fyodor's growth, is nonetheless subordinate to a traditional quest myth portrayed mock-heroically. D. Barton Johnson's discussion of "The Ambidextrous Universe of Nabokov's *Look at the Harlequins!*" contributes substantially to the understanding of Nabokov's "scientific art," demonstrating that Nabokov dramatizes in his fiction several hypotheses of twentieth-century physics, and tracing the "development of the ambidextrous universe theme" through the novels. Ellen Pifer's discussion of "Nabokov and the Art of Exile" definitively establishes ways in which the life of the artist and the life of the émigré impinged on each other.

While the debate between those who view Nabokov as a humanist and those who argue that he is "merely" a player of sophisticated literary games should itself be played out—although further, more historically and philosophically informed discussion of what constitutes literary realism and reflexivity would be profitable—new areas for fruitful scholarship and debate are appearing. The publication of *The Nabokov/Wilson Letters* and the three volumes, with the possibility of more to come, of Nabokov's lectures on literature should occasion further study of Nabokov in the context of several literary traditions. Work needs to be undertaken, too, on the roles of the women characters in Nabokov's fiction, an area of critical neglect only now beginning to be remedied.[189] And, as several critics have demonstrated, Nabokov's "scientific art" should be investigated more thoroughly, including further study not only of Nabokov and the natural and physical sciences but also of Nabokov and psychology: Claude Mouchard's essay on "Doctor Froid," translated here for the first time, raises several significant questions about the references to psychoanalysis in Nabokov's novels and about the ultimate relation of psychoanalytic interpretation to artistic creativity. Several critics in America are now exploring this relation, with at least one dissertation on Nabokov and Freud being completed at present. And, of course, far more scholarship is required to explicate the linguistic and literary complexities of the texts; clearly such work is under way, for an annotated *Pnin* will appear in dissertation form at least.[190]

Most exciting to a student of Nabokov is the sense that, with almost the entire Nabokov canon in English, and with "critical crotchets"[191]—both Nabokov's and his readers'—now clearly in view and, one hopes, in perspective, future scholars can follow the directions signaled by the best approaches of their predecessors: specifically, the thorough, careful study of the play of languages, style, and structure, and the sensitive probing of the relations between the life of the fiction and the art of the author which together constitute Nabokov's distinctive signature and the basis of his literary eminence.[192]

Work on *Critical Essays on Vladimir Nabokov* was supported by Skidmore College Faculty Research Grants and completed with the unstinting assistance of the reference librarians at Skidmore's Lucy Scribner Library. I wish especially to express my gratitude to J. D. O'Hara for the challenging introduction to Nabokov he gave me, to Ralph A. Ciancio who has been unfailingly generous in his support of my research on Nabokov, and to the many additional Nabokov scholars and admirers whose contributions to Nabokov criticism are responsible for the publication of this collection.

PHYLLIS A. ROTH
Skidmore College

Notes

1. Subsequently published as *Nabokov: The Man and His Work*, ed. L. S. Dembo (Madison: Univ. of Wisconsin Press, 1967), pp. 226–27; all references are to the Dembo edition.

2. Alfred Appel, Jr., offers an interesting perspective on this process in *Nabokov's Dark Cinema* (New York: Oxford Univ. Press, 1974) and in "The Road to *Lolita*, or the Americanization of an Émigré," *Journal of Modern Literature*, 4 (1974), 3–31.

3. Andrew Field argues that Nabokov "is not as he is usually called, a Russian-American author, but rather, he is an American-Russian writer, and was that long before he began to write in English, or had come to America." And he quotes Nabokov as describing himself as "an American writer, born in Russia and educated in England where I studied French literature, before spending fifteen years in Germany" (*Nabokov: His Life in Art* [Boston: Little, Brown, 1967], pp. 64–65). In an interview reprinted in *Strong Opinions*, Nabokov says he is "as American as April in Arizona" ([New York: McGraw-Hill, 1973], p. 98).

4. D. Barton Johnson, "Nabokov as a Man of Letters: The Alphabetic Motif in His Work," *Modern Fiction Studies*, 25 (Autumn 1979), 397.

5. *Keys to* Lolita (Bloomington: Indiana Univ. Press, 1968), p. 5.

6. George Steiner, "Extraterritorial," *TriQuarterly*, 17 (Winter 1970), 123.

7. New York: McGraw-Hill, 1973.

8. See note 3 above.

9. See issues 8 and 9 (Spring and Fall 1982) of the *Vladimir Nabokov Research Newsletter* for Juliar's "Notes from a Descriptive Bibliography." The Spring 1983 issue includes a discussion between Michael Juliar and Brian Boyd which provides a good indication of the significance and complexity of the scholarly issues at stake in Nabokov's bibliography. Any issue of the *Newsletter* demonstrates the value of the service Stephen Parker is providing Nabokov scholars and critics.

10. The issue was put in just these terms at the 1982 Nabokov section held in conjunction with the Conference of the American Association of Teachers of Slavic and East European Languages and moderated by Samuel Schuman.

11. See *Nabokov: His Life in Art*, p. 54, for a listing of Nabokov's pen names. According to Field, "It is generally true that works written in Russia prior to 1940 are signed with the *nom de plume* V. Sirin, and that works written in English after this date are signed Vladimir Nabokov. However, there are exceptions (early works signed V. V. Nabokov and Russian poems signed Vaseli Shiskov and Vivian Calmbrood. . . .)" (*Nabokov: A Bibliography*, p. xxii).

12. Foster's essay was originally published in *Russian Literature TriQuarterly*, 3 (1972), 330–41 and reprinted in *A Book of Things about Vladimir Nabokov*, ed. Carl R. Proffer (Ann Arbor: Ardis Inc., 1974), pp. 42–53. In her essay, Foster, who is the compiler of a *Bibliography of Russian Émigré Literature, 1918–1968*, 2 vols. (Boston: G. K. Hall, 1971), traces émigré critical response to Nabokov from 1923 to 1968 and finds a total of only thirty-one reviews and articles published in the journals. Marina Naumann's discussion, emphasizing the last two decades of émigré criticism, appears in *Russian Language Journal*, 99 (1974), 18–26.

13. In his foreword to *The Complection of Russian Literature: A Cento*, where these reviews appeared for the first time in English, Field explains that the volume is a "cento, and not a translation in any traditional understanding of that term. . . . Essays have been shortened, portions of them have been rearranged. . . ." ([New York: Atheneum, 1971], p. xiv). Nikolay Andreyev's essay is shortened from his piece in *Nov'*, 3 (1930). Vladimir Weidle's piece is shortened from his review in *Krug*, 1 (1936).

14. *TriQuarterly*, 17 (Winter 1970), 96–101.

15. Khodasevich, p. 97.

16. Ibid., p. 101.

17. *Books Abroad*, 28 (Autumn 1954), 402.

18. Adamovich's "Vladimir Nabokov," is translated in *Twentieth Century Russian Literary Criticism*, ed. V. Ehrlich (New Haven: Yale Univ. Press, 1975), pp. 219–31; reference here is to p. 220. In *Nabokov: His Life in Art*, Field provides background for Adamovich's views of Nabokov, citing a feud between the two in émigré publications as one cause of Adamovich's hostility. See Field, pp. 51f, 86ff.

19. Review of *Laughter in the Dark*, Nabokov's translation of *The Song of Igor's Campaign*, and *Poems* (April 7, 1961), p. 218. This sense of oppression felt by critics who perceive a lack of compassion—for both characters and readers—persists in the criticism through the years. See also Hortense Calisher, "The Young Magician Trying his Tricks," *New York Times Book Review*, January 9, 1972, p. 36; Anatole Broyard, "A Feudal Lord of Fiction" (review of *A Russian Beauty and Other Stories*), *New York Times*, May 11, 1973; and William Gass, "Mirror, Mirror," *New York Review of Books*, 10 (June 6, 1968), 4, reprinted in Gass's *Fiction and the Figures of Life* (New York: Random House, Vintage Books, 1972).

20. "Strictly One-Sided," *Nation*, 159 (November 25, 1944), 658.

21. *Commonweal*, 88 (September 6, 1968), 604.

22. *Speak, Memory*, pp. 12–13.

23. See, in particular, *American Literary Scholarship: An Annual* (Durham: Duke Univ. Press), beginning with 1963, which is especially useful for English-reading critics in its discussions of essays and books published in other languages.

24. Boston: G. K. Hall, 1979. A short version of this bibliography appears in *Modern Fiction Studies*, 25 (1975), 527–54. As with Field's *Bibliography*, Schuman's *Reference Guide* can be supplemented by listings in the *Vladimir Nabokov Research Newsletter*.

25. Vol. 29, pp. 316–19.

26. *Otchayanie* in Russian, published in Berlin in 1936; published in English in London (1937); the revised edition with which American readers are familiar was serialized in *Playboy* in 1965–66 and published in a single volume by G. P. Putnam's in 1966.

27. Originally published in Paris in 1932, published in English translation by Winifred Roy in 1936 and as *Laughter in the Dark* in Nabokov's translation in New York in 1938.

28. Clifton Fadiman, "Books," *New Yorker*, 14 (May 7, 1938), 92.

29. Samuel Nock, "Tragicomedy in Berlin," *Saturday Review*, June 18, 1938, p. 16.

30. Harold Strauss, *New York Times*, May 8, 1938, p. 7.

31. See *Speak, Memory* (Putnam's 1966 edition, p. 275) for Nabokov's description of the arcs of the spiral of his existence.

32. Walter Allen, *Spectator*, No. 6149 (May 3, 1946), 464.

33. Kay Boyle, "The New Novels," *New Republic*, 106 (January 26, 1942), 124.

34. Babette Deutsch, "Creator of Dead Souls," *New York Herald Tribune Weekly Book Review*, December 24, 1944, p. 8.

35. Bernard Guilbert Guernay, "Great Grotesque," *New Republic*, 111 (September 25, 1944), 376.

36. Marjorie Farber, "Nikolai Gogol the Man—and His Nightmares," *New York Times Book Review*, November 5, 1944, p. 29.

37. Edmund Wilson, "Nikolai Gogol—Greek Paideia," *New Yorker*, 20 (September 9, 1944), 72.

38. Published in New York by Henry Holt (1947) and reprinted by Time, Inc. in 1964 with a new introduction by Nabokov.

39. See, for example, Richard F. Patteson, "Nabokov's *Bend Sinister*: The Narrator as God," *Studies in American Fiction*, 5 (1977), 241–53.

40. "Superior Amusement," *Time*, June 16, 1947, pp. 104f.

41. New York: Harper & Bros., 1951.

42. Maurice Hindus, "Gentle Russian Yesterdays," *Saturday Review*, 34 (April 14, 1951), 29.

43. Marc Slonim, "Glimpses into a Vanished World," *New York Times Book Review*, February 18, 1951, p. 7.

44. Readers who enjoy neither Nabokov's narrators nor even his language, will find a sympathetic voice in Richard G. Stern's "*Pnin* and the Dust-Jacket," *Prairie Schooner*, Summer 1957, pp. 161–64.

45. Granville Hicks, "Chaplin with a Russian Accent," *New York Times Book Review*, March 10, 1957, p. 4.

46. Victor Lange, "A Saint of the Comic," *New Republic*, 136 (May 6, 1957), 17.

47. At least one long volume could be published reprinting the discussions of these issues. Schuman's bibliography describes many of the relevant reviews and essays and there are several other useful summaries; "Lolita's Creator—Author Nabokov, a 'Cosmic Joker,' " *Newsweek*, 59 (June 25, 1962), 51–54; "The Lolita Case," *Time*, 72 (November 17, 1958), 102; and especially F. W. Dupee's "Lolita in America," *Encounter*, 12 (February 1959),

30–35, with which is printed a page of excerpts from responses in England. Perhaps the most extended consideration of the pornography issue and defense of *Lolita* is a pamphlet entitled *L'Affair Lolita: Defense de l'ecrivain*, ed. F. W. Dupee et al. (Paris: Olympia Press, 1957). The review of *Lolita* by V. S. Pritchett in *New Statesman* (January 10, 1959, p. 38) is among the best to consider the pornography question, for Pritchett actually troubles to discuss the unusual strengths of Nabokov's narrative strategies.

48. See, for example, Robert Hatch, "Books in Brief," *Nation*, 187 (August 30, 1958), 97, and Kingsley Amis, "She Was a Child and I Was a Child," *Spectator*, No. 6854 (November 6, 1959), 635–36.

49. Elizabeth Janeway, "The Tragedy of Man Driven by Desire," *New York Times Book Review*, August 17, 1958, p. 25.

50. John Hollander, "The Perilous Magic of Nymphets," *Partisan Review*, 23 (Fall 1966), 560.

51. "On a Book Entitled *Lolita*," Nabokov's Afterword to the novel, first appearing, with excerpts of *Lolita*, in the *Anchor Review* (1957).

52. Orville Prescott, "Books of the Times," *New York Times*, August 18, 1958, p. 17.

53. "A Sense of the Absurd," *Times Literary Supplement*, November 13, 1959, p. 657.

54. W. B. Fleishmann, *Books Abroad*, 34 (Spring 1960), 180.

55. See especially Paul Pickrel, "Vintage Nabokov," *Harper's*, 169 (November 1959), 104; and Ronald Bryden, "Quest for Sebastian," *Spectator*, No. 6900 (September 23, 1960), 454.

56. "Briefly Noted," *New Yorker*, 35 (November 28, 1959), 241.

57. John Wain, "Nabokov's Beheading," *New Republic*, 141 (December 21, 1959), 18.

58. Malcolm Bradbury, "New Fiction," *Punch*, 237 (April 20, 1960), 562. Similarly, V. S. Naipaul contends: "The skill with which Mr. Nabokov creates his effects of fantasy is remarkable: an oblique narrative method coupled with a minute exploration of small scenes, precise detail upon precise detail, again and again dissolves reality into nightmare. But the effort is too cerebral to arouse immediate response" ("New Novels," *New Statesman*, 59 [March 26, 1960], 461).

59. W. L. Webb, "In Glorious Nabokolor," *Manchester Guardian Weekly*, 82 (March 24, 1960), 11.

60. Frank Kermode, "Aesthetic Bliss," *Encounter*, 14 (June 1960), 81–86; reprinted in his *Puzzles and Epiphanies* (London: Routledge & Kegan Paul, 1962); citation here is to p. 85.

61. Dwight Macdonald, "Virtuosity Rewarded, or Dr. Kinbote's Revenge," *Partisan Review* (Summer 1962), 439.

62. See "Zemblances," *New Statesman*, 64 (November 9, 1962), 671–72; reprinted in Kermode's *Continuities* (New York: Random House, 1962).

63. Macdonald, p. 437. Only of slightly greater interest now are the debates about the primary author of *Pale Fire*. In "Vladimir Nabokov's *Pale Fire*: The Composition of a Reading Experience," (*Literatur in Wissenschaft and Unterricht*, 10 [1977], 31–40; reprinted as "Vladimir Nabokov: Reader Beware," in his *The Story of Identity: American Fiction of the 60's* [Stuttgart: Matzler, 1979], pp. 194–210), Manfred Putz provides a helpful summary of the evidence that has been adduced for the arguments—is Shade Kinbote or Kinbote Shade, or perhaps they are both someone neither of them knows? See also D. Barton Johnson, "Index of Refraction in Nabokov's *Pale Fire*," *Russian Literature TriQuarterly*, 16 (1979), 33–49. Carol T. Williams' " 'Web of Sense': *Pale Fire* in the Nabokov Canon" (*Critique*, 6 [1963], 29–45) provides an early synthesizing, rather than reductive, reading of the narrators' relationship.

64. New York: Atheneum, 1971, pp. 3–11. See also *TriQuarterly*, 17.

65. George Steiner, "Lament for Language Lost," *Reporter*, 26 (June 27, 1962), 45.

66. Donald Malcolm, "Noetic License," *New Yorker*, 38 (September 22, 1982), 166–75.

67. See Field's bibliography for the publishing history and Nabokov's preface to the novel for the ironies of that history.

68. Hilary Corke, "Nabokov: Old News from Old Prospero," *New Republic*, 149 (July 6, 1963), 25–27; Donald Malcolm, "A Retrospect," *New Yorker*, 40 (April 25, 1964), 198–205.

69. See, for example, William Barrett's "Reader's Choice," *Atlantic Monthly*, 214 (November 1964), 197–99.

70. Malcolm Bradbury, "Grand Master," *Spectator*, No. 7116 (November 13, 1964), 634.

71. John Updike "Grandmaster Nabokov," *New Republic*, 151 (September 26, 1964), 15–18; reprinted in Updike's *Assorted Prose* (New York: Alfred A. Knopf, 1965), pp. 318–27—citation here is to p. 319.

72. Updike, pp. 322–23.

73. "Nabokov's Game," *New York Review of Books*, January 14, 1965, pp. 18–19.

74. In the one superb review occasioned by the publication of *The Eye*, Julian Moynahan argues that the dearth of reviews was caused by the book's appearance during a newspaper strike in New York but, given the lack of attention this novel has elicited since then, that can only be a partial explanation. Moynahan's review, actually an appreciation of Nabokov's achievement as a whole, is well worth reading; see "Speaking of Books: Vladimir Nabokov," *New York Times Book Review*, April 3, 1966, pp. 2, 14.

75. Originally published in New York Times Book Review, May 16, 1966, pp. 5, 25.

76. The *Speak, Memory* published in London and reprinted in New York in 1960 is simply a retitled *Conclusive Evidence*.

77. "Nabokov's Look Back, a National Loss," *Life*, 62 (January 13, 1967), 11; reprinted as "Mnemosyne Chastened," in Updike's *Picked Up Pieces* (New York: Alfred A. Knopf, 1975), pp. 191–92.

78. Appel, "Nabokov's Puppet Show—I," *New Republic*, 156 (January 14, 1967), 30. Eight years later, Dabney Stuart elaborated this argument in "The Novelist's Composure: *Speak, Memory* as Fiction," *Modern Language Quarterly*, 36 (June 1978), 177–92, an expanded version of which is the final chapter of his *Nabokov: The Dimensions of Parody* (Baton Rouge: Louisiana State Univ., 1978). See also, Patricia Bruckmann, "Echoes of the Pram-Pushers' Knack: Some Facts in Nabokov's Self-Fiction," in *Figures in a Ground: Canadian Essays on Modern Literature*, ed. Diane Bessai and David Jackel (Saskatoon, Saskatchewan: Western Producer Prairie Books, 1978), pp. 32–41.

79. V. S. Pritchett, "Exile," *New Statesman*, 74 (July 21, 1967), 89.

80. See Andrew Field's *Nabokov: His Life in Art* and Phyllis Roth's "Toward the Man Behind the Mystification" in *Nabokov's Fifth Arc*, ed. J. E. Rivers and Charles Nicol (Austin: Univ. of Texas Press, 1982), pp. 43–62.

81. The clearest articulations of the latter position are those of Philip Toynbee in "This Bright Brute is the Gayest," *New York Times Book Review*, May 12, 1968, p. 5 and William Gass in "Mirror, Mirror" (see note 19 above).

82. Denis Donoghue, "Bright Brute," *Listener*, 80 (October 10, 1968), 480.

83. "Nabokov's Waterloo," *TLS*, October 2, 1969, p. 1121.

84. *New York Times Book Review*, April 18, 1971, pp. 2–18.

85. Robert Alter, "Nabokov's Ardor," *Commentary*, 48 (August 1969), 49; greatly expanded as "*Ada*, or the Perils of Paradise" in *Vladimir Nabokov: A Tribute*, ed. Peter Quennell (New York: William Morrow, 1980), pp. 103–18. See also Robert M. Adams, "Passion

Among the Polyglots," *Hudson Review*, 22 (1969), 717–24; and Alfred Appel's review in the *New York Times Book Review*, May 4, 1969, p. 37—a much expanded version of this review was published as "*Ada* Described," in *TriQuarterly*, 17 (Winter 1970), 160–86.

86. Leslie Fiedler, "The Profanation of the Child," *New Leader*, 41 (June 23, 1958), 26–29; all citations here are from p. 29; reprinted in *No! in Thunder* (Boston: Beacon Press, 1960), pp. 289–90 and, with revisions, in *Love and Death in the American Novel* (Cleveland: World Publishing, 1964), pp. 326–28.

87. Dupee, "A Preface to *Lolita*," in *"The King of the Cats" and Other Remarks on Writers and Writing* (New York: Farrar, Straus & Giroux, 1965), pp. 128–29.

88. Translated by Richard Howard (New York: Pantheon Books, 1963), p. 41; see pp. 41–54 for the focus on *Lolita*. The chapter including the discussion of *Lolita* was originally published in French in 1959.

89. de Rougement, p. 47.

90. *New World Writing*, 16 (1960), 58–84.

91. *Critical Quarterly*, 6 (1964), 35–48; reprinted in *The World and the Book* (Stanford, 1971).

92. *Western Humanities Review*, 18 (1964), 234.

93. *The Hollins Critic*, 3 (June 1966), 1–12; reprinted in *The Sounder Few: Essays from* The Hollins Critic, ed R. H. W. Dillard, George Garrett, and J. R. Moore (Athens: Univ. of Georgia Press, 1971), pp. 139–71; citation here is to p. 2 in *The Hollins Critic*. For a different but equally solid overview of Nabokov's work, see Henry Grosshans, "Vladimir Nabokov and the Dream of Old Russia," *Texas Studies in Literature and Language*, 7 (1966), 407.

94. *English Literary History*, 33 (1966), 198–227; citation here is to p. 217.

95. Levine, p. 224.

96. "Vladimir Nabokov's Novel *Dar* as a Work of Literary Criticism," *Slavic and East European Journal*, 7 (1963), 284–90.

97. See Schuman's entries for 1964 for annotations of the critical pieces and Beverly Clark in the present volume for a discussion of Robbe-Grillet's piece on *Lolita*.

98. New York: The Dial Press, 1966; Apollo paperback edition, 1969. References here are to the latter, in this case, p. 13.

99. Stegner, p. 40.

100. Field, p. 180.

101. Proffer, p. 82. An important question has been raised recently about Proffer's calendar for *Lolita*, a question which suggests that Nabokov's careful use of dates indicates that Humbert invented Quilty. See Christine Tekiner, "Time in *Lolita*," *Modern Fiction Studies*, 25 (Autumn 1979), 463–69.

102. *Novel*, 1 (Fall 1967), 12.

103. (New York: W. W. Norton & Co., 1967), p. 168.

104. *Atlantic*, 220 (August 1967), 29. Also published in 1967, Robert Scholes' study of writers he calls *The Fabulators*, briefly mentioning Nabokov as one of the number, identifies characteristics similar to those discussed by others writing on "post-modernist" fiction. "Fabulations," surely a more cheerful conception of art than "the literature of exhaustion," nonetheless designates the same emphases on verbal and structural artifice, on "delight in design." Moreover, in connecting fabulation to fables, Scholes is able to locate its "didactic quality": thus, "Modern fabulation, like the ancient fabling of Aesop, tends away from the representation of reality but returns toward actual human life by way of *ethically controlled fantasy*" (*The Fabulators* [New York: Oxford Univ. Press, 1967], pp. 10–11; my italics).

105. Barth, p. 31.

106. Evanston: Northwestern Univ. Press, 1970.

107. "Extraterritorial," p. 123.

108. Steiner, p. 124.

109. "*Invitation to a Beheading*; Nabokov and the Art of Politics," p. 42.

110. Alter, p. 56.

111. Ibid., p. 46.

112. Gillian Tindall, "Past Eternal," *New Statesman*, 81 (February 19, 1971), 244.

113. However, for excellent reviews, see Robert Alter, "Mirrors for Immortality," *Saturday Review*, 55 (November 11, 1972), 72–76; and Simon Karlinsky, "Russian Transparencies," *Saturday Review of the Arts*, 1 (January 1973), 44–45.

114. J. D. O'Hara, review of *Glory*, in *Saturday Review*, January 15, 1972, pp. 41, 36.

115. Two provocative reviews of *LATH!* provide a microcosm of the world of critical discord. See Richard Poirier's, "Nabokov as his own Half-Hero," *New York Times Book Review*, October 13, 1974, pp. 2–4; and Dabney Stuart's review in *Georgia Review*, 29 (1975), 743–47. See also John Updike, "Motley But True," in *Picked Up Pieces*, pp. 215–20, a reprint of "Motlier than Ever" which appeared in *New Yorker*, November 11, 1974, pp. 209–112.

116. See note 113 above.

117. A dissertation remake published by Cornell Univ. Press which I reviewed too harshly but not inaccurately in *Studies in American Fiction*, 3 (Sring 1975), 109–11.

118. *Vladimir Nabokov* (New York: Frederick Ungar, 1974).

119. Boston: G. K. Hall.

120. The Hague: Mouton.

121. London: Marion Boyars. Hyde pursues a line of argument similar to Lee's Twayne volume, that Nabokov is as much a moralist as a master of language, and he usefully attempts to define Nabokov's Russian heritage. For lengthier discussions of Grabes and Hyde, see Charles S. Ross, "Nabokov's Mistress/Muse Metaphor: Some Recent Books," *Modern Fiction Studies*, 25 (Autumn 1979), 514–24.

122. See note 2 above.

123. New York: New York Univ. Press, 1971. See Nabokov's Response, "Rowe's Symbols," *New York Review of Books*, 17 (October 7, 1971), 8. In the main, Rowe's other reviewers concur with Nabokov. See, for example, Phyllis Roth in *Studies in American Fiction*, 1 (Spring 1973), 116–18.

124. See Schuman's *Reference Guide* for bibliographic data and a summary.

125. Readers especially interested in this topic should consult the relevant essays in *TriQuarterly*, 17; Alexandr D. Nakhimovsky, "A Linguistic Study of Nabokov's Russian Prose," *Slavic and East European Journal*, 21 (Spring 1977), 78–87; Carl R. Proffer's "From *Otchaianie* to *Despair*," *Slavic Review*, 27 (June 1968), 258–67; and *An English-Russian Dictionary of Nabokov's* Lolita," compiled by A. Nakhimovsky and S. Paperno (Ann Arbor: Ardis Inc., 1982).

126. Ann Arbor: Ardis Inc., 1974, p. 50.

127. New York: Viking Press, 1977. See the review by Phyllis Roth in *Studies in American Fiction*, 6 (Autumn, 1978), 245–47.

128. Others include Tony Tanner's *City of Words: American Fiction 1950–1970* (London: Jonathan Cape, 1971); John Stark's *The Literature of Exhaustion: Borges, Nabokov, Barth* (Durham: Duke Univ. Press, 1974); Patricia Drechsel Tobin's *Time and the Novel: The Genealogical Imperative* (Princeton: Princeton Univ. Press, 1978); and Ronald Wallace's *The Last Laugh: Form and Affirmation in the Contemporary American Comic Novel* (Columbia: Univ. of Missouri Press, 1977). This list is by no means exhaustive.

129. *Partial Magic* (Berkeley: Univ. of California Press, 1975, 1978), p. x.

130. Alter, p. 215.

131. Ibid., p. 180.

132. Ibid., p. 182.

133. Ann Arbor: Ardis Inc.

134. *Modern Fiction Studies*, 25 (Autumn 1979), 397. A related discussion of Nabokov's unique imprint appears in the same issue in David I. Sheidlower's discussion of the chess theme in *Bend Sinister*, an excellent discussion of Nabokov's "subtle and precise interrelation of life, art and chess" (p. 424).

135. See also Johnson's "Spatial Modeling and Deixis: Nabokov's *Invitation to a Beheading*," *Poetics Today*, 3 (Winter 1982), 81–98.

136. *Novel*, 4 (Spring 1971), 197–208.

137. *Modern Language Quarterly*, 34 (June 1973), 180–90. Though he does not refer to Bruffee's analysis, Lawrence Buell is describing much the same category, using many of the same texts as examples including *The Real Life of Sebastian Knight*, in his "Observer-Hero Narrative," *Texas Studies in Literature and Language*, 211 (Spring 1979), 93–111.

138. "The Moral Rhetoric of Nabokov's *Lolita*," *Four Quarters*, 22 (Spring 1973), 13–14. Rackin's reference to Green is to Martin Green, "The Morality of *Lolita*," *Kenyon Review*, 28 (June 1966), 352–77, a complex essay worth reconsidering.

139. Rackin, p. 18.

140. *Twentieth Century Literature*, 21 (1975), 428. See also Max F. Schultz, "Characters (Contra Characterization) in the Contemporary Novel," in *The Theory of the Novel: New Essays*, ed. John Halperin (New York: Oxford Univ. Press, 1974), pp. 141–54.

141. *Poetics Today*, 1 (Autumn 1979), 65–83.

142. *Criticism*, 17 (1975), 227. Flower's perspective recalls the distinctions offered by R. H. Stacy's *Russian Literary Criticism: A Short History*, published by Syracuse Univ. Press in 1974. Stacy comments that "Nabokov, despite his emphasis on strangeness and the irrational, is a stickler for accuracy in *realia*. . . ." (p. 249). Stacy's volume provides a context in Russian literary criticism for Nabokov's attitude toward social realism, a helpful summary of Nabokov's critical views, and a chapter on Nikolay Chernyshevsky which is useful for readers of *The Gift*.

143. *Essays in Literature*, 2 (Fall 1975), 209–29.

144. *PTL: A Journal for Descriptive Poetics and Theory of Literature*, 1 (1976), 489–512.

145. *Studies in American Fiction*, 4 (Autumn 1976), 215.

146. *The French-American Review*, 1 (Fall 1977), 173–97.

147. D. Barton Johnson's book, *Worlds in Regression: Some Novels of Vladimir Nabokov*, which includes many of the essays referred to here, will be published by Ardis within the year.

148. *Style*, 5 (Winter 1971), 57–69.

149. *Slavic Review*, 32 (1973), 79–90.

150. *Contemporary Literature*, 18 (Autumn 1977), 518.

151. *PTL: A Journal for Descriptive Poetics and Theory of Literature*, 2 (1977), 73–87.

152. "On Human Freedom and Inhuman Art: Nabokov," *Slavic and East Euopean Journal*, 22 (1978), 57.

153. Pifer, p. 60.

154. *Nabokov: The Dimensions of Parody* (see note 78 above), p. 50.

155. Stuart, p. 88. For the same argument, see also Max F. Schultz, "Characters (Contra Characterization) in the Contemporary Novel" mentioned in note 140 above.

156. Stuart, p. 133.

157. "Nabokov's Performative Writing," in *Les Américanistes: New French Criticism*

on Modern American Fiction, ed. Ira D. Johnson and Christin Johnson (Port Washington, N.Y.: Kennikat Press, 1978), p. 158.

158. Couturier, pp. 180–81.

159. "Mimesis and the Motive for Fiction," *TriQuarterly*, 42 (Spring 1978), 241.

160. Alter, p. 242.

161. "Nabokov's *Invitation:* Literature as Execution," *PMLA*, 96 (October 1981), 360–83.

162. New York: William Morrow & Co., Inc., 1980; originally published in Great Britain by Weidenfeld and Nicolson, 1979.

163. See, for example, Daniel Albright, *Representation and the Imagination: Beckett, Kafka, Nabokov, and Schoenberg* (Chicago: Univ. of Chicago Press, 1981), and Sylvia Paine, *Beckett, Nabokov, Nin: Motives and Modernism* (Port Washington, N.Y.: Kennikat Press, 1981).

164. (Lewisburg: Bucknell Univ. Press, 1981), p. 15. See also Bruss's essay in *Nabokov's Fifth Arc*, entitled "The Problem of Text: Nabokov's Last Two Novels."

165. Bruss, p. 29.

166. See, for example, Arthur Mizener, "The Seriousness of Vladimir Nabokov," *Sewanee Review*, 76 (1968), 655–64.

167. *Vladimir Nabokov: The Structure of Literary Desire* (Columbia: Univ. of Missouri Press, 1982), p. 21.

168. Packman, p. 45.

169. In *Nabokov and Others* (Ann Arbor: Ardis Inc., 1979), pp. 175–82.

170. *Nabokov's Spectral Dimension* (Ann Arbor: Ardis Inc., 1981).

171. "Nabokov's Philosophical World," *Southern Review* (Adelaide, Australia), 14 (November 1981), 260–98.

172. *Nabokov's Novels in English* (Athens: Univ. of Georgia Press, 1983).

173. "Introduction," *Nabokov's Fifth Arc* (Austin: Univ. of Texas Press, 1982), p. xiv.

174. "Nabokov's Assault on Wonderland," pp. 63–74.

175. "The Cartesian Nightmare of *Despair*," pp. 82–104.

176. "*Invitation to a Beheading* and Kafka," pp. 105–21.

177. "Toward the Man Behind the Mystification," pp. 43–62.

178. In *Nabokov: The Man and His Work*, pp. 183–94.

179. Review of *Poems and Problems* in the *New York Times Book Review*, July 25, 1971, p. 4.

180. "New Sidelights on a Lepidopterist," *TLS*, April 7, 1961, p. 218.

181. "The Anguish of the Spirit and the Letter," *Hudson Review*, 12 (1959–60), 594.

182. "Nabokov's Verse Shows Rare Wit," *Richmond News-Leader* (Va.), September 16, 1959, p. 13.

183. See, for example, Helen Muchnic's review of *Details of a Sunset and Other Stories*, *New York Review of Books*, May 27, 1976, pp. 22–24; Elizabeth Pochoda's review of *Tyrants Destroyed*, *New Republic*, 172 (March 29, 1975), 31–32; and Howard Nemerov on *Nabokov's Dozen* (also published as *Spring in Fialta*), "The Ills of Missing Dates," in Nemerov's *Poetry and Fiction: Essays* (New Brunswick. Rutgers University Press, 1963), p. 267.

184. L. L. Lee's "Duplexity in Vladimir Nabokov's Short Stories," *Studies in Short Fiction*, 11 (Summer 1965), 307–35, contains a superb analysis of this story and a discussion of the unique use of doublings in several others.

185. See Tuuli-Ann Ristok, "Nabokov's 'The Vane Sisters': 'Once in a thousand years of fiction,' " *University of Windsor Review*, 11 (February 1976), 27–48; David Eggenschwiler,

"Nabokov's 'The Vane Sisters': Exuberant Pedantry and a Biter Bit," *Studies in Short Fiction*, 18 (Winter 1981), 33–39; and Isobel Murray, " '*Plagiatisme*': Nabokov's 'The Vane Sisters' and *The Picture of Dorian Gray,*" *Durham University Journal*, 70 (December 1977), 69–72.

186. In "A Guide to Nabokov's 'A Guide to Berlin,' " *Slavic and East European Journal*, 23 (1979), 353–61, D. Barton Johnson argues that this story, unlike others in *The Return of Chorb* collection, foreshadows the stylistic and thematic complexities of the later novels.

187. "Signs and Symbols," probably the most widely anthologized of Nabokov's stories, has also received the lion's share of attention. See, John V. Hagopian, "Decoding Nabokov's 'Signs and Symbols,' " *Studies in Short Fiction*, 18 (Spring 1981), 115–19; Geoffrey Green, "Nabokov's Signs of Reference, Symbols of Design," *College Literature*, 7 (1980), 104–12; and Paul J. Rosenzweig, "The Importance of Reader Response in Nabokov's 'Signs and Symbols,' " *Essays in Literature*, 7 (1980), 255–60. Additionally, several of the collections of essays on Nabokov include pieces on this story.

188. New York: New York Univ. Press, 1978.

189. The earliest piece I have located with such a focus is James Twitchell's "*Lolita* as *Bildungsroman*," *Genre*, 71 (September 1974), 272–78; it is joined now by some recent discussions of Ada and Lucette, and the Nabokov session to be held at the 1983 MLA convention will explore the function and characterization of women in Nabokov's art.

190. Jenefer P. Shute, "Nabokov and Freud: The Play of Power," for completion of the degree at the University of California, Los Angeles; Gene Barabtarlo's dissertation on *Pnin* will be completed at the University of Illinois. For both references, see the *Vladimir Nabokov Research Newsletter*, 10 (Spring 1983), 9.

191. I am appropriating the title of Leon Edel's review of Nabokov's *Lectures on Russian Literature* (*New Republic*, 185 [December 23, 1981], 35–36) which takes on Nabokov taking on Freud.

192. Since the present volume initially went to press, another important collection has been published of which Nabokovians should be aware. *Nabokov: The Critical Heritage*, edited by Norman Page (London: Routledge and Kegan Paul, 1982), is an invaluable collection of seventy-five reviews, including several of the most well known and several others previously difficult to find, spanning the years 1934 to 1977. The volume also includes a lengthy survey of these reviews and others, but does not treat any other critical material and is therefore rather mistitled.

Notes and Comment

John Updike*

Vladimir Nabokov's most recent novel, on one of its last pages, invites us, "Imagine me, an old gentleman, a distinguished author, gliding rapidly on my back, in the wake of my outstretched dead feet, first through that gap in the granite, then over a pinewood, then along misty water meadows, and then simply between marges of mist, on and on, imagine that sight!" This man had imagined death so often, from Luzhin the chessmaster's fall into a chasm of "dark and pale squares . . . at the instant when icy air gushed into his mouth" to Cincinnatus C.'s false beheading ("A spinning wind was picking up and whirling: dust, rags, chips of painted wood, bits of gilded plaster, pasteboard bricks, posters; an arid gloom fleeted") and to the reported demise of Mrs. Richard F. Schiller, née Dolores Haze, yclept Lolita, while "giving birth to a stillborn girl, on Christmas Day 1952, in Gray Star," and on to the death by gunshot of the poet John Shade and by "time-and-pain" of Van Veen—Nabokov had imagined death so often, so colorfully and variously and searchingly, that we felt him to be exempt, having already passed through, into that Switzerland he inhabited as a chocolate-box province of immortality, the last and most playful of his exiles. His death, at the ripe age of seventy-eight, comes too soon, too coarsely—an ugly footnote to a shimmering text, reality's thumbprint on the rainbow.

Posterity's judgment can sort out the best: in English, "Lolita," perhaps, and, in Russian, "The Gift" ("Дар"). What matters now is that the least of his writings offered a bygone sort of delight: a sorcerer's scintillant dignity made of every sentence a potentially magic occasion. He wanted the reader to share his extraordinary intimations; this generosity gave even his scholarly dissertations and diatribes a certain spaciousness, a giddying other dimension. He lived in the world, and more peripatetically and traumatically than many of us, yet in his art declined to submit to the world; rather, he asked that the world submit to the curious, spotty evidence of its own mimetics, its streaks of insane tenderness, its infinitely ingenious interior markings. Few minds so scientific have deigned to serve the gods of fancy; with his passion for precision and for the complex design, he mounted for display the crudest, most futile lurchings of the human heart—lust, terror, nostalgia. The violence and violent comedy of his novels strike us, in the main, as merely descriptive, the way the violences of geology are. He saw from a higher altitude, from the top of the continents he had had to put behind him.

Though some of his asides sounded arrogant, and even peevish, his life in its actions demonstrated immense resilience and a robust optimism. Few men who have lost so much have complained so little. He brought to America the body of a forty-one-year-old man of genius in his native

*From *New Yorker*, 53 (July 18, 1977), 21–22. Reprinted by permission;

language, but offered no excuse of exhaustion; the same active mind that entertained his insomnia with the invention of chess puzzles now turned to inventing himself anew, as an American writer. That he succeeded, and taught us new ways to use our language and to experience our milieu, is perhaps less remarkable than his willingness to try, when a hundred college Slavic Languages Departments held shelter against the raging of the strange democratic culture whose uncodified quirks swarmed about him. On page 53 of "Lolita," as Humbert Humbert's love-fever comes to a boil, there is a sudden list of forty names, beginning

> Angel, Grace
> Austin, Floyd
> Beale, Jack

and ending

> Williams, Ralph
> Windmuller, Louise.

It is, the author explains, "a poem, a poem, forsooth!" It is one of Lolita's class lists; it is, with the odd chiming of its relentless alphabetization of fuzzy, budding souls, the class list all Americans have been part of. We have sat in those classes, Nabokov had not; yet it was he who put one into literature, along with so many other comic, correct details of his adopted "lovely, trustful, dreamy, enormous country." His patriotism won him few friends in our literary establishment, but it gave his American novels the fervor of the explicit. His most gracious compliment to the United States was to merge it, in "Ada," with the Russia of his memory to make one paradisiacal Antiterra.

His prose was festive, though his characters were doomed. Now he has joined them, in that state he so often imagined—sometimes as the blackest of blacknesses and at other times as a transformation as harmless and amusing as that from chrysalis to butterfly. In his youthful novella "The Eye," the hero shoots himself and reports, "Some time later, if one can speak here of time at all, it became clear that after death human thought lives on by momentum." Nabokov's momentum originated at the beginning of the century and should continue to its end and beyond. Gentleman, aesthete, metaphysician, wit: the words to describe him have an old-fashioned ring. The power of the imagination is not apt soon to find another champion of such vigor. He was one of the last delegates from the nineteenth century; he takes with him the secret of an undiscourageable creativity, he leaves behind a resplendent oeuvre.

ON SIRIN

". . . The author that interested me most was naturally Sirin. He belonged to my generation. Among the young writers produced in exile he turned out to be the only major one. Beginning with the appearance of his first novel in 1925 and throughout the next fifteen years, until he vanished as strangely as he had come, his work kept provoking an acute and rather morbid interest on the part of critics. Just as Marxist publicists of the eighties in old Russia would have denounced his lack of concern with the economic structure of society, so the mystagogues of émigré letters deplored his lack of religious insight and of moral preoccupation. . . . Conversely, Sirin's admirers made much, perhaps too much, of his unusual style, brilliant precision, functional imagery and that sort of thing. . . . Across the dark sky of exile, Sirin passed . . . like a meteor, and disappeared, leaving nothing much else behind him than a vague sense of uneasiness. . . ."

from *Conclusive Evidence* (1951)

"None of my American friends have read my Russian books and thus every appraisal on the strength of my English ones is bound to be out of focus."

from "On a Book entitled *Lolita*"
November 12, 1956

[*Review of Mashen'ka (Mary)*]

Mikhail Osorgin
(Mikhail Andreevich Il'in,
1878–1943)*

Mary is not a novel but a very fine novella of the customs and manners of émigré life. In Berlin, in a Russian pension with windows looking out on the railway tracks there live, "in an iron draft," some insignificant people: the vulgar little "gentleman"-operator Alfyorov; "the old Russian poet" Anton Podtyagin; the full-busted young lady Klara; the ballet dancers Kolin and Gornotsvetov; and the story's hero Ganin.

The blabbermouth and vulgar Alfyorov, a man with a murky past, is awaiting the arrival from Russia of his young little wife Mary—about whom he keeps talking to everyone. The elderly poet Podtyagin is trying to leave for Paris and is helplessly bogged down with visas and other documents. Klara, a very cozy and sentimental girl, leads a loveless existence, while her neighbor Ganin is having a chance affair with her friend Lyudmila, a stupid, "uncozy," tiresome girl. The dancers are more or less satisfied with life and with one another. Ganin must be—according to the obvious thought of the author—a positive type or hero. For this he is endowed with a store of physical strength, life experiences, good sense, and positive views on life. Being an intelligent man, he has managed to have tried his hand at everything: laborer, waiter, movie "extra"—never shying away from work, yet never deriving any particular pleasure from life. The settled way of life wearies him as does any lasting attachment. Émigré surroundings obviously oppress him; his disease is "a desire for a change of scene." For some reason he drags on his affair with Lyudmila, putting off from one day to the next his departure—for parts unknown. In effect, he lives quite senselessly for a positive type.

It comes to light, by chance, that Alfyorov's wife, about whose arrival he has been dinning everyone's ears, is the very same girl Mary whom Ganin had loved in Russia and for whom alone he has preserved tenderness and a wealth of memories. Ganin recognizes her from a snapshot. Thus a significant part of the novella is devoted to Ganin's recollec-

*From *Sovremennye Zapiski* [Contemporary annals], 28 (1926), 474–76, translated by Marina Turkevich Naumann.

tions of his youthful affair, which on the whole has been a very ordinary one.

He conceives a daring plan and nearly carries it out. The plan consists in meeting Mary before her husband does and carrying her off with him, from Alfyorov. A drinking bout in the pension, arranged by the dancers, comes to aid the plan: Ganin gets Alfyorov drunk and puts him to bed to sleep it off. He then sets the alarm clock a few hours back, so that Alfyorov will be late for the train to meet Mary. And then, grabbing his suitcase, Ganin leaves the pension for good. He sets off to meet Mary and to carry out his plan.

But in the days before Mary's arrival Ganin has had a chance not only to relive his youthful affair with her in his recollections, but to exhaust all the feeling which he once had for her. That which has been—is beautiful; but now, it will not return. Her image has become a shadow, just as shadowy as the pension, recently abandoned by him, with all of its petty people; just as all the past has faded before a vision of the future—of new paths, new homelands, a new fight for life. Ganin hails a cab and goes . . . to another station to set off for somewhere in the south, to the seashore. "How long it was since he had felt so fit, strong and ready to tackle anything."

The novella's hero, his strength and well-being, his search for life and struggle—all this in the novella is quite controversial and unjustified. One has to take the author's word for it, while in fact Ganin is just as much a wandering émigré, living as aimlessly, as are all the other inhabitants of the pension "in the iron draft,"—only he is a bit younger, physically a bit stronger, a bit more agile. He knocks about out of ennui and tedium; he is mischievous out of aimlessness; in his soul there is a void. As is to be expected from a Russian author—the positive type does not work out.

But for Sirin something else does work out, and it works out very well indeed: the trivia of daily life and surroundings. The small pension, inhabited by unneeded people, accommodates perfectly the great melancholy, rootlessness, senselessness of the refugee way of life; its spiritual exhaustion; its weak-willed vulgarity. True, from the complex phenomenon of emigration Sirin has taken only the refugees, the mass, a way of life without an existence, an inertia without an idea. Nevertheless, he incarnates this portion of emigration almost exhaustively in a few figures, which are drawn artistically and are complete as types.

The finest figure of his novella is "the old Russian poet" Podtyagin, who never does get off to Paris and ends his life in the pension where Ganin has left him dying. The several tragic—in all their quotidian pettiness—pages of the novella, devoted to the old man-poet, compensate for the novella's shortcomings and in part the failure of the "hero" figure.

Mary is written with rare simplicity and in a fine literary language. It absolutely does not pay to stop at the individual controversial or unsuccessful expressions. . . . *Mary* may be acknowledged as one of the most successful novellas written in the "Emigration." What is splendid is the absence of all political tendentiousness and that cheap journalism which spoils artistry in contemporary Russian literature, both abroad and in Russia itself.

[Review of "Terror"]

Iulii Isaevich Aikhenval'd (1872–1928)*

Sirin's little story "Terror" reproduces precisely that terror which occurs when a person experiences a sudden feeling of alienation; when he wonders about himself, about his face, about his being and existence, about other people, about the whole world in general; when everything for him unexpectedly takes on some sort of excruciatingly odd and strange appearance. However, Mr. Sirin's hero experiences not just this fear of life. He also experiences the fear of death—in those nocturnal hours he recalls his mortality when "my soul would choke for a moment," when "one tells oneself that death is still far away, that there will be plenty of time to reason everything out, and yet one knows that one never will do it," because "in the dark, from the cheapest seats, in one's private theater" "warm live thoughts about dear earthly trifles" interfere with this. The double terror in Sirin's sketch would have brought the hero to madness, but this time the death of his beloved saved him. "Plain human grief filled my life so completely there was no room left for any other emotion." Here is the story's precept and wisdom: unwarranted mystical terror yields to the simple terror of human grief, and another's death cures one of the fear of one's own death. In our terrifying reality mystical terror is sort of a luxury. Similarly, madness also is a unique luxury. You withdraw into it as into tight agony and insanity closes you off from others; from the near ones, from the rest of the world. Real misfortune and compassion do not make allowances for madness. The lunatic is guilty before the community. At the dying woman's bedside "it never occurred to me to analyze the meaning of being and nonbeing and no longer was I terrified by those thoughts." On a couple of Sirin's pages we are presented with great content. But here psychological analysis and vital artistry are not all sufficiently coordinated everywhere—are not in complete accord. And several lines are too rich and heavy because of their erudition. They resemble excerpts from a psychology textbook. True, in similar textbooks there is no elegant picturesqueness and expressiveness as, for example, in the figure of the heroine. While sitting on a crimson little sofa in the vestibule of the theater loge and taking off huge gray snowboots, she extricated "her

*From Aikhenval'd's column "Literaturnye zametki" (Literary notes), in *Rul'* (The rudder), February 2, 1927, p. 2, translated by Marina Turkevich Naumann.

slender silk-clad legs—and I thought of delicate moths that hatch from bulky shaggy cocoons." Or: "the rosy abyss of the house," "a solid old screen with pale-gold decorations depicting scenes from various operas." Or: in "the misty winter sky [was] the inflamed little eye of the sun, which kept up with the train," and "the white snow-covered fields which kept endlessly opening up like a giant fan of swan's down."

[Review of *Vozvrashchenie Chorba (The Return of Chorb)*]

A. Savel'ev
(Savelii Grigor'evich Sherman)*

V. Sirin, in his newly published book, engagingly tells us about the artist Shock who transformed his entire life into sheer mystification: "he resembled a poet more than a stage magician, and demonstrated his skill with a sort of tender and graceful melancholy. . . ." And in another story Sirin complains that, like Shock, life itself mystifies poets, enticing them by an idea which, it would seem, has a logical conclusion. But, at the last minute, life suddenly and incomprehensibly changes it into something unforeseen, "a hundred times nicer," and "much more subtle and deep. . . ."

Sirin's stories and poems attest to such a bold and unexpected trick created by life. This trick, like Shock's, is not devoid of a distant echo of sorrow. Life's intention here is risky, odd, and cruel; but apparently this time it works out brilliantly.

In the early period of an artist's maturation—when with his delicate roots the artist greedily absorbs the juices of his native soil which is endlessly pliant to intuitive comprehension, when his hearing bathes them in the speech of his fathers and grandfathers, speech which is so intimately close to the images arising in his soul and resonant to them—at this critical time for Nabokov, life cruelly ripped out his tender roots. And it gave them up to the will of a hurricane. Thus they were carried off to a chance hard rock and were enveloped in a cold blanket of forsakenness, alienation, nonbeing. Then suddenly, like a fakir's sapling, his talent revealed a blooming, ripening creativity which was full of the bright strength of joyful contemplation and unexpected well-being.

The past is absent in Sirin's book. He does not work over the deep recesses of memory and the associations carried off with it—whence the precious metal of the writers of the generation of Bunin, Kuprin, and Zaitsev was extracted. And the library, so necessary for Aldanov's work, is also alien to him. Russia penetrates his pages in special ways. It weaves

*From *Rul'* (The rudder), December 31, 1929, pp. 2–3, translated and edited by Marina Turkevich Naumann.

through his lyric poetry, hovers as a bright specter, passes on as disturbing and sorrowful dreams, but, as with the heroine of *Mary*, Russia is not visible to the reader. The developing strength of youthful talent strains toward what is directly given, to the river of life which seethes all around. However, placed in extraordinary conditions, torn from the surrounding way of life and, as if raised above them, Sirin develops in himself an unusual perceptiveness and an extraordinary ability to look at things from afar and to sense in them "the fragrant tenderness that only posterity will discern and appreciate in the far-off times when every trifle of our plain everyday life will become exquisite and festive in its own right." He is a "chance spy" "among strange people." He can even glimpse "somebody's future recollection." Incisively and wonderfully he perceives not Berlin alone. In his book a small German town, "where the very air seemed a little lusterless and where a transverse row of ripples had kept shading gently the reflected cathedral," benevolently lights up in a new way. So does London "on that smoke-blue day, in the August sun" when it "was particularly lovely"; as well as the hot lane of the Mediterranean port where "the stream and sun, and violet shadow all flowed, and streamed down to the sea" and a "dense sapphire brilliance grew from the depths between the walls" and where it would be easy to meet a Negro in a colonial uniform "with a face like a wet galosh."

The author is gripped by a greedy, insatiable curiosity to become acquainted with life's inner essence. . . . As the author knows that "life's performance is too sweeping, too uneven," he is tormented that often "her works are untranslatable, undescribable." But in the search for the solution to the "translatable and describable" of the surroundings, he turns off onto narrow paths, onto several ways which are not open for all. In Sirin's restless curiosity there is some sort of barely mocking smile which never leaves him. At times it appears to be a reflection of an inner chill. He needs it in order to preserve the sharpness of his vision and the subtlety of his hearing, which might deaden "compassion and anger." Caustically investigating everything thoroughly, getting his teeth into life, and feeling each bit of trivia, Sirin often stumbles upon incomprehensible existence and upon still-indigestible forms of alien culture. Like the root of a mountain pine which has encountered a rock, he skirts it, going into the depths, into the secret, hidden low places over which neither forms of culture nor existence have power.

All the stories, beginning with the first—an exquisite masterpiece completely beggaring retelling and giving the name to the entire collection—and concluding with the last one ("Terror"), use psychological material which is common to all mankind, because of the impossibility of distinguishing it as the property of certain peoples or a certain epoch. Sirin is frequently drawn to sick souls ("Bachmann"), and yet he is often bright and devoid of torment. Most importantly, he experiments with his heroes with the greatest care. Intensely sharp, he is filled with piety toward life's creation and, most of all, is afraid, through his willfullness, of insulting this creation. At moments of his heroes' highest spiritual tensions, the author seems to withdraw to the side, as if he were only a modest scribe of the great invisible and featureless experimenter. "I imagine for some reason. . . ." "I think that these two, the deranged musician and the dying woman, that night found words the greatest poets never dreamed of. . . ." One often runs into this form of narrative in Sirin.

The high level of his stories is so even and there is so little material in them for negative judgments, that they seem to be selected from a reserve which is rich in quality and quantity. Only rarely does one sense a strained construction (in the story "An Affair of Honor"); or for an instant the author's eye ceases being submissive to any aesthetic flair ("And with its thick, spongy tongue, suggesting somehow that of a cacological idiot slackly vomiting his monstrous speech").

The cruel experiment which Sirin performs upon himself does not poison him with bitterness. On the contrary, in places ("A Letter that Never Reached Russia") Sirin almost unnecessarily underlines his joy at being exceptional ("absently sensing the lips of dampness through my worn soles, I carry proudly my ineffable happiness. . . . My happiness will remain . . .").

But in the lyrics, in the marvelous, deeply sincere melodious verses a quiet groan is occasionally heard: ". . . I overnight with strangers, / I gaze upon my fellow travelers, / I catch the flat sound of their voices . . . / I demand fatal signs as to who will see the homeland; who will not; / who will fall asleep on non-Russian soil? . . . / Even for those who believe and wait— / even for me—it is occasionally sad. / At times only dreams console. / It is not into *oblasts* and towns or *volosts* and villages that / all Russia is divided, but into dreams."

Sirin's verses not only are good in their unique and, at the same time, unusually clear and transparent form. (In the realm of form many other poets are successful nowadays.) But, what appears to be a priceless rarity is that each of his poems, in its thought and subject, is a consummately finished creation, full of substance. The poem "Dream" is amazing for its form and keenness of psychological penetration.

Nikolay Andreyev on Vladimir Sirin (Nabokov) *and* Vladimir Weidle on Sirin

Andrew Field, trans.*

NIKOLAY ANDREYEV ON VLADIMIR SIRIN (NABOKOV)

Sirin is an émigré. This elementary definition refers not only to his temporary geographical location (Berlin), but in a real sense to the spirit and substance of his works. The emigration I have in mind is not a political one, but, rather, the one of adopting the culture of Western Europe, something that we see reflected in Sirin's artistic devices, his themes, his subject material (the setting, the plot, the hero's psychology) and perhaps in his style as well. More than a few critics, indeed, have seen in Sirin the influence of recent German and French writing.

But regardless of the foreign influences upon him (and whether, in fact, there have been such influences at all), Sirin's work is, to my way of thinking, the most important and interesting contribution to new Russian prose. He is a writer whose remarkable and promising silhouette made its appearance in our years of exile and combined our cultural heritage with the spirit of the new generation, the Russian literary tradition with bold innovation, the Russian propensity toward psychoanalysis with the Western regard for subject and pure form. Sirin's example shows clearly that it is wrong and superficial to believe that literary art, once the writer has been deprived of his native land, is fated to wither and perish or is limited to talented but impotent remembrance.

The older generation of Russian writers in emigration, for that matter, has also proved the view that foreign air is artistically sterile to be a false one. One can scarcely deny (even unfree Soviet criticism does not do this) that the best works of Bunin, the radiant heights of his brilliant, ever-so-slightly cold, wholly Olympian art, were written in emigration; that Remizov also refined his clever verbal art in emigration; that the striking and piercing poems of Marina Tsvetaeva, a most intricate, virtuosolike, and intelligent Russian poetess whose art is technically thorough and masculine and who possesses both the boldness of a great talent and the fineness of feminine intuition, were created in the smoke of Prague and on Parisian boulevards; that Vladislav Khodasevich, Georgy Adamovich, Zinaida Gippius, Georgy Ivanov all still have not ceased to make rare but culturally significant appearances in Russian print abroad.

But in the older generation there has been a fracture. The Russian tragedy has not left this generation unscarred. This generation's abrupt change of concern from pure art to political matters is a clear and easily

*From *The Complection of Russian Literature: A Cento*.

understood phenomenon. Their concern with ordinary life in emigration, which has been cultivated so assiduously by the older generation of exiled writers, is similar to "the art of embalming," as one Soviet critic wrote about Bunin. One cannot forever remember, ceaselessly sigh, and interminably sorrow over the past. Vital art cannot do without the vitality of the present. Sirin, more than any of his other young contemporaries, has shown how Russian literature may live abroad and live without relying upon the traditional descriptive modes, and has shown those directions which have contributed and may still contribute to the creative structure of new Russian prose.

The first book which made Sirin's name known—before it there had been two little-noticed books of poems—was his novel *Mashenka* (English title: *Mary*), which Mikhail Osorgin called "a tale of emigration." *Mashenka* is an extremely interesting novel in both its conception and its structure. Although the book is entitled after its heroine, it in fact does not have a heroine. All the action takes place on two planes: in reality (contemporary existence) and in recollection. The voice of the past penetrates the present, grows ever stronger, and finally smothers the boring existence of Berlin life. The plot, at first invisible, proceeds in a concealed, furtive manner and then suddenly hurries forward; obstacles, turns, and complications present themselves, and then everything is resolved in an unexpected but, in literary terms, logical and psychologically justifiable manner.

The novelty consists not, as often happens, in primitive (and sometimes extremely artificial) word play, but in a unique handling of normal vocabulary. The language of *Mashenka*, subtly vivid but without the protruding elbows of effort, intellectually refined, works toward the author's intent: one link is joined with the next, and the impact of his epithets is unexpectedly fresh.

The author strives to avoid the appearance of trying too hard. Many details of the story find their justification in the unnoticed turn of the tale (the face in the photograph that Alfyorov has, the "dovelike happiness" of the acrobatic roommates). The world of things (his descriptions of rooms and furniture are poems in themselves) is animated and breathes, and this provides a particularly highly charged, purposeful dynamism which, again, is part of the author's technique of employing the unexpected and the novel (for example, the smoothly rotating columns instead of the spokes of the bicycle passing them). In general the play of details in this novel, accompanying the theme of remembrance, is particularly well-suited and expressive.

But *Mashenka* also has faults. Sometimes there is an excess of separate detail. In places the author's tone gives way to intonations which are not his own. Sometimes we hear Gogol when Sirin leaps into lyrical digressions about Berlin at eventime.

Ganin, the novel's hero, is an attempt to depict a man of extremely strong character. But, interestingly, this is not what comes through most strongly in him, but rather it is his determined flight, characteristic of all Sirin's heroes, into his own special imaginative world which produces Ganin's romance with Mashenka (a charming and ephemeral image) and turns real life into the unreal. The only world that has life for Ganin is the one for which his soul grieves. And it is only one step from allegory: Mashenka is Russia. One direct statement seems to indicate such a thought on the author's part: "Fate on this final August day allowed him to taste in advance his future separation from Mashenka, from Russia." But my feeling is that this understanding was not the author's intention (if it were, then from a literary point of view it would have coarsened the novel) so much as it is Ganin's own unconscious feeling.

The novel is unusual. Precisely in this unusualness, in those simple Berlin days with a slightly retouched air about them, lies the novel's principal danger. The novel is refined from a literary point of view, gives promise of great possibilities, is lyrical and tender, but, because of all this, it may be mistakenly taken to be cold play with art. It is that, but only in order to conceal the author's emotional excitement.

In *King, Queen, Knave* one is struck by the virtuosity of stylization in the milieu depicted, but the stylization is not linguistic but rather a stylization of mood and spiritual atmosphere. For this reason it is understandable and, perhaps, pardonable to argue stupidly, as several literary criticasters have, that this book has the air of a German translation. The novel is set in present-day Germany and reflects bourgeois life in Berlin, which in itself distinguishes the novel as an interesting attempt by a Russian author to depict foreign life "from the inside out."

The banal and tragic combination of three playing-card figures symbolically reveals the inescapably gloomy sensuality and the impersonality of such human existence. Their turgid, lacquered lives, which glitter on the surface, burst to reveal disgusting and nauseating interiors, which Franz (the Knave) once properly sensed in childhood. Not surprisingly, in this gray-green slimy morass Dreyer (the King) instinctively tries to retire into his quiet world of fantastic invention, ironic observation, quest for the amusing, all the while donning the outward appearance of a smiling mannikin. Immersed in his dreams, Dreyer, who is saved by fate and the author, happily for himself never wakes up; perhaps it is a reward for his unassuming latent humanity. And even matter-of-fact Marta (the Queen) in the lightest and most delicious minutes of her earthly love tries involuntarily (for this urge is inherent in all human souls) to create and guard her own brittle happiness.

Moving with stressed coolness, mathematically, inexorably, Sirin reveals the absurdity of philistine life as though it were a chess problem, and the reader is left stunned and weary. The world of man is repulsive and coarse carnality. Maybe there is more sense and delight in the world of things, which are submissive, secretive, and alive in their own way.

Even whimsy can turn into a distorted grimace, as we see, for example, in the giggling old man who is Franz's landlord, or in Marta's plots. This banal handful of "cards" forms a merciless judgment, but without pretending to form any general conclusion for the reader's convenience. Sirin's heroes are always unique. But there are short glimpses of clear sky even in such a story: as a result of the sadness which oppresses these souls, they grow slightly more refined. The ever-heightening sorrow removes even Marta's icy mask for a moment.

King, Queen, Knave turns into a common crime novel before the end, and this is appropriate for the intentionally elementary, immobile, and fixed skeleton of the action (humdrum life is this way). The author adds intricate and inventive zigzags so that at the decisive moment everything will hinge on the simplest, most banal, and therefore most unforeseen occurrence, which is for that very reason Sirin's chosen fictive path.

The reader is subjected to two optical illusions. One's initial impression is that the action is quite complicated, whereas in fact one finds a simplicity and almost primitiveness in the silhouette of the plot. The second optical illusion is that the author's true interest is in existence laid bare. This is a mistake.

There are many fine things in *King, Queen, Knave*. In places the visual intensity of the text is stunning: it seems that one may really feel objects (the scene in the railway car when Franz loses his eyeglasses). There are many memorable details such as "the strange man" whom Marta meets after her first love assignation—her husband.

Sirin's collection of short stories and poems *The Return of Chorb* allows us to draw close to the writer and see the sympathy that is difficult to discern in his novels because of their blinding glitter. We see here how Sirin is consistently attracted to unusual people who fly toward fantastic worlds (the magician Shock, the Potato Elf, Mark, Erwin, Bachmann), how cautiously and wisely he treats the spiritual sadness and weariness of his characters, and how gifted he is in the seemingly endless verbal diversity of his descriptions. This book refutes the opinion expressed by one critic in the Paris paper *Russia and Slavdom* that Sirin's world is an unhealthy one. Sirin's world is full of color, breath, fragrance, which all come through these pages in spite of the dull sadness inherent in dark human acts.

The Defense, Sirin's most recent novel, is something extraordinary not only for Sirin, but also in all contemporary Russian prose. Everything is fresh, finished, and perfectly blended: it is an unexpected and exhilarating joy in the midst of the ordinariness and averageness of this literary period. Even the subject of *The Defense* is a happy discovery. The story tells about the life of a chess player of genius who is sentenced by fate, as is the case with any true gift, to his ghostly and unreal art (it is not for nothing that Luzhin remarks several times, "What a dubious thing chess is"), about the inspired and mad world of chess which insinuates itself into all actual reality, about his stubborn and tragic defense against the evil unknown things in this world that seek to imprison him and subject his free personality, and about delirium in the soul of an extraordinary man.

And this extremely complex story turns out to be simply a trampoline enabling Sirin to make a brilliant leap into breathtaking expanses of art and deep secrets of human psychology.

This novel, so wonderfully (another, less ecstatic term does not come to mind) written, bypasses all generally accepted structural forms. The narrative is broken chronologically several times, but artistically it remains unbroken. The gradual increase in the action does away with all conventional measures by chapter. This architectonic novel is a superb spectrum which, thanks to Sirin's talent, does not break down into separate colors, but, rather, unites all colors in the stream of art. Demanding the reader's maximum attention every moment, the story reflects in its extrinsic structure the internal tension of Luzhin, this strange and attractive hero whose pale prototype appeared in the "Bachmann" story in the collection *The Return of Chorb*. But there is not much point in singling out separate features, because this entire novel is an endless succession of striking innovations.

From a formal point of view Sirin represents a synthesis of Russian moods and West European forms. Sirin, more clearly and successfully than any other Russian writer, has fulfilled the well-known call of Mayakovsky's companion, the late Lev Luntz—"To the West!" And this has been done while perpetuating the principle direction of Russian literature. The brilliance of his writing, his departure from the canons, his engaging play with themes, his bold shuffling of parts, his witty deceptions, the false clue which leads to something unexpected, the freshness of his language and images, and his remarkable narrative ease—all this remarkable literary achievement carries within it clear waftings from the West. But no matter how paradoxical such an assertion may seem, it is precisely this feature of Sirin's writing which causes some to react with dubiousness toward him. This is understandable. The surface gloss of technical perfection has always been foreign to Russian literature. We loved and still love solidity, simplicity, the interior, and the serene flame of the trepidating thoughts and the sorrowful soul. We do not approve of reserve, and irony is foreign to us. We love prophets and psalm singers. And the more excited and passionate, possibly even the more formless their dire prophecies, the more quickly and closely we accept them.

VLADIMIR WEIDLE ON SIRIN

Together with *The Defense*, *Despair* seems to me to be the most characteristic of the Sirin novels, the closest to the central core of his art.

But one should not speak of it in isolation, apart from the other books of this very complex writer who is customarily judged in a sweeping fashion, his partisans and his opponents repeating almost the same clichés. He clearly deserves greater critical attention from his émigré audience.

There is really no point in writing reviews about *Despair*. Everyone who has not yet lost interest in Russian literature either has read this novel or will read it. All who still respond to literary innovation and sharpness in Russian prose will acknowledge its author's enormous gift. Beyond that, differences of opinion will arise which are not fruitful to weigh in regard to this one book. I shall limit myself, therefore, to pointing out one particular feature common to both *Despair* and *The Defense*.

The theme of Sirin's art is art itself—this is the first thing that one must say about him. Smurov, the protagonist of *The Eye*: the chess player Luzhin in *The Defense*; the butterfly collector Pilgram in the short story "The Aurelian"; the murderer who is the protagonist-narrator of *Despair*; Cincinnatus, sentenced to death in *Invitation to a Beheading*: all are diverse but generically related symbols of the creator, artist, and poet. Sirin's attention is turned not so much on the world around him as on the particular "I" which is fated, as a result of its creative calling, to reflect the images, apparitions, and shades of this world. The works which I have cited show us the unconscious or conscious torments of this "I," its somehow powerless total authority, its unasked-for power over things and people which are in reality not at all things or people but merely the products of its own fancy, although there is nowhere for this "I" to hide from them. Of course, this does not limit the outward form of the tale, and the motif of the artist unites (in *Invitation to a Beheading*, for example) with motifs of a different order. Sirin's other books, those which are basically more autobiographical (such as *Mashenka* and *The Exploit*) or those which reflect directly the mechanized contemporary world (such as *King, Queen, Knave* and *Laughter in the Dark*), in spite of all their virtues, are not central to his creation.

The plot of *Despair*, an intricately planned crime which nonetheless fails as a result of a trivial inadvertence, would seem at first glance to be completely intellectual and worthy of any detective novel. However, there is an excitement which infects the very rhythm of the narrative and its language, and this alone testifies to the many levels in Sirin's artistic structure. The intense tone winds from the first lines to the point of maximum tension and proceeds not only from the hero but also from the author. The urge to cross over into one's own double, as Hermann wishes to do in *Despair*, to turn the reality around the narrator topsy-turvy, to commit a murder that is, as it were, a frustrated suicide, and finally the failure of the whole plan, the coming to light, behind all the fictions and apparitions, behind the disintegrating reality and the destroyed dream, of the bare, trembling, condemned-to-death spiritual protoplasm—is not all this an intricate allegorization concealing not the despair of a hardened murderer but the despair of a creator incapable of believing in the object of his creation? *This* despair is the basic motif of the best that Sirin has created. It gives him a place among the most provocative writers in contemporary European literature and a place in Russian literature which he occupies alone.

ON NABOKOV

"I have always maintained, even as a schoolboy in Russia, that the nationality of a worthwhile writer is of secondary importance. The more distinctive an insect's aspect, the less apt the taxonomist is to glance first of all at the locality label under the pinned specimen in order to decide which of several vaguely described races it should be assigned to. The writer's art is his real passport. . . ."

Strong Opinions, p. 63.

". . . the main favor I ask of the serious critic is sufficient perceptiveness to understand that whatever term or trope I use, my purpose is not to be facetiously flashy or grotesquely obscure but to express what I feel and think with the utmost truthfulness and perception."

Strong Opinions, p. 179.

Lolita Lepidoptera

Diana Butler*

Vladimir Nabokov is a passionate collector of butterflies. Although he is well known as a lepidopterist, his interest in butterflies is more than scientific—it is poetic, emotional, and obsessive.

To Nabokov, the primary purpose of life is the attainment of moments of ecstacy. He tells us he finds such moments in art, in capturing butterflies, and in intricate games of deception.

Of art, he says in the author's note at the end of *Lolita*, "For me a work of fiction exists only insofar as it affords me what I shall bluntly call aesthetic bliss, that is a sense of being somehow, somewhere, connected with other states of being where art (curiosity, tenderness, kindness, ecstasy) is the norm."

Of butterflies, to which he devotes the sixth chapter of his autobiography, *Conclusive Evidence* (1951), he says, "I discovered in nature the nonutilitarian delights that I sought in art. Both were a form of magic, both were a game of intricate enchantment and deception. Few things indeed have I known in the way of emotion or appetite, ambition or achievement, that could surpass in richness and strength the excitement of entomological exploration." He concludes this chapter with a moment of ecstasy, the capture of a butterfly in the mountains of Colorado:

> And the highest enjoyment of timelessness—in a landscape selected at random—is when I stand among rare butterflies and their food plants. This is ecstasy, and behind the ecstasy is something else, which is hard to explain. It is like a momentary vacuum into which rushes all that I love. A sense of oneness with sun and stone. A thrill of gratitude to whom it may concern—to the contrapuntal genius of human fate or to tender ghosts humoring a lucky mortal.

And writing of the game of chess, he refers in his autobiography to

> the ecstatic core of the process and its points of connection with various other, more overt and fruitful, operations of the creative mind, from the charting of dangerous seas to the writing of one of those incredible novels

*From *New World Writing*, 16 (1960), 58–84. Reprinted by permission of the author, Diana Butler Thomson.

> where the author, in a fit of lucid madness, has set himself certain unique rules that he observes, certain nightmare obstacles that he surmounts, with the zest of a deity building a live world from the most unlikely ingredients—rocks, and carbon, and blind throbbings.

It is no coincidence, given Nabokov's desire for ecstasy, his passion for butterflies, and his penchant for intricate deception in art, that the dictionary definition of "nympholepsy," the exact science of debauchery that obsesses the hero of *Lolita*, should be "a state of rapture supposed to be inspired in men by nymphs; hence, an ecstasy or frenzy, esp. that caused by desire of the unattainable." Nor is it a coincidence that one of the meanings of "nymph," the object of Humbert Humbert's passion, should be a "a pupa," or "the young of an insect without complete metamorphosis"—as Lionel Trilling has pointed out, in a recent issue of *Encounter*. For in *Lolita* Nabokov has transposed his own passion for butterflies into his hero's passion for nymphets. At least on one level, and as part of an elaborate literary game, little Dolores Haze is a butterfly.

This hypothesis may dispel some of the aura of mystery which still surrounds *Lolita*. The sexual aspects of the novel are disconcerting, but equally so are the sly explanations to the reader that seem to explain nothing, the mass of clues that seem to disclose no mystery, and Nabokov's helpful note which has been no help at all. However, if *Lolita* is approached as a form of literary game, in which the nature of illicit passion is equated with Nabokov's own passion for butterflies, the mystifications begin to make sense.

The butterfly has often been used in literature as the symbol of the unattainable, combining matter and an appearance of spirituality, but eluding the grasp of man. In Conrad's *Lord Jim*, for example, there is a significant chapter in which Stein offers advice on Jim's romanticism out of his own passion for butterflies.

Conrad does not employ the butterfly as an abstraction or a convention—nor does Nabokov. The latter's professed hatred of literary symbolism is not belied by our finding butterflies in *Lolita*. For to Nabokov, butterflies are a physical reality, objects to which he has attached his own deepest emotions. They may easily possess more sensuous reality for him than twelve-year-old girls.

Apparently feeling that readers of the original edition published in Paris had not understood *Lolita*, Nabokov wrote a brief comment, printed at the end of the American edition, which offers some obvious clues to its interpretation. He draws attention to the nonsexual aspects of the novel, in the same manner as that in which his hero insists he is not primarily concerned with sex. Nabokov says the book "had grown in secret the claws and wings of a novel"—butterflies have claws as well as wings. He mentions "a suburban lawn, a mountain meadow" as the North American sets he needed to create—both happy hunting grounds for lepidopterists. He says, "But in regard to philistine vulgarity there is no intrinsic difference between Palearctic manners and Nearctic manners" —these terms are used to differentiate European and American butterflies.

Nabokov lists the ten most important scenes, the "nerves of the novel" (none of which portray the sexual act) and ends with "the tinkling sounds of the valley town coming up the mountain trail (on which I caught the first known female of *Lycaeides sublivens* Nabokov)."

And he tells us—with no apparent reason for being so specific:

> Every summer my wife and I go butterfly hunting. The specimens are deposited at scientific institutions, such as the Museum of Comparative Zoology at Harvard or the Cornell University collection. The locality labels pinned under these butterflies will be a boon to some twenty-first century scholar with a taste for recondite biography. It was at such of our headquarters as Telluride, Colorado; Afton, Wyoming; Portal, Arizona; and Ashland, Oregon, that *Lolita* was energetically resumed in the evenings or on cloudy days.

One century too soon, I would like to report that a single small drawer at the Harvard Museum of Comparative Zoology contains butterflies caught by Nabokov at Telluride, Colorado; Afton, Wyoming; and Portal, Arizona. At Telluride, in July of 1951, Nabokov made the most significant capture of his career as a lepidopterist: the first known females of *Lycaeides sublivens* Nabokov. And, in describing the capture in volume VI of the 1952 *Lepidopterists' News*, Nabokov identifies the town of Telluride, Colorado, as a "cul-de-sac . . . at the end of two converging roads, one from Placerville, the other from Dolores."

Not only is Dolores the given name of the heroine of *Lolita*, but the town of Dolores, Colo., is used in the book three times, as a clue: in the demonic list of home addresses by which Humbert attempts to identify his rival; as the only one of these clues which the hired detective discovers to be based on fact; and as the means by which Humbert identifies himself to his rival, Clare Quilty. " 'Quilty,' I said, 'do you recall a little girl called Dolores Haze, Dolly Haze? Dolly called Dolores, Colo.?' "

The foreword to *Lolita*, by the fictitious John Ray, Jr., says the names and places in the novel have been carefully disguised—all but one. "While 'Haze' only rhymes with the heroine's real surname, her first name is too closely interwound with the inmost fiber of the book to allow one to alter it; nor (as the reader will perceive for himself) is there any practical necessity to do so." This last sly dig at the reader may refer to the fact that although the town of Dolores is used as a clue, the reader will probably not guess the connection. Furthermore, as John Ray tells us, "Haze" rhymes with Lolita's real surname. Butterflies, like people, have two names, but the last, or generic, name—as of Nabokov's find, *Lycaeides*—precedes the first, or specific, name—*sublivens*. A classical

Latin pronunciation of *Lycaeides* rhymes well enough with Haze to make us wonder.

Apropos of John Ray, Jr., it is worth noting that John Ray was an eminent seventeenth-century English natural historian, the chief founder of systematic biology. The bulk of his work on insects was done on butterflies. He assumed the job of posthumously editing his partner's work, as the fictional John Ray assumes the posthumous editing of *Lolita*. And both John Rays are prone to moralizing about their work.

Humbert Humbert moralizes very little. His attitude is a scientific one, whether the science be nympholepsy or lepidoptery. Even the most "pornographic" passages of *Lolita* depict the heroine with scientific detachment, and her extraordinary charm is rendered by the use of minute specific details.

These specific details coincide with the markings of the most important butterfly of Nabokov's life. We are not subjected to raptures about Lolita's hair, breasts, or the usual barrage of femininity. Instead, Nabokov repeatedly mentions the golden-brown color of her arms and legs. The upperwings of the female of *Lycaeides sublivens* Nabokov are the color of a summer tan. Nabokov stresses the minute downy hairs on Lolita's arms and legs. The scales of a butterfly are modified hairs, and the word "pubescence," so often applied to Lo, means literally the soft downy hairs on an insect such as a butterfly. The whitish background of the underwings of *Lycaeides sublivens* recalls Lo's white shorts, white shirts, white socks, and the untanned white parts of her body. The small dark spots on this butterfly's underwings are seen in the asymmetrical freckles of her nose, her assorted bruises and moles.

Nabokov stresses the "reverse" side of his heroine, as if recalling the two sides of his butterfly, brown and white. He speaks of "Brown, naked, frail Lo, her narrow white buttocks to me" (p. 139) and of her "honey-brown body, with the white negative image of a rudimentary swimsuit patterned against her tan" (p. 127).

He tells us she is shameless in matters of leg show, but admires the "sudden smooth nether loveliness" (p. 46). Nabokov speaks of Lolita's arms and legs collectively, as one thinks of a butterfly's wings: "how I longed to enfold them, all your four limpid lovely limbs."

Lolita's eyes are wide-spaced and poor-sighted, like a butterfly's. Her smile seems hardly human: "While the tender, nectared, dimpled brightness played, it was never directed at the stranger in the room but hung in its own remote flowered void, so to speak, or wandered with myopic softness over chance objects" (p. 288).

Different butterflies have different characteristic resting positions. The Lycaenidae, to which family Nabokov's butterfly belongs, according to Klots's *Field Guide to the Butterflies*, upon alighting "hold the forewings together over the back, spread the hindwings slightly out at the sides, and then rub the hindwings forward and back alternating them with each other." Here is Lolita in an identical movement (p. 189): "her feet gestured all the time: she would stand on her left instep with her right toe, remove it backward, cross her feet, rock slightly, sketch a few steps, and then start the series all over again."

Like butterflies, Lolita's favorite food is fruit. Even when, as an all-American girl, she drinks Coke and eats sundaes, she prefers them with fruit syrup. The first sign Humbert sees of the heroine when he enters the Haze house is the brown core of an apple. Later on in Kasbeam (pp. 214–217), "I must say she was very sweet and languid, and craved for fresh fruits. . . . She became aware of the bananas. . . . Lo applied herself to the fruit."

Butterflies employ odors to attract a mate. In his autobiography Nabokov describes the "subtle perfume of butterfly wings on my fingers, a perfume which varies with the species—vanilla, or lemon, or musk, or a musty sweetish odor difficult to define."

Humbert prides himself on his well-developed sense of smell, and has even inherited a perfume business. He describes the scent of his first love, Annabel, as "a sweetish, lowly, musky perfume," and says Lolita "smelt almost exactly like the other one, the Riviera one, but more intensely so, with rougher overtones—a torrid odor that at once set my manhood astir" (p. 44). In helping one of Lo's fellow nymphets to play tennis, Humbert would "inhale her faint musky fragrance as I touched her forearm and held her knobby wrist, and push this way or that her cool thigh to show her the backhand stance" (p. 164).

Humbert's science of nympholepsy has much in common with lepidoptery. The notebook he keeps during his first days at the Haze house contains the essential data of a lepidopterist's field notebook: descriptions of locale and terrain, weather conditions, and vantage points, as well as the minute details of appearance already noted. For example, "*Thursday*. Very warm day. From a vantage point (bathroom window) saw Dolores taking things off a clothesline" (p. 43). Or, "*Sunday*. Heat ripple still with us; a most favonian week. This time I took up a strategic position . . ." (p. 44).

Humbert says he copied out his entries "with obvious abbreviations"; in referring to names of states, he also uses the standard abbreviations employed by butterfly collectors in identifying specimens. The Latin names of butterflies are written in italics, and Humbert tells us on his first night alone with Lolita "A breeze from wonderland had begun to affect my thoughts, and now they seemed couched in italics" (p. 133).

Humbert, buying clothes for Lolita, laboriously lists for us her "January measurements: hip girth, twenty-nine inches; thigh girth (just below the gluteal sulcus), seventeen; calf girth and neck circumference, eleven"; etc. (p. 109). Just such lists of precise measurements are included in scientific papers on butterflies.

Humbert says of his arctic expedition, "I felt curiously aloof from my own self. No temptations maddened me. . . . Nymphets do not occur in polar regions" (p. 35). Butterflies are only absent from the regions around the poles.

Humbert presents us with the scientific methods of nympholepsy. He tells us that not all girl-children are nymphets, but that only an expert can be sure of detecting the difference between a nymphet and an "ordinary, plumpish" little girl (p. 19). "Neither are good looks any criterion." "You have to be an artist and a madman . . . in order to discern at once, by ineffable signs—the slightly feline outline of a cheekbone, the slenderness of a downy limb, and other indices which despair and shame and tears of tenderness forbid me to tabulate—the little deadly demon among the wholesome children. . . ." Humbert's distinctions between nymphets and non-nymphets echo the distinctions between moths and butterflies, which together comprise the order Lepidoptera. Although moths are big-bodied and butterflies are slender-bodied, some moths are more beautiful than butterflies, and only an expert can be sure of telling them apart.

All the women Humbert hates are fat. His first wife is "my fat Valeria," "a large puffy, short-legged, big-breasted and practically brainless *baba*." Humbert describes the unsatisfactory nature of his marriage in these terms: "moth holes had begun to appear in the plush of matrimonial comfort" (p. 29).

Humbert's second wife, Charlotte, who is always on a diet, is described at Hourglass Lake with "thick thighs" and "plump wet back." Says Humbert, "still I could not make myself drown the poor slippery big-bodied creature" (p. 89). But there are similarities between Charlotte and her daughter: "She was my Lolita's big sister—this notion, perhaps, I could keep up if only I did not visualize too realistically her heavy hips, round knees, ripe bust . . ." (p. 74).

Humbert's final mistress, Rita, is picked up "at a darkishly burning bar under the sign of the Tiger-moth" (p. 260). She keeps being drawn back to her home town like a moth to a flame: "it was a fatal attraction; and before she knew what was what, she would find herself sucked into the lunar orbit of the town, and would be following the flood-lit drive that encircled it—'going round and round,' as she phrased it, 'like a God-damn mulberry moth.' "

Not only are the women Humbert loathes likened to moths; moths are used directly in the novel as a symbol of disgust. At the Enchanted Hunters, Humbert says, "I left the loud lobby and stood outside, on the white steps, looking at the hundreds of powdered bugs wheeling around the lamps in the soggy black night, full of ripple and stir. All I would do—all I would dare do—would amount to such a trifle . . ." (p. 128). As Humbert goes to kill Clare Quilty, he notices "in front of me, like derelict snowflakes, moths drifted out of the darkness into my probing aura. . . . There was still that stream of pale moths siphoned out of the night by my headlights" (pp. 294–5).

The enchanted hunter and his attempt to capture his prey is a major theme of the novel. The plot of *Lolita* is that of an extended search. Humbert likens himself to the traditional predators upon butterflies. He is a toad, an ape or monkey, a spider, and a hummingbird. Hummingbirds will upon occasion attack a butterfly; Humbert's name is mistaken by headmistress Pratt as "Hummer" (slang for hummingbird) and "Humbird," the 1634 usage for hummingbird (pp. 179–180). The spider metaphor is stressed most strongly: "I am like one of those inflated pale spiders you see in old gardens. Sitting in the middle of a luminous web and giving little jerks to this or that strand . . . one has to feel elsewhere about the house for the beautiful warm-colored prey. Let us have a strand of silk descend the stairs" (p. 51). Another day, the hero terms himself "Humbert the Wounded Spider" (p. 56).

And Lolita is again and again termed his prey: "like some predator that prefers a moving prey to a motionless one" (p. 44); or "I overtook my prey (time moves ahead of our fancies!)" (p. 113); or "Finally, the sensualist in me (a great and insane monster) had no objection to some depravity in his prey" (p. 126).

Weather conditions are crucial in capturing butterflies. In his autobiography Nabokov speaks of waking up each morning as a child hoping for sunny, good weather for butterfly hunting. Throughout a large portion of his article in *The Lepidopterists' News*, Nabokov fulminates against the poor weather which interfered with his search for the female of *Lycaeides sublivens*. He especially singles out for hatred the "daily electric storm, in several installments, accompanied by the most irritatingly close lightning I have ever encountered anywhere in the Rockies . . . and followed by cloudy and rainy weather throughout the rest of the day." In his note to *Lolita*, Nabokov tells us that the novel was written while he was collecting butterflies, but at times when butterfly collecting was impossible: "*Lolita* was energetically resumed in the evenings or on cloudy days."

In the novel, rain interferes more than once with Humbert's plans to seduce Dolores at Hourglass Lake, and it is raining during his discouraging visit to his married darling, Dolly Schiller. Thunderstorms are a constant threatening leitmotiv in the novel. Humbert's mother was killed by one, after Charlotte's death Humbert leaves the Haze house during a thunderstorm, a thunderstorm interferes with the performance of *The Enchanted Hunters*, and a thunderstorm accompanies Humbert on his way to kill Clare Quilty. Humbert says (p. 219), "As happens with me at periods of electrical disturbance and crepitating lightning, I had hallucinations. Maybe they were more than hallucinations." Lolita doesn't like thunderstorms either: " 'I am not a lady and do not like lightning,' said Lo, whose dread of electric storms gave me some pathetic solace" (p. 222).

This accumulation of butterfly data, which is much more extensive than I have had space to indicate, could be mere coincidence, or the unconscious contribution of a lepidopterist's mind, if there were not evidence that Nabokov has included it out of conscious artistry. Two groups of material seem to prove that these butterfly parallels were deliberately "planted" by the author: the section of clues by which Humbert unsuccessfully attempts to identify his rival, and the ten scenes which Nabokov has singled out as "the nerves of the novel."

In describing Humbert's state of mind as he tracks his rival, and Humbert's perception of the workings of his rival's mind, Nabokov has told us about the workings of his own mind. Only by such a bizarre mode of mental operation, such "lucid madness"—the means by which an author composes the works of art he so much admires—could Nabokov have written a deceptive game of the magnitude of *Lolita*.

In terms of the plot, this section of clues and description of mental operation (pp. 249–254) is unnecessary. Humbert does not identify his rival by these clues, and finally must rely on Dolly Schiller to supply the name of Clare Quilty. The clues are suspended in a vacuum. The section has been included for the use of the reader.

> I could not hope, of course, he would ever leave his correct name and address; but I did hope he might slip on the glaze of his own subtlety . . . leaving me with the sportive hope . . . that he might give himself away next time. He never did—though coming damn close to it. We all admire the spangled acrobat with classical grace meticulously walking his tight rope in the talcum light; but how much rarer art there is in the sagging rope expert wearing scarecrow clothes and impersonating a grotesque drunk! *I* should know.
>
> The clues he left did not establish his identity but they reflected his personality, or at least a certain homogenous and striking personality; his genre, his type of humor—at its best at least—the tone of his brain, had affinities with my own. He mimed and mocked me. His allusions were definitely highbrow. He was well-read. He knew French. He was versed in logodaedaly and logomancy. He was an amateur of sex lore. . . .
>
> His main trait was his passion for tantalization. Goodness, what a tease the poor fellow was! He challenged my scholarship. I am sufficiently proud of my knowing something to be modest about my not knowing all; and I daresay I missed some elements in that cryptogrammic paper chase.

This description of mental operation might have been written by a lively imagination with the aid of a pathology textbook. The clues, if they are not nonsense, must have been composed by a mind prone to "lucid madness." Their underlying scheme is the search for an ideal, and competition for that ideal, mingled with references to Nabokov's own ideal, the butterfly *Lycaeides sublivens*.

It is emphasized, by means of a moonlight bribe to a nurse who cared for Lolita in the hospital, that Humbert is the "brother" of "Dr. Gratiano Forbeson, Mirandola, N.Y." Mirandola refers to the Neoplatonist philosopher, Pico della Mirandola. Nabokov mentions "Italian Comedy connotations" for this clue, and may have in mind Gratiano in *The Merchant of Venice*, whose most important speech is "All things that are / Are with more spirit chased than enjoyed." (Like Lolita and butterflies.) As to the remaining elements, "Dr. . . . Forbeson . . . N.Y.": one of the most important single works on butterflies, certainly well known to Nabokov, is Dr. William Forbes's *The Lepidoptera of New York*.

"Quelquepart Island" was one of the rival's "favorite residences," we are told, and " 'Aubrey Beardsley, Quelquepart Island' suggested more lucidly than the garbled telephone message had that the starting point of the affair should be looked for in the East." Aubrey here refers to Aubrey McFate, the personification of fate that haunts Humbert, and Beardsley is the town in which Humbert and Lolita lived. There is no real "Quelquepart Island" that I can discover, but there is a Quelpart Island off the coast of Korea—in the East. Nabokov, in a monograph published by the Harvard Museum of Comparative Zoology on *The Nearctic Members of the Genus Lycaeides Hübner* (which includes *sublivens*), indicates that some of the few Asian specimens of this butterfly were captured on Quelpart Island.

We are told of "such assumed names as 'Arthur Rainbow'—plainly the travestied author of *Le Bateau Bleu*—let me laugh a little too, gentlemen—and 'Morris Schmetterling' of *L'Oiseau Ivre* fame." These, unscrambled, give us Arthur Rimbaud's *Le Bateau Ivre* and Maurice Maeterlinck's *L'Oiseau Bleu*. "Maeterlinck-Schmetterling," Clare Quilty mentions just before his death, and there are other references to Quilty's similarity to Maeterlinck. *Schmetterling*, of course, is German for butterfly.

"I noticed that whenever he felt his enigmas were becoming too recondite, even for such a solver as I, he would lure me back with an easy one. 'Arsène Lupin' was obvious to a Frenchman who remembered the detective stories of his youth. . . ." A Frenchman would detect that *lupin* is French for lupine—the host plant of the butterfly *Lycaeides sublivens*. To a lepidopterist, this would be an easy clue and a significant one, for once you have found a butterfly's own special host plant, you have only to wait by that plant until the butterfly shows up to lay some eggs—and be captured.

So to "Phineas Quimby, Lebanon, NH": Quimby was, in reality, an American mental healer devoted to mesmerism—which may have a connection with Humbert's consideration of "Mesmer Mesmer" as a pseudonym. And the mythical character Phineus was always having his food taken away by the Harpies as he was about to eat; it was he who gave directions to Jason on how to find the Golden Fleece. Lebanon is the next town down the road from Dolores, Colo.

Those license numbers "such as 'WS 1564' and 'SH 1616', and 'Q32888' or 'CU88322')" refer to William Shakespeare's birth in 1564 and death in 1616, and to the playwright Clare Quilty, whose nickname is "Cue," or "CU." It may be no coincidence that the CU_1 cell is the significant single cell on the hindwing of a butterfly by which entomologists classify a specimen; however, the meaning of the second pair of numbers escapes me.

Nabokov has even included an anagram: "Ted Hunter, Cane, NH" equals "enchanted hunter." And we come again to "Horribly cruel, forsooth, was 'Will Brown, Dolores, Colo.' " Forsooth—in truth—brown is the color of the upperwings of the female *Lycaeides sublivens*, and Dolores is the town next to which the butterfly was caught. This is the one direct clue.

This same mode of mental operation, this devising of a hidden game, has also been applied to the plot of the novel. We may find evidence of it in the ten key scenes Nabokov lists in his note: "These are the nerves of the novel. These are the secret points, the subliminal co-ordinates by means of which the book is plotted—although I realize very clearly that these and other scenes will be skimmed over or not noticed."

He tells us he finds the book to be "a delightful presence now that it quietly hangs about the house like a summer day which one knows to be bright behind the haze." Perhaps the haze he mentions is the overt sexual meaning of the book—perhaps the brightness is its hidden butterfly pattern.

Nabokov points out that a pornographic novel is generally expected to contain a "rising succession of erotic scenes" and suggests that this lack of a crescendo line in *Lolita* may disappoint his readers. It is true that the eroticism of the book follows, rather, a diminuendo line. In the first portion of the book, Nabokov engrosses the reader so thoroughly in the sexual content of the book that he is numbed and unable to investigate the nonsexual interstitial material. But we must concentrate upon this interstitial material to understand *Lolita*.

The scenes Nabokov selects as important have very little to do with the manifest sexual content of the book. They tell the story of his search for *Lycaeides sublivens*.

Two scenes Nabokov lists are "the pictures decorating the stylized garret of Gaston Godin" (p. 183) and "the Kasbeam barber (who cost me a month of work)" (p. 215). Godin and the barber are not butterfly collectors, but their own passions have the same absorbing intensity in their lives that nymphets have for Humbert, or that butterflies have for Nabokov. Gaston's predilection for young boys, and the barber's obsession with the memory of his son, are two of many similar obsessions in the book: the dentist's with teeth, Charlotte's with material goods, Farlow's with his second wife. In effect, Nabokov tells us that the object of a passion is unimportant, but that the nature of passion is constant. In *Lolita* he has depicted the nature of passion. It may be a sense of the interchangeability of passionate objects that has enabled Nabokov to write simultaneously of a passion for young girls and a passion for butterflies.

Nabokov also lists two scenes dealing with Humbert's two wives: "Mr. Taxovich" (p. 30) and "Charlotte saying 'waterproof' " (p. 91). Here we have Mr. Taxovich's passion for Valeria, and Charlotte's passion for American material goods. But even more significantly, it is at these two points in the novel that Humbert's disgust with the moth-like nature of non-nymphets is most strongly emphasized.

Nabokov selects "that class list of Ramsdale School" (p. 53) as one of the ten scenes. He says "there was a mimeographed list of names referring, evidently, to her class at the Ramsdale school. It is a poem I know already by heart." Nabokov lists the names of forty students, with last names first (like butterflies). By weighting the list toward the beginning of the alphabet, Nabokov manages to have "Haze, Dolores" appear as number 22.

The *Encyclopedia Britannica* gives a simplified list of the orders of insects and places Lepidoptera as number 22 in a list of twenty-five. The three other lists I have seen also place Lepidoptera in 22nd place, just like Dolores Haze. The *Encyclopedia Britannica* mentions, however, that lists now in technical usage would include thirty or forty orders. I have not been able to discover the list of forty that Nabokov has used, but if it could be found it might yield a correlation between the different orders of insects and the different pupils in Lolita's class. "Duncan, the foul-smelling clown" might even turn out to be a stink-bug.

But even ruling out this hypothesis, Humbert's rhapsodies suggest what may be Nabokov's feelings when he sees the object of his passion, *Lycaeides sublivens*, included in a scientific list.

> I am trying to analyze the spine-thrill of delight it gives me, this name among all those others. What is it that excites me almost to tears (hot, opalescent thick tears that poets and lovers shed)? What is it? The tender anonymity of this name with its formal veil ("Dolores") and that abstract transposition of first name and surname, which is like a pair of new pale gloves or a mask? . . . Is it because there is always delight in the semitranslucent mystery, the flowing charshaf, through which the flesh and the eye you alone are elected to know smile in passing at you alone?

Nabokov lists "Lolita in slow motion advancing toward Humbert's gifts" (p. 122). This happens on Humbert's and Lolita's first night together, at the Enchanted Hunters. The entire scene is composed in terms of predator and prey, and of Humbert's emotions before possessing the object of his passion. Lolita, advancing toward the gifts, is described:

> Oh, what a dreamy pet! She walked up to the open suitcase as if stalking it from afar, at a kind of slow-motion walk, peering at that distant treasure box on the luggage support. (Was there something wrong, I wondered, with those great grey eyes of hers, or were we both plunged in the same enchanted mist?) She stepped up to it, lifting her rather high-heeled feet rather high, and bending her beautiful boy-knees while she walked through dilating space with the lentor of one walking under water or in a flight dream.

The flight dream may suggest Lolita flying, like a butterfly. Her myopic butterfly-eyes are stressed. But here Lolita is more the hunter than the prey, and new clothes are the closest she comes to a passionate obsession. Her attitude toward the gifts is identical with Humbert's attitude toward her during this first night—the predator and the prey:

"Lust is never quite sure—even when the velvety victim is locked up in one's dungeon—that some rival devil of influential god may still not abolish one's prepared triumph." "Should I wait a solid hour and then creep up again? The science of nympholepsy is a precise science." "Now and then it seemed that the enchanted prey was about to meet halfway the enchanted hunter."

And Humbert says, "I am not concerned with so-called 'sex' at all. Anybody can imagine those elements of animality. A greater endeavor lures me on: to fix once for all the perilous magic of nymphets." Perhaps Nabokov is not concerned with sex—perhaps, in directing us to these enchanted hunters, he means to emphasize the emotions of the search, the attitudes with which the enchanted butterfly hunter stalks his prey.

Nabokov lists "Lolita playing tennis." This scene (pp. 232–36) is the most complete portrayal the novel holds of Lolita's butterfly nature, and it recreates a moment of ecstasy, in the same mountainous region of Colorado where Nabokov captured *Lycaeides sublivens:*

> But all that was nothing, absolutely nothing, to the indescribable itch of rapture that her tennis game produced in me—the teasing delirious feeling of teetering on the very brink of unearthly order and splendor. . . . No hereafter is acceptable if it does not produce her as she was then, in that Colorado resort, between Snow and Elphinstone, with everything right: the white wide little-boy shorts, the slender waist, the apricot midriff, the white breast-kerchief whose ribbons went up and encircled her neck to end behind in a dangling knot leaving bare her gaspingly young and adorable apricot shoulder blades with that pubescence and those lovely gentle bones, and the smooth, downward-tapering back.

The colors of the butterfly's wings, white and apricot-tanned, and that pubescence (the downy hair on a butterfly rather than Lolita's age), even the slender waist, gentle bones, and tapering back, agree with a butterfly's physique. (Nabokov has elsewhere told us that Lolita has a large chest and small *derrière*, which agree with the proportions of a butterfly's mesothorax and metathorax.)

"Her tennis was the highest point to which I can imagine a young creature bringing the art of make-believe, although I daresay, for her it was the very geometry of basic reality. . . . Her form was, indeed, an absolutely perfect imitation of absolutely top-notch tennis, without any utilitarian results."

Lolita's tennis form is beautiful, for her the geometry of basic reality, but as ineffectual for winning tennis as the form of a butterfly. She always lets her opponent win. In this passage she is playing opposite Humbert and Humbert is winning. The passage depicts the capture of a butterfly, complete with net:

> She who was so cruel and crafty in everyday life, revealed an innocence, a frankness, a kindness of ball-placing, that permitted a second-rate but determined player, no matter how uncouth and incompetent, to poke and cut his way to victory . . . any abrupt attack, or sudden change of tactics on her adversary's part, left her helpless. . . . Her dramatic drives and lovely volleys would candidly fall at his feet. Over and over again she would land an easy one into the net—and merrily mimic dismay by drooping in a ballet attitude, with her forelocks hanging.

Says Humbert, "on that particular day, in the pure air of Champion, Colorado . . . I felt I could rest from the nightmare of unknown betrayals within the innocence of her style, of her soul, of her essential grace."

The passage ends with a single short sentence, standing in a paragraph by itself and not apparently connected with the scene: "An inquisitive butterfly passed, dipping, between us."

Like all bliss, this bliss passes. Next Nabokov lists "the hospital at Elphinstone" from which Lolita is taken by Humbert's rival, Quilty. With "Lolita ill. Lolita dying," the spector of death enters. Humbert's guilt over killing rises from this point until the end of the book.

In his autobiography Nabokov tells of his horror of killing butterflies. The emotional shift from the moment of ecstasy on the tennis court to Lolita's illness recreates, perhaps, Nabokov's guilt at attaining ecstasy by the capture of a rare butterfly, and then being forced to kill his specimen. It may also reflect his reluctance to turn over his beloved *Lycaeides sublivens* to the banal clutches of other lepidopterologists.

Lycaeides sublivens is one of the genus of butterflies commonly termed "the blues" by imprecise lepidopterists. Nabokov's chief scientific work has been the reclassification of this group of butterflies, and he has contempt for the slip-shod old-style classification.

At the Elphinstone hospital (p. 242), Lolita is turned over to "Blue, the best man in the district." "Dr. Blue, whose learning, no doubt, was infinitely inferior to his reputation, assured me it was a virus infection, and when I alluded to her comparatively recent flu, curtly said this was another bug, he had forty such cases on his hands." Dr. Blue may be the ignorant scientist who calls these butterflies "the blues" and who sees *Lycaeides sublivens* Nabokov as just "another bug." We may recall the Ramsdale class list, with its forty varieties of bugs.

Lolita is handed over just as a butterfly is handed over to a museum, complete with receipt—just as Nabokov deposited his specimens of *sublivens* at Harvard and Cornell. "I signed the very symbolic receipt, thus surrendering my Lolita to all those apes." Again, apes appear as predators.

Nabokov lists, as the ninth of his ten scenes, "pale, pregnant Dolly Schiller dying in Gray Star (the capital town of the book)." Dolly's death in Gray Star is mentioned only in John Ray's foreword, right after he has given us the earlier-mentioned clues about her real name. Humbert's visit to pale, pregnant Lolita (pp. 271–82) describes the death of the butterfly within the body of the novel. Lolita has ceased to be a nymphet. "Her bare shins and arms had lost all their tan"—the distinguishing characteristic of Humbert's tanned adolescent, and Nabokov's brown-winged butterfly. Instead we are told of Dolly's ears, armpits, glasses, hairdo, and rope-veined hands—all physical attributes ignored while she was still a butterfly. A butterfly dead and pinned to a board is dramatically suggested: "Against the splintery deadwood of the door, Dolly Schiller flattened herself as best she could . . . and was crucified for a moment . . . her watered-milk-white arms outspread on the wood."

Humbert, perhaps with guilt for killing butterflies, says "I have hurt too much too many bodies with my twisted poor hands to be proud of them." He says he still loves Dolly Schiller "more than anything I had ever seen or imagined on earth, or hoped for anywhere else. She was only the faint violet whiff and dead leaf echo of the nymphet I had rolled myself upon with such cries in the past. . . ." "Faint violet whiff"—violet is one of the butterfly odors Nabokov has mentioned. "Dead leaf echo"—"dead leaf" is a term used for the whitish color of the underwings of *Lycaeides sublivens.*

Nabokov's list of vital scenes ends up with "the tinkling sounds of the valley town coming up the mountain trail (on which I caught the first known female of *Lycaeides sublivens* Nabokov)."

The place is Telluride, Colorado, where Nabokov caught the butterfly. In the geography of the novel, Humbert could easily have returned to the site of Lolita's tennis game. The final moment of ecstasy is a flashback in the mind of Humbert, just before his capture by the police (pp. 309–10).

There is a fusion of past and present, and all the major emotions of the novel are resolved by this "last mirage of wonder and hopelessness":

> As I approached the friendly abyss, I grew aware of a melodious unity of sounds rising like vapor from a small mining town that lay at my feet, in a

> fold of the valley. . . . And soon I realized that all these sounds were of one nature, that no other sounds but these came from the streets of the transparent town, with the women at home and the men away. Reader! What I heard was but the melody of children at play, nothing but that. . . . I knew that the hopelessly poignant thing was not Lolita's absence from my side, but the absence of her voice from that concord.

In this epiphany, this moment of ecstasy, Humbert's predatory passion for Lolita changes to unselfish love, as he feels genuine remorse for what he has done to her childhood.

But more is accomplished by this attainment of ecstasy on the spot where Nabokov attained the long-sought object of his passion. In terms of butterfly hunting—and this is conjecture on my part—the capture of *Lycaeides sublivens* may well have been a final attainment of what Nabokov sought. In his autobiography he tells us,

> Nothing in the world would have seemed sweeter to me than to be able to add, by a stroke of luck, some remarkable new species to the long list of Pugs already named by others. And my pied imagination, ostensibly, and almost grotesquely, groveling to my desire (but all the time, in ghostly conspiracies behind the scenes, coolly planning the most distant events of my destiny), kept providing me with hallucinatory samples of small print: ". . . the only specimen so far known . . ."

It would seem that capture of this unique specimen, the female of *Lycaeides sublivens*, may have satisfied Nabokov's desire to capture the first known specimens of a butterfly. Once this had been accomplished, it is possible that the reluctance to kill his specimens became stronger in his mind than his desire to capture more butterflies. It is significant that since this major capture, Nabokov's contributions to published entomological literature have shown a marked decrease.

The paragraph following the epiphany, in *Lolita*, says, "This then is my story. I have reread it. It has bits of marrow sticking to it, and blood, and beautiful bright-green flies. At this or that twist of it I feel my slippery self eluding me, gliding into deeper and darker waters than I care to probe. I have camouflaged what I could so as not to hurt people. . . ."

It may be that Nabokov has camouflaged what he could so as not to hurt himself. He has written a highly passionate novel about incest and sexual perversion, employing an elaborate parallel with butterfly collecting perhaps—if for no other reason—as a psychic defense for himself. Such intricate deception, such an involved literary game, provided him with obstacles to be overcome, and the process of surmounting these odds may have protected him from a too-constant awareness of the sexual theme.

Nabokov is an old hand at the fusion of disparate elements, and it is one of his most important artistic techniques. He tells us in his note that he "has to rely on such ancient terms as Interreaction of Inspiration and

Combination—which, I admit, sounds like a conjuror explaining one trick by performing another." The statement is not as ironical as it sounds, for in *Lolita*, inspiration (the butterfly-nymphet analogy) inter-reacts with combination (the American scenes Nabokov has created).

In the novel Humbert facetiously describes (p. 262) an essay he published in the *Cantrip Review*, entitled "Mimir and Memory," in which he suggested a "theory of perceptual time based on the circulation of the blood and conceptually depending (to fill up this nutshell) on the mind's being conscious of its own self, thus creating a continuous spanning of two points (the storable future and the stored past)." Beneath the spoofing of literary explanations, Nabokov is telling us the means by which his own mind, drawing on memory, can effect such a fusion as he has accomplished in *Lolita*, superimposing one part of the pattern upon another, uniting the sexual story with the hidden butterfly story.

By announcing his hostility to literary interpretations, Nabokov has forced his readers to accept *Lolita* at its erotic face value. Now he seems to be sorry. He has included a comment, with clues, in the American edition of *Lolita.* A prize has been offered to "puzzle-minded readers of Nabokov" who discovered the puzzle hidden in his story "The Vane Sisters," published in the *Hudson Review* and in the March, 1959, *Encounter.* He has reprinted his note on the novel in the April, 1959, *Encounter*. He seems to be asking his readers to look below the surface and discover how much else his novel contains.

Lolita contains much more, still undiscovered. The novel's importance rests on the elaborate literary technique that Nabokov has employed, as well as on its luminous sexuality. The fusion of the obvious erotic meaning with Nabokov's search for *Lycaeides sublivens* is only one element in *Lolita*'s brilliance; and this hidden butterfly pattern does not contradict, but supplements, Nabokov's exposition of the nature of passion and the attainment of moments of ecstasy.

Vladimir Nabokov's Great Spiral of Being

L. L. Lee*

We seek the explanatory image of the author's works: the river, the hourglass, the knotted string, the circle. But it is Nabokov himself who offers us the figure for his novels. In his memoir, *Conclusive Evidence*, he says that he sees his life as a "colored spiral in a small ball of glass," and that the spiral is the circle "set free" to give us a visual form for the Hegelian triad, thesis, antithesis, synthesis. All things, he adds, are essentially spiral "in their relation to time."

*From *Western Humanities Review*, 18 (1964), 225–36. Reprinted by permission of the journal.

Still, to assert that the figure an author applies to his life also applies to his art is not, of course, sufficient. Does it really apply and does it explain? Would it help us to understand, for instance, a novel like *Pale Fire*?

For the moment, let me say that the spiral does throw light on those mirror-reflections, doppelgängers, chess games, spelling reversals, puns, repetitions of situations, sexual ambivalences, echoes of names that we find in the fiction. For the spiral is like the circle, but less exact, less rigid; it is time recurring and yet not quite; events that are repeated but only partially; mirror images that are of necessity distorted because they exist at different moments. The spiral is the figure of space and time unified, but a figure that allows multiplicity in its unity. The "V" (Vladimir?) of *Sebastian Knight* says that, to Knight, "time and space were . . . measures of the same eternity." And, in *Lolita*, Humbert Humbert points out to his reader that "I substitute time terms for spatial ones."

The spiral offers us an explanation, also, of the "marrowsky" (Nabokov defines his word in *Pale Fire* as "a rudimentary spoonerism"). A marrowsky is, almost, Makarovski, Macaronski, Skomorovski, and Komarov; Kinbote is Botkin, Botkine, Bodkin, and, with a leap, Nabokov.

To say "Nabokov" is no violation of the truth, for the "marrowsky," the similarity of word to word, is the "marrow" of his work. Moreover, it is obvious that Nabokov makes use of his own life story in his fiction. *The Gift* is filled with the events and people who are to be found also in *Conclusive Evidence*. We find echoes of that memoir in *Pnin*, in the poems, in *Pale Fire*, in even *Lolita*. And Nabokov's own qualities are plainly those of some of his characters—what Humbert Humbert says of Clare Quilty is true of their creator: "The tone of his brain . . . had affinities with my own. He mimed and mocked me. . . . he was versed in logodaedaly and logomancy." Too, Nabokov's great passions, butterflies and chess, are so often used in his works that one is tempted to look to them for keys to his meanings.

Can we not then guess that Nabokov may be writing a kind of *A la recherche du temps perdu*? Indeed, he makes references to Proust in *Pale Fire*, in *Lolita*, in *Sebastian Knight*. Could he be trying to recapture his past by some oblique method?

An author's past experiences and observations, and his imagination working on those experiences are without doubt the source of most of his material and, in a way, he is always recapturing it. "Madame Bovary, c'est moi," says Flaubert. But Nabokov's memoirs as he recreates them are not the past recaptured as Proust would have it. One must agree when Louis D. Rubin denies that *Lolita* is an autobiographical work (God save us!) "because no authorial personality is involved; the dimension of memory, the recapture of events for the sake of recapture, has not been created for us by the author."[1] Nabokov has another purpose.

That purpose is expressed by one of the author's fictional people—Nabokov, like his own creature, the writer Sebastian Knight, not only gives his qualities to his characters but also his ideas. Joan Clements, in *Pnin*, speaks of an unnamed author (Nabokov himself) and asks, "But don't you think . . . that what he is trying to do . . . practically in all his novels . . . is . . . to express the fantastic recurrence of certain situations?" Recurrence, yes, but in a different form. What we perceive is the echo of an inside arc of a spiral by an outside arc; it is a kind of relativity. Physical time, says Pnin in his discourse on *Anna Karenina*, is not the same as "spiritual time."

But why use the past if not to recapture it for its own sake? One finds the reason in Nabokov's attitude toward language and toward time. When Mary McCarthy speaks of the "burden" of *Pale Fire* as "love," she is quite right, but she seems to limit that "burden" to love between human beings.[2] Let me make a narrower and then a much broader generalization. Nabokov is speaking of *his* love for language, and then of all things in the universe that language can represent, *i.e.*, everything. In the poem "An Evening of Russian Poetry," he says that he speaks of words instead of "*knowledge nicely browned* / Because all hangs together—shape and sound, / heather and honey, vessel and content." Words are "shells that hold a thimble and the sea." In brief, Nabokov is not writing autobiography for the purpose of autobiography, unless we use those vague words "spiritual autobiography." He is showing that the world, and the language one uses to *create* the world, are intricately, inextricably, interwoven. What one does is not to recapture just past action, nor even past meaning, but to capture, again and again, the order of the world in an artistic form. Or rather, art shows the form of and gives form to the world.

This idea offers an explanation for Nabokov's use of actual events and actual names in his novels, even though one should remember that he doesn't always stick to the "historical" truth. The fictional world can absorb the actual, since fiction, form, is as real as the actual—the actual is part of the fiction in that everything is related. Nabokov illustrates this point within his works. Maud Shade in *Pale Fire* is a "poet and a painter with a taste / For realistic objects interlaced / With grotesque growths and images of doom." In the same novel, the painter Eystein's paintings contain actual objects. And the painter Lake, in *Pnin*, teaches that a work of art can and must be a part of the natural world. A motor car as a subject for a painting becomes a part of nature by having "the scenery penetrate the automobile. . . . This mimetic and integrative process Lake called the necessary 'naturalization' of man-made things." The artistic process is a search for correspondences that give structure. The novel, then, offers us a kind of esthetic completeness in itself—in its finding forms for the rest of the world it makes a complete form. A novel is not a social report, not a myth, not allegory, Nabokov says in the epilogue to *Lolita*. Still, one must insist that it always has a subject. That subject is form itself, although form here means more than just a pleasingly regular structure. Nabokov, citing a "critic" who says that *Lolita* was the "record of my love affair with the romantic novel," adds, "The substitution 'English language' for 'romantic novel' would make this elegant formula more correct."

Now, the world and words *are* involved in time, in something that seems separate from them. However, in *Conclusive Evidence*, Nabokov tells the story of one of his butterfly hunts. The boy Nabokov starts off across a Russian bog and comes out on the other side, not in Russia, but in Colorado perhaps forty years later. And he says, "I confess I do not believe in time. I like to fold my magic carpet, after use, in such a way as to superimpose one part of the pattern upon another," and then he expresses gratitude "to the contrapuntal genius of human fate. . . ." It is timelessness that he is praising; the purpose, the structure, and the texture of his novels are searches for timelessness, not just for time past, but for all time *now*. Timelessness is unity. Sebastian Knight announces, "The only real number is one, the others are mere repetition." History is one because history does repeat itself.

Nevertheless, we, being in time, should remember that the author is *making* the world he offers us. He creates his spiral, his correspondences. These correspondences may say that the actual world is held together but, above all, they hold the individual work together, just as a painter's lines hold his painting together. And, of course, these correspondences reach from one work to another. One cannot speak of Nabokov's novels (at least his English novels) in isolation from the others. They are all part of the same made object, the one work of art.

II

No one will claim that Nabokov writes "naturalistic" novels, novels that are a photograph of a certain place at a certain time with carefully motivated, thoroughly human, perhaps thoroughly dull, characters. Oh, yes, Nabokov is a formidable social critic; *Pale Fire* is, among other things, a satire on such papers as this. But it is not an abdication of his power and his duty for the artist to refuse to write topical novels about facts or ideas; it is his duty to create a world.

Let us look, then, at *Pale Fire*. Surely it is about something, as well as being something. The reviewers, the critics, have seen it as this and that: as hoax, funny no doubt, but a hoax; as a pleasant or unpleasant puzzle to be deciphered; as something inhuman (one or two reviewers were repelled by its [lack of] "moral" qualities). Its structure seems chaotic; its people, except for the Shades, non-human; its values unclear. But. . . .

Pale Fire is about Nabokov's loves: language and memory (or timelessness); it is about "American and European" things. In a note, Charles Kinbote (who is a "spiral" image of John Shade and of Nabokov himself) remarks upon Shade's lines about the exile dying who "conjures in two tongues": "English and Zemblan, etc.," Kinbote says, repeating

"English and Russian" four times in sixteen sets of "English and. . . ." He ends, of course, with a seventeenth: "American and European." And the Zemblan language that Kinbote "speaks," although based upon a Teutonic grammar, has a Teutonic and Russian vocabulary—it is a verbal blending of Nabokov's American and European worlds, it is "the tongue of the mirror."

The construction of *Pale Fire* may also help to clarify its meaning. It is a commonplace to say that a novel is built on many levels, but the commonplace is patently true of *Pale Fire*. But the "true" level of *Pale Fire* is difficult to find. There is the obvious story: the scholar Charles Kinbote offers us a foreword to the poem *Pale Fire* by the American poet John Shade, who has been killed by a homicidal maniac named Jack Grey; gives us the poem; and then writes "explanatory" notes for the poem. But the notes reveal another story: the story of Charles Xavier Vseslav the Beloved, exiled from his "distant northern" kingdom of Zembla by an Extremist (*i.e.*, Communist) revolution. We learn, also, that Kinbote is Charles in disguise. But we must, on this level, ask ourselves if Kinbote may not be mad, if he is not, in fact, a paranoid who is making up his story of Charles. Mary McCarthy suggests that Kinbote is not only mad, but that he is really V. Botkin, "a harmless refugee pedant" (the name is given in the "index" of the novel but is mentioned only once in the body of the story—a questioner asks Kinbote if his name is not "a kind of anagram of Botkin or Botkine." Indeed, it is. It is a marrowsky). Miss McCarthy adds, however, that "each plane or level in its shadow box proves to be a false bottom." My point is that each level is quite as true as the next. The novel is an order within itself, an esthetic order created by the author. What the events represent, on the deepest level, is the author's vision of the world. In *Conclusive Evidence*, Nabokov speaks of the poet experiencing in one moment of time "an instantaneous and transparent organism of events, of which the poet (sitting in a lawn chair, at Ithaca, New York) is the nucleus." As artist, he is at the center of his spiral.

A glance at the structure of *Pnin* and *Lolita* will show that this order is repeated again and again in Nabokov's works. *Pnin*, although apparently only a series of short stories, interlinked to be sure, is a novel in Nabokov's fashion. The first story tells of Pnin's mishaps on his journey to Cremona to give a lecture on "Are the Russian People Communist?"; the novel ends with Jack Cockerell, head of the English department at Waindell College, about to give an imitation of Pnin about to give the wrong lecture at the Cremona Women's Club. The novel has gone, not full circle, but full spiral. The same event will be repeated but not in the same form. We are not told in the first story that Pnin will give the wrong lecture; he worries about it, almost misses the lecture because he makes an error in the manuscripts he carries, but the story ends as Pnin is being introduced. We can guess, though. And particular images reinforce the novel's shape. Lake conceives of the solar spectrum not as a circle, starting with red on one end and going through violet on the other to return to red, but as a spiral, going beyond violet to a "lavender gray" and then off into "Cinderella" colors beyond the range of "human perception." Lake is one of the few people in the novel of whom Nabokov approves; his idea is Nabokov's idea.

The organization of *Lolita* is not so neat; it is, in fact, much like that of *Pale Fire*. John Ray, Jr., writes his preface after Humbert and Lolita are both dead. He says that Humbert has written a novel, a "moral" novel. During this "novel," Humbert makes use of not only his memories but parts of a journal which he had kept (which, by the way, he tells Charlotte Haze is to be part of a novel—a lie, yes). Humbert also refers to his story as a novel. But, as Rubin suggests, the past is not there for the sake of the past, but to create Humbert's character. It is also there for the sake of form. The novel is not, certainly, a moral novel, it is a design.

Humbert tells the story of his pubertal love for Annabel (surely there is a rather mocking use of Poe here) as a pre-figuring of his love for Lolita; his love for Lolita is the love for Annabel in a monstrous shape. I trust no one will accuse me of thinking that Nabokov is writing autobiographically if I point out that the story of H.H.'s adolescent love is a variant of Nabokov's love for Colette as he gives it in *Conclusive Evidence*. This illustrates once again that the author is not using his past to recapture it; he is using it to make word contain fact, event contain event—but not quite.

For the novel is circular, or rather, spiral. The introduction is, in point of time, after the rest of the work; we end the story and return to the introduction, or, to our memory of it. It fades off into another, but related, space just as *Pnin* does.

Pale Fire orders itself in the same manner. The foreword which introduces the book was written after the rest, at least in the fictive world—one can only guess what the actual author wrote first—the poem, which comes second, was written first; and the notes, which come last, were written second. The parts are in a 3-1-2 order, although the notes sometimes refer us back to the foreword. In short, the novel is, like *Lolita*, a time spiral.

III

It is not, then, just the story that the author is concerned with, but with the telling of the story. Nabokov, for instance, offers most of *Laughter in the Dark* in the first paragraph, most of the story, that is. His real concern is with the presentation and discovery of order and delight.

We see this play of relationships even in the names of Nabokov's characters and places. In *Pnin*, the American railway employee Bob Horn, of the first story, is echoed by the Russian steward, Robert Karlovich Horn, of the last story. Gerald Emerald of *Pale Fire*, who dresses in "a cheap green jacket," is repeated by Izumrodov, the Shadow, who is dressed in a green velvet jacket. Not too surprisingly, *izumrud* is Russian for "emerald, smaragdite." We have a Doctor Starov in *Sebastian Knight*, and then an astronomer of Russian descent named Starover Blue in *Pale Fire*. The name Starover, says Kinbote, is not English; it is derived from a Russian word meaning "old believer," and the "Blue" is a translation of the Russian "siniy." Still, an astronomer named Starover yokes, perhaps a little violently, English and Russian together. The author puns again, but more obscurely, in the name of Blue's wife, Stella Lazurchik. Stella, of course, is the Latin for star, but we find that *lazur* in Russian means "sky-blue, ultramarine." Is there not also a pun on lazuli, and *l'azur*? The murderer Gradus stays at the Hotel Lazuli in Nice after having landed at the Cote d'Azur airport. And Shade begins his poem:

> I was the shadow of the waxwing slain
> By the false azure in the window pane. . . .

Miss McCarthy suggests that there may be a logical pattern in Nabokov's use of colors, certain shades being associated with certain people and perhaps certain moral judgments. I should say that there is a pattern, but not one that makes divisions. It is a pattern of surprise, one that shows that good and evil characters are connected by the same colors, that good and evil are much alike in the end. The same applies to the names: Odon has his wicked half-brother Nodo; Baron Radomir Mandevil has, in another back-spelled name, his wicked cousin Baron Mirador Mandevil. The "man-devil" playing in this name is obvious, as well as the allusion to Sir John de Mandeville, that classic liar who sometimes told some truth. Dolores Haze is perhaps not a mirror image of Hazel Shade, but the names connect two novels—and the "haze" element has a certain foggy ambiguity about it.

Nabokov uses the numbers in the same way—they are not magic numbers, symbolic numbers, but connectives, linking this to that. Lolita leaves H.H. on July 5; the birthday of John Shade, of Gradus, and of Kinbote is July 5 (unless we agree that Kinbote is simply mad and making up his facts, but if so we have a case history and the novel is nonsense). Pnin's birthday is February 15; on February 15 his happy life at the home of the Clementses is ended by the return of their daughter; he is "driven" from Waindell by the "I" of the novel who is going to give a lecture on February 15. Pnin lives, in his last Waindell house, at 999 Todd Road; John Shade's poem has 999 lines (or maybe 1000)—and Shade says, in the poem "The Nature of Electricity," that lamps may house souls and that "maybe [streetlamp] / Number nine-hundred-ninety-nine / . . . is an old friend of mine." He is indeed.

Names, colors, and numbers, then, we can call marrowskies. But, if a name is marrowsky, "a rudimentary spoonerism," it is a shade or shadow of the other name, a repetition in an altered form. The title of *Pale Fire* comes from *Timon of Athens*, IV, ii:

> The sun's a thief, and with his great attraction
> Robs the vast sea; the moon's an arrant thief,
> And her pale fire she snatches from the sun.

Miss McCarthy, explaining the meaning of this thief imagery to the novel, says that *Pale Fire* is about many kinds of theft, including literary theft. So it is. But one must notice that the image from Shakespeare is that of a cycle, a going from one thing to another, not exactly circular, for different things are stolen, but nearly. The pattern is complex at first sight, although its basis is simple: it is a repetition with alterations. It is the extension of the marrowsky into the spiral. And such a pattern sometimes reverses things. Kinbote tries to remember certain lines from *Timon* but he does not have the original with him and has to translate back from the Zemblan. He is quoting the above passage, but it is so changed in "translation" that one can hardly recognize it:

> The sun is a thief: she lures the sea
> and robs it. The moon is a thief:
> he steals his silvery light from the sun.
> The sea is a thief: it dissolves the moon.

The "pale fire" disappears. But, more important, the genders of the sun and moon are reversed. Gender, in Nabokov's work, is an ambiguous thing. It is ambiguous because Nabokov is attacking the clear, divisive, and perhaps untrue categories of simple common sense. The artistic pattern is like the pattern of the universe: a thing exists but it is not simple. And it looks different from a different position. And so reversals and coincidences are not chance alone.

Shade, speaking of the meaning of his world and of death, says that the "contrapuntal theme" of existence is:

> not text, but texture; not the dream
> But topsy-turvical coincidence,
> Not flimsy nonsense, but a web of sense.

And for himself as an individual it would be right and sufficient if he could discover:

> Some kind of link-and-bobolink, some kind
> Of correlated pattern in the game,
> Plexed artistry, and something of the same
> Pleasure in it as they who played it found.

Texture, topsy-turvical coincidence, not text, not message, not sociological reporting is what he is presenting. Shade says what Nabokov says:

The Message Man, the owlish Nincompoop
And all the Social Novels of our age
Leave but a pinch of coal dust on the page.

The mirror images of the book can be seen, then, as an integral part of its form and meaning. They help make up the altered coincidences. In *Conclusive Evidence*, Nabokov remarks on the novels of the Russian emigre Sirin (Nabokov's *nom de guerre* for his Russian works) that "the real life of his books flowed in his figures of speech which one critic [no doubt Nabokov himself once more] has compared to 'windows giving upon a contiguous world . . . a rolling corollary, the shadow of a train of thought.' " This quotation means more than it says directly, for it offers us the source and perhaps the significance of some of the images elsewhere. In the same book, Nabokov describes a scene on a train: his mother and he are playing cards—and all this is reflected in the window and, so, superimposed upon the scene outside. John Shade begins his poem *Pale Fire* with just such a reflection: the room he lived in as a boy is repeated in a window and stands "upon that snow, out in that crystal land" of the winter outside. The "crystal land" is a number of things, *i.e.*, the actual winter outside, Kinbote's Zembla, and Nabokov's Russia. The important thing is, though, that the room and the world outside are nearly one.

Shade's name also enters into this pattern. Puns on the name are made throughout the book, *e.g.*, the chief Extremists are Shadows, but one of the hidden word plays brings the name and mirror images together. Kinbote speaks of the "anonymous [Zemblan] masterpiece," the *Kongs-skugg-sio* which he translates as *The Royal Mirror. Kongs* is Zemblan for "king's" or "royal," *skugg* is Zemblan for "mirror." But we find that there is a Swedish word *skugga* which means shade or shadow. Shade is mirror, and both are the king's. The two are nearly one.

Discussing butterflies in *Conclusive Evidence*, Nabokov speaks of the pleasure that mimicry in insects gives him. He points out that often such mimicry goes far beyond any protective need and so "I discovered in nature the nonutilitarian delights that I sought in art. Both were a form of magic, both were a game of intricate enchantment and deception." Therefore, he seeks the magic and the intricacy. Who else would find the *Vanessa atalanta*, the Red Admirable (Admiral) butterfly in Swift's poem "Cadenus and Vanessa"?

When, Lo! *Vanessa* in her bloom
Advanced like *Atalanta*'s star (*PF*, 172)

For the "true artist," Kinbote says, will "pounce upon the forgotten butterfly of revelation, wean" himself "abruptly from the habit of things, see the web of the world, and the warp and the weft of that web." Gradus, in *Pale Fire*, is Jack Grey, "no fixed abode, except the Institute for the Criminal Insane," but he is also Jakob Gradus, Jack Degree, Jacques de

Grey, Sudarg of Bokay ("a mirror maker of genius"), and d'Argus. In *Laughter in the Dark*, the usherette Margot works at a movie theater called the Argus. And the key element in the names of certain genera of butterflies on which Nabokov is an expert is "argus." All these things, too, are nearly one.

But they are nearly one because the author so perceives them. Nabokov says, "In a sense all poetry is positional: to try to express one's position in regard to the universe embraced by consciousness, is an immemorial urge. The arms of consciousness reach out and grope, and the longer they are the better" (*CE*, 155). And though he says that in making up chess problems he was always willing to give up form "to the exigencies of fantastic content" (*CE*, 219), he does not really sacrifice form anywhere: he invents new and strange forms, spiral ones, combinational ones, ones that encompass more and more of the universe. For, as John Shade writes:

> I feel I understand
> Existence, or at least a minute part
> Of my existence, only through my art,
> In terms of combinational delight.

And Charles Kinbote, V. Botkin, and by marrowsky V. Nabokov, claims ambiguously, "I have no desire to twist and batter an unambiguous *apparatus criticus* into the monstrous semblance of a novel."

"Semblance" is of course a key word in the novel. Zembla, Kinbote states, is not derived from the Russian *zemlya* meaning "earth" (although we know that it is—in part), but from "Semblerland, a land of reflections, of 'resemblers'. . . ." And Shade adds that "resemblances are the shadows of differences. Different people see different similarities and similar differences." A shadow of a difference—remember the puns on Shade—is a difference, but not entirely so. It is a matter of position on the spiral. We can see the pleasure that Kinbote (and Nabokov) takes in the *korona-vorona-korova* series in Russian that by some almost incredible chance is echoed in their English equivalents: crown-crow-cow. The tiny shifts in the spelling of the words make for great differences in meaning. But we must also pay attention to the words themselves. They make resemblances where they do not exist in the actual world. Or, rather, they find resemblances. John Shade speaks of "playing a game of worlds." Of "words"—and worlds. And later he suggests:

> Maybe my sensual love for the *consonne*
> *D'appui*, Echo's fey child, is based upon
> A feeling of fantastically planned,
> Richly rhymed life.

Art and life are almost one; they echo one another as well as having echoes within themselves.

In a rejected draft, Shade says:

> I like my name: Shade, *Ombre*, almost "man"
> In Spanish . . . (174)

By a marrowsky, he is linking himself with the universal. He does not symbolize *man*, he is part of man, a part of the whole that makes up man. It is in this way that one can hold that Kinbote and Shade are "spiral" images of Nabokov, that art and life are almost one.

But one can be more concrete. Kinbote, Shade, and Gradus were, as we have noted, all born on July 5th. Shade was born July 5, 1898; Kinbote and Gradus were both born on July 5, 1915. The *Kongs-skugg-sio* means "the mirror and the shadow" of the king. Kinbote claims to be a king; Shade's name is involved with Kinbote's kingship.

Moreover, Shade speaks thus to his wife Sybil in his poem:

> We have been married forty years. At least
> Four thousand times your pillow has been creased
> By our two heads.

Kinbote remarks in a note that in the morning hours of July 5, 1959, he observed the Shades' house and, seeing the light on in their bedroom, "smiled indulgently, for, according to my deductions, only two nights had passed since the three-thousand-nine-hundred-ninety-ninth time—but no matter." He is writing this after reading the poem, true, but he is speaking of his thoughts on a night when he could *not* have known what Shade had written. In short, he knew what was going on in Shade's house because he is, in a sense, Shade. And even if Kinbote is mad, he and Shade are still similar—Shade, talking of a madman who thought himself God, says that the man was "a fellow poet." And gods, of course, create worlds. Gradus as Jack Grey is also mad. And Gradus, Argus, repeats Nabokov's interest in butterflies. More to the point, however, is Nabokov's own poem," "An Evening of Russian Poetry." The speaker, who is, as I have already said, Nabokov himself, announces, "all hangs together—shape and sound, / heather and honey, vessel and content." And

> My back is Argus-eyed. I live in danger.
> False shadows turn to track me as I pass
> and, wearing beards, disguised as secret agents,
> . . . warily they linger
> or silently approach the door and ring
> the bell of memory and run away (*Poems*, 22).

The speaker is Argus, Gradus, himself, pursued by *shadows* or *shades* that are his own memories. But these memories are out of time; it is himself who pursues himself. And behind him, in Russia, the speaker says that he leaves a kingdom, a kingdom that is of language, not of political power:

> Beyond the seas where I have lost a sceptre,
> I hear the neighing of my dappled nouns . . . (*Poems*, 21).

He is Kinbote the exiled king, Kinbote who translates his name as regicide or "king's destroyer," for "a king who sinks his identity in the mirror of exile is in a sense just that." But the name Kinbote is also related to the Anglo-Saxon *cyn* which means kind or relative and to *bote* which means reward. He has been paid back in a sense, or in kind. "I have lost a sceptre," the speaker of the poem says. But Charles Kinbote announces, "You will never find our crown, necklace and sceptre," for they are too well hidden. In the "index" of *Pale Fire*, the reader is sent from Crown Jewels to Hiding Place to Potaynik to Taynik which is Russian for "secret place." But the word also introduces a common Russian phrase that means "the secret recesses of the heart." The sceptre then, which is one of language, still exists in the heart and memory of the speaker. It still exists, for everything that was still is. Everything exists and is related, as the points on a spiral are.

IV

The poem *Pale Fire* is, in actuality, the work of Vladimir Nabokov. He gives it to a fictional character named John Shade. But Shade is Nabokov's American disguise, the other half or third of Nabokov's world. He speaks of his Russian, his Western Europe, and his American worlds, and says that he "invented" them (*Lolita*, 314). He invented them in two senses of the word: first, he discovered them, and second he fabricated them.

And who speaks at the end of *Pale Fire*? Is it Kinbote alone who says: "I shall continue to exist. I may assume other disguises. . . . I may turn up yet, on another campus, as an old, happy, healthy, heterosexual Russian, a writer in exile, . . ." an "old Russian" who may write a play, "with three principles" (not principals, but *principles*): "a lunatic who intends to kill an imaginary king, another lunatic who imagines himself to be that king, and a distinguished old poet who stumbles by chance into the line of fire, and perishes in the clash between the two figments"? We cannot doubt that this is Nabokov talking about his own work.

The writer is saying once more that the same pattern may be repeated—although changed. Nabokov's belief in spirality is not, it must be emphasized, deterministic. There is freedom in that belief, just as there is order and yet freedom in art. Toward the close of *Conclusive Evidence*, he recurs to the image and says that, "if, in the spiral unwinding of things, space warps into something akin to time, and time, in its turn, warps into something akin to thought, then, surely another dimension follows," a dimension that could be better, "unless spirals become vicious circles again."

But no matter what, the image informs Nabokov's art. We might guess, too, that it has informed his life. It is delightful to discover that Vladimir Nabokov was born April 23, 1899. One does not need to be reminded who else was, traditionally, born and who died on April 23. But we must remember that he offers Nabokov a title for his novel. Whether *Pale Fire* is Nabokov's *Timon of Athens* is another thing, though.

And, of course *Pale Fire*, as well as Nabokov's other novels, is something more than just a spiral, it is something more than a statement about "the essential spirality of all things in their relation to time." But, if the novel is also a satire upon literary commentators, we Kinbotes, despite the slangs and errors of outraged authors, must say what a work means essentially.

Notes

1. Louis D. Rubin, Jr., "The Self Recaptured," *The Kenyon Review*, XXV (Summer, 1963), p. 403.

2. Mary McCarthy, "Vladimir Nabokov's *Pale Fire*," *Encounter*, XIX (October, 1962), p. 81.

Nabokov's Russian Games

Simon Karlinsky*

After the Soviet cosmonaut Gherman Titov returned to earth from outer space not so many years ago, he vividly described his overwhelming experience of seeing the enlarged moon pass alarmingly close to his spacecraft. The sight reminded him of Gogol, Titov said. His impressions were front-page news and his remark was picked up by newspapers everywhere. One of the San Francisco papers that reported it felt obliged to explain to its readers that Nikolai Gogol was a Russian writer, gave his dates and, apparently exhausting its stock of information, ventured that Gogol was noted for his descriptions of the rising of the moon.

Titov was using a ploy that is fairly traditional among his countrymen: he was establishing his credentials as a man of culture and education by making an oblique and not fully stated literary allusion, paying his audience the compliment of assuming that they did not require a more explicit identification. He knew that he could trust his description of the huge moon and the mention of the author's name to lead all literate Russians to Gogol's tale "Christmas Eve," popular both in its own right and as the basis of two well-known operas: Rimsky-Korsakov's "Christmas Eve" and Tchaikovsky's "The Golden Slippers," sometimes called "Oksana's Caprices."

The hero of Gogol's tale, a Ukrainian village blacksmith, captures a devil and on his back flies to St. Petersburg to visit Catherine the Great.

*From the *New York Times Book Review*, April 18, 1971, 2–18. © 1971 by New York Times Company. Reprinted by permission.

During his flight, the smith passes the moon at such close range that he has to stoop to avoid having his fur cap knocked off. Within the Russian cultural framework, Titov's allusion was both apt and accessible. It did not occur to him that he might also be stumping the copy desk of a California newspaper.

The situation in which Titov's offhand remark had put the unsuspecting American copyreaders is not unlike the position in which many American literary critics and scholars find themselves with the advent of Vladimir Nabokov as a major phenomenon on today's literary scene. A writer of wide-ranging, international culture Nabokov delights in projecting his literary likes and dislikes into his fiction, in interlarding his narratives with thinly disguised bits of literary criticism and in playing a variety of literary games involving allusion to and parody and citation of other men's writings.

In their turn, academic-minded American reviewers and exegetes, trained on Joyce and Eliot, love nothing better than unraveling this sort of literary puzzle for the edification of their readers and their less-informed colleagues. Thus, very soon after "Lolita" was published and acclaimed, several American commentators stepped forward to point out the numerous allusions to the work of Edgar Allen Poe in that novel; traces and paraphrases of Swift and Pope were quickly discovered in "Pale Fire"; and the better reviews of "Ada" emphasized the importance of its Byronic references and explained the several sets of variations on themes by Chateaubriand that the book contains.

But Nabokov was an accomplished, fully formed Russian writer before he ever wrote anything in English and it was in his Russian novels (which now, in translation, form an indispensable part of his total *oeuvre*) that he developed his art of incorporating literary allusion and reference as an inherent device of fictional narration. He drew mostly on Russian literature for this purpose in his early novels, and he continues to do so now that he writes in English. But competent critics, perfectly able to do the brilliance of Nabokov's verbal style and the elegance of his plotting full justice and to discern the subtlest and most veiled evocations of, say, Mérimée's "Carmen" or Poe's "Annabel Lee," have been known to stumble and fall on their faces the moment Nabokov mentions some work of Russian literature familiar to any child in the Soviet Union (or to any American college student who has taken a survey course on Russian literature in translation).

T. S. Eliot's absurdly uninformed dictum, enunciated in the 1920's, that Russian literature consists of half-a-dozen good novelists and possesses no poets or any other writers of note, may not necessarily be endorsed by most people who teach American literature or write about it today, but it does describe the extent of their factual grasp of it. This is why Matthew Hodgart, reviewing "Ada" for The New York Review of Books, was able to see significance in the similarity of the heroine's name to that of Lord Byron's daughter, but was thrown completely off the scent by the novel's subtitle, "A Family Chronicle."

Sergei Aksakov's "A Family Chronicle" is, of course, one of the most famous works of Russian 19th-century literature, long available in English translation and in no way minor or obscure. It is on that book's depiction of the leisurely and patriarchal life on a remote country estate in early 19th-century Russia that Nabokov draws for both the nostalgic and the parodistic aspects of "Ada's" quasi-Russian landed gentry setting. To drive the point home, he introduces into the novel minor characters named Aksakov and "Bagrov's grandson," the latter being the hero of Aksakov's sequel to "A Family Chronicle," "The Childhood Years of Bagrov-Grandson." Not aware of any of this, Mr. Hodgart decided that the subtitle "A Family Chronicle" indicated that "Ada" was a parody of the turn-of-the-century "family novel" of Galsworthy and Thomas Mann.

In a manner reminiscent of Alfred Hitchcock's celebrated walk-on scenes in every one of his films, Nabokov includes some Russian literary game in almost every one of his novels. Still, the unwary reader may miss the cryptic reference to a poem by Tiutchev in "Invitation to a Beheading" or fail to grasp the complex Franco-Russian puns in "Bend Sinister," which revolve around the Russian wording of Hamlet's soliloquy, and nevertheless have unimpeded access to the content of the novel. In three essential works, however, the quoted Russian literature serves as such a basic and central component, that to miss its significance is to miss much of the book's meaning. These works are "The Gift," the still-untranslated play "The Event" and the recent best-selling novel "Ada."

In the science-fiction-like narrative fabric of "Ada," the social and literary reality of 19th-century Russia is projected against the background of mid-20th century America, with results not unlike a double-exposed photograph. Russian language and literature (and to a lesser extent, French language and literature) permeate the verbal texture of the novel. Russian words and phrases are quoted, translated accurately, translated obliquely or deliberately mistranslated for punning or humorous effect. Quotations from Pushkin's "Eugene Onegin," from Griboedov's "The Misfortune of Being Clever," from Tolstoy, from several plays by Chekhov and from Russian poets too numerous to mention, are worked into the author's narration and into the characters' dialogue, with or without identification. Russian literary scholarship and scholars are twitted in ways that only they themselves could possibly perceive.

The lengths to which Nabokov can go in his verbal-literary games in "Ada" can be illustrated by his casting a girl named Dawn in the role of Natasha in a production of Chekhov's "Four Sisters" ("Three Sisters," plus Varya from the same author's "The Cherry Orchard") in which the heroine of the novel also appears. This enables Van to remark later: "Dawn *en robe rose et verte*, at the end of Act One," unexpectedly juxtaposing for those who know about such things, the pink dress with its inappropriate green sash worn by Chekhov's vulgar Natasha with the rosy and green robe of Charles Baudelaire's shivering dawn (in his poem "Le Crépuscule du Matin") flying over the deserted Seine. The chapter wherein Van takes Ada and Lucette to a Russian-style New York nightclub gives Nabokov a chance to produce a series of virtuoso translations into English of the better-known torch songs of the Russian-Gypsy repertoire; however, the English of one of these translations, if read with a broad enough accent, will yield the Russian text of a popular song by Bulat Okudzhava, the current Soviet equivalent of Bob Dylan.

All this sort of thing did not prevent intelligent reviewers, such as Robert Alter and Alfred Appel Jr., from writing of "Ada" with distinction and perception, without delving too deeply into its Russian thickets; nor did this literary underbrush turn away thousands of satisfied readers, who found enough sustenance in the novel's other riches to ignore the cultural obstacles, which they for the most part did not even notice. But a very basic dimension of "Ada" was, however, almost universally overlooked by both critics and readers, despite Nabokov's numerous literary clues, and that was the demonic origin and nature of both the hero and the heroine.

The father of Ada and of Van is nicknamed Demon and the text of the novel constantly likens him to the hero of Mikhail Lermontov's *magnum opus* "The Demon," an iridescent-hued and somewhat tinseled narrative poem set in the Caucasus about the love of a Byronic demon for the ethereal Georgian girl Tamara, whom he kills with his kiss once she is able to reciprocate his love. The Russians also know this poem through Anton Rubinstein's bombastic opera, which they still inexplicably like, and through the series of beautiful, genuinely visionary oils and watercolors of the Demon by the turn-of-the-century painter Vrubel.

Although Nabokov draws heavily on both Lermontov and Vrubel ("I, Demon, rattling my crumpled wings" is a description of one of those paintings, and later on Ada herself refers to her father's portrait by Vrubel), his Demon Veen emerges both Victorianized and vulgarized when compared to his prototype in Lermontov. This is most clear in the passage (p. 180) where he is seen accompanied by a "temporary Tamara" (Lermontov's princess demoted to a harlot), and the pristine Caucasus landscape against which Lermontov's Demon is first glimpsed, the diamond-like facets (*gran' almaza*) of Mount Kasbek, is tellingly reduced to Demon Veen's ostentatious jewelry ("He wore a diamond ring blazing like a Caucasian ridge") and his companion's cheap cosmetics (her "kasbek rouge" and "Caucasian perfume, Granial Maza, seven dollars a bottle").

It is their descent from Demon that gives Van and Ada their superhuman stature, their immunity to scruples, and delivers their nondemonic half-sister Lucette into their power. The title "Ada or Ardor" may also refer to the heroine's infernal origin, but it may also be a rhyming device, designed to prevent the reader from pronouncing her name as Eh-dah. If the Lermontov references were more widely understood by the American reviewers of "Ada," the ridiculous comparisons of the diabolical sibling-lovers to the novelist himself and his wife in which some of these reviewers indulged would be instantly seen in all of their glaring absurdity.

While the Russian literary components in "Ada" are a part of an elaborate artistic game and a mechanism of plot structure, the similar component in the earlier novel, "The Gift," provides us with basic insights into Nabokov's views on the uses of literature and literary criticism and contains an explanatory key to many of Nabokov's controversial literary, political and social opinions. When the English translation of "The Gift" first appeared in 1963, it was greeted in the daily press with review headings such as "Early Nabokov Tale Wordy, Confusing" and "Nabokov's Merry Pranks Hard to Follow in 'Gift'."

Even the remarkably eloquent and hugely favorable reviews of the novel by Granville Hicks and Stanley Edgar Hyman indicated that there was a dimension to the novel that they wished they had understood. Stephen Spender, writing in The Times Book Review, confessed that he had to read "The Gift" three times "in order to obtain an idea of the kind of novel it was." All reviewers read the book as an almost plotless record of a young émigré poet's solitary life in Berlin. None of them seemed to notice the exciting and eventful intellectual plot of the novel, dealing with the hero's literary researches, or that in fact, "The Gift" belonged to a totally new hybridized genre, combining as it does traditional fictional narration with lengthy sections of literary criticism and cultural history (a hybridization that was later continued in "Pale Fire").

What serves as the "internal" plot in "The Gift" is the hero's gradual discovery of some inescapable facts of Russian 19th- and 20th-century intellectual history and especially the oppressive character of the "men of the [eighteen-] sixties," the traditionally admired radical anti-government literary critics. As Fyodor plunges into his research on the life and writings of N. G. Chernyshevsky (1828–89), a figure almost unknown abroad, but venerated by Russians of every persuasion as a saint of human progress, the hero and the reader become convinced that it was Chernyshevsky (rather than his volatile, simple-minded predecessor Belinsky) who was the true originator of that grim anti-art, anti-beauty, anti-joy tradition in 19th-century Russian criticism which decreed any literature not aiding the cause of the oppressed Russian people in some universally perceptible and immediately relevant way to be harmful and in need of extermination.

The triumph of that tradition in the intellectual life of the country was what delayed the recognition of Dostoevsky's true stature for decades, caused generations of progressive university students to prefer a succession of now-forgotten Populist novelists to Tolstoy and to shun Chekhov as irrelevant and harmful. It was the great feat of Russian Symbolists at the turn of the century to break the stranglehold of Chernyshevskianism and to bring back complexity, mysticism, joy and literary craftsmanship as again respectable and desirable.

But the generation of Lenin (whose favorite novelist and critic Chernyshevsky was) was deeply imbued with the ideas of the late sixties. The Soviet-Marxist aesthetics owes far more to the ideas of Chernyshevsky than to anything to be found in Marx and Engels. Where Chernyshevsky and his followers could only decry literary originality and independence as irrelevant and socially harmful in their editorials, their linear descendants of the 1930's, the decade when Nabokov wrote "The Gift," extended their methods of literary criticism to physical annihilation of excessively complex writers, such as Mandelstam and Babel.

Written when it was, "The Gift" is certainly the most engagé work Nabokov ever wrote. Its portrait of the morally righteous, aesthetically unimaginative Chernyshevsky fighting oppression and sowing the seeds of a later tyranny he could not have possibly imagined is all the more persuasive for the parodistic and burlesque terms in which Nabokov chose to couch it. Nabokov's daring challenge of some sacred traditions in "The Gift" caused a liberal émigré journal that first published it to delete an entire chapter from this novel.

It is a book that still makes elderly anti-Bolshevik Russian socialists, living in retirement in New York, to spit at the mention of Nabokov's name, and it has been known to move Soviet mathematicians visiting an American campus to break into an improvised dance of glee after perusing a few pages of the Chernyshevsky chapter. It is also, as Ellendea Proffer's recent article told us, Nabokov's most highly valued work among his underground fans in the Soviet Union. But until someone does "The Annotated Gift" (similar to Alfred Appel Jr.'s recent "The Annotated Lolita"), American critics and readers will continue closing this masterpiece of 20th-century Russian literature with a bored yawn.

Because of his paradoxical situation between Russian and American literatures, Nabokov will pose formidable problems to any American or British scholar who attempts to establish his literary genealogy and trace the influences that contributed to the formation of his art. The problem will have to be faced because of Nabokov's pervasive influence on literature written in English: from Stephen Schneck's gross "The Nightclerk" to John Fowles's elegant "The French Lieutenant's Woman," the Nabokov imprint is unmistakably there on any number of important novels of the last decade. But turning to Tolstoy and Turgenev for comparison, as some have tried, is fruitless: Nabokov was not directly influenced by them any more than James Joyce was by Dickens. Apart from his enormous debt to Pushkin, the roots of his innovative art are closer to us in time.

Although one would never know it from reading Sholokhov, the Russian novel was as thoroughly reformed in the first decade of our century as the Western European novel was to be reformed a decade or two later by Proust, Joyce and Kafka. The three key writers of that Russian reformation have been so systematically downgraded or ignored by the neo-Chernyshevskians in their native country that the outside world is hardly aware of them, but those who care about Russian literature were never in doubt about their importance.

There was Fyodor Sologub, whose novel of transcendental evil, "The Petty Demon," written five decades before "Lolita," features a sexual affair between a 13-year-old boy and a sophisticated young woman of 25 and whose trilogy of novels, "The Created Legend," is situated partly in Russia during the revolution of 1905 and partly on a distant imaginary planet in a way that is reminiscent of "Ada." There was Andrei Belyi, who, had he written in any language other than Russian, would have long since received his due as one of the greatest novelists of the century and whose experimental novelistic techniques, tricky plot structures and shifting narrative viewpoints affected every Russian writer who wrote in the 1920's. And there was Alexei Remizov, a sort of Russian combination of Gertrude Stein and Raymond Queneau, whose writing career began in 1906 and ended with his death in Paris in 1957, and whose unique verbal art, based on the spoken rather than the written language, is so hypnotic that it can make one wonder whether anyone ever lived who knew Russian as well as this eccentric, half-blind man.

Nabokov has proclaimed his admiration for Belyi in a television interview, claiming for his novel "Saint Petersburg" a place on a par with Proust and Joyce; he mentions Remizov, whom he knew in Paris, in various memoirs, as one of the more important of Russian exiled writers; as to Sologub, chances are that his mysticism and fascination with absolute evil bore Nabokov. But whatever his current attitude may be, as a young beginning writer in 1916 he was sure to have been aware of the innovative novelists of the astounding Silver Age of Russian literature as he was certainly aware of its poets.

It is in the work of these predecessors, to whom he had to react either in imitation or rejection, that the origins of Nabokov's admired craftsmanship, verbal flair and thematic novelty are to be sought. By contributing to his formation, those Russian pioneers, banned or reviled in their own land are now indirectly helping to turn the English and American novel to new and undreamed-of paths, enriching these two literatures with what the intolerant Soviet literary establishment forced Russian literature to reject. One handsome way that Nabokov's readers and critics could repay for all this largesse would be to learn a little more about the magnificent and much put-upon literature that so unexpectedly provided the English-speaking world with its currently reigning literary figure.

Pnin's History

Charles Nicol*

"The history of man is the history of pain!"—Timofey Pnin

Pnin, one of Vladimir Nabokov's most approachable novels, may be read enjoyably on an elementary level for its "human interest"—those quotation marks, and that sneer, belong to Nabokov himself. Consequently, some critics have praised *Pnin* out of all proportion, and Nabokov's best critics have tended to over-react and slight this delightful novel. A book that can be enjoyed by simple people is not necessarily a simple book, and *Pnin* is as complicated as a pet snake.

Timofey Pnin, a pathetically comic Russian émigré, teaches his native language at Waindell College, somewhere in New England. His ineffectual English makes him the butt of countless jokes; amid this alien corn Pnin wanders with apparent cheer, but cannot always avoid hearing the mockery of his numerous mimics on campus. Far from a cliché clown, Pnin is inescapably comic because he is a penguin out of water, a man who had the world pulled out from under him. Among fellow Russian émigrés a highly intelligent, articulate, polite, scholarly student of the social sciences, among Americans he appears an incoherent fool, unschooled in the simplest of the mores of "unpredictable America." As a whole, Pnin's life may be tragic, but in its visible fragments it is either comic or pathetic. Nabokov thoroughly exploits these dual possibilities, continually shifting his focus and our allegiance.

While the views of Pnin are ambivalent, they are rarely ambiguous; the distinction is between Pnin fooled and Pnin hurt. In the first chapter we witness Pnin's comic misadventures with American trains, busses, and women's clubs, as well as his pathetic heart attack. The second chapter includes his hilarious encounters with a washing machine and a heartbreaking visit from his cruel, thoughtless, exploitative ex-wife. The quiet third chapter records his comic battles with the college library as well as the loss of his pleasant room and his failure to recognize his own birthday. The fourth chapter begins a rising movement in Pnin's fortunes: he meets his ex-wife's son Victor to their mutual delight. The comedy of this chapter involves Pnin's—or America's—confusion between football and soccer, the vagaries of Jack London's literary reputation, and Victor's height; a comic fall gives Pnin a later, pathetic backache. The fifth chapter, Pnin with fellow émigrés, shows him at his best: the comedy involves not just Pnin lost in the Catskills, but also Pnin marvellously talented at croquet; the pathos is Pnin's remembrance of a childhood sweetheart who died in a Nazi concentration camp. The sixth chapter begins a corresponding falling movement. The comedy is again on Pnin's side, the triumph of his little party. The emotion catches us rather off-

*From *Novel*, 4 (Spring 1971), 197–208. Reprinted with permission of the author and of the journal.

guard, for just as Pnin is feeling most at home in his new house and in Waindell College, he is informed that he is about to lose his job. The seventh chapter details how Pnin first met his cheaply poetic and intellectual ex-wife Liza, and how now, on his birthday, Pnin leaves Waindell College with no particular destiny in mind and no new job in sight (in *Pale Fire* we find that Pnin did eventually find a better job). In this last chapter what humor there is, is deliberately flat.

That four of its seven chapters appeared first as separate stories in *The New Yorker* tends to reinforce the impression that this short novel is marvellously realized throughout, but fails to progress; though his circumstances have changed, Pnin at the end of the novel may seem much the same as at its beginning. Lost: his position at Waindell. Gained: friendship with Victor and the completion of an extensive piece of research. But because of these two (closely related) gains, Pnin's character does indeed change. After Liza's visit in the second chapter, the utter loneliness of Pnin comes home to him and he yields to his grief: " 'I haf nofing,' wailed Pnin between loud, damp sniffs, 'I haf nofing left, nofing, nofing!' " In contrast, at the end of the sixth chapter when he again seems to have nothing left, neither job, house, nor punch-bowl, "bracing himself" he stoically continues washing dishes. Pnin's progress, the gains which brings about this character change, are the subject of this paper.

Many of Nabokov's novels have men of letters as their subjects, fictional authors whose projected writings reveal something about themselves. Naturally, these works often also inform us of Nabokov's own intentions; *The Real Life of Sebastian Knight* mirrors the novels supposedly written by its title figure, and Humbert's writings on psychology, Proust, and memory provide insights into *Lolita*. In like manner, the research of modest and scholarly Timofey Pnin provides another dimension for our view of *Pnin*.

The content of Pnin's research is a bit hard to establish, however, since it is only mentioned twice, first in the third chapter:

> He contemplated writing a *Petite Histoire* of Russian culture, in which a choice of Russian Curiosities, Customs, Literary Anecdotes, and so forth would be presented in such a way as to reflect in miniature *la Grande Histoire*—Major Concatenations of Events. He was still at the blissful state of collecting his material; and many good young people considered it a treat and an honor to see Pnin pull out a catalogue drawer from the comprehensive bosom of a card cabinet and take it, like a big nut, to a secluded corner and there make a quiet mental meal of it, now moving his lips in soundless comment, critical, satisfied, perplexed, and now lifting his rudimentary eyebrows and forgetting them there, left high upon his spacious brow where they remained long after all trace of displeasure or doubt had gone.

Note for later reference the simile of the card catalogue, "like a big nut," and its further development where Pnin becomes, metaphorically, a squirrel. In the next paragraph we find Pnin consulting a "voluminous work . . . on Russian myths," but we find out no more about that research until the sixth chapter, several years later, when we are told that the project is practically finished:

> Index cards were gradually loading a shoe box with their compact weight. The collation of two legends; a precious detail in manners or dress; a reference checked and found to be falsified by incompetence, carelessness, or fraud; the spine thrill of a felicitous guess; and all the innumerable triumphs of *bezkorïstnïy* (disinterested, devoted) scholarship—this had corrupted Pnin, this had made of him a happy, footnote-drugged maniac who disturbs the book mites in a dull volume, a foot thick, to find in it a reference to an even duller one.

And this is all. Two mentions, separated by almost half the novel. There are no other references to Pnin's research, and the trail of his little history grows cold.

And yet—we all know that when a man is wrapped up in his studies, some of that wrapping unwinds wherever he goes. At his own party, over-wound Pnin suddenly explodes into suspiciously detailed, very pedantic footnotes about the Cinderella fairy-tale:

> . . . Professor Pnin remarked . . . that Cendrillon's shoes were not made of glass but of Russian squirrel fur—*vair*, in French. It was, he said, an obvious case of the survival of the fittest among words, *verre* being more evocative than *vair* which, he submitted, came not from *varius*, variegated, but from *veveritsa*, Slavic for a certain beautiful, pale, winter-squirrel fur, having a bluish, or better say *sizïy*, columbine, shade—from *columbia*, Latin for "pigeon," as somebody here well knows—so you can see, Mrs. Fire, you were, in general, correct.

Here, suddenly and clearly, is an example of Pnin's research on his *Petite Histoire*, an example that corresponds perfectly to Nabokov's second mention of that research (see above), for it includes not only "the collation of two legends" and "a precious detail in manners or dress," but even, most compactly, those index cards "loading a shoe box"!

So Pnin has discovered how Cinderella's shoes changed from squirrel to glass. In his projected book, this little discovery will provide a model for some major trend in Russian history; however, it also illustrates a Major Concatenation of Events in the Life of Timofey Pnin: squirrel to glass.

For there can be no doubt that Pnin is associated with squirrels throughout the novel. In the first chapter Pnin suffers a heart attack that recalls a childhood delirium; then in his fever he had felt that a squirrel drawn on a screen by his bed held the answer to the world's riddle. That remembered picture overlaps Pnin's confused perception of his present surroundings, a park where a gray squirrel sits in front of him, emblematically holding a peach stone. In the second chapter, in a second park, Pnin gives a third squirrel water from a drinking fountain, thinking "she has fever, perhaps." In the third chapter, a squirrel crosses the snow in front of the college library, and later Pnin is directly compared to a squirrel (in the extended description, already quoted, of Pnin investigating a catalogue drawer). The fourth, central chapter is as much about young Victor Wind as it is about Timofey. And when Pnin begins writing to Victor, he follows his first letter with "a picture postcard representing the Gray Squirrel." It is, in a sense that Pnin himself does not understand, Pnin's calling card. (The Gray Squirrel, *Sciurus carolinensis*, is the uniquely American squirrel. Might Pnin's squirrels, or Pnin himself, belong to a special Nabokovian sub-variety, American-Russian, *Carolina Slavsky*—the name of a minor character in *Pnin*?) "Victor," we are told, "was glad to learn that 'squirrel' came from a Greek word which meant 'shadow-tail.' " We shall return later, first to Victor, then to shadow-tail. The fifth chapter begins with Pnin somewhere in New England, lost; after a hunter fires at a squirrel and misses, Pnin finds his road. The sixth chapter contains the history of Cinderella's shoes, which we have already mentioned; Pnin demonstrates that they were originally made from Russian squirrel fur. The seventh, last chapter contains the narrator's glimpse of young Pnin's Russian schoolroom, where a stuffed squirrel stands among the toys and books.

Victor, Liza's son by Eric Wind while she was still Mrs. Pnin, is associated with glass, for he is, thematically, the later version of Cinderella's slipper. Glass can reflect and refract events, as well as shadow them, and all of Victor's painting and drawing is concerned with optical effects; for instance, he spends much time observing the appearance of various objects through the distortion of a glass of water. One of his ancestors was "a stained-glass artist in Lübeck." Victor, at St. Bart's, learns from Lake, his art teacher, that

> the order of the solar spectrum is not a closed circle but a spiral of tints from cadmium red and oranges through a strontian yellow and a pale paradisal green to cobalt blues and violets, at which point the sequence does not grade into red again but passes into another spiral, which starts with a kind of lavender gray and goes on to Cinderella shades transcending human perception.

Pnin approaches the Cinderella tale through history and legends; Victor approaches the same material through art, and eventually sends Pnin a beautiful punch-bowl of aquamarine glass. One of Pnin's guests, admiring this gift, also uses the Cinderella description: "when she was a child, she imagined Cinderella's glass shoes to be exactly of that greenish blue tint." These words prompt Pnin's discussion of Cinderella's shoes. Squirrel, glass, we have come full circle again.

It should be made clear at this point that squirrels are not symbols for Pnin, shorthand to represent him, or reductions of him, but only themes associated with him. Nabokov's method of associational cross-references, "not text but texture," is uniquely non-reductive, non-levelling. If one thing can be reduced to another, then the first item has no independent value; if one thing stands for another, then the system is itself unnecessary. Nabokov clearly objects to all reductive systems, particularly Freudian and Marxian, that treat art as source materials for ideas, denying creation its essential dignity.

Nabokov investigates events not in their reduction to a hidden simplicity, but in their hidden complexity. Drunk on Pnin's punch, one of the guests at Pnin's party asks it this way: "But don't you think—haw—that what he is trying to do—haw—practically in all his novels—haw—is—haw—to express the fantastic recurrence of certain situations?" This calls to mind Nabokov's discussion (in his autobiography) of his two memories of General Kuropatkin, and how these memories are both associated with sulfur matches. "What pleases me," Nabokov wrote, "is the evolution of the match theme"—and then comes one of the organizing principles of his art: "The following of such thematic designs through one's life should be, I think, the true purpose of autobiography."[1] Following such designs is also for Nabokov a rationale of fiction, and the relationship of Timofey and Victor may be obliquely described as the evolution of the Cinderella's slipper theme.

We may note in passing that the Cinderella motif apparently fascinates Nabokov, for Cinderella stories are hidden in at least two other novels. In *Bend Sinister*, Mariette, the amoral girl who spies on Krug, keeps house for him, and nearly becomes his mistress, is the youngest of the three Bachofen sisters. A young policeman once calls her by "a secret diminutive which none knew, which he had somehow divined." That diminutive is "Cin."[2] In *Ada* there are numerous Cinderella references: in the garbled play of the second chapter the servant girls are described as "Cinderellas"; the curtain falls with an actor "holding the glass slipper." And the servant girl Blanche is throughout *Ada* described as Cinderella or "Cendrillon." Once "she rushed down the corridor and lost a miniver-trimmed slipper on the grand staircase, like Ashette in the English version."[3] She is, of course, another totally false Cinderella: she suffers from venereal diseases and eventually marries a man named Fartukov.

Is there a Cinderella story in *Pnin*? If so, it is not a parody as in *Bend Sinister* and *Ada*, but a transfiguration. In most older versions of the Cinderella tale, Cinderella is befriended not by a fairy godmother but by a helpful animal, which frequently has to be killed for its magic to take effect.[4] Pnin is indeed befriended by a series of uncanny squirrels in the novel, he makes the necessary sacrificial connection in his rather far-fetched insistence that the fur of Cinderella's slippers was squirrel fur, and he possesses "frail-looking, almost feminine feet." We also identify with him in his frequent humiliations in the same way we identify with Cinderella in the ashes. But this seems inadequate evidence. This brings us to the possibility that Victor is the "male Cinderella." The most famous version of Cinderella, "Cendrillon" by Perrault, is the version that Pnin discusses at his party. Perrault introduces the glass slipper to the story, and Pnin's guess that he confused *vair* and *verre* is accepted scholarship.[5] Victor, as we have said, is associated with glass, and consequently with this version of the tale. Perrault's version also includes the fairy godmother, and to some extent Pnin fills this role for Victor—he may also be the fairy-tale prince, since in Victor's dream Pnin is the King. Further, Victor is kept at St. Bart's for a day of his vacation as punishment for smoking; telltale ashes had been found in the attic, and ashes are Cinderella's trademark. But again, it is dangerous to press the case for Victor as Cinderella too far. It is clear that we do not have an especially strong case for either Pnin or Victor as Cinderella; what we do have is a substantial comparison of early and late artifacts of the Cinderella tale, with the representatives of the two versions trading emblems: Pnin sends Victor a card with a squirrel on it, while Victor sends Pnin a glass punch-bowl of "Cinderella" color. We do not have the evolution of a story, but the evolution of a theme in that story.

The card that Pnin sends Victor, carefully chosen from "an educational series depicting Our Mammals and Birds," tells us that "squirrel" comes from the Greek for "shadow-tail." The Greek for shadow is *skia*. We know from *Pale Fire* the importance to Nabokov of Shade and Shadow; it is therefore fitting that, just as this card helps begin the relationship of Victor and Pnin, this word as a "thematic design" helps demonstrate their deep natural affinity. In the very first section of the first chapter, we are told that Pnin can "shadowgraph with his knuckles a rabbit (complete with blinking eye)." Here, "shadowgraph" has a perfectly clear meaning. Compare the same word, at a different stage in its etymological history, applied to Victor:

> He studied his mediums with the care and patience of an insatiable child—one of those painter's apprentices (it is now Lake who is dreaming!), lads with bobbed hair and bright eyes who would spend years grinding colors in the workshop of some great Italian skiagrapher, in a world of amber and paradisal glazes.

Here, with "shadow" moved back into Greek, Nabokov seems to be referring to some highly technical artistic process. But there is apparently no such term as "skiagrapher" in the history of art—although Victor is indeed visiting Italy with his mother at the end of the novel. It is, rather, an early term for a Roentgen photographer; that is, a skiagrapher is an X-ray technician. ("Pnin said, laughing, that every time *he* was X-rayed, doctors vainly tried to puzzle out what they termed 'a shadow behind the heart.' ") But while there has been no such term in art, Nabokov demonstrates that there easily *could* be. A skiagrapher might project shadows, or sketch shadows, or draw silhouettes. Pnin, as we have seen, does the first. Victor does the second:

> He never went through that initial stage of graphic activity when infants draw *Kopffüsslers* (tadpole people), or humpty dumpties with L-like legs, and arms ending in rake prongs; in fact, he avoided the human form altogether and when pressed by Papa (Dr. Eric Wind) to draw Mama (Dr. Liza Wind), responded with a lovely undulation, which he said was her shadow on the new refrigerator. . . . And at six, Victor already distinguished what so many adults never learn to see—the colors of shadows, the difference in tint between the shadow of an orange and that of a plum or of an avocado pear.

Thus Pnin and Victor are both practitioners of the art of skiagraphy. Amusingly, so is Nabokov, who chooses the third and, he admits, easiest method of skiagraphy to end his fifth chapter:

> On the distant crest of the knoll, at the exact spot where Gramineev's easel had stood a few hours before, two dark figures in profile were silhouetted against the ember-red sky. They stood there closely, facing each other. One could not make out from the road whether it was the Poroshin girl and her beau, or Nina Bolotov and young Poroshin, or merely an emblematic couple placed with easy art on the last page of Pnin's fading day.

Of course Nabokov is a far better shadowgrapher when he so chooses. Indeed, the references to shadows in all the novels continually reinforce our impression that Nabokov is in total control, that his characters are only shades, shadows, figments of the imagination of "an anthropomorphic deity impersonated by me,"[6] with no independent life of their own. They are but Nabokov's shadows on the page, and their existence has no reality apart from the whims of their creator.

In the undercurrents of this novel, Pnin and young Victor are related by the Cinderella story and by shadowgraphy. What that relationship approximates is obvious even on the novel's surface: father and son. The thematic designs run in harmony with the flow of the novel. Pnin's triumph is that eventually he and Victor qualify as father and son under every test but flesh itself.

Approached directly, the relationship is a reasonable one. Liza, Victor's mother, was at the time of her pregnancy Pnin's wife. (One analysis of *Pnin* incorrectly states that when she married Pnin, Liza was already pregnant.[7] Since she married Pnin on the rebound from her affair with the narrator, and since the narrator seems to be Nabokov himself, this would indeed be a fascinating situation. The chronology is, however, impossible.) Although Liza eventually marries Eric Wind, Victor's actual father, still later she takes for granted that Pnin will help finance the education of a boy he is not related to and has never met, simply because the relationships of Victor and Pnin to Liza make them father and son by extrapolation. And when Liza, Timofey, and Eric all came to America on the same ocean liner, Liza and Eric both seemed more than willing to include Pnin in their parenthood. When Eric referred to "our child," Nabokov tells us, "the 'our' sounded tri-personal." Given Pnin's wide sympathies, his innocence and openness, his plans at the end of his European career to raise then-unborn Victor as his own, and his still firm attachment to Liza, Pnin's acceptance of Victor as a son is effortlessly believable.

The problem is Victor himself. Victor is a very talented youth, possibly a genius; like Pnin he is a loner; before he meets Pnin Nabokov confides about him, "I do not think he loved anybody." Yet, almost purely through indirection, Nabokov has convinced us by the end of the novel that Victor, in spite of his "amicable aloofness," thinks of Pnin as his proper father. This involves a careful predisposing of Victor's fantasies, tastes, and opinions.

Victor's relationships with Eric and Liza are hardly satisfactory: "Both parents, in their capacity of psycho-therapists, did their best to impersonate Laius and Jocasta, but the boy proved to be a very mediocre little Oedipus." Considering Nabokov's well-known attitude toward Freud, this statement is hardly surprising. What is surprising is that Andrew Field, perhaps our foremost Nabokov expert, has in his study of Nabokov come close to reproducing, this "modish triangle of Freudian romance." Victor has a recurring fantasy about "the King, his father." Because in these dreams the man who has married Liza resembles Victor "as that underformer imagined he would look at forty himself," Field assumes that Victor wishes to elevate himself to the role of "the King, his more plausible father."[8] But this would mean that Victor wishes to replace his father in his mother's affection, and has in his imagination destroyed his father (Eric is non-existent in the dream) in order to marry his mother (the photograph of the King's wife is clearly of Liza—but she is dead also). Since Field failed to comment on these Oedipal implications, perhaps he did not realize the consequences of his reading of Victor's fantasy.

Victor's dream is not, as Field apparently reads it, a boy's fantasy about being king, but a more significant fantasy on the subject of an ideal father. Logic would dictate to Victor that his father should resemble himself. While the "residue of various family allusions of long standing to the flight of Russian intellectuals from Lenin's regime" has its place in the dream, the other "obvious sources" include "an Italian film, made in Berlin for American consumption," "an anonymous Kafkaesque story," and *The Scarlet Pimpernel*. Curiously, Nabokov fails to mention here the

Shakespearean sources for the king pacing "a beach on the Bohemian Sea, at Tempest Point." Prospero in *The Tempest* is an exiled duke, while the geographically absurd Sea of Bohemia is found in *Winter's Tale*, whose plot deals in part with a princess exiled from birth and her eventual reunion with her father the king. At any rate, if we follow Victor's dream to that "crucial flight episode when the King alone . . . paced a beach on the Bohemian Sea," we find it merging with Pnin's dream that ends the chapter. Pnin's dream apparently occurs on the coast of that same "hopeless sea," so it is no wonder that his friend has gone home to get a map. (This theme of the impossible voyage occurs also in the middle of the chapter in the legendary float trip of Saint Bartholomew's casket from the landlocked Caspian Sea to the coast of Sicily.) Pnin, who has escaped from a palace in his own dream, must also be the king, the "more plausible father," in Victor's dream, for the dream has insistently recurred to Victor ever since Liza, her marriage to Eric breaking up, first

> informed him [*Victor*] that she had been Mrs. Pnin before she left Europe. She told him that this former husband of hers had migrated to America too—that in fact he would soon see Victor; and since everything Liza alluded to . . . invariably took on a veneer of mystery and glamour, the figure of the great Timofey Pnin . . . acquired in Victor's hospitable mind a curious charm, a family resemblance to those Bulgarian kings or Mediterranean princes who used to be world-famous experts in butterflies or sea shells.

Thus, even before meeting him, Victor's choice for father (and king) is a tentative Pnin.

Their first meeting, in chapter four, is "extremely satisfactory." Because of this meeting, the chapter has the underlying theme of the cross, or intersection at right angles (the intersection on a map in the first part, Jung's mandala in the third, a Celtic cross of stone in the fourth). Because Pnin is Victor's "water father"—an insistent reference in the novel—it rains throughout this chapter, even in dreams. And of course, it is a tremendous formal and psychological reinforcement that at the end of the chapter Pnin picks up the dream where Victor left off at the beginning of the chapter. With this device, the central chapter of the novel circles back on itself, the same way the entire novel circles back when Jack Cockerell's story "of Pnin rising to address the Cremona Women's Club and discovering he had brought the wrong lecture," the last words of the book, reminds us of, and brings us back to, the first chapter, where Pnin prepares to deliver that lecture.

There is plenty of room for Pnin in Victor's life, for his attitude toward his indifferent, "real" parents is quite clear. Eric, "a cranky refugee doctor, whom the lad had never much liked and had not seen now for almost two years," is hardly a rival for Liza's affections, since he now lives in South America and Liza is about to marry for a third time. And the narrator expressly rejects the possibility that Victor is jealous about his mother's love: "In his attitude toward his mother, passionate childhood affection had long since been replaced by tender condescension." Victor has no Oedipus complex.

But this condescension apparently does not extend to Liza's appearance, for the desk photograph in Victor's dream indicates that he and his mother share the same opinion of her beauty and of her style, "those great blue eyes, that carmine mouth (it was a colored photo, not fit for a king, but no matter)." Compare the emphasis in a poem that Liza wrote in Paris: "No jewels, save my eyes, do I own, but I have a rose which is even softer than my rose lips." Dismissing those jewel eyes but keeping in mind both pairs of rose lips, we may further note that Liza's early collection of Russian poems is entitled *Dry Lips*, and that she inscribes them to the narrator in "dark-red ink." With this emphasis in mind, we realize that Victor's own poem is not just about da Vinci's painting, but about his mother (Liza of course equals Lisa; indeed, Pnin's proposal of marriage addresses her as "Lise"):

> Leonardo! Strange diseases
> strike at madders mixed with lead:
> nun-pale now are Mona Lisa's
> lips that you had made so red.

And now that, in Victor's poem, this contrast of nun-like appearance and lurid reality has been added to the mix, notice that the same pattern comes up in Liza's own poem, the one she recites to Pnin at Waindell:

> I have put on a dark dress
> And am more modest than a nun;
> An ivory crucifix
> Is over my cold bed.
>
> But the lights of fabulous orgies
> Burn through my oblivion,
> And I whisper the name George—
> Your golden name!

Clearly, Victor understands his mother's character. Incidentally, the ultimate joke in this particular thematic complex threatens to be a private one for Russians, for Liza's poems are described as being unoriginal in a special way, "the kind of stuff that émigré rhymsterettes wrote after Akmatova." Twice in *Pnin* Liza's poems are described as weak imitations of Anna Akhmatova, and Akhmatova was herself notoriously denounced by Zhdanov (Stalin's sub-dictator in matters of culture) in 1946 as "a mixture of nun and harlot."[9] Nabokov's joke is that this parody of criticism does apply perfectly to the poetry of Liza, herself a parody of a poetess.

In these family relationships, *Pnin* can be profitably compared to Joyce's *Ulysses*, one of the few twentieth-century works for which Nabokov has unrestrained admiration—a comparison one critic has already pointed out.[10] Liza, like Molly Bloom, is an unfaithful Penelope to her Odysseus, while Pnin is the "true" father of Victor, as Bloom is of Stephen. Victor is also more autobiographical than he first appears (extending the comparison with Joyce's Stephen) since Nabokov was almost by mistake christened Victor (according to the autobiography, at least), and was expected to become not a writer but a painter.[11] Victor, then, embodies two alternative paths, or "time-forks," in Nabokov's life. Although he insists that the biography of the artist is ultimately irrelevant to fulfilled art, one suspects that Nabokov has a control over his biography that rivals his control over his fiction, and that these little references were not intended to go forever unnoticed.

"It is for the sake of the pages about David and his father that the book was written and should be read," Nabokov wrote in a preface to *Bend Sinister*,[12] and the father-son relationship is also important in *Pnin*. If that relationship has been over-emphasized in this paper, it is because the thematic strands investigated here all led back to Pnin's "family." The relationship to Victor is not Pnin's whole history, but it is a major factor in Pnin's progress. Hopefully the reader is by now convinced that the book is an intricate webbing of cross-references, a fully realized novel rather than a series of casually connected sketches.

There is more to Pnin. His full character development lies in his rejection of Nabokov—or, purists will insist, of Nabokov's *persona*. Several commentators have, rightly, been intrigued with the particularly wobbly lines between the author, the narrator, and ultimately the character in the novel who seems to be Nabokov. That is precisely the point: Pnin rejects them all. This devilish composite personality I shall simply call Nabokov.

Nabokov, author and narrator, leads Pnin through innumerable agonies of fever, seizure, "pain and panic" in the first chapter; in the second he dredges up Liza and reduces Pnin to his nadir. In the third chapter, Nabokov the narrator warns the "careless reader" that it is Pnin's birthday, but no one warns Pnin. "And where will fate send me?" Pnin wonders, following the thought of the Pushkin poem he has just taught in class; he fails to find out. He is unknowingly preparing for a Pushkinian "future anniversary," the birthday several years later when he will leave Waindell College. Pnin has now begun his research on the *Petite Histoire* in earnest, storing up fragments against his ruin. In the fourth chapter, Pnin affirms the new pattern of his life through meeting and cherishing Victor. The fifth chapter provides Pnin with a breathing space, the semblance of a full life, visiting Russian friends, talking about Victor, showing his mental and physical prowess. But Nabokov is mentioned during a conversation, and unfortunate, not-quite-so-innocent Pnin says, "I have always had the impression that his entomology was merely a pose." "Oh no," replies Pnin's best friend Chateau, continuing rather ominously,

"You will lose it some day," referring to "the Greek Catholic cross on a golden chainlet" that Pnin has temporarily taken off. Whether or not we take this as a threat from an insulted author, the next, sixth chapter includes another attempt to reduce Timofey to nothing. Herman Hagen tells vulnerable Pnin that he will almost certainly be fired when a new chairman takes over. When Hagen reveals that Nabokov will be a lecturer in the English Department and a potential employer, Pnin insists, "I will never work under him." Possibly because Pnin has rejected the author's conciliatory gesture, a further disaster now occurs: quietly washing dishes, Pnin drops a nutcracker into the water, "where an excruciating crack of broken glass followed upon the plunge." The "melodious" punch-bowl, Pnin's most precious possession, his Cinderella link to Victor, seems to have been broken. Nabokov has slipped tremendous importance into that aquamarine punch-bowl, invisible in a sink full of water. And Pnin rises magnificently to the occasion. In *The Real Life of Sebastian Knight*, only after merging the experience of two lives is the narrator able to speculate on the possibility of Nabokov's existence. In *Bend Sinister* Nabokov confronts the hero on a "beam of pale light" and drives him mad. Stupendous Pnin, standing once again in the wreckage of his life, confronts fate, chance, Nabokov with all the energy in his zig-zag soul, and drags his punch-bowl back from Hades:

> Pnin hurled the towel into a corner and, turning away, stood for a moment staring at the blackness beyond the threshold of the open back door. A quiet, lacy-winged little green insect [*an emblem of entomologist Nabokov, this bug is the signature, the evidence of Nabokov's presence in the scene*] circled in the glare of a strong naked lamp above Pnin's glossy bald head. He looked very old, with his toothless mouth half open and a film of tears dimming his blank, unblinking eyes.

Pnin seems dead himself on his return from this "duration," this long moment where we feel time in our bones, but at this crucial moment of time suspension to which the novel has led, he has confronted Nabokov and won: his punch-bowl is intact.

In the last chapter Nabokov emerges from his den, striking in all directions, and takes on the definite shape of a character. He visits a direct hit on Pnin's past by telling us that it was his own affair with Liza that precipitated her into marriage with Pnin. We hear Pnin call Nabokov "a dreadful inventor"—to his face. We find Pnin and Nabokov cheerfully riding a New York bus together. It is clear that Nabokov and Pnin have ambivalent feelings toward each other, but Nabokov, as author as well as narrator and character, is ultimately always in control; we are perhaps annoyed by his tone of sympathetic superiority, as well as moved by his disappointment at not gaining Pnin's confidence. It is here that we begin to suspect our author's attitude toward his unfortunate character, and that suspicion flows backwards to color our impression of the entire novel.

It is a remarkable technical feat. Then Nabokov visits the campus for a lecture and a personal confrontation with his victim. But Pnin flees, escaping on his birthday while Nabokov is busy with a decoy, Jack Cockerell, the false Pnin who "had acquired an unmistakable resemblance to the man he had now been mimicking for almost ten years." Surging up the hill, Pnin is "free at last"—free of his author. But Nabokov will neither retire his puppet to his box, nor let him go, a real live boy, on his earned escape. Pnin will re-appear briefly in *Pale Fire*, carefully trimmed back to comic Russian, "fantastic pedant," stock figure trapped in an enormous burlesque.

Notes

1. *Speak, Memory: An Autobiography Revisited* (New York, 1966), p. 27.
2. *Bend Sinister* (New York, 1964), p. 186.
3. *Ada* (New York, 1969), p. 114.
4. Marian Roalfe Cox, *Cinderella* (London, 1893), *passim*.
5. Stith Thompson, *The Folktale* (New York, 1946), p. 127.
6. *Bend Sinister*, p. xviii.
7. Page Stegner, *Escape Into Aesthetics: The Art of Nabokov* (New York, 1966), p. 93.
8. Andrew Field, *Nabokov: His Life in Art* (Boston, 1967), p. 138.
9. Alexander Werth, "Akhmatova: Tragic Queen Anna," *London Magazine*, VI (December 1966), 88.
10. Ambrose Gordon, Jr., "The Double Pnin," in *Nabokov: The Man and His Work*, ed. L. S. Dembo (Madison, Wisconsin, 1967), pp. 144–156.
11. *Speak, Memory: An Autobiography Revisited*, p. 21; Field, p. 30.
12. *Bend Sinister*, p. xiv.

A Personal View of Nabokov

Joyce Carol Oates*

The world of art offers us an astonishing galaxy of personalities—artists expressing their self-images in a vast multiplicity of styles, some of them linked firmly to a place and a time, the "self" imagined as an embodiment of a certain era, some of them quite divorced from any earthly, temporal dimension at all. At one extreme is that entirely American personality, Walt Whitman, whose "Song of Myself" is hardly a song of Whitman *himself*; at the other extreme, almost inaccessible to us, is Samuel Beckett, whose monologue novels are an expression of a particular self, almost selfless, pared to an existence devoid of the "world" as we know it. Nabokov is closer to Beckett, of course, but his genius is far more exciting than Beckett's because he has the ability—which is sometimes

*From *Saturday Review of the Arts*, 1 (January 6, 1973), 36–37. Reprinted by permission of the author and the journal.

dizzying—to reach into the world for sights, sounds, words, hints, to use the world for his own purposes, to ransack the world of what he would, contemptuously, call "ordinary," unsubjective reality. *Lolita* is one of our finest American novels, a triumph of style and vision, an unforgettable work, Nabokov's best (though not most characteristic) work, a wedding of Swiftian satirical vigor with the kind of minute, loving patience that belongs to a man infatuated with the visual mysteries of the world. Yet when Nabokov talks of the work, we are disappointed, for there is an arrogant, contemptuous side of his nature that tends to distract us from his genuine accomplishments—"Nothing is more exhilarating than philistine vulgarity," he says, in explaining his use of "North American sets" for the work. And he needed this stimulus, this "exhilarating milieu," or he could not have written the novel.

Marx saw history as the process of men pursuing their goals, in action. It is possible to see "literature" as the process of an infinite number of individuals pursuing their "images" of themselves and of their eras, each work of art expressing the artist's nature at the time of its execution. Yet it is necessary to realize how incredibly different we all are, how violently differing are our visions of reality—so that "reality" itself must be, in some fantastic Einsteinian paradox, an event multiplied endlessly, in each of our brains, an event split up into many fragments, *which are all equal.* The world of literature may be divided very loosely into those writers who believe this, enthusiastically, recognizing divinity everywhere—literally everywhere—like the American Transcendentalists, like Dostoevsky, like all mystics; into those who deny it flatly, and believe that they, as isolated individuals, possess all that is sacred or at least important, in themselves, and who truly do not need any sense of communion or kinship with other people. In fact, it is not really possible for these writers to feel this communion, because they do not believe—not fully—that other people exist. Nabokov has stated that ordinary reality will begin to "rot and stink" unless a subjectivity is imposed upon it. This means, of course, that ordinary human beings—not so enchanting as Lolita or the other feminine targets of Nabokov's powerful, lustful imagination—will also begin to rot and stink unless someone comes along to give them value. Their "value" does not exist in themselves and certainly not in nature—it can only be given to them, assigned to them, *imagined* in them, by a confident, powerful, Magus-like personality. Who is this godly creature? Who, reading Nabokov's most revealing works (*Speak, Memory* and *Ada*), can doubt that it is only Nabokov himself?

In discussing Nabokov, I must analyze my own reactions. I believe that, as an artist, as a conscious—obsessively *conscious* artist—he is as exciting as any writer who has ever lived. There are critics, such as Mary McCarthy, who, recoiling from the tedium of *Ada*, began to wonder whether, perhaps, earlier works like *Pale Fire* were really as good as they had believed, but I think it is unnecessary, and perhaps unfair, to put much emphasis upon a writer's weakest books. We all want to be judged by our highest accomplishments, and so we should extend to others this generosity. So there are the intensely personal, obsessive, brilliant esthetic accomplishments of Nabokov—arrangements of words on paper, exercises of skill that bear relationship, of course, to the game of chess. If he had written only *Lolita*, *Pnin*, and *Speak, Memory*, he would be the "Nabokov" he is today, eccentric and brilliant. We all honor Nabokov the artist.

But my deeper and, admittedly, very personal reaction to Nabokov is quite different. To me he is a tragic figure, heroic in his isolation perhaps, or perhaps only sterile, monomaniacal, deadening to retain for very long in one's imagination. He is far more depressing than Kafka, who believed that the "divine" was everywhere *except* in himself, but who did believe passionately that he might gain access to it somehow, at some point in his life. Nabokov empties the universe of everything except Nabokov. He then assigns worth—which may seem to us quite exaggerated, even ludicrous, as in *Ada*—to a few selected human beings, focusing his powerful imagination upon the happy few, lavishing contempt and energetic humor upon most other people. Nabokov exhibits the most amazing capacity for loathing that one is likely to find in serious literature, a genius for dehumanizing that seems to me more frightening, because it is more intelligent, than Céline's or even than Swift's. Reeling from the depths of Swift's unarguable hatred for much of life, one can always rationalize that probably—perhaps—there was a political reason for his extraordinary vigor in attacking people who seem to us harmless or even sympathetic; and when Céline's loathing crystallized into a historical political philosophy, fascism, we could dismiss it, or at least assign it to some temporary pathology of his era. But of Nabokov, what excuses can we make?—that his early years were tragic indeed, that he suffered the loss of his father, his homeland, his entire way of life, his "untrammeled, rich, and infinitely docile Russian tongue"?—that, ultimately, he *is* not American, and his scorn for the democratic ideal is something as deep in him, as natural, as his genius for words, for chess, and for the capturing of butterflies?

Still, assuming the immense differences between Nabokov, as an exiled Russian, and us, as Americans, we must admit that he is not really Russian either. He "is" only, supremely, himself. Therefore, it is understandable that he should despise certain "mediocrities"—Stendahl, Balzac, Zola, Dostoevsky, Mann—not because they are really mediocre but because they are not Nabokov. Dostoevsky especially arouses his contempt, for Dostoevsky lavished love on everyone—prostitutes, drunkards, bullies, saints, the mad, the diseased, *even* those who might have been hilarious targets for satire—transcending any particular embodiment of "self" to create a work like *The Brothers Karamazov*, in which "self" expands to contain the entire world and from which no one is really excluded. With his fastidious concern for esthetic form and the manipulation of words, Nabokov could not possibly sympathize with or even comprehend the nature of what Dostoevsky accomplished.

Yet Nabokov should have the last word, in this lovely and revealing passage from *Speak, Memory*, in which he compares the pleasure he feels upon examining a butterfly's organs under a microscope with the pleasure he derives from art. For Nabokov the butterfly must die and be dissected "for cool study," and its death is justified by the esthetic pleasure he feels as a man who has conquered one tiny aspect of nature—"In the glass of the slide, meant for projection, a landscape was reduced, and this fired one's fancy; under the microscope, an insect's organ was magnified for cool study. There is, it would seem, in the dimensional scale of the world a kind of delicate meeting place between imagination and knowledge, a point, arrived at by diminishing large things and enlarging small ones, that is intrinsically artistic."

Postscript to A Personal View of Nabokov

Joyce Carol Oates*

Nearly a decade later, while I still agree, more or less, with the "personal view" here expressed, I'm not sure that I agree at all with the impulse to commit it to print; or with the generally reprehensible error of confusing opinions with literally criticism. Why I should have wished, or imagined I wished, the idiosyncratic and incontestably brilliant Vladimir Nabokov to be a species of *Dostoyevsky*, or *Mann*, or more egregious yet, *myself*, I can't comprehend. Nabokov did the work he was born to do, and fulfilled what the sentimental among us persist in calling his destiny; to create the work he had to be that man, and to live that life, and to rejoice or despair in his unique nature: and so it's quite beside the point, and futile besides, to wish him otherwise. Since January 1973 I've either come to be more latitudinarian in my own literary tastes, or more "Nabokovian,"—alternatives that are, of course, mutually exclusive, yet mutually attractive; and wonder if the "contempt" Nabokov lavished upon so many of his fictional characters really matters all that greatly, so long it gave him the emotional and psychological leverage to write his books. *Pale Fire*, which seems to me his masterpiece, is a beautiful, multifaceted work of art, which hides, at its core, as if deep inside the dazzingly ornate carapace of certain species of turtle, a very tender, and very vulnerable, heart: which is precisely why the novel was written with the elaborate care and cranky, fastidious concern with which it was written. Loathing, contempt, an amusing inflation of the self, a penchant for punishing, or

*This postscript was written specifically for this volume and appears here by permission of the author.

even violence, or whatever, are certainly easier to discern than this secret pulsing heart, but hardly more significant. Whether Nabokov forged for himself the greatness he seems to have aspired to, I can't judge, but he certainly forged for himself *Vladimir Nabokov*—which is quite an achievement.

August 24, 1981

Problems of Voice in Nabokov's *The Real Life of Sebastian Knight*

Shlomith Rimmon*

The Real Life of Sebastian Knight[1] is a maddening labyrinth, a "hell of mirrors,"[2] its complexity deriving mainly from the multiplication and collision of narrative levels and from the ambiguous status of the narrator. It is because of these factors that the novel seems at first sight to defy, or at least render problematic, some of the major distinctions in Genette's seminal *Figures III.*[3] Particularly vulnerable seems the key-notion of the diegetic level or *récit premier* (the level of the primary fictional events), since the novel appears to yield two alternative primary narratives, and *Figures III* seems to offer no criteria for choosing between them or for confirming the equal plausibility of both (and hence the ambiguity of the novel).

Further perusal, however, reveals that although *The Real Life of Sebastian Knight* is more complex than the examples Genette gives, its complexity can profitably be accounted for with the help of Genette's categories, since it is with such categories (though of course not in Genette's terms) that the novel plays. There is, we discover, only one *récit premier* here, and in general the only feasible criterion for the *récit premier* (or diegetic level) is the relational one implied in Genette's definition, namely its being narrated by the extradiegetic narrator.[4] But the primacy of the primary level is challenged by Nabokov's ambiguous treatment of hetero/homodiegetic narration, and the whole notion of the separateness of levels is simultaneously affirmed and denied.

To begin, let me recapitulate Genette's main points about voice. *Figures III* distinguishes among three narrative levels: extradiegetic, intradiegetic (or diegetic) and metadiegetic. The extradiegetic level is external to the primary fictional events and is concerned with their narration. The intradiegetic (or diegetic) level is that of the fictional events narrated in the primary narrative (*récit premier*), and the metadiegetic level is a narrative within a narrative, a second degree of fictionality. The act of narration of the real author is external to all these levels of fictionality and is therefore rightly excluded from Genette's list.

*From *PTL: A Journal for Descriptive Poetics and Theory*, 1 (1976), 489–512.

Adding to these levels the factor of participation or absence of participation on the part of the speaking voice in the *histoire* (*diegesis*) he narrates, Genette arrives at four types of narrators:

(a) extradiegetic-heterodiegetic, i.e., an "external" narrator who is not a fictional character in the *histoire* he narrates;

(b) extradiegetic-homodiegetic, i.e., an "external" narrator who narrates his own story;

(c) intradiegetic-heterodiegetic, i.e., a fictional narrator (or "second degree" narrator) who narrates events in which he does not participate;

(d) intradiegetic-homodiegetic, i.e., a fictional narrator (or "second degree" narrator) who tells his own story.

Homodiegetic narrators can be either protagonists (autodiegetic narration) or witnesses.

The narratee, the addressee of the narrative discourse, is always located at the same fictional level as the narrator, and we can thus distinguish between an extradiegetic and an intradiegetic narratee. The extradiegetic narratee is what Anglo-American criticism calls "the implied reader," addressed by the extradiegetic narrator. The intradiegetic narratee, on the other hand, is an addressee who is himself a fictional character addressed by a fictional intradiegetic narrator.

1. NARRATIVE LEVELS OR "THE MERGING OF TWIN IMAGES"

"Reality," said Nabokov, "is an infinite succession of levels, levels of perception, of false bottoms, and hence unquenchable, unattainable."[5] Nothing can illustrate this statement better than the Chinese-boxes structure of *The Real Life of Sebastian Knight.*

The outer box, the extradiegetic level, is concerned with V's narration and his thoughts about methods of composition and difficulties involved in writing a biography.

The intradiegetic (or diegetic) level, the events related by the extradiegetic narrator, consists of V's quest for his half brother Sebastian's real life. Thus V has a double role: that of an extradiegetic narrator and that of an intradiegetic character-focus.

Sebastian's life story is not told directly by the extradiegetic narrator, but in a mediated way through conversations between V as fictional character with other fictional characters (Sebastian's governess, Sheldon, Miss Pratt, Nina Rechnoy-Lecerf, etc.), or through V's own memories of his half brother (and in this case V is still a fictional character). The conversations are sometimes rendered in the form of a scene, with V as intradiegetic narratee, and sometimes summed up by V. Thus Sebastian's life becomes a metadiegetic level, a story narrated by fictional characters. That a person's "real life" should be a doubly-fictional narrative (the novel we read and, to boot, a metadiegetic level in it) tells us something about the reality of fiction and the fiction of reality. It also puts in doubt the validity of every piece of information we get about Sebastian. V formulates this pervasive doubt in the passage where he hears a mysterious voice in the mist, the voice of conscience wanting to know "Who is speaking of Sebastian Knight":

> It was but the echo of some possible truth, a timely reminder: don't be too certain of learning the past from the lips of the present. Beware of the most honest broker. Remember that what you are told is really threefold: shaped by the teller, reshaped by the listener, concealed from both by the dead man of the tale (44).

Within V's quest—the *récit premier*—there are other metadiegetic levels in addition to Sebastian's life, some taking the form of written documents, some essentially non-verbal and only translated by writing. To begin with, there is V's report of Mr. Goodman's book, *The Tragedy of Sebastian Knight* which V abolishes and finally labels *The Farce of Mr. Goodman.*[6] Then there are notes, like Sebastian's final letter to his half brother or Dr. Starov's telegram to V, and (of a different order, closer to the meaning of meta-language in linguistics and logic) V's ideas about poetics. Of the non-verbal kind are V's prophetic dream about his half brother and Roy Carswell's portrait of Sebastian.

But this is not all. If Sebastian's life is a metadiegetic level, his novels—often narrated in detail and "quoted from"—constitute a meta-metadiegetic level. And if Sebastian's life is a fiction not to be trusted, Sebastian's novels are self-declared fictions closer to his "real life" than his day-to-day reality reconstructed through V's conversations with the various informants. As in Derrida, here too *l'écriture* is more reliable than *la parole*. "Who is speaking of Sebastian Knight?" the passage quoted above continues:

> Who indeed? His best friend and his half brother. A gentle scholar, remote from life, and an embarrassed traveller visiting a distant land. And where is the third party? Rotting peacefully in the cemetery of St. Damier. Laughingly alive in five volumes (44).

But even Sebastian's fictional works do not really yield the final truth for, as Sheldon suggests "his novels and stories were but bright masks, sly tempters under the pretence of artistic adventure leading him unerringly towards a certain imminent goal" (87). The real face cannot be seen; behind every mask there is another mask; behind every sign another sign, and the *signifié final* is as elusive as ever (if I dare again rephrase the idea in Derridan vocabulary).[7]

Within [Sebastian's] novels there is a further meta-level consisting of letters of his metadiegetic characters to their metadiegetic addressees (the love letter and the business letter in *Lost Property*). A dazzling and puzzling succession of levels.

As if to complicate matters, the different levels are made analogous to each other, sometimes so much so that they seem identical; and the borders between them are often blurred by the penetration of one level into the other.

A. Analogy Between Levels

Perhaps the most striking are the analogies between Sebastian's novels (a meta-metadiegetic level) and V's quest (the diegetic level), and many of them have already been pointed out by various critics.[8]

The Prismatic Bezel, is, among other things, "a rollicking parody of the setting of a detective tale" (76) and hence full of "false scents" and delays: "Owing to a combination of mishaps (his car runs over an old woman and then he takes the wrong train) [the detective] is very long in arriving" (77). V's quest is similarly a process of detection (minus the parody) with its own false scents, like Mr. Goodman, and its own delays, like Mme. Lecerf and the various obstacles put in V's way to the dying Sebastian: a slow car, a wrong turning, and all the rest of the conventional retardatory apparatus. In any self-respecting detective novel, the murderer turns out to be the one least suspected by the police and the reader. *The Prismatic Bezel* takes this device to a ridiculous extreme. The corpse is that of an art dealer called G. Abeson. In the crowd there is a passer-by, the harmless old Nosebag with a passion for collecting snuff-boxes. When the detective finally arrives and starts cross-questioning everybody, a policeman suddenly informs him that the corpse is gone. Old Nosebag now steps forward, taking off his beard, wig and spectacles, revealing the face of G. Abeson. The most harmless looking among the crowd turns out to be not the murderer, as in the conventional detective story, but the murdered. The newly resurrected corpse then goes on to explain: "You see [. . .], one dislikes being murdered" (79), and therefore Abeson's death is transcended by his identification with the living Nosebag. A similar situation, in a serious vein, occurs at the beginning of V's quest.[9] Sebastian is no more and because one dislikes being dead, he is continued by a death-transcending duplicate in the person of his half brother, V: "I am Sebastian Knight."[10] Note also that in both cases the identification is connected with the names of the two parties. "Nosebag" is the exact anagram of "G. Abeson," and V's identification with Sebastian is implicitly and indirectly hinted at in the doctor's telegram (a second degree of the metadiegetic) which spells Sebastian's name in the Russian way—"Se*v*astian's state hopeless come immediately Starov"—and "for some reason unknown" makes V stand for a moment in front of the looking glass (160, my emphasis on *v*).

In addition, *The Prismatic Bezel* abounds in situations whereby strangers discover that they are related to each other, just as V's quest leads him to discover that Nina Rechnoy and Mme. Lecerf are one and the same person.

Success is a novel of quest, with an obvious Percival Q. as the researcher. It is thus analogous to V's quest both in its very subject and in its use of false scents and delays.[11] In addition to this basic theme, *Success* contains a series of near meetings between its protagonists, a phenomenon which may parallel V's near meeting with the unwitting Clare in the street (65).

The Back of the Moon, a short story,[12] contains one of Sebastian's most lively characters, "a meek little man," called Siller, who helps three miserable travellers while waiting for a train (86). His physiognomy includes a bald head, a big strong nose, bushy eyebrows, and a constantly moving Adam's apple (86). This meek and helpful Mr. Siller becomes Mr. Silbermann at the diegetic level of V's quest. Like Siller, Silbermann helps a miserable traveller (V) on a train, and like Siller, Silbermann has "a pink bald head" (104), "a big shiny nose" (104), "bushy eyebrows (103), and an Adam's apple which keeps "rolling up and down" (105). As if to clinch the analogy, the diegetic Silbermann advises V to stop searching for his brother's fatal woman because one cannot see "de odder side of de moon" (105), thus reminding us of the story in which his metametadiegetic counterpart "makes his bow, with every detail of habit and manner" (86).

In *Lost Property*, Sebastian's most autobiographical novel, the narrator tells the story of a profound experience he had while visiting the small hotel at Roquebrune where his mother had died. Later, he adds, he mentioned this experience to a relative in London only to learn that he had made a dreadful mistake: "but it was the other Roquebrune, the one in the Var" (17). The experience, nevertheless, was real. V has an analogous "wrong-right" experience when he sits by the bed of a dying man, believing that it is Sebastian (who, in fact, is already dead) and feeling, as he had never done before, intense affinity with his half brother. It is this experience that gradually leads V to the climactic recognition of interchangeability and identification:

> So I did not see him after all, or at least I did not see him alive. But those few minutes I spent listening to what I thought was his breathing changed my life as completely as it would have been changed, had Sebastian spoken to me before dying. Whatever his secret was, I have learnt one secret too, and namely: that the soul is but a manner of being—not a constant state—that any soul may be yours, if you find and follow its undulations. The hereafter may be the full ability of consciously living in any chosen soul, in any number of souls, all of them unconscious of their interchangeable burden. Thus—I am Sebastian Knight (172).

Sebastian's last novel, *The Doubtful Asphodel*, yields an even greater number of analogies with V's quest. The subject of the novel is a dying man who has a secret, an absolute truth, to divulge and who dies before uttering the word which would have changed the lives of all those who could have benefited from the disclosure. In a similar fashion, V tries desperately to reach the dying Sebastian in the belief that "He had something to tell me, something of boundless importance" (162), but Sebastian dies, and it is too late for the extraordinary revelation expected to come from his lips. Within this analogy there is one crucial difference, however: V does discover a secret—not from Sebastian's mouth but from the silent breathing of the "wrong Sebastian" in the wrong room.

Around the central character in *The Doubtful Asphodel* there are other lives, constituting "but commentaries to the main subject":

> We follow the gentle old chess player Schwarz, who sits down on a chair in a room in a house, to teach an orphan boy the moves of the knight; we meet the fat Bohemian woman with that grey streak showing in the fast colour of her cheaply dyed hair; we listen to a pale wretch noisily denouncing the policy of oppression to an attentive plainclothes man in an ill-famed public house. The lovely tall prima donna steps in her haste into a puddle, and her silver shoes are ruined. An old man sobs and is soothed by a soft-lipped girl in mourning. Professor Nussbaum, a Swiss scientist, shoots his young mistress and himself dead in a hotel room at half past three in the morning (147).

Most of these people are analogous, to the point of identity, with minor characters in V's search. Schwarz, the chess-player, is—with a simple translation of the name—Uncle Black at the Rechnoy house, and Rechnoy himself opens the door to V, holding "a chess-man—a black knight—in his hand" (118).[13] Note that this is not only analogous to the diegetic level of V's quest but also to the metadiegetic level of Sebastian's life: Sebastian's name is Knight and he used to sign his English poems with "a little black chess-knight drawn in ink" (15). Later in V's quest, it is again chess that helps him remember the name of Sebastian's hospital: in the telephone booth "some anonymous artist had begun blacking squares—a chess board, *ein Schachbrett, un damier*" (166), hence St. Damier.

The orphan boy in *The Doubtful Asphodel* parallels the one who opens the door at Helene Grinstein's, and the "soft lipped girl in mourning" (147) is Helene herself (111–112). The "fat Bohemian woman" is Lydia Bohemsky of V's quest and the "plainclothes man" may again be Silbermann (105). There is no parallel in V's quest to the man who denounces the policy of oppression. The "lovely prima donna" is analogous to Helene von Graun who has "a splendid contralto" (109) and who, like the prima donna of the novel, steps into a puddle when she arrives at Mme. Lecerf's country house. And finally, the episode of Professor Nussbaum and his young mistress is parallel to the story the hotel manager at Blauberg tells V: "In the hotel round the corner a Swiss couple committed suicide in 1929" (102).[14]

The similarities between *The Doubtful Asphodel* and V's quest are so close to identity that one feels not only an analogy between the levels but also an imminent collapse of the distinctions between them. One also feels as if Sebastian's novel dictates the development of V's quest. It is not only that the quest has "that special 'Knightian twist' about it," as V puts the idea during his visit to Mme. Lecerf (131); the quest is actually made to duplicate Sebastian's novel, manifesting, I believe, the mastery of fiction over reality, except, of course, that the reality is also fiction, and the fiction is supposed to yield the "real" life of its protagonist.

So far I have concentrated on the analogies between the diegetic level of V's quest and the meta-metadiegetic level of Sebastian's novels. The same meta-metadiegetic level (Sebastian's fictional works) is also parallel to the metadiegetic level of Sebastian's life. Thus we are told, in rather vague way, that a certain passage in *Success* is "strangely connected with Sebastian's inner life at the time of the completing of the last chapter" (82), but no details are given as to the specific nature of the connection. Wiliam, the protagonist of this novel, suffers from his heart and consults a doctor named Coates (82). Like him, Sebastian had a heart disease, and his doctor is called Oates (88).[15] Another anology may be discerned between the unrealized meetings in *Success* (81) and the near confrontation between Sebastian and Clare by the Charing Cross bookstall (154).[16]

The "meek little man" in *The Back of the Moon* is not only analogous to Silbermann at the level of V's quest but also to the "meek little man" who provoked a tremendous scene of rage and fury by unwittingly interrupting Sebastian in his work (85).

Lost Property is said to be an autobiographical novel and hence generally similar to Sebastian's life. Particularly analogous is the situation of a man breaking up a happy love affair for the sake of a fatal and miserable one, "the damned formula of 'another woman' "(93). The letter written by the meta-metadiegetic character on this occasion is considered by V to resemble what Sebastian felt about Clare or perhaps even wrote to her, although the "twin" character is a faintly absurd one.

Doubtful Asphodel, composed when Sebastian is mortally ill, reenacts the anxiety of a man who fears he will die before revealing the great truth he has glimpsed. Small details in this novel also parallel Sebastian's life, like Clare's silver shoes (147, 86) and the feeling of regret for not giving a penny to an old beggar (148, 90).

In addition to the analogies between Sebastian's novels (a meta-metadiegetic level) and V's quest (the diegetic level) and to those between Sebastian's novels and Sebastian's life (a metadiegetic level), there are also parallels between Sebastian's life (metadiegetic) and V's life (diegetic). Clare was, in a sense, Sebastian's muse; in the period of their alliterative life together he wrote most of his novels, and she participated, lending her imagination and her English to the creative enterprise. In a minor way, Clare has also become V's muse, since it was the half-meeting with her that has inspired the writing of the chapters devoted to her life with Sebastian (75).[17] Nina Rechnoy-Lecerf, Sebastian's second love, is attractive enough to V so that, for a split second, he contemplates making love to her. V, who works at an office, finally writes *The Real Life of Sebastian Knight*, thus emulating his half brother's profession. Moreover, Sebastian had a plan of writing "a fictitious biography" (34), and after his death it is V who writes such a biography about him. Thus V's life is dictated not only by Sebastian's novels but also by Sebastian's life. The diegetic level is manipulated and molded by the metadiegetic and the meta-metadiegetic.

Another influence of the metadiegetic on the diegetic is found in the parallel between Roy Carswell's portrait of Sebastian and V's discovery of Mme. Lecerf's real identity. In Carswell's portrait, the portrait which should have included the shadow of the destructive woman, Sebastian's face is seen as if mirrored in clear water "with a very slight ripple on the hollow cheek, owing to the presence of a water-spider which has just stopped and is floating backward" (99). When V suspects Mme. Lecerf, he tricks her in Russian, and in reaction to her attempt to remove something from her neck, he triumphantly explains: "I have just been telling this Russian gentleman that I thought there was a spider on your neck. But I was mistaken, it was a trick of light" (144).

V's dream, another "transcribed" non-verbal metadiegetic level, also parallels a central situation in his quest, the diegetic level, as well as in Sebastian's *Doubtful Asphodel*, a meta-metadiegetic level:

> I knew he [Sebastian] was calling me and saying something very important—and promising to tell me something more important still, if only I came to the corner where he sat or lay, trapped by the heavy sacks that had fallen across his legs (159)

—another search for an absolute truth which ends in a similar way to the anticlimax of *The Doubtful Asphodel* and of coming too late to Sebastian's bedside: V wakes up with a nonsensical sentence which he knows to be "the garbled translation of a striking disclosure" (160) but which he cannot decipher.

Having seen parallels between the diegetic, the metadiegetic, the meta-metadiegetic and the meta-meta-metadiegetic levels, it is now the time to include the extradiegetic level as well. And indeed there are analogies between Sebastian's novels and V's narration or, more precisely, its product: V's novel, the novel we read.

V's comments about the poetics of Sebastian's novels are equally applicable to his own novel. To prove this I would have to give an exhaustive analysis of all the aspects of V's novel, a task clearly transcending the limits of this paper. I shall therefore trace most of the analogies without supporting them by all the desired evidence.

Talking about *The Prismatic Bezel* V explains:

> I should like to point out that *The Prismatic Bezel* can be thoroughly enjoyed once it is understood that the heroes of the book are what can be

> loosely called "methods of composition". It is as if a painter said: Look, here I'm going to show you not the painting of a landscape, but the painting of different ways of painting a certain landscape, and I trust their harmonious fusion will disclose the landscape as I intend you to see it (79).

The same subordination of psychology to composition, reminiscent of Propp's view of character[18] is effected in *The Real Life of Sebastian Knight*. Moreover, instead of directly painting a landscape, directly unfolding Sebastian's life story, V paints different ways of painting this landscape, different accounts of Sebastian's life by different people who knew him in different ways, and the real Sebastian, to the extent that he emerges at all, is a result of the harmonious fusion of all these accounts. The emphasis is thus put not on the referential status of the character but on the medium through which he is characterized; on what Jakobson calls "the poetic function."

It is the poetic function that justifies another of V's comments, this time about *The Doubtful Asphodel*, a comment analogously adequate for V's own novel: "I don't know whether it makes one 'think,' and I don't much care if it does not. I like it for its own sake. I like its manners" (153).

One of the ways of effecting "a set towards the message as such" (to use Jakobson's phrase) is by creating a central gap, a gap you cannot ape without filling it in somehow,[19] a gap which forces your attention on every detail in the texture. This V does through the central enigma of the "real life," and this Sebastian does in *The Doubtful Asphodel*:

> The man is dead and we do not know. The asphodel on the other shore is as doubtful as ever. We hold a dead book in our hands. Or are we mistaken? I sometimes feel when I turn the pages of Sebastian's masterpiece that the 'absolute solution' is there, somewhere, concealed in some passage I have read too hastily, or that it is intertwined with other words whose familiar guise deceived me. I don't know any other book that gives one this special sensation, and perhaps this was the author's special intention (151).

For the same reason V's novel, like *The Doubtful Asphodel*, is characterized by the fact that "It is not the parts that matter, it is their combinations" (148).

Like Sebastian, V uses "parody as a kind of springboard for leaping into the highest regions of serious emotion" (76) and, like Sebastian, V takes pleasure in "the gleeful bathos" (7). To pick one example out of many: The story in *Lost Property* about the Englishman who survived an aircrash and, asked whether he was badly hurt, succinctly replied: "No [. . .] toothache. I've had it all the way" (93) is paralleled by V's account of the honorable and courageous duel fought by his father, culminating in death . . . of the common cold.[20]

Delays and reversals, a central technique in Sebastian's detective and quest novels, and a major stage in V's search, is also prominent in V's novel, and in two ways. First, owing to the order of the *récit* (a pseudo-temporal phenomenon), every delay for V is also a delay for the reader (the extradiegetic narratee). Or, put in formalist terms, the structural delay is realistically motivated by V's ignorance of the truth. The mistakes and delays are experienced by V the character and focus, not by V the extradiegetic narrator. At the stage of writing the book the narrator already knows the truth, and if he chooses to withhold and delay information (to restrict the manifestation of his omniscience) it is, I believe, in order to reproduce in the narratee the Roquebrune-like twist experienced by the focus. But it is not only the realistically motivated "delays-revelations," like the visit to Rosanov, the visit to Rechnoy and the encounters with Mme. Lecerf, that produce in the reader an experience analogous to that undergone by V. Compositionally motivated delays operate in the same way. Thus, from the point of view of the quest as well as from that of the unfolding of Sebastian's life story, the long summaries of and quotations from Sebastian's novels constitute tantalizing delays, halting the reader on his way to the desired information (e.g., who was Sebastian's fatal love?). But these delays are in fact revelations, bringing us closer to Sebastian's life than many of the details unearthed by conversations with people.

Another kind of "twist" at the level of narration has to do with the use of what V, talking about one of Sebastian's novels, defines as "the problem of blending direct speech with narration and description which an elegant pen solves by finding as many variations of 'he said' as may be found in the dictionary between 'acceded' and 'yelped' " (77). Since *The Real Life of Sebastian Knight* is based on information collected by V from various sources, the problem of where and how to introduce the informant arises repeatedly. Sometimes the informant is preposed to the information, as for example on the very first page: "An old Russian lady who for some obscure reason begged me not to divulge her name, happened to show me in Paris the diary she had kept in the past" (5), and the details follow (see also 8, 63, 84, 98). But often the identity of the informant is either embedded in the information or postposed to it, so that the reader must retrospectively correct his impressions about the source of information. Thus, for example, in the middle of what seems Sheldon's attempt to guess at Sebastian's past thoughts while sitting on a fence near the Cam, an embedded exclamation tells us that the thoughts attributed to Sheldon are actually V's: "Oh, how much I would give for such a memory coming to him" (41; see also 11, 70, 72, 73). Perhaps the best example of the misleading effect created by post-posing the informant is the end of Chapter V and the beginning of Chapter VI. Chapter V ends with the following words: " 'Sebastian Knight?', said a sudden voice in the mist. 'Who is speaking of Sebastian Knight?' " (43), a question which encourages the reader to believe that somebody overhears V's conversation with Sheldon and tries to interfere. This impression is maintained and reinforced by the beginning of Chapter VI: "The stranger who uttered these words now approached" (44), only to be shattered by the sequel: "Oh, how I sometimes yearn for the easy swing of a well-oiled novel! [. . .] That Voice in the Mist rang out in the dimmest passage of my mind" (44; see also 36–37, 75, 92, 96).

Throughout this section I have referred to the novel we read as V's novel, because V is its declared author. But behind this fictional author there is also the real author, Vladimir Nabokov, and although Nabokov is not a part of any of the text's narrative levels, it may be interesting to note that he has made Sebastian's life analogous to his own. Thus both Sebastian and Nabokov were born in 1899 in St. Petersburg; both left Russia in 1919, moved to England and studied in Cambridge. Like Sebastian's mother, Nabokov's mother used to tie her own wedding ring to her husband's with a black ribbon, and, like Sebastian, Nabokov experienced the end of his first love with the bitterness attached to the girl's betrayal. "Sebastian's Russian was better and more natural to him than his English" (71), and Nabokov repeatedly said the same thing about himself. Sebastian wrote his novels under his mother's maiden name (Knight) and Nabokov did the same in his Russian novels (Sirin). Many more similarities can be discerned by perusing Nabokov's autobiographical *Speak, Memory* but these will suffice as indications of the general principle of analogy, a principle which may help us understand the last part of the crucial revelation. "I am Sebastian, or Sebastian is I, or perhaps we both are someone whom neither of us knows" (173), this "someone" being perhaps Vladimir Nabokov.

If the levels mirror each other in such a way, perhaps their separateness is an illusion, a straitjacket devised by the human mind for its convenience but constantly broken by reality and by art. This feeling is reinforced by the interpenetration of the various levels in *The Real Life of Sebastian Knight.*

B. Interpenetration of Levels

The diegetic V is not only analogous to various elements of the metadiegetic level of Sebastian's life, but is also infused into one of them. The description of Sebastian's last meeting with his first love, as rendered by Natasha Rosanov, unwittingly uses the narrator's name as part of the scenery: "A last change: a V-shaped flight of migrating cranes; their tender moan melting in a turquoise-blue sky high above a tawny birch-grove" (114–115). A similar use of the name is made at the meta-metametadiegetic level of the letter written by the fictional character in Sebastian's *Lost Property*: "Life with you was lovely—and when I say lovely, I mean doves and lillies, and velvet and that soft pink 'v' in the middle" (93).[21] It is not only V's initial but also other features of his personality that are evoked in this letter by way of association and analogy.

Thus the broken-hearted lover knows that he will nevertheless "joke with the chaps at the office" (94), and we know that V works at an office. Similarly, the character in the letter has not been able to bring some business to a satisfactory end (94), and V too is unsuccessful in clinching some bureaucratic matter (151–152).

It is interesting to note that *Lost Property* contains another interpenetration of elements, though they both belong to the same level. Among the letters found in the aircrash, one is addressed to a woman and begins "Dear Mr. Mortimer" while another is addressed to a firm of traders and contains a love letter. Not only did the letters get confused, but the one contains details from the other. Thus we read in the love letter: "and I have not been able to clinch the business I was supposed to bring 'to a satisfactory close', as that ass Mortimer says" (94).

V's description of *The Doubtful Asphodel* treats the book itself and the events narrated in it as if they belonged to the same level: "A man is dying, and he is the hero of the tale; [. . .] The man is the book; the book itself is heaving and dying, and drawing up a ghostly knee" (147). The intermingling of the book and its narrative reaches a metaphoric climax when the landscape (itself used as a comparison) is described in terms of vowels, consonants and sentences:

> The answer to all questions of life and death, 'the absolute solution' was written all over the world he [the dying man] had known: it was like a traveller realizing that the wild country he surveys is not an accidental assembly of natural phenomena, but the page in a book where these mountains and forests, and fields, and rivers are disposed in such a way as to form a coherent sentence; the vowel of a lake fusing with the consonant of a sibilant slope; the windings of a road writing its message in a round hand, as clear as that of one's father; trees conversing in dumb-show, making sense to one who has learnt the gestures of their language. . . . (150).[22]

Knight's act of narration is also treated as if it were at the same level as the events it narrates, so that the author, his narrator, and his hero are almost fused:

> And now we shall know what exactly it is; the word will be uttered—and you, and I, and everyone in the world will slap himself on the forehead: What fools we have been! At this last bend of his book the author seems to pause for a minute, as if he were pondering whether it were wise to let the truth out. He seems to lift his head and to leave the dying man, whose thoughts he was following, and to turn away and to think: Shall we follow him to the end? Shall we whisper the word which will shatter the snug silence of our brains? We shall. We have gone too far as it is, and the word is being already formed, and will come out. And we turn and bend again over a hazy bed, over a grey, floating form—lower and lower. . . . But that minute of doubt was fatal: the man is dead (151).

The "you" and "I" refer simultaneously to the intra- and the extra-diegetic narratee, and the author's lifting his head seems to be at the same fictional level as the visions of the dying man. It is as if a pause at the level of writing actually causes the death at the level of the *histoire*.[23]

A similar collision occurs in *The Real Life of Sebastian Knight* when its characters are treated as real people who can read the novel in which they appear. Thus V says about the Russian lady whose diary he studied: "That she will ever read this book seems wildly improbable" (5). Similarly, he wishes that the Blauberg hotel manager would "never read these lines" (101), and on the other hand wonders whether he should "send [Silbermann] this work when it is finished" (110) and definitely decides to give Nina a copy (145). From one point of view, these references do not transgress the boundaries between levels, since the book is presented as a biography and the characters are meant to be considered as real people. But, on the other hand, for the real reader, outside the "game" of narrative levels, the characters—including Sebastian and V—are fictional, and therefore cannot really read the book we hold in our hands.

The levels thus collide, intersect, mirror each other, shattering the illusion of their separateness, implicitly declaring with Lacan "il n'y a pas de méta-langage," providing, through the "game of writing" (*écriture*) the "mental jerk" V speaks of, the jerk which would set free the imprisoned human brain "encompassed by an iron ring, by the close-fitting dream of one's own personality" (150). But in order to shatter the illusion of levels one has to recognize it in the first place, and it is here that Genette's classification has proved so useful.

The attempt to transcend "the close-fitting dream of one's own personality" also takes the form of the interchangeability of souls glimpsed by V toward the end of the novel (see quotation on page 184 above). And the same principle of analogy, mirroring, intermingling operates here, creating a pervasive pattern of "the merging of twin images." And again, for the "merging" to occur, the "twin images" must first be, or at least seem, separate. Thus, in *The Prismatic Bezel*, G. Abeson, the corpse, and old Nosebag, the innocent passer-by, turn out to be the same person. And at the level of V's quest, Nina Rechnoy and Mme. Lecerf are the same woman, and furthermore, when Nina speaks about Helene von Graun's love affair, she is actually speaking about herself.[24] Thus the narrator intuits one part of a tripartite identification when he thinks:

> Very curious, I mused: there seemed to be a slight family likeness between Nina Rechnoy and Helene von Graun—or at least between the two pictures which the husband of one and the friend of the other had painted for me (136).

Using various *leurres*, the text takes great pains to keep the three "images" distinct, so that the "merging" will be a surprise to both V and the extradiegetic narratee.[25] The image Rechnoy paints seems to V to be too obvious to have pleased Sebastian. Nina says she doesn't much like Russians (141), and her Frenchness is insisted on again and through V's impressions of her (e.g., 125, 129, 131, 140). Sebastian's beloved was definitely Russian, and thus Nina deceives V, V deceives himself, and the text (or the narration) deceives the implied reader (or the narratee). In addition, Mme. Lecerf asks V whether he saw "the Rechnoy woman" (131), a question which forestalls any suspicion of a connection between the two. And the same Mme. Lecerf is seen by V as "a nice quiet, quietly moving person" (127), a description which could not tally less with an image of a woman who smashes a man's life. But the *leurre* becomes the reality, the seeming delay yields the truth: Mme. Lecerf, the "wrong woman," the purely useful informant, turns out to be the right woman, and Nina Rechnoy, the "wrong woman," the stereotype, proves to be Mme. Lecerf and hence again the "right woman."[26] Moreover, Mme. Lecerf's unwitting betrayal of her identity—"once upon a time [. . .] I kissed a man just because he could write his name upside down" (143)—is linked with the Rechnoy house where Uncle Black performs this unusual feat (119). Thus V has never been closer to "the Rechnoy clue" than when he thinks he can drop it altogether (136).

It is interesting to note that in the middle of the conversations with Mme. Lecerf there is a momentary identification of V with Sebastian, anticipating perhaps their final identification. Nina is painting an atrocious picture of "her friend's" affair with the man who may be Sebastian, and when V looks particularly pained, she comments: "you look as if my friend were your own sweetheart" (130). In other words, V looks as if he himself were Sebastian. The irony is twofold: Nina here reproaches V for reacting as if he were Sebastian while at the same time she keeps acting as if she were somebody else. Moreover, V almost does reenact Sebastian when he contemplates making love to Mme. Lecerf (140).

Among Sebastian's books there is a classic of the *doppelgänger* genre, *Doctor Jekyll and Mr. Hyde*; and *Lost Property* describes the merging of two manifestations of the self:

> I seem to pass with intangible steps across ghostly lawns and through dancinghalls full of the whine of Hawaiian music and down dear drab little streets with pretty names, until I come to a certain warm hollow where something like the selfest of my own self sits huddled up in the darkness. . . .(58).[27]

This brings me to the most crucial "merging of twin images" in the novel, the identification between V and Sebastian, a fusion which is not only a metaphoric event but also a crucial aspect of the status of the narrator.

But before broaching this last subject of the present analysis, I would like to point out that the principle of self-reflecting levels and of merging characters is best described with the help of mirror-imagery. Thus V meditates about the mirror relationship between a man and the date of his birth:

> He [Sebastian] died in the very beginning of 1936, and as I look at this figure I cannot help thinking that there is an occult resemblance between a man and the date of his death. Sebastian Knight d. 1936. . . . This date to me seems the reflection of that name in a pool of rippling water. There is something about the curves of the last three numerals that recalls the sinuous outlines of Sebastian's personality (154).[28]

Roy Carswell's portrait of Sebastian also uses the principle of reflection:

> These eyes and the face itself are painted in such a manner as to convey the impression that they are mirrored Narcissus-like in clear water—[. . .] Thus Sebastian peers into a pool at himself (99).

And when V receives the telegram about Sebastian's imminent death, the telegram with the 'v' in the middle, he goes to the bathroom and stands there for a moment in front of the looking glass, enacting the identification between Sebastian and himself.[29] It is tempting to relate the mirror motif to Lacan's "stade du miroir,"[30] but this will take me too far afield.

2. THE STATUS OF THE NARRATOR, OR "WHO IS SPEAKING OF SEBASTIAN KNIGHT?" (43, 44)

"The Real Life of Sebastian Knight," the title, arouses in the extradiegetic narratee expectations of a biography, whether fictional or real. He therefore looks forward to a gradual process of getting acquainted with Sebastian Knight through the mediation of a narrator who will be either extradiegetic-heterodiegetic or if intradiegetic, either heterodiegetic or homodiegetic of the witness-type. In other words, the implied reader expects either an "external" narrator who will recount the life of Sebastian Knight in the fashion of an historical biography, reducing his own role to that of a compiler and writer, or a character-narrator whose involvement in the events narrated is either null or that of an observer. However, the more one reads the novel, the more these expectations are frustrated. True, the narrator, the fictional V, does prove to be the compiler and writer of the biography, as is emphasized both by direct statements like "Two months had elapsed after Sebastian's death when this book was started" (28; see also 5, 29, 101, 110, 145) and by recurrent accounts of his thoughts about the difficulty of this task as well as about his adequacy (or inadequacy) for performing it. But all the other expectations seem to be belied by the text, for on the one hand, as Charles Nicol puts it, "the more V talks about his half brother the less we seem to know about him,"[31] and on the other hand, the more V talks about his half brother the more we seem to know about V.[32] Put differently, the speaking voice appears to be that of an intradiegetic-homodiegetic *protagonist* narrator—a surprising "twist" to the genre of fictional biography. But the situation is even more complex, and here Genette's distinction between "voice" and "mode" has proved illuminating. The intradiegetic protagonist who participates in the events narrated, perhaps to the extent of becoming more central than the purported subject of his narrative, is not V the narrator, but V's younger self. Throughout this retrospective *récit*, focus and voice are distinct, with varying degrees of temporal distance between them (considerable when V as focus is a child, small when V narrates his adventures after Sebastian's death). The narrator is therefore extradiegetic, but the question which remains to be asked—and it is a key question—is the following: Is the narrator heterodiegetic or homodiegetic? Or, formulated differently: Is the novel about Sebastian's life or about V's quest for Sebastian's life? Thus the question of hetero- or homodiegetic narration parallels the question of the primacy of the diegetic or the metadiegetic level.

As was observed above, the title, in general a good indicator of primacy, suggests Sebastian's preeminence, but the very first paragraph reverses this impression with seven pronouns relating to the narrator ("I," "my," "me") and only two mentions of Sebastian.

A possible, though not sufficient, way of approaching the problem is basically quantitative. If we can determine how many events or situations focus (in a non-Genettian sense) on Sebastian and how many on V, we may then be able to hazard a hypothesis as to primacy. With this rather primitive idea in mind, I have divided the text into narrative segments, each encompassing one event, episode, or situation (e.g., "V's meeting with Mr. Goodman" or "Sebastian's trip with the poet Pan and his wife"). The segments differ in length as well as in the diegetic duration they cover, but I have tried to preserve the same level of abstraction throughout. The result is 44 segments focussing on Sebastian's life story, 51 segments focussing on V's quest, and 17 focussing equally on both.[33] In other words, an almost complete balance, with a marked predominance of V towards the end of the novel (which does not coincide with the end of the *histoire*). The numbers should be taken as no more than a general indication, since errors in segmentation or in level of abstraction are quite possible, as is the attainment of a different result (though not substantially different, I believe) by a division of each unit into its smallest irreducible components (if such a division is at all possible).

Another, perhaps more reliable, criterion is subordination, but, unfortunately for the desired solution, V and Sebastian are completely interdependent. On the one hand, Sebastian's life depends on V's quest for its revelation and exists only in so far as it unfolds in the process of this quest. And, on the other hand, V's quest depends on Sebastian's life for its object and would have no purpose without it. The two depend on each other for their existence, and subordination can therefore be no help in determining primacy.

Perhaps chronology can be a better help? If we can show that the order of the *récit* follows either Sebastian's life or V's quest, this may be a clue to the question of hetero- or homodiegetic narration. What we find in the text, however, is a pattern of "rhythmical interlacements" (113) of the time of V's quest (1936) and the chronology of Sebastian's life. Each temporal line is told more or less chronologically although there are significant distortions of order even in the unfolding of each story separately, but the two lines alternate in the pseudo-temporal disposition of the *récit*.[34] To illustrate let us take a short chapter, Chapter 2, and trace its order of presentation:

(1) Non-temporal: thoughts about Goodman's book.
(2) 1910–1919: Sebastian's childhood.
(3) 1919: Sebastian leaves for England. His verse in English.
(4) Non-temporal: V's reservations about the biography he writes.
(5) Non-temporal: the Roquebrune story from Sebastian's *Lost Property*.
(6) Non-temporal: V about Goodman's book.
(7) Non-temporal: V's discussion of different kinds of biography.
(8) 1936: V travels to Lausanne to find Sebastian's governess.
(9) 1914: Governess left the Knight family.
(10 Non-temporal. V's general comments about Swiss governesses in Russia.
(11) Before 1914: Governess's constant complaints.
(12) Non-temporal: general comments again.
(13) 1936: V's meeting with the governess.

It is worth noting that in about two-thirds of the novel the order is dictated more by Sebastian's life than by V's quest and then the proportion is reversed, with an explicit explanation of the reversal:

> A more systematic mind than mine would have placed them [the details about Sebastian's first love] in the beginning of this book, but my quest had developed its own magic and logic and though I sometimes cannot help believing that it had gradually grown into a dream, that quest, using the pattern of reality for the weaving of its own fancies, I am forced to recognize that I was being led right, and that in striving to render Sebastian's life I must now follow the same rhythmical interlacements (113).

And if the reader hopes that this shift in order from a predominance of Sebastian's life to a predominance of V's quest is an indication of the development of the text as a process of substituting one "centre" for another, he is bound to be frustrated when he reaches the very last lines of the novel. Far from opting for one of the possibilities, the last statement is symmetrical in structure ("I am Sebastian, or Sebastian is I") and cannot solve the "doubleness" except by leaving it open through a figurative "duplication."

Feeling uneasy with the double status of the narrator, traditional Nabokov critics try to resolve the ambiguity by opting for one of the two alternatives. To do so, each of them interprets the last paragraph in a conclusive way which he subsequently projects back onto the novel as a whole. Thus Stuart:

> For the narrator, the person whose perspective we are left with at the end of the novel, is, as we discover, Sebastian himself.[35]

Later in the article Stuart modifies this view, but Andrew Field firmly reiterates the same position:

> Is it possible that *The Real Life of Sebastian Knight* is not a biography at all, but a fictional autobiography, another of Knight's novels? It is more than possible.[36]

Explicitly arguing with the Stuart-Field hypothesis, Bruffee says:

> Clearly neither critic is willing to accept the narrator's assertion of his own identity. Both are more willing to believe in the existence of Sebastian, whom we never see and whom in fact the narrator himself has not seen for several years, than to believe in the existence of the muddle-headed narrator, who calls himself simply 'V,' yet is our constant companion as we read the novel [. . .] Certainly this novel is not the fictional biography it claims to be. The title is a ruse. Sebastian Knight is not the center of attention at all, although he is, or *was*, the narrator's center of attention. Field is correct in saying that the novel is fictional autobiography. Its subject is V, the narrator. And Stuart is correct in saying that Sebastian has no life apart from the person who composes him, the narrator, V. Whether Sebastian "really existed" or not has little importance.[37]

What these diametrically opposed views have in common is the tendency to solve the problem of double status by opting for one of the alternatives and by identifying the narrator and the "center of attention." Thus the first view makes Sebastian both the narrator and the center of attention, while the second view attributes both roles to V. Equally similar is the way in which these contrasted readings see the structure of the novel or, better, its narrative continuum. According to both, *The Real Life of Sebastian Knight* is an inverted story, reversing at the end the impressions it has promoted throughout, though subtly intimating the final reversal at various points along the narrative continuum.[38] Thus, on one view, our assumption about the narrator is finally shattered when we discover that it is Sebastian, and not V. And, on the other view, our assumption about the "center of interest" is reversed when we find out that the novel is not Sebastian's biography but V's autobiography.

By literally identifying V and Sebastian, the above critics have made the narrator, whether V or Sebastian, homodiegetic (without using Genette's term, of course), thus solving the problem of his double-status with the help of the convincing device of reversal, convincing because—as we have seen—it is prominent at other levels of the text as well. But they have achieved this solution at the cost of ignoring the basic data of the novel. It seems to me illegitimate to forget that Sebastian is dead when V starts his quest; that the two have different mothers, different jobs (V works at an office, Sebastian is a novelist), different life stories; that V lives in Paris and studied at the Sorbonne while Sebastian studied at Cambridge and lived in London; that V met Clare in Paris as Sebastian's girlfriend, not his own, etc., etc. There is no use in accumulating details; the point is clear: at the literal level V and Sebastian can in no way be one and the same person. Just as the levelling of narrative levels presupposes their initial separateness, so the fusion of V and Sebastian depends on their being two different people. V himself formulates this similarity-in-difference at an early stage of the *récit*:

> And the more I pondered on it, the more I perceived that I had yet another tool in my hand: When I imagined actions of his [Sebastian's] which I heard of only after his death, I knew for certain that in such or such a case I should have acted just as he had. Once I happened to see two brothers, tennis champions, matched against one another; their strokes were totally different; and one of the two was far, far better than the other; but the general rhythm of their motions as they swept all over the court was exactly the same, so that had it been possible to draft both systems two identical designs would have appeared. I daresay Sebastian and I also had some kind of common rhythm; this might explain the curious "it-has-happened-before feeling" which seizes me when following the bends of his life (28–29).

The identification at the end can only be taken figuratively and, far from solving the problem of the double-status of the narrator, it leaves it open and "justifies" the doubleness. We cannot decide whether the narrator is heterodiegetic or homodiegetic because this is an impossible decision to make. By setting on a quest you discover yourself but the self you discover is to a large extent formed by the object of your quest: "I am Sebastian, or Sebastian is I, or perhaps we both are someone whom neither of us knows."

The fusion is figurative, and the choice of the merging characters' names is another sign of Nabokov's playful inventiveness. "V" is both the beginning and the end of "Vladimir Nabokov," and "S" is the beginning of "Sirin"; thus both of them are indeed "someone whom neither of us knows," the real author of this novel. But V and Sebastian are also twin characters in a Shakespearean play about mistaken identities and identifications. The Shakespearean brothers are Sebastian and Viola and the play in which they appear is homonymous with Sebastian's second name—*Twelfth Night.*

Notes

1. Vladimir Nabokov, *The Real Life of Sebastian Knight* (London: Penguin, 1971). All subsequent references will appear in the text.

2. Vladimir Nabokov, *The Eye* (New York: Pocket Books, 1962), x.

3. Gerard Genette, *Figures III* (Paris: Seuil, 1972); for a detailed summary of *Figures III* see Shlomith Rimmon, "A Comprehensive Theory of Narrative: Genette's *Figures III* and the Structuralist Study of Fiction," *PTL* I, 1 (1976), 333–62.

4. I hereby retract my criticism ("A Comprehensive Theory of Narrative . . . ," pp. 359–60) of Genette's allegedly incomplete discussion of narrative levels and his failure to provide criteria by which one could recognize the *récit premier*. The problem still remains in novels where there is only an intradiegetic narrator. What will the diegetic level be in such cases?

5. Peter Duval Smith and Vladimir Nabokov, "Vladimir Nabokov on His Life and Work," *The Listener*, 68 (1962), 856.

6. In "*The Real Life of Sebastian Knight*: Angles of Perception" [*Modern Language Quarterly*, 29 (1968), 312–328], Dabney Stuart defends Goodman's biography and argues that V's own book relies on the same methods which he criticizes in Goodman.

7. Jacques Derrida, *De la grammatologie* (Paris: Minuit, 1967) and *L'ecriture et la difference* (Paris: Seuil, 1967). It is interesting that all the authors in this novel wear masks. Goodman wears a black mask (48, 49, 50) which the narrator pockets in the hope that "it might come in usefully on some other occasion" (50). Sebastian's novels are a mask, and at the end V says: "for, try as I may, I cannot get out of my part; Sebastian's mask clings to my face, the likeness will not be washed off" (173). This point was also made by Stuart, p. 325.

8. Julia Bader, *Crystal Land: Artifice in Nabokov's English Novels* (Berkeley: University of California Press, 1972), 17–24; Charles Nicol, "The Mirrors of Sebastian Knight," in L. S. Dembo, ed. *Nabokov: The Man and His Work* (Madison: University of Wisconsin Press, 1967), 87–93; Susan Fromberg, "The Unwritten Chapters in *The Real Life of Sebastian Knight*," *Modern Fiction Studies* 13 (1967), 434–436. Critics tend to lump all the levels together, not noticing the "hierarchy" from the extradiegetic to the third degree of metadiegetic.

9. This is the beginning from the point of view of the chronology of the *histoire*, not from that of the disposition of events in the *récit*.

10. Note the difference between a literal identification (Abeson and Nosebag) and a figurative one (V and Sebastian). More about V and Sebastian will be said later.

11. The expression "false scent" is used in connection with *Success* (80) and in connection with V's meeting with Goodman (50).

12. The title is underlined in Nabokov's text.

13. Uncle Black, named after the black chess figures, is the one who could write his name upside down, and the expression recurs, albeit in a completely different context, in *The Doubtful Asphodel*: "physical growth considered upside down" (148).

14. There may also be a sound similarity between Nussbaum and Nosebag of *The Prismatic Bezel*.

15. It may be interesting to note that a similar name is also connected with V's quest: one of the names given by the hotel manager is Professor Ott.

16. We remember that there was also a near meeting between V and Clare.

17. Fromberg, p. 433.

18. Vladimir Propp, *Morphology of the Folktale*, Louis A. Wagner and Alan Dundes, trans. (*Publications of the American Folklore Society*, Bibliography and Special Series 9); Indiana University Research Center in Anthropology, Folklore, and Linguistics 10 (Austin–London: University of Texas Press, 1968).

19. Roman Jakobson, "Linguistics and Poetics," in T. Sebeok, ed., *Style in Language* (Cambridge, Mass.: MIT Press, 1960), 30.

20. Bathos also exists in another metadiegetic level relating to Sebastian: his letter to V. After about half the letter, phrased as a serious entreaty, there comes the following anticlimactic sentence: "This letter was begun almost a week ago, and up to the word 'life' it had been destined [*prednaznachalos*] to quite a different person" (156). And in a fictional letter of one of Sebastian's fictional characters: "This blot is not due to a tear. My fountain-pen has broken down and I am using a filthy pen in this filthy hotel room" (93).

21. Note the alliteration of "v" in "velvet."

22. Note how the use of alliteration, e.g., "sibilant slope" and "winding"—"writing" enacts what it talks about.

23. In some sense it really does, since it is the author who decides to "kill" the character, but this causal relationship is denied in the above passage by the impression of unwittingness: the pause was fatal; it accidentally caused the man's death.

24. About the similarities between Nina and Sebastian's mother, see Fromberg, p. 440.

25. The term "leurre" is borrowed from Roland Barthes, S/Z (Paris: Seuil, 1970).

26. As was hinted above, this identification is also related to the pattern of "wrong-right" reversals (the wrong Roquebrune; V by the bed of the wrong man) as well as to the recurrent use of seeming delays which actually yield invaluable information (like Sebastian's novels; like V's visit to Rosanovs). Thus V has never been closer to the truth than when he believes he is being detained from it.

27. Note also that Clare married a man with the same name (Bishop) and that the narrator identifies the husband's cold with the one Clare had twelve years earlier (65). Some kind of identification between Clare and Sebastian is also hinted at (see, in particular, 68, 73, 74).

28. Note also that the date of Sebastian's death is mirrored in a jumbled way by the phone number of Dr. Starov: Jasmin 61–93 (1936). I owe this point to Stuart, p. 314.

29. Note also (a) the reflection of the talc powder-tin in the mirror in Sebastian's flat (31). On this tin violets are painted, and violets are another recurrent motif in the novel (9, 15, 16, 31, 70, 143); (b) the distorted reflection at the editor's office in *Lost Property* (57); (c) the related image of a "cherry stone and its tiny shadow" (150) in connection with *The Doubtful Asphodel.*

30. Jacques Lacan, *Ecrits I* (Paris: Seuil, 1966).

31. Nicol, p. 88.

32. Nicol makes the above comment in brackets.

33. This does not cover all the segments of the text. There are segments of yet different kinds, like the plots of Sebastian's novels.

34. The handling of time in *The Real Life of Sebastian Knight* is an interesting subject in itself, but it lies beyond the scope of the present study.

35. Stuart, p. 313.

36. Quoted in K. A. Bruffee, "Form and Meaning in Nabokov's *The Real Life of Sebastian Knight*: An Example of Elegaic Romance," *Modern Language Quarterly*, 34 (1973), 181.

37. Ibid. See Fromberg for a compromise view.

38. They do not use the term which I borrow from Menachem Perry, "The Inverted Poem: On a Principle of Semantic Composition in Bialik's Poems," *Ha-Sifrut* 1 (1968–69), 607–631 (Hebrew), 767–768 (English summary).

Doctor Froid

Claude Mouchard*

The first chapters of *Ada* are a jumble of international, geographical, temporal, and, in particular, familial items.

Agua, an imaginary mother and supposedly mother of one of the novel's bright protagonists, dies in that section of the book, an insane suicide victim. In the establishment where she is presumably cared for, she has only been able to gather up the "two hundred pills and tablets" necessary for her last "little huckleberry banquet" by altering for her own use the methods and manias of a certain Dr. Froid.

The name of "Froid" is identical in the English text and in the translation. It is a question, if you wish, of a French word in the English text; but inversely, I expect one must keep an English pronunciation in French—by which the word approximately recaptures the German pronunciation of the name Freud.

(On the whole, the novel plays on several languages. Its English is filled with French or Russian expressions; and it is, for example, in a complex oscillation between French and English that the two incestuous lovers, Ada and Veen, will discover the ultimate refinement of their cryptographic systems . . . simultaneous languages, superimposed structures, borderline systems. We will discover a little later, when discussing the question of the very existence of literature, some partially analogous effects.)

This separation between the spelling and the pronunciation of the name is but one of the ways in which the absurd therapist is reduced to dust. There he is, suddenly optional between his negligently created doubles turned upside down before our eyes. Dr. Freud "was perhaps, the emigrant brother—with the patronym corrupted by a passport misfortune—of the Doctor Froid from Signy Mondieu-Mondieu in the Ardennes mountains, or he was even Doctor Froid himself, since both of them came from Vienne [trans. Vienna], a subprefecture of Isère, and moreover, both were only sons."[1] In addition to "Sig-mund," the name of Signy Mondieu-Mondieu calls to mind "signify," and this word, ending on "Mondieu-Mondieu" [trans. My God or Good heavens], reminds us that Sig's theory could only cheat someone out of their salvation and be an ultimate interpretive bigotry inviting one to search for the supreme ambiguous meaning. The suggestion is confirmed a bit later by the name "Heiler"—where the "Heil" balances between medical rescue and spiritual salvation. Heiler is, of course, another avatar of Doctor Froid, "Another agent or double of the Isère professor, a certain Doctor Sig

*From *Critique: Revue Générale des Publications Françaises et Etrangères*, 32 (1976), 311–16. Reprinted by permission of the journal. Translated from the French by Lynne L. Gelber.

Heiler, whom everyone venerated as a whiz, an ace, a kind of genius (in the sense in which one says 'kind' of champagne" [p. 24]).

It is not polemically irrelevant that chapter 3 of *Ada* dissolves into indeterminate proliferation the very person to whom he attributes the desire to interpret and guide on the basis of a fixed system. Elsewhere the determination of the Freudians appears as vain as the tenacity of a swarm of flies, "The Freudians buzz all around [my book] with caution and greed, devoured by a burning need to deposit their eggs there. . . ."[2]

The interest of Freudians in symptomatic acts, dreams, and transference will be recognized in the practice of the "sagacious Siggy." The patients who were considered as being well on the way to a cure "gave evidence, through spasms in the eyelids and in other parts below the waist observed by the medical students, that the great Sig (slightly deformed, although still a good-looking, gay blade) figured in their current dreams in the guise of "Papa Figue," ["Fig" in the English edition] the great spanker of girls and valiant user of spittoons" (p. 24). In fact, Sig only uses the therapeutic situation to embody his own fantasy, to see himself and be seen under the features of the truculent Papa Figue. In one fell swoop, the sentence claims to turn around and to conclude the analytic situation: there would be nothing else to decipher, in the dreams of the patients, except those of the so-called therapist—vague, unsatisfied boy scout "dressed in shapeless khaki shorts."

The challenge to the "Freudians" in Nabokov's works, and especially in his prefaces, is almost an obligatory rite of passage. The introduction to *Mary* (the English translation of *Mashen'ka* which appeared in Russian in 1926) written in 1970, ends with this remark: "Although a complete fool would venture to emphasize that 'orange' is the dream-like anagram for 'organ,' I would not advise the members of the delegation from Vienna to waste their precious time analyzing Klara's dream at the end of chapter IV of the present book."[3] This time it is a question of short circuiting any eventual analytic investigation. The plot of ground laid claim to being uncovered with painstaking care, an unwieldy plot of a Viennese from Isère, has, I believe, never been concealed. Perhaps there is a pot of gold at the end of the rainbow only for imbeciles. Wouldn't a mystery that had to be brought to the light of day serve only to justify the existence of some pedants?

As for the jibes depicting analysts as retards who would be the last to understand that which is clear to everybody else, the response of the Freudians has been ready for a long time it seems to me. It would maintain a certain balance between the jeering rejections and the overly officious acceptances. Both adversaries and admirers would seek to uncap the question opened up by psychoanalysis by reducing it to scholarship which one could then easily claim to anticipate or rejoin.

So be it. One can play the points game. But this description of a fight, for which one could end up translating some of Nabokov's pages or sentences into too systematic a language, leaves aside almost entirely that which is central for both sides, and for those in between. . . .

The anti-Freudian remarks of Nabokov often coincide with those characteristics and places where the novel seeks to regain something of its own possibilities. When Van Veen affirms, in discussing dreams, that, "Nothing in these disorganized visions . . . can be deciphered by a Shaman . . ." (p. 304), it is not just a question of refusing psychoanalysis, it is also an elaboration of a paradoxical empiricism where everything is immediate, perceptible, material reality—objects, words, thoughts, time, space, etc.: conditions which the novel seeks to keep hidden for itself.

As for the "Freudians" and for *the* psychoanalysis which Nabokov mocks, it is certainly impossible, for the purposes of a rhetorical joust, to envelop in a single, stable definition their divisions and displacements where, to be precise, the definition of their discipline itself can only remain an open question.

Therefore, rather than improve in a heavy-handed way on the thin, fictional skirmishes of Nabokov, one should encompass the battle over territories and language, their respective styles of resolution and justification, the question for each one of them of their very existence and their duration or their decay.

For what wanders throughout Nabokov's scintillating perfidies is perhaps this enormous, vague, question: can psychoanalysis be the death of literature?

Would Doctor Froid (this time with a pronunciation as French as the spelling) . . . finally be a question of a replica of the murderer of the poet Shade assassinated in *Pale Fire*? Froid [trans. cold], shade, flame's pallor are all phantasmic combats.

The question of the death of literature has, occasionally, been able to be asked and to be limited in terms of a so-called choice by an individual between poetry and psychoanalysis: Rilke's or perhaps Michaux's. But from its formless menace one could possibly extract some lesson only by questioning the cultural fantasy which it manifests.

As clumsy as the question in this form is, one couldn't eliminate it simply by adopting a wrathful and ecumenical point of view. Freud and Thomas Mann did not always escape that tone in their accounts: summit conferences, geniuses with pensive countenances managing vast sectors of universal culture. To consider the intellectual "turfs" as existent is always to be taken in by a certain cultural prejudice. And why, moreover, by what claim would we want to be sure to keep score and share harmoniously the diverse types of ideas and discourse?

But, on the other hand, what then is the mythic position of literature, a position whereby this "turf" could divulge its specific feature only by exposing itself as being threatened by reabsorption or destruction through proximity, for example, to the philosophical or to the theoretical in general?

It often happens that Freud (in his sketch on Leonardo da Vinci for example) makes use of an art-science duality conceived in terms of competition and where one feels the mark of a particular historical situation—about which, moreover, we do not yet know what to say.

For a novel like *Ada*, underlining the slanderousness of any theoretical view which one would take regarding it (as if we living things were afraid to be devoured by biology), and claiming to elude the designs on it, is also to revive the uproar over its own consistency. This little scene is assembled, for example, in the exhibition of Van Veen who, using a pseudonym, has become an acrobat and illusionist, "Thus, the intoxication which the young Mascodagama felt when conquering gravity, was linked to the intoxication of artistic revelation considered in a meaning totally unsuspected by the simpletons of criticism, by commentators on the social scene, by moralists, by manufacturers of ideas, etc. On the stage, Van accomplished organically what his parts of speech should accomplish later in his life . . ." (*Ada*, p. 157).

There is no cause, certainly, to neglect those brilliant areas, those little strategies, those brief skirmishes against the nearest and most incompatible theory. But it would be absurd to give them currency, to elevate them to the level of a vision equal to those accounts of realms which can only be largely imaginary.

If, after all, these somewhat too highly colored and slightly varnished productions cannot be considered a global definition of literature, they are not specifics of literature either. One would say that texts proclaimed as literary are charged with exhibiting and circumscribing in a particular light a question which is certainly posed, although in very different terms, for all fields: that of their persistence, their validity, their limits, and their demise.

Van Veen and Ada, whose fictive lives as adolescents or old people lengthen when approaching death, do not play just with the pleasure of "hatching" words in a literary way; they do not just enjoy a typically poetic, narcissistic security; they also manipulate a question which fluctuates for other types of discourse and other linguistic games and which is perhaps unformulatable anywhere other than at the heart of literature.

Concerning this question of validity, specificity of fields, and their eventual reabsorption, there is no decision possible at the core of a given domain, no imminent mastery of one's own existence. Nor would one know how to elect some prevalent interdisciplinary point of view which would have to be aware of the legitimacy of diverse claims.

No place exists for this question, a question neither naive nor multiple. Nor shall we make decisions about duplications or faults in cultural territory or eventual new distributions of interest—even if in this regard all our actions are conclusive.

Notes

1. References here are to *Ada or Ardor, A Family Chronicle*, translated into French by Gilles Chanine and J. B. Blandenier and revised by the author (Fayard, 1975), p. 23. [Since Mouchard's essay is closely attentive to the language of the French translation, passages from *Ada* cited here are translated directly from the article.] All subsequent references to this edition will appear parenthetically.

2. Foreword to *Le Guetteur*, p. 13 [editor: translated by George Magnane (Paris: Gallimard, [(1968]). Nabokov's English translation is as follows: "Freudians flitter around [my books] avidly, approach with itching oviducts, stop, sniff, and recoil" (*The Eye* [New York: Pocket Books, 1966], ix).]

3. *Mary*, Penguin Books, p. ii.

Proust, Nabokov, and *Ada*

J. E. Rivers*

In 1966, in a televised interview, Vladimir Nabokov stated that the "greatest masterpieces of twentieth-century prose are, in this order: Joyce's *Ulysses*; Kafka's *Transformation*; Bely's *St. Petersburg*; and the first half of Proust's fairy tale, *In Search of Lost Time*."[1] Nabokov's admiration for Proust is thus a matter of public record. Nabokov's critics, however, have done very little toward pursuing the implications of that admiration. To be sure, several critics have commented on the frequency with which Nabokov mentions and alludes to Proust.[2] Others have linked Proust and Nabokov as writers who share an interest in the nature of time and memory.[3] And still others have noticed parallels between Proust's philosophy of love and the view of love developed in *Lolita* and elsewhere.[4] The subject of Nabokov's relation to Proust remains, nonetheless, largely uncharted and unexplored. The work that has been done is brief and tentative. It oversimplifies the obvious parallels and neglects the less obvious ones. More seriously, it fails to take full account of the differences between Proust and Nabokov, differences that are, finally, just as important as the similarities.

Did Proust influence Nabokov? The question must be approached with caution, since Nabokov mockingly repudiates the suggestion that he owes a debt to any writer, living or dead. In the Foreword to the English translation of *Invitation to a Beheading* he comments: "Incidentally, I could never understand why every book of mine invariably sends reviewers scurrying in search of more or less celebrated names for the purpose of passionate comparison. During the last three decades they have

*From the *French-American Review*, 1 (Fall 1977), 173–97. Reprinted by permission of the author and of the journal.

hurled at me (to list but a few of these harmless missiles) Gogol, Tolstoevski, Joyce, Voltaire, Sade, Stendahl, Balzac, Byron, Bierbohm, Proust, Kleist, Makar Marinski, Mary McCarthy, Meredith(!), Cervantes, Charlie Chaplin, Baroness Murasaki, Pushkin, Ruskin, and even Sebastian Knight. One author, however, has never been mentioned in this connection—the only author whom I must gratefully recognize as an influence upon me at the time of writing this book; namely, the melancholy, extravagant, wise, witty, magical, and altogether delightful Pierre Delalande, whom I invented."[5] Indeed, the more obvious the affinity seems to be, the more vehemently Nabokov denies it. To a critic who attempted to establish a relationship between Borges and Nabokov, Nabokov replied: "I owe no debt whatsoever . . . to the famous Argentine essayist and his rather confused compilation 'A New Refutation of Time.' "[6] And when an interviewer asked Nabokov about his Proustian sense of places," he responded: "My sense of places is Nabokovian rather than Proustian."[7] Throughout Nabokov's writing and public utterances he heaps scorn upon influence studies of any sort—especially those that suggest that aspects of his own vision have been shaped by the achievements of other writers.[8]

One can understand Nabokov's desire to emphasize the originality of his work. And one can also understand his protest against the type of comparative study that glibly suggests (without offering any proof) that an author found such-and-such a theme in this or that other book. This does not mean, however, that the methods of comparative literature are inappropriate for studying Nabokov's novels and his place in modern literature. Though he disassociates himself from all schools and movements, and though he discourages attempts to compare him with any other writer, the truth is that Nabokov's achievement is in many ways an achievement of literary synthesis. To read a novel by Nabokov is to be exposed to a wide spectrum of allusions to and parodies of other authors, and occasionally to passages of explicit literary criticism. Nabokov's literary references display, moreover, a cavalier disregard for barriers of language and national frontier. Portions of *Ada* are written in Russian and French; the dialogue is studded with multilingual literary puns; and the exposition is filled with allusions to writers as diverse as Marvell, Baudelaire, Tolstoy, Pascal, and Henry Miller. Indeed, the first part of *Ada*, as critics have recognized,[9] parodies the entire history of the novel. Nabokov constantly reminds us of the similarities and differences between what his characters are thinking and doing and what other characters, in other works of literature, have thought and done. Literature—its nature, its uses, its history—is one of his principal themes.

The work of Marcel Proust is a recurrent topic whenever Nabokov writes about literature. Sometimes Nabokov pays homage to Proust; sometimes he quarrels with him; sometimes he makes fun of him; but always he is aware of him. What Nabokov calls in *Ada* the "mauve [shade] of Monsieur Proust"[10] haunts both the surface and the sub-surface of Nabokov's major works. In *The Real Life of Sebastian Knight* Mr. Goodman singles out "the French author M. Proust" as one "whom Knight consciously or subconsciously copied."[11] And, indeed, Sebastian Knight lapses self-consciously into the Proustian style in one of his letters. "You seem to wonder," Knight says, "what on earth could make me, a budding author (as you say—but that is a misapplied term, for your authentic budding author remains budding all his life; others, like me, spring into blossom in one bound), you seem to wonder, let me repeat (which does not mean I am apologizing for that Proustian parenthesis), why the hell I should take a nice porcelain blue contemporary . . . and let him drop from the tower of my prose into the gutter below" (p. 54). Similarly, in *Lolita*, Humbert Humbert borrows (and parodies) Proust's characteristic, tentative speculation about psychological motives. "Into the fifty days of our cohabitation," Humbert says, "Charlotte crammed the activities of as many years. The poor woman busied herself with a number of things she had foregone long before or had never been much interested in, as if (to prolong these Proustian intonations) by my marrying the mother of the child I loved I had enabled my wife to regain an abundance of youth by proxy."[12] Moreover, Humbert's unsuccessful attempt to keep Lolita a captive of his love—subjecting her the while to constant jealous surveillance—repeats the pattern of Proust's narrator's love for Albertine. In *La Prisonnière* Albertine's flight from the Paris apartment is foreshadowed by the sound of a window violently opening in her room. The incident is echoed in *Lolita* just before Humbert's nymphet changes, in her turn, from prisonnière to fugitive. "Downstairs the screen door banged. Lo? Escaped? . . . I had no other alternative than to pursue on foot the winged fugitive" (p. 208). A little later Humbert underscores the Proustian pattern of his love by alluding to the original French title (*Albertine Disparue*) of the work we know as *La Fugitive*. "Now . . . I have reached the part which (had I not been forestalled by another internal combustion martyr) might be called *Dolorès Disparue*" (p. 255).[13]

Nabokov also reproduces in *Lolita* Proust's well-known view of the personality as multiple, discontinuous, and constantly changing. At one point Humbert receives a letter revealing that John Farlow's life has taken a totally unexpected course—a revelation that, Humbert says, serves to "Proustianize" his fancy. He explains as follows: "I have often noticed that we are inclined to endow our friends with the stability of type that literary characters acquire in the reader's mind. . . . Thus X will never compose the immortal music that would clash with the second-rate symphonies he has accustomed us to. Y will never commit murder. Under no circumstances can Z ever betray us. . . . Any deviation in the fates we have ordained would strike us as not only anomalous but unethical. We would prefer not to have known at all our neighbor, the retired hot-dog stand operator, if it turns out he has just produced the greatest book of poetry his age has seen" (p. 267).

In what ways does this meditation "Proustianize" the narrative? First of all, the style is Proustian: Humbert uses the first person plural in the same way Proust uses it to formulate his "general laws" of human conduct. Furthermore, Humbert's examples of (in Proustian terms) disjunction between the social mask and the *moi profond* all have close analogues in Proust's writing. Swann regards Vinteuil as an "old fool";[14] and yet this same Vinteuil composes music that reveals to Swann profound truths about suffering and love. (Swann never discovers that the "old fool" and the inspired composer are one and the same).[15] In the essay "Sentiments filiaux d'un parricide," Proust writes of his amazement on discovering that one of his friends, who seemed a model son, has suddenly killed his mother and committed suicide.[16] And again, in *Un Amour de Swann*, Swann struggles with the duality of human nature after receiving a vicious, anonymous letter about Odette. He searches his mind to discover who could have sent it and considers, among others, M. de Charlus. "After all, M. de Charlus was fond of him, had a good heart. But he was also a neuropath, perhaps tomorrow he would weep to discover that Swann was ill, and today, through jealousy, through anger, through some sudden idea that had taken hold of him, he might have decided to do Swann some injury" (I, 357). Bergotte, the writer whose books so charm the young narrator, is the equivalent of Nabokov's retired hot-dog stand operator who turns out to be the greatest poet of his age. The narrator envisions Bergotte as a "sweet Singer with white hair"; but when he finally meets him, Bergotte proves to be the antithesis of the narrator's mental picture: "a young man, rigid, short, heavy-set, near-sighted, with a red nose shaped like a snail shell and a black goatee" (I, 547).

Obviously, then, Nabokov is intimately familiar with both the style and the substance of Proust's writing. And obviously he holds Proust's work in very high regard. In *Pale Fire* the poet John Shade imagines that one of the rewards of the afterlife might be "talks / With Socrates and Proust in cypress walks."[17] And yet Nabokov's admiration for Proust is not without qualification. After all, he places *A la recherche* last in his list of the four greatest masterpieces of modern prose; and he also says that only the first half of *A la recherche* achieves greatness (by the first half Nabokov means those volumes Proust lived to revise and see through publication: *Du côté de chez Swann* through *Sodome et Gomorrhe*).[18] On this score Nabokov has aimed some very telling (and very humorous) barbs at what he regards as Proust's most glaring peculiarities and excesses as a man and a writer. In *Ada* he speaks archly of "crusty Proust who liked to decapitate rats when he did not feel like sleeping" (p. 73).[19] In *Pale Fire* he makes fun of the happy coincidences which seem always to place Proust's narrator outside a window at just the right moment to make some startling discovery—as when he spies on Mlle Vinteuil at Montjouvain and Charlus in Jupien's brothel. "Windows, as well known, have been the solace of first-person literature throughout the ages," says Charles Kinbote. "But this observer never could emulate in sheer luck the eavesdropping *Hero of Our Time* or the omnipresent one of *Time Lost*" (p. 87). In the same spirit, the index to *Pale Fire* identifies "Marcel" as "the fussy, unpleasant, and not always plausible central character, pampered by everybody in Proust's *A la Recherche du Temps Perdu*" (p. 310). More seriously, Nabokov in *Ada* criticizes Proust's Albertine as a sexual transposition lacking in verisimilitude, a female character too obviously based on a real-life male lover. "It makes sense," says Van Veen, "if the reader *knows* that the narrator is a pansy, and that the good fat cheeks of Albertine are the good fat buttocks of Albert. It makes none if the reader cannot be supposed, and should not be required, to know *anything* about this or any other author's sexual habits in order to enjoy to the last drop a work of art" (p. 169).

Nabokov's feeling about Proust has, then, a positive side and a negative side. How might we summarize his evaluation of Proust as a writer? On August 11, 1973, I spent an afternoon talking with Nabokov at his hotel in Montreux, Switzerland. In my letter I had mentioned that I would like to talk about Marcel Proust. When Nabokov, accompanied by his wife, came down to meet me, he was carrying a copy of *Pale Fire* into which he had placed a white index card to mark a certain passage. When the conversation turned to Proust, he said: "Perhaps you have read this little book of mine, *Pale Fire*." He went on to say that the passage he had marked gave the best summary he knew of his current opinion of Proust and *A la recherche*. I opened the book to the page Nabokov had indicated; it described the revenge Charles Kinbote takes on Sybil Shade for not inviting him to John Shade's birthday party. On the morning after the party from which Kinbote has been excluded, Kinbote brings over a present for Shade and hands it to Sybil, asking her "And how did the party go?" When Sybil begins to make the excuse Kinbote has anticipated—"We did not ask you because we knew how tedious you find such affairs"—Kinbote reaches into his pocket "for another book—a book she did not expect." The narrative continues with Kinbote addressing Sybil as follows:

> "Speaking of novels," I said, "you remember we decided once, you, your husband and I, that Proust's rough masterpiece was a huge, ghoulish fairy tale, an asparagus dream, totally unconnected with any possible people in any historical France, a sexual *travestissement* and a colossal farce, the vocabulary of genius and its poetry, but no more, impossibly rude hostesses, please let me speak, and even ruder guests, mechanical Dostoevskian rows and Tolstoian nuances of snobbishness repeated and expanded to an unsufferable length, adorable seascapes, melting avenues, no, do not interrupt me, light and shade effects rivaling those of the

> greatest English poets, a flora of metaphors, described—by Cocteau, I think—as 'a mirage of suspended gardens,' and, I have not yet finished, an absurd, rubber-and-wire romance between a blond young blackguard (the fictitious Marcel), and an improbable *jeune fille* who has a pasted-on bosom, Vronski's (and Lyovin's) thick neck, and a cupid's buttocks for cheeks; but—and now let me finish sweetly—we were wrong, Sybil, we were wrong in denying our little *beau ténébreux* the capacity of evoking 'human interest': it is there, it is there—maybe a rather eighteenth-centuryish, or even seventeenth-centuryish, brand, but it is there. Please dip, or redip, spider, into this book [offering it], you will find a pretty marker in it bought in France, I want John to keep it. . . ."
>
> I am a very sly Zemblan. *Just in case*, I had brought with me in my pocket the third and last volume of the *Bibliothèque de la Pléiade* edition, Paris, 1954, of Proust's work, wherein I had marked certain passages on pages 269–271. Mme. de Mortemart, having decided that Mme. de Valcourt would *not* be among the "elected" at her soirée, intended to send her a note on the next day saying "Dear Edith, I miss you, last night I did not expect you too much (Edith would wonder: how could she at all, since she did not invite me?) because I know you are not overfond of this sort of parties which, if anything, bore you."
>
> So much for John Shade's last birthday. (pp. 161–163)

As Nabokov once told an interviewer, he occasionally—but not always—assigns to the characters in his novels opinions which are totally congruent with his own.[20] And in the passage quoted above, Nabokov told me, he allows Charles Kinbote to state his own opinion of Marcel Proust.

Once again, of course, the mention of Proust is couched in a mock-Proustian style. The 199-word sentence with which the passage begins is a masterful parody of the lengthy, rolling Proustian period, meandering as it does through an intricate succession of subordinate clauses and parenthetical interjections before finally coming to rest. The remarks contain, too, the ambivalence we have seen to be typical of Nabokov's statements about Proust. Nabokov, through Kinbote, praises the imagination and the metaphorical vision of *A la recherche* and refers to the work (as he also did in his television interview) as a "fairy tale."[21] This, coming from Nabokov, is great praise indeed: when Nabokov taught literature at Cornell, he began his lectures by declaring that "great novels are above all great fairy tales."[22] And yet there is a parodox. Nabokov admires the fantastical inventiveness of *A la recherche*, but he also takes the novel to task for what he regards as faulty realism and characterization. Once again he pronounces the love affair between the narrator and Albertine an unconvincing sexual *travestissement*; and he asseverates that, in general, the characters in this "asparagus dream"[23] are "totally unconnected with any possible people in any historical France." He suggests, too, that Proust's skillful and ornate imagery, though admirable, ultimately represents "the vocabulary of genius and its poetry, but no more." And he claims that the novel is too long. Having said all this, however, he concludes with a demonstration of how, after all, Proust's novel contains passages of acute and genuine insight into human motives and conduct, so much so that Kinbote is able to offer *A la recherche* as a mirror wherein Sybil Shade can read the story of her own hypocrisy.

We can partially agree with some of Nabokov's objections to *A la recherche*. Proust's imagery—his "adorable seascapes," "melting avenues," and "light and shade effects rivaling those of the greatest English poets"—sometimes approaches a reveling in metaphor for its own sake, as in the elaborate transformation, in *A l'ombre des jeunes filles en fleurs*, of the restaurant at Rivebelle into a model of the Ptolemaic uiniverse. Every reader, too, has felt the burden of the Proustian *longueurs*; and many have wondered, along with Nabokov, whether all the "nuances of snobbishness" analyzed in the novel need to be "repeated and expanded" to such "an unsufferable length." As Edmund Wilson remarks, sometimes in Proust we "feel ourselves going under in the gray horizonless ocean of analysis."[24] We can agree, too, that the "sheer luck" that consistently places Proust's narrator in front of the right window at the right time sometimes seems a little contrived.[25] But when Nabokov asserts that the characters of *A la recherche* are "totally unconnected with any possible people in any historical France," and when he insists that "the good fat cheeks of Albertine are the good fat buttocks of Albert," his criticism begins to falter.

These pronouncements are, of course, characteristically Nabokovian overstatements.[26] And, for all their sweeping generality, they do contain a grain of truth. Proust perceives the personality as elusive and ultimately unknowable. As a consequence, he sometimes presents his characters as phantoms unfixed in time and place. When Swann searches for Odette after failing to find her at the Verdurins', the narrative takes on a mythic dimension that frees it from its historical context and transforms it into an archetypal journey through the underworld, a journey in which the people of Paris become as shadowy and inscrutable as Odette herself is now becoming in Swann's mind. "Swann brushed anxiously against all these obscure bodies as if, among the shades of the dead, in the realm of darkness, he was searching for Eurydice" (I, 230). But Proust's novel is not all fairy tale, not all mythic archetype. There are many ways in which it is firmly rooted in its time and place, ways in which, in fact, it cannot be understood without explicit knowledge of that time and place. Bloch's Homeric language, which echoes and parodies Leconte de Lisle; Mme de Guermantes' distaste for the "Empire style"; Françoise's peasant dialect; the division of characters into Dreyfusists and anti-Dreyfusists; Charlus' discourse on the trial of Prince Eulenberg—these and many other aspects of *A la recherche* show that Proust is as much cultural historian as fabricator of fiction. And he is much more successful than Nabokov allows at combining these two basic novelistic functions.

Perhaps Nabokov's most serious charge against *A la recherche* is his idea that the character of Albertine arises from a sexual transposition and is therefore unconvincing as a portrayal of a woman. This, of course, is a criticism frequently brought against *A la recherche.*[27] It is, however, a criticism which fails to grasp the full significance of Albertine as a "goddess of Time" (III, 387) who illustrates the many planes of being which converge and interact in the human personality. Of course Albertine is sexually ambiguous; but she is ambiguous in many other ways as well. In one particularly revealing vision she appears to the narrator as simultaneously lesbian and heterosexual, inanimate and animate, animal and human, mortal and divine (III, 527–528). True, the narrator's love for Albertine is partly based on Proust's love for Alfred Agostinelli; and it probably contains traces of Proust's other homosexual love affairs as well. But, as most students of Proust know, Albertine has female as well as male models and becomes, finally, larger and more complex than any of them. Furthermore, as Eric Bentley points out in a recent interview, "there is *creativity* in the characterization [of Albertine] . . . Proust has not tried to give the character what a man would have said and done on all occasions. . . . Now even if Albertine is a man without a penis, that still isn't a woman. But it isn't Albertine either; she has positive feminine traits."[28] Albertine escapes not only from the limits of gender but from any attempt to categorize and contain her. She represents the flux of time and the pluralistic structure of the self as it exists in time.[29] In this regard, she has many identities, many modes of being. Her sexual ambiguity—that she seems to be something other than purely and stereotypically female—is part and parcel of this overall meaning. It is a meaning Nabokov seriously misconstrues when he asserts that Albertine must be understood as "really" a man before the novel makes sense.[30]

Nabokov's statements about Proust may be read and evaluated (as I have done in part above) as literary criticism in their own right. But they are a special kind of criticism—criticism that exists in, and functions as a part of, a work of creative art. Nabokov attempts in his novels to judge Proust and *A la recherche* critically and objectively. But he also uses Proust and his work creatively, as metaphors for particular views of experience and particular approaches to reality, many of which Nabokov embraces, but some of which he rejects. Nabokov told me in Montreux that he first read Proust with his wife around 1935–1936, at which time, he said, he had already been formed as a writer and was immune to outside influences.[31] This comment requires of us a careful and subtle distinction. Though Proust's work obviously influences the shape and tone of Nabokov's fiction by its presence therein, it does not exert a direct influence upon Nabokov's aesthetic philosophy or upon the formulation of his central themes. Nabokov's references to Proust are not admissions of literary debt. Like his allusions to and parodies of other writers, they are exercises in metacriticism through which he tries to define his own place in literary history. Nabokov's literary references are deliberate reminders of what he has in common with the literature that precedes and surrounds him; and they are also signposts—implanted as much for Nabokov's own benefit as for that of his readers—outlining the areas he must avoid and the frontiers past which he must forge if he is to achieve artistic originality. When Nabokov reflects upon Proust, he is almost always reflecting upon the aims and aspirations of his own art.

Nabokov's recent novel *Ada* (1969)—which bore for a time the working title *The Texture of Time*—is, of all Nabokov's works, perhaps the most steeped in Proust. It can serve, therefore, as a useful example of Nabokov's affinities with and challenges to the Proustian aesthetic. Like *A la recherche*, *Ada* is a novel that describes its own coming into being. The hero of the book, Van Veen, is also (with help from his sister and lover Ada) its narrator and putative creator, as is also the case with Proust's protagonist. *Ada*, like *A la recherche*, is both *Künstlerroman* and *Bildungsroman*. It tells the story of how its central character acquires the artistic sensibility that will allow him to write a novel about how he acquired an artistic sensibility.

In *Ada* Nabokov exploits with a vengeance a device the Russian Formalist critic Victor Shklovsky calls *ostraneniye* ("making strange" or "defamiliarization"). Van and Ada grow up not on Earth but on a parodic double of Earth known as Antiterra, a place where history has warped to interfuse Russian, French, and American culture. Their childhood is spent in the nineteenth century, but a nineteenth century in which time is strangely out of joint: Proust has already written his masterpiece, and people drink Coca-Cola, go to the movies, and travel on flying carpets known as "jikkers." The Proust of Antiterra is almost, but not quite, the Proust of Terra (the rival planet in which only lunatics and artists believe). Just as Henry Miller appears on Antiterra as Heinrich Müller, *Un Amour de Swann* is known there as *Les Malheurs de Swann* (an apt title, and one which Proust himself might well have used).[32] Life on Antiterra proliferates with similar kinds of anachronisms and distortions of the familiar. Antiterra may be, in fact, nothing more than Van's artistic reimagining of life on Earth, though this is never explicitly stated in the novel.[33]

Whether or not Van has reimagined the universe, Nabokov certainly has. And in this sense *Ada* represents the logical fulfillment of the Proustian notion that each individual artist breaks down the elements of ordinary life and recombines them to create new worlds, new universes. In *A l'ombre des jeunes filles en fleurs* Proust's narrator speaks of Elstir's studio as "the laboratory of a sort of new creation of the world"; and he says that "if God the Father created things by naming them, it was by taking away their name, or by giving them another, that Elstir created them anew" (I, 834–835; cf. I, 349–350; III, 257–258). Nabokov's creation of characters who exist, *a priori*, outside the usual limits of chronological time is also, of course, a refraction of one of Proust's chief artistic goals: to find ways of voyaging freely through time and escaping from its sequential, forward thrust.

Not surprisingly, Nabokov establishes at the outset of the novel that Van and Ada are on very familiar terms with the work of Proust, as were Sebastian Knight, Humbert Humbert, John and Sybil Shade, and Charles Kinbote before them. Mlle Larivière, the French governess, remembers Van as a precocious "*bambin angélique* who adored à *neuf* ans . . . Gilberte Swann *et la Lesbie de Catulle*" (p. 66).[34] And in discussing the entomological entries in Ada's diary, the narrative voice informs us that "At ten or earlier [Ada] had read—as Van had—*Les Malheurs de Swann*, as the next sample reveals" (p. 55). There follows a passage in which Ada describes the "noble larva of the Cattleya Hawkmoth (mauve shades of Monsieur Proust) . . . rearing its hyacinth head in a stiff 'Sphinxian' attitude" (p. 56). When Van later looks in upon Ada's larvarium, he discovers that "the Odettian Sphinx had turned, bless him, into an elephantoid mummy with a comically encased trunk of the guermantoid type" (pp. 56–57).

This passage is as dense in allusions as any selection from *Finnegans Wake*. Here we can pursue only the reference to Proust. The Cattleya, of course, is the exotic orchid (named for the English botanist William Cattley) which Proust's Odette wears on her bodice and which Swann "arranges" as a prelude to love.[35] The larva of the Cattleya Hawkmoth thus becomes, in Nabokov's allusive language, an "Odettian Sphinx." Its cocoon, moreover, has a "comically encased trunk of the guermantoid type"—a reference to Proust's famous family of aristocrats, and possibly to the fact that Proust attributes to the Duchesse de Guermantes a prominent nose and a bird-like profile.

In the very act of alluding to Proust, however, Nabokov accomplishes something entirely original. Nabokov's personal interest in lepidopterology is well known. In his novels, Nabokov sometimes uses entomological metamorphosis as an image for the passage of time and the metamorphosis of reality that accompanies artistic creation.[36] In *Ada* Dr. Krolik, who helps Ada with her entomology, is referred to as "le Docteur Chronique," Dr. Chronos, Dr. Time (p. 49). The Proustian allusions introduce the theme of time and its relationship to art. But they are enclosed in an aura that is purely Nabokovian, and their ultimate purpose is to throw into relief a highly individual aspect of Nabokov's imagery and vision of the world. As always in Nabokov, the shared meanings of literary culture illuminate and explicate the private language of the Nabokovian universe; and the private language, in turn, widens the meanings of literary culture.

The same could be said of the role of painting, and of color in general, in *Ada*. These motifs are introduced, again, in a Proustian allusion. Toward the beginning of the novel Van mentions that Demon Veen, his father, "preferred to stay by the sea, his dark-blue great-grandmother" (p. 8). On the next page he takes up "the dark-blue allusion, left hanging" and explains it as follows:

> A former viceroy of Estoty, Prince Ivan Temnosiniy, father of the children's great-great-grandmother, Princess Sofia Zemski (1755–1809) . . . had a millennium-old name that meant in Russian "dark-blue". . . . Van could not help feeling esthetically moved by the velvet background he was always able to distinguish as a comforting, omnipresent summer sky through the black foliage of the family tree. In later years he had never been able to reread Proust (as he had never been able to enjoy again the perfumed gum of Turkish paste) without a roll-wave of surfeit and a rasp of gravelly heartburn; yet his favorite purple passage remained the one concerning the name "Guermantes," with whose hue his adjacent ultramarine merged in the prism of his mind, pleasantly teasing Van's artistic vanity. (p. 9)[37]

Nabokov is alluding to Proust's synaesthetic description of the name Guermantes, the sound of whose final syllable suggests to the narrator of *A la recherche* a color described sometimes as orange, sometimes as purple ("amarante") (I, 171; II, 209). Van's aesthetic sensibility is stimulated by the thought that his aristocratic ancestry boasts a name with similar associations; and the Proustian reverie leads him to visualize his past—his family tree—as a tableau dominated by the dark blue color of his great-great-grandmother's maiden name.

Once again, Nabokov uses an allusion to Proust as a starting point for the delineation of a highly original vision. Nabokov once told an interviewer, "I think I was born a painter";[38] and *Ada* represents the most serious attempt since *A la recherche* to combine the aesthetics of painting and the aesthetics of literature. Both Proust and Nabokov practice what Nabokov calls at another point in *Ada* "iridian recall" (p. 469); that is, they strive to recreate the *colors* of the past, as well as its tastes, sounds, textures, and smells. For both writers, an ability to reproduce the variegated hues of an experience is a touchstone of the fidelity of memory to that experience. In the half-waking state described at the beginning of *A la recherche*, the narrator recalls Combray only as a shadowy vision in black and white (I, 43); but in the rush of involuntary memory unleashed by the tea and madeleine, he is able to see Combray in its full panoply of color, the way it actually was (I, 47). Proust's skillful and thoroughgoing use of color as a means of vividly recreating the past is, of course, one of the most famous characteristics of his style, one that has received extensive commentary from his critics.[39] As many of these critics have pointed out, it often seems that Proust, with his elaborate and extensive color imagery, is attempting to rival with his pen the resources of the painter's brush and palette. Immediately before his death Proust's Bergotte views a little patch of yellow wall in a painting by Vermeer; and the thoughts that painting inspires in Bergotte seem in many ways a statement of one of Proust's own artistic goals: "I should have written like that. . . . My last books are too dry, I should have given them several layers of color, should have rendered my sentence precious in itself, like this little patch of yellow wall" (III, 187).[40]

The attempt to do with words what the painter does with color is also one of the primary artistic ambitions of *Ada*. A great deal of the novel can, in fact, be interpreted as an original variation on Proust's "purple passage" on the colors inherent in the name Guermantes. At one point in the novel Demon Veen is described as a "talking palette" (p. 437). The phrase could easily be applied to the novel as a whole. "Hue or who?" Ada writes in the margin of the manuscript (p. 9), and her query points to one of *Ada*'s central aesthetic equivocations. Many of the characters in the novel have color names and function simultaneously as psychological entities and as splashes of verbal color. First of all, of course, there is the "dark-blue great-grandmother" Temnosiniy. There are also the brothers known as Raven Veen and Red Veen, and the sisters Aqua and Marina, who merge to form aquamarine (p. 419). The ostensible editor of Van's novel is named Ronald Oranger; and Van dictates the manuscript to a typist named Violet Knox. Van's Negro nurse is named Ruby Black, and she is later doubled by a Negro maid named Rose.

Characters who do not have color names are often associated with specific colors, which appear whenever the characters themselves appear. Lucette is repeatedly presented as a study in russet, gold, and green (e.g., p. 36; p. 198). Ada most frequently appears in black and white: creamy skin, black hair, and black clothes (e.g., p. 37; p. 39). Van's love for Ada leads him to explore the nature of time; and it is perhaps no accident that he later imagines time as being grayish in color—a merging of Ada's characteristic colors of black and white (p. 538; p. 569). If time drains color from the past, however, the artist can restore that color by reproducing in art the varied hues which live on in memory. Van speaks at one point of "the colored contents of the Past" (p. 547); remarks that "thoughts are much more faintly remembered than shadows or colors" (p. 280); and points out that "one's memory speak[s] in the language of rainbows" (p. 469).

With so much overlapping of character and color, pen and paintbrush, it is no wonder that Nabokov, like Proust, often presents his characters either as escapees from famous paintings (Swann visualizes Odette as Botticelli's Zipporah) or as tending to recreate scenes from famous paintings in their relationships with each other (the father of Proust's narrator looks, in the scene of the goodnight kiss, like "Abraham in the engraving after Benozzo Gozzoli . . . telling Sarah she must leave the side of Isaac" [I, 36–37]). In *Ada*, Van feels himself transferred into a painting by Caravaggio one afternoon when he makes love to Ada in Ardis Park. And after describing the love scene, the narrative voice inquires: "Whose brush was it now? A titillant Titian? A drunken Palma Vecchio?" (p. 141). The act of love itself is compared to the act of painting when Lucette, describing her lesbian encounters with Ada, says: "If my skin were a canvas and her lips a brush, not an inch of me would have remained unpainted and vice versa" (p. 382). Later, after describing a scene in which Van, Ada, and Lucette seem to meld into a painting as they lie in bed together, the narrative voice comments: "That about summed it up" (p. 420). Such descriptions do, indeed, sum up the relationship between "iridian recall" and the novel's many allusions to painters and painting.[41]

This obsession with the past and with the various ways it can be recalled and recreated in art is the primary trait Nabokov shares with Proust. *Ada*, like *A la recherche*, is a work of nostalgia; it follows the lives of its two main characters from childhood into their nineties, at which time Van undertakes an artistic chronicle of his love for his sister in an attempt to defeat time and immortalize their past in art. Throughout the novel Proust and *A la recherche* appear as recurrent metaphors for this type of artistic enterprise and as constant reminders that the theme of time lost and regained is also one of the chief concerns of the novel now before us. At a dinner given at Ardis the menu will include, we are told, "that special asparagus (*bezukhanka*) which does not produce Proust's After-effect, as cookbooks say" (p. 254). The reference is to Proust's description of the rainbow-hued asparagus which, in the words of Proust's narrator, "all night following a dinner at which I had partaken of it . . . played, in poetic and scurrilous pranks such as one might find in a fairy scene by Shakespeare, at transforming my chamber pot into a fragrant urn" (I, 121). This allusion to the urine-scenting asparagus of *A la recherche* seems at first to be only a literary joke. But it takes on a special resonance when we realize that this dinner at Ardis is filled with other, more significant kinds of Proustian after-effects. One of the most important of these is the description of the reaction of Demon and Marina when they meet again many years after their love has died. Their meeting poses, in miniature, the essential question of *Ada*, which is also the essential question of *A la recherche*: How can the destructive action of time be halted or reversed? "It aggrieved him," the narrative voice says of Demon's reaction to Marina, "that complete collapse of the past, the dispersal of its itinerant court and music-makers, the logical impossibility to relate the dubious reality of the present to the unquestionable one of remembrance" (p. 251). The cinema actress Marina, for her part, views the past as a badly made film in need of editing and revision: "Someday, she mused, one's past must be put in order. Retouched, retaken. Certain 'wipes' and 'inserts' will have to be made in the picture; certain telltale abrasions in the emulsion will have to be corrected; 'dissolves' in the sequence discreetly combined with the trimming out of unwanted, embarrassing 'footage' and definite guarantees obtained; yes, someday—before death with its clapstick closes the scene" (pp. 253–254). The language is Nabokovian;[42] but the thought is Proustian and is highly reminiscent of the race with death Proust's narrator undertakes at the end of *A la recher-*

che in an attempt to finish his novel before death plunders and destroys the accumulated riches of memory.

Neither Demon nor Marina, of course, succeeds in translating the past into a more meaningful or enduring form. This is a task that only Van—with the help and inspiration of Ada—can accomplish. And he accomplishes it by writing a novel whose story is the story of his own life. Like Proust's narrator, Van and Ada draw nearer and nearer to death, but never actually die in the novel. The end of *Ada*, like the end of *A la recherche*, folds back upon the beginning, implying and demonstrating the victory of art over the inevitable extinction of the personality and the memory. "One can even surmise," says the narrative voice of *Ada*, "that if our time-racked, flat-lying couple ever intended to die they would die, as it were, *into* the finished book, into Eden or Hades, into the prose of the book or the poetry of its blurb" (p. 587).

The poetry and prose of *Ada* play a key role in releasing the story from the dominion of time. "I wonder," says Ada at the end of Part IV, "if the attempt to discover those things is worth the stained glass. We can know the time, we can know a time. We can never know Time. Our senses are simply not meant to perceive it. It is like—" (p. 563). Ada's sentence breaks off; but, as critics have recognized, it refers to the entirety of the preceding narrative, and particularly to the metaphorical language that narrative applies to time. In Van's novel time becomes a painting, a bad movie, a great expanse of the color gray, and "much, much more" (p. 589). Time, in other words, can best be apprehended and controlled through metaphor. And in this respect Nabokov echoes one of Proust's most famous pronouncements in *A la recherche*: "truth begins only at the moment when the writer takes two different objects, establishes their relationship . . . and encloses them in the necessary rings of a beautiful style . . . releases their common essence in uniting them one with another in order to remove them from the contingencies of time, in a metaphor" (III, 889).

In *Ada*, as in *A la recherche*, the passage of time inevitably results in human suffering, and suffering, in turn, becomes a necessary prelude to artistic creation. The conclusion of *Ada* equates time and pain: "In the latest *Who's Who* the list of [Van's] main papers included by some bizarre mistake the title of a work he had never written, though planned to write many pains: *Unconsciousness and the Unconscious*. There was no pain to do it now—and it was high pain for *Ada* to be completed" (p. 587). Art, for both Proust and Nabokov, is palliative and redemptive. It eases the suffering of existence; and it redeems the life of the individual by revealing its larger, universal meaning: "Ideas are the successors of griefs," says Proust's narrator as he contemplates his plans for his novel; "at the moment when these latter change into ideas, they lose a part of their harmful action over our heart" (III, 906). Similarly, Van and Ada find that the book on which they collaborate is the only means they have of relieving their suffering and guilt over Lucette's suicide. After Lucette's death, Ada writes to Van that "we never learned in the arbors of Ardis that such unhappiness could exist" (p. 500). And Van, reflecting on his relationship with Lucette, decides that "he understood her condition or at least believed, in despair, that he *had* understood it, retrospectively, by the time no remedy except Dr. Henry's oil of Atlantic prose could be found in the medicine chest of the past with its banging door and toppling toothbrush" (p. 485). In Proust, as in Nabokov, the balm of prose is the only palliative for the wound of time. "I will . . . redeem our childhood," says Van to Ada, "by making a book of it" (p. 406).

For all the Proustian parallels in *Ada*, the novel also contains important divergences from and challenges to the Proustian outlook. Proust, as is well known, distinguishes two types of memory, voluntary and involuntary; and he exalts the latter over the former as a tool for exploring the past. In *A la recherche* voluntary memory, the memory of the intelligence, produces only an imperfect picture of the past; but involuntary memory, the type of memory set in motion by the tea and madeleine, brings back the past in all its complex variety (cf. I, 344–345). Nabokov, like Proust, writes about both kinds of memory. But, unlike Proust, he sets them on equal footing and draws upon them simultaneously in his attempts to recapture the past in art. In his autobiography, *Speak, Memory*, Nabokov writes: "I discovered that sometimes, *by means of intense concentration*, the neutral smudge [of memory] might be *forced* to come into beautiful focus" (p. 12; italics mine). At the same time, Nabokov's works are filled with moments when, with no concentration or mental effort whatsoever, a random taste or smell or sight suddenly and inexplicably recalls the past to vivid life. Toward the end of his poem, "An Evening of Russian Poetry"—a poem dealing among other things with his exile from Russia—Nabokov writes as follows:

> And now I must remind you in conclusion,
> that I am followed everywhere and that
> space is collapsible, although the bounty
> of memory is often incomplete:
> once in a dusty place in Mora County
> (half town, half desert, dump mound and mesquite)
> and once in West Virginia (a muddy
> red road between an orchard and a veil
> of tepid rain) it came, that sudden shudder
> a Russian something that I could inhale
> but could not see.[43]

In *Ada*, as elsewhere in Nabokov, voluntary and involuntary memory work in concert. "It did not matter, it did not matter," Van thinks at one point. "Destroy and forget. But a butterfly in the Park, an orchid in a shop window, would revive everything with a dazzling inward shock of despair" (p. 324). And just as important as the memory that arrives unbidden is the memory consciously willed to appear. "Not only in their ear-trumpet age—in what Van called their dot-dot-dotage—but even more so in their adolescence (summer, 1888), did they seek a scholarly excitement in establishing the past evolution (summer, 1884) of their love, the initial stages of its revelations, the freak discrepancies in gappy chronographies. . . . 'And do you remember . . . (invariably with that implied codetta of 'and,' introducing the bead to be threaded in the torn necklace) became with them, in their intense talks, the standard device for beginning every other sentence" (p. 109).

Nabokov challenges the reader to participate in these attempts to summon up the past—to become, in effect, a collaborator in Van's and Ada's exercises in memory and, by extension, a collaborator in the creation of the novel itself. On one occasion Van and Lucette quarrel and Van walks angrily away: " 'I apollo, I love you,' she whispered frantically, trying to *cry* after him in a *whisper* because the corridor was all door and ears, but he walked on, waving both arms in the air without looking back" (p. 467). Later in the novel Nabokov asks the reader to remember the details of this scene. Van calls after Ada in a whisper and the narrative voice poses the question: "who, and where in this tale, in this life, had also attempted a *whispered cry*?" (p. 520). Throughout the novel the narrative voice tests the reader's memory with similar interjections. "Now who pronounced it that way? Who?" (p. 381); "last call for that joke" (p. 558); "the third blind character in this chronicle" (p. 468).

These demands on the reader's memory reach levels of great complexity in *Ada*. Late in the novel Lucette walks in on Van and Ada as they are having intercourse bent over a bathtub (p. 392). The scene doubles an earlier one in which Lucette spies on Van and Ada as they are making love by a brook in the woods (p. 267). But the congruence of scenes is only hinted at—"and now their four eyes were looking again into the azure brook of Pinedale" (p. 392)—and is left for the reader to identify. If the reader succeeds in establishing the parallel, he will find that the earlier scene is a reduplication of a still earlier scene, as we discover if we turn back and review the scene by the brook. There we read: "Something of the sort had happened somewhere before; he did not have time to identify the recollection" (p. 267). Once again it is up to the reader to establish the memory and recall a third scene, still further removed in time, which occurs when a very young Van and Ada, on an outing near the bank of a brook, invent a game to get rid of Lucette so they can make love (pp. 142–145). These triply echoed episodes are designed to produce in the reader what Nabokov calls elsewhere in the novel "a faint paramnesic tang" (p. 510). But the *déjà vu* must be accompanied by a conscious effort of memory in order to grasp the details of the structural reduplication. By thus drawing the reader into the network of voluntary and involuntary memory. *Ada* creates a past for the reader at the same time that it creates a past for its central characters. The ideal reader of *Ada* does not simply read about time; he participates in it, he voyages through it, along with Van and Ada.

To be sure, there are many scenes that echo and reecho each other in *A la recherche* and that produce a similar sensation of an accumulated past. But Proust does not issue the same impish challenge to the reader's memory. Rather, he constantly reminds and instructs his readers about what is being recalled and where similar scenes have unfolded. René Girard has well described this aspect of *A la recherche* in a comparison of Proust and Dostoyevsky:

> [In Dostoyevsky] the reader is supposed to recollect; it is not the author who does the remembering for him, as in Proust. The development of the novel can be compared to a game of cards. In Proust the game proceeds slowly; the novelist constantly interrupts the players to remind them of previous hands and to anticipate those to come. In Dostoyevsky, on the contrary, the cards are laid down very rapidly. . . . one must give to the novel the attention which Veltchaninov gives to "the eternal husband," the attention of a witness who is not sure he understands and is afraid of missing the slightest detail that might enlighten him.[44]

Though Nabokov would resent the comparison to Dostoyevsky, whom he holds in very low esteem, the same distinction could be drawn between Proust and Nabokov.

Regardless of their different treatments of voluntary and involuntary memory, the primary function of memory is the same in Proust and Nabokov: it offers proof of the existence and the continuity of the self. The first version of Nabokov's *Speak, Memory* was entitled *Conclusive Evidence*—"conclusive evidence of my having existed," Nabokov declared in the Foreword to the revised version (p. 11). Similarly, in *Ada*, we read that "time is but memory in the making" and that " 'to be' means to know one 'has been' " (p. 559). Such ideas are, of course, Proustian in the extreme. When Proust's narrator asks the painter Elstir whether he regrets the frivolous life he formerly led in Mme Verdurin's salon, Elstir replies: "I understand how the image of what we have been in an early period might be unrecognizable and at all events displeasing. It must not be denied, however, because it is a testimony that we have really lived" (I, 864).

Toward the end of *Ada*, as toward the end of *A la recherche*, the narrative gives way to a long meditation on time and its relation to the artistic vocation. In *Ada* this section takes the form of a work-within-the-work, Van's quasi-philosophical treatise, *The Texture of Time*, which is excerpted in Part IV of the novel. The time Van discusses in Part IV of *Ada* is, Nabokov has said, "something quite different from what Proust called 'lost time.' "[45] When I asked Nabokov how, precisely, Van's time was different from Proust's lost time, he replied: "Van is talking about time such as you know it in the dentist's chair." And in 1970 he explained

Van's time as follows: "It is precisely in everyday life, in the waiting rooms of life's stations that we can concentrate on the 'feeling' of time and palpate its very texture."[46] In his attempt to palpate the texture of time, Van decides that "Time is rhythm: the insect rhythm of a warm humid night . . . the drum in my temple. . . . Yes. Maybe the only thing that hints at a sense of Time is rhythm; not the recurrent beats of the rhythm but the gap between two such beats, the gray gap between black beats: the Tender Interval. The regular throb itself merely brings back the miserable idea of measurement, but in between, something like true time lurks" (pp. 537–538).

Nabokov has remarked that the "only rightful field" for discussing Van's concept of time "is Part Four and not the entire novel."[47] And, indeed, we have seen that the idea of "lost time," though it does not occupy Van in Part IV, plays a fundamental role in the rest of *Ada*. Part IV, however, is an attempt to forge beyond the concept of lost time and to formulate a different perspective on temporality. Here Van attempts not to recapture time but to scrutinize it in and of itself. He states: "I wish to examine the essence of Time, not its lapse, for I do not believe that its essence can be reduced to its lapse. I wish to caress Time" (pp. 536–537). Van decides that, in order to experience time in its essence, he must get rid of the relativist concept of space-time. His attitude toward relativity, he says, "is not sympathetic" (p. 543). He speaks of "Space-Time—that hideous hybrid whose very hyphen looks phoney" (p. 543). And he says that "one can be a hater of Space, and a lover of Time" (p. 543).

Van apparently regards Proust as a representative of the relativist tendency to spatialize time, for he warns himself to "beware . . . of the marcel wave of fashionable art, avoid the Proustian bed" (p. 541). And, indeed, many critics have spoken of Proust's affinities with the theory of relativity and have analyzed the tendency to equate space with time in *A la recherche.*[48] On the other hand, Roger Shattuck has recently shown that time cannot be successfully reduced to and identified with space in Proust's novel. "The *Search* affirms *both* perspectives," Shattuck writes. "Time and space do not try to elbow one another aside in the *Search* in order to dominate the scene. They perform an elaborate and moving saraband that leaves both on stage and in full possession of their powers."[49] Predictably, then, Van's attempt to avoid the Proustian bed and jettison the space half of the space-time hybrid is not totally successful. Eventually he, like Proust, finds that space and time are mutually dependent concepts and that each is necessary to illuminate the other. Van writes: "The sharpest feeling of nowness, in visual terms, is the deliberate possession of a segment of Space. . . . This is Time's only contact with Space, but it has a far-reaching reverberation. To be eternal the Present must depend on the conscious spanning of an infinite expansure. Then, and only then, is the Present equatable with Timeless Space. I have been wounded in my duel with the Imposter [Space]" (p. 551). Van's conclusion about time is similar to that presented in the famous closing paragraph of *A la recherche*, where time and space, the past and the present, unite in another "conscious spanning of an infinite expansure," another equation of the present with timeless space. Proust's narrator concludes his novel with the resolution to "describe men (even if this should make them resemble monstrous creatures) as occupying a very considerable place, beside the restrained place which is reserved for them in space, a place on the contrary prolonged beyond measure—since simultaneously, like giants plunged into the years, they touch upon epochs so distant one from another, among which many years have come to take their place—in Time" (III, 1048).[50]

Ada's most fundamental challenge to Proust occurs not in its treatment of time but in its treatment of love. In *Lolita*, as we have seen, Nabokov echoes the Proustian concept of the loved one as an *être de fuite*, a fugitive creature impossible to possess and to comprehend. In *Ada*, however, Nabokov reverses this pessimistic view and presents love as the ultimate reality in a world of illusion. To be sure, it seems for a while that Van might fall victim to Proustian jealousy, as did Humbert Humbert in *Lolita*. The possibility is raised when Van suspects Ada and Cordula of having a lesbian relationship. Van tries to convince himself that lesbianism is no cause for alarm, that he need not torment himself as does Proust's narrator in his suspicions about Albertine's affairs with women. "Did he feel any Proustian pangs? None. On the contrary: a private picture of their fondling each other kept pricking him with perverse gratification" (p. 168). Van, unlike the protagonist of *A la recherche*, finds himself sexually aroused by the idea of lesbian love. He argues that Proust's "detailed description of a heterosexual male jealously watchful of a homosexual female is preposterous because a normal man would be only amused, tickled pink in fact, by his girl's frolic with a female partner" (p. 169).[51] Nevertheless, there remains an undertow of jealousy; and in this case as well Van discovers that he is unable totally to dodge the marcel wave. He wonders: "What, exactly—not that it mattered but one's pride and curiosity were at stake—what exactly had they been up to, those two ill-groomed girls, last term, this term, last night, every night, in their pajama-tops, amid the murmurs and moans of their abnormal dormitory?" (p. 168).

The desire to know "what, exactly" occurred between two other people at a specific point in the past is, of course, the hallmark of Proustian jealousy. For Proust, this is the aspect of jealousy that makes it a valuable tool for the artist, since it leads the artist to scrutinize the lives of others with passionate and unrelenting curiosity (I, 274). The same is true of Van's jealousy in *Ada*, and it becomes one of the primary motives behind Van's exploration and reconstruction of the past. When Van meets Greg Erminin in Paris in 1901, Greg reminisces about life at Ardis, about his own love for Ada, and about the "numerous" other lovers she had in those days. Van wonders: "Numerous? Two? Three? Is it possible [Van] never heard about the main one?" (p. 454). Greg goes on to say that his former love for Ada is "so odd to recall! It was frenzy, it was fantasy, it was reality in the x degree. I'd have consented to be beheaded by a Tartar, I declare, if in exchange I could have kissed her instep. . . . you can't understand that obsession. Ah, those picnics! And Percey de Prey, who boasted to me about her, and drove me crazy with envy and pity, and Dr. Krolik who, they said, also loved her, and Phil Rack, a composer of genius—dead, dead, all dead!" (pp. 454–455). Van, of course, *can* understand Greg's obsession, since, unknown to Greg, he has shared it. But in order to understand it as fully as possible, in order to save it from becoming "dead, dead, all dead," Van will have to reconstruct, in a more thorough exploration of the past than Greg is able to perform, his own envy, his own jealousy, his own "frenzy and fantasy." Like the narrator of *A la recherche*, Van writes his novel in order to preserve and define "this reality which we run a great risk of dying without having known and which is, quite simply, our life" (III, 895).

Though jealousy functions in *Ada*, as it also does in *A la recherche*, as a kind of artistic inspiration, Van's love for Ada is ultimately non-Proustian, even anti-Proustian. Proust equates love with suffering and disappointment and repeatedly dramatizes the failure of his characters to understand each other. Proustian love is an allegory of the inability of the mind to know reality. The closer the lover approaches to the loved one, the more mysterious the loved one seems to become, as in the tragi-comic scene where Proust's narrator tries to kiss Albertine and finds to his chagrin that, viewed from close range, she is not the same girl she appears to be when viewed from afar. Proust is, as André Maurois has stated, "the Zeno of love." And Maurois continues: "Albertine's kiss, like the movement of Zeno's arrow, is annihilated by reason. [In Proust] love will never catch up with jealousy, just as Achilles will never pass the tortoise."[52]

Nabokov's final vision of love in *Ada* is a resounding denial of Proust's conception. True, Nabokov shares Proust's suspicion that the mind can never grasp the *Ding an sich*, that, indeed, there is perhaps no *Ding an sich* to be grasped. Nabokov has stated repeatedly that the word reality should properly be written in quotation marks;[53] and his novels dramatize the idea that there is no single reality but rather a multitude of realities, an infinite regression of illusions and *trompe l'oeil* effects. But in *Ada* the relationship of the two central characters—which easily transcends petty jealousies and endures in strength and tenderness into extreme old age—functions as an antidote for the elusiveness of reality in general. "What, then, was it that raised the animal act to a level higher than even that of the most exact arts or the wildest flights of pure science? It would not be sufficient to say that in his love-making with Ada he discovered the pang, the *ogon'*,[54] the agony of supreme 'reality.' Reality, better say, lost the quotes it wore like claws" (pp. 219–220). In another, equally anti-Proustian statement, the narrative voice observes that "[Van's] love for Ada was a condition of being, a steady hum of happiness. . . . He saw reflected in her everything that his fastidious and fierce spirit sought in life" (p. 574). The love of Van and Ada outlasts sexual desire and becomes, itself, a way of defeating time, a way of regaining youth through shared memories and continuing tenderness. When Ada grows old "nothing remained of her gangling grace"; but Van "loved her much too tenderly, much too irrevocably, to be unduly depressed by sexual misgivings" (pp. 556–557). And when an Englishman sitting near the old lovers in a restaurant comically mistakes *ananas* for bananas on the menu, "Young Van smiled back at young Ada" (p. 557). Finally, the two personalities meld in the dual narrative consciousness of the novel: "Actually, the question of moral precedence has now hardly any importance. I mean, the hero and heroine should get so close to each other by the time the horror begins, so organically close, that they overlap, intergrade, interache, and even if Vaniada's end is described in the epilogue we, writers and readers, should be unable to make out (myopic, myopic) who exactly survives, Dava or Vada, Anda or Vanda" (p. 584). On the subject of love, *Ada* provides the most convincing rejoinder to Proust to be found in modern literature.

Nabokov has confronted Proust's literary achievement more steadily and more thoroughly than any other twentieth-century novelist. He has parodied it, paid tribute to it, and challenged it. By so doing, he has incorporated Proust into a new fictional universe, the universe of novels by Vladimir Nabokov, and thereby extended Proust's meaning and significance. The recurring presence in Nabokov's fiction is a testimony to the profound impact of *A la recherche* on the modern sensibility: for if Proust is one of the first great modernists, Nabokov is undoubtedly, in the words of Charles Nicol, "the last great modern author."[55] We have seen that Nabokov's literary personality was formed before he read Proust and that, in the relationship of the two authors, there is no genetic influence in the usual sense. Should Proust, then, be considered a precursor of Nabokov? Only, we can conclude, in the sense in which Borges defines the term in a famous essay: "The fact is that every writer *creates* his own precursors. His work modifies our conception of the past, as it will modify the future."[56]

Notes

1. Quoted in Vladimir Nabokov, *The Annotated Lolita*, ed. Alfred Appel, Jr. (New York, 1970), p. 398 (note 209/3).

2. *The Annotated Lolita*, p. 339 (note 18/4); and Julia Bader, *Crystal Land: Artifice in Nabokov's English Novels* (Berkeley, 1972), pp. 131–132.

3. Julian Moynahan, *Vladimir Nabokov* (Minneapolis, 1971), p. 5; Yvette Louria, "Nabokov and Proust: The Challenge to Time," *Books Abroad*, 48 (Summer, 1974), 469–476;

and Nancy Anne Zeller, "The Spiral of Time in *Ada*," in *A Book of Things About Vladimir Nabokov*, ed. Carl R. Proffer (Ann Arbor, 1974), pp. 280–281.

4. Octavio Mello Alvarenga, "Proust e Nabokov: Aproximações" *Revista do Livro*, 5 (June, 1960), 85–98; David L. Jones, "*Dolorès Disparue*," *Symposium*, 20 (1966), 135–140; Andrew Field, *Nabokov: His Life in Art* (Boston, 1967), pp. 344–346.

5. Vladimir Nabokov, *Invitation to a Beheading* (New York, 1959), p. 6. After the first footnoted reference, references to works by Proust and Nabokov will be given in parentheses in the text.

6. Vladimir Nabokov, "Anniversary Notes," *TriQuarterly*, 17 (Winter, 1970), p. 6.

7. Vladimir Nabokov, *Strong Opinions* (New York, 1973), p. 197.

8. Cf. *The Annotated Lolita*, p. 18.

9. Alfred Appel, Jr., "*Ada* Described," in *Nabokov: Criticism, Reminiscences, Translations, Tributes*, ed. Alfred Appel, Jr. and Charles Newman (London, 1970), p. 170 ff.; and Bader, p. 127 ff.

10. Vladimir Nabokov, *Ada* (New York, 1969), p. 56.

11. Vladimir Nabokov, *The Real Life of Sebastian Knight* (Norfolk, Conn., 1941), p. 116.

12. *The Annotated Lolita*, p. 79.

13. For further thoughts on Proust and *Lolita* see Jones, "*Dolorès Disparue*."

14. Marcel Proust. *A la recherche du temps perdu*, 3 vols. (Paris, 1954), I, 214. Translations of Proust are by the author.

15. In *Ada*, the musician Mr. Rack is a Vinteuil-like character. We first meet him as "an insignificant but on the whole likable young musician" who gives piano lessons to Lucette (p. 197). As a composer, he is regarded as second-rate; but he gains critical acclaim after his death (pp. 334–335) and is gradually recognized as a "composer of genius" (p. 455). The life of Proust's Vinteuil follows essentially the same pattern.

16. Marcel Proust, "Sentiments filiaux d'un parricide," in "*Contre Sainte-Beuve*" *précédé de "Pastiches et mélanges" et suivi de "Essais et articles*," ed. Pierre Clarac and Yves Sandré (Paris, 1971), pp. 150–159.

17. Vladimir Nabokov, *Pale Fire* (New York, 1962), p. 41.

18. Nabokov clarified this point for me in a private conversation in Montreux, Switzerland on August 11, 1973.

19. The story of Proust's sadistic experiments with rats is, of course, one of the most famous bits of gossip in literary history. Proust's biographer George Painter argues that the story is true, though there remains some room for reasonable doubt. For the fullest available account see George Painter, *Proust: The Later Years* (Boston, 1965), pp. 268–269. In her article, "Proust and Nabokov: The Challenge to Time," Yvette Louria asserts that the reference to Proust and the rats in *Ada* is "borrowed from Painter's own descriptions" (p. 471). This seems extremely doubtful. Painter says that Proust had rats brought to him and pierced with hatpins to indulge a repressed hatred for his parents; Painter says nothing about Proust's "decapitating rats" as an insomniac diversion (the decapitation seems to be Nabokov's embellishment of the traditional form of the story). Furthermore, the legend of the rats and the hatpins is well known and is repeated in many sources outside Painter.

20. *Strong Opinions*, p. 18.

21. "Ghoulish," of course, because of all the cruelty and suffering depicted in it, in such scenes as Françoise's slaughter of the chicken in *Combray* and Charlus' flagellation in *Le Temps retrouvé*.

22. Appel, "*Ada* Described," p. 160.

23. An allusion to Proust's lyrical descriptions of the asparagus served at Combray (I, 121).

24. Edmund Wilson, *Axel's Castle* (New York, 1931), p. 153.

25. For a more general and more sympathetic view of Proust's use of windows see Randi Marie Birn, "The Windows of Imagination in *A la recherche du temps perdu*," *Pacific Coast Philology*, 5 (April, 1970), 5–11.

26. Cf. Nabokov's extravagant judgment of Freud as "the Viennese quack" (*Strong Opinions*, p. 47) and his comment in *Speak, Memory* (New York, 1966) that "I reject completely the vulgar, shabby, fundamentally medieval world of Freud, with its . . . bitter little embryos spying, from their natural nooks, upon the love life of their parents" (p. 20).

27. The first critic to present this criticism in the form of serious scholarly argument was Justin O'Brien in "Albertine the Ambiguous: Notes on Proust's Transposition of Sexes," *PMLA*, 64 (December, 1949), 933–952.

28. "An Interview With Eric Bentley," conducted by Rictor Norton, *College English*, 36 (November, 1974), 296.

29. For a detailed exploration of this idea see Carl John Black, Jr., "Albertine as an Allegorical Figure of Time," *Romantic Review*, 54 (October, 1963), 171–186.

30. Nabokov's biographer Andrew Field has, unfortunately, followed Nabokov's lead in oversimplifying the role of homosexuality in Proust's life and art. Field writes that "in place of Albertine we must always read Albert, for *Remembrance of Things Past* is, above all, a glorification of homosexual love," (p. 345). One must wonder whether Field has actually read Proust, or whether he is simply taking his cue from Nabokov. Anyone familiar with the grotesque comedy of *Sodome et Gomorrhe I*, or with the horrible physical and moral degeneration of the Baron de Charlus, could scarcely speak of Proust's work as "above all, a glorification of homosexual love." For a bracing antidote to this pont of view, see Harry Levin's "Proust, Gide, and the Sexes," *PMLA*, 65 (June, 1950), 648–652. Nabokov is, in general, hostile to the idea of homosexuality, and this may account in some measure for his view that Proust's homosexuality invalidates his portrait of Albertine. As Julian Moynahan points out, a recurring motif in Nabokov's work is the celebration of "marital love" (p. 16). And Douglas Fowler comments in *Reading Nabokov* (Ithaca, 1974) that "homosexuality [is] always an aspect of sterility and monstrosity in Nabokov's world" (p. 114).

31. Nabokov said during the same conversation that he began to "dig in" to Proust seriously when he reread him in prepration for his lectures on literature at Cornell, where he taught from 1948–1959 (with an intermittent guest lectureship at Harvard from 1951–1952). Nabokov has made similar statements about his relation to James Joyce. See *The Annotated Lolita*, pp. 398–399 (note 209/3); and *Strong Opinions*, pp. 102–103.

32. In his notes to the British paperback edition of *Ada* (Harmondsworth, England, 1970), Nabokov explains that *Les Malheurs de Swann* is a "cross between *Les malheurs de Sophie* by Mme de Ségur (née Countess Rostopchin) and Proust's *Un amour de Swann*" (p. 465, note to p. 50).

33. The question of whether we should understand Antiterra as an actual place or simply as a figment of Van's imagination is one critics are just beginning to debate. Bobbie Ann Mason argues the latter point of view in *Nabokov's Garden: A Guide to Ada* (Ann Arbor, 1974), p. 12; and Charles Nicol advances a similar argument in "*Ada* or Disorder," a paper presented before the special session on Vladimir Nabokov at the 1976 convention of the Modern Language Association.

34. Nabokov told me in private conversation that, while he regards Albertine as an utterly unconvincing character, he views the young Gilberte as one of the most skillfully drawn characters in literature.

35. On the Cattleya and its role in Proust see Annie Barnes, "Le Jardin de Marcel Proust," *Modern Language Review*, 64 (1969), 548 ff. Odette's Cattleya has "large mauve petals" (I, 234); hence the "mauve shades of Monsieur Proust" in Ada's larvarium. Annie Barnes identifies Odette's cattleya as the *Cattleya elegans* (a variety of the *Cattleya superba*).

36. *The Annotated Lolita*, p. xxii and pp. 340–341 (note 18/6); and see Diana Butler, "Lolita Lepidoptera," *New World Writing 16* (New York, 1960), pp. 58–84.

37. The surname Temnosiniy does in fact mean "dark-blue" in Russian, as noted by Carl Proffer in "*Ada* as Wonderland: A Glossary of Allusions to Russian Literature," *Russian Literature Triquarterly*, 17 (1970), 403 (note 9/14 [18]).

38. *Strong Opinions*, p. 17.

39. See for instance Ninette Bailey, "Le rôle des couleurs dans la genèse de l'univers proustien," *Modern Language Review*, 60 (April, 1965), 188–196.

40. Cf. Proust's narrator's observation that "style for the writer, like color for the painter, is a question not of technique but of vision" (III, 895). In *Ada* Nabokov remarks that "originality of literary style . . . constitutes the only real honesty of a writer" (p. 471).

41. For further thoughts on the role of color in Nabokov (and especially in *Speak, Memory*) see D. Barton Johnson, "Synthesia, Polychromatism, and Nabokov," in *A Book of Things About Vladimir Nabokov*, pp. 84–103.

42. Alfred Appel, Jr. studies Nabokov's relation to the cinema in *Nabokov's Dark Cinema* (New York, 1974).

43. *The Portable Nabokov*, ed. Page Stegner (New York, 1971), p. 524.

44. René Girard, *Deceit, Desire, and the Novel: Self and Other in Literary Structure*, tr. Y. Freccero (Baltimore, 1965), p. 246.

45. "Anniversary Notes," p. 5.

46. "Anniversary Notes," p. 5.

47. "Anniversary Notes," pp. 5–6.

48. See for instance Georges Poulet, *L'Espace proustien* (Paris, 1963); and Maurice J. Beznos, "Aspects of Time According to the Theories of Relativity in Marcel's Proust's *A la recherche du temps perdu*," The *Ohio University Review*, 10 (1968), 74–102.

49. Roger Shattuck, *Marcel Proust* (New York, 1974), pp. 117, 119.

50. For further thoughts on the role of time in *Ada* see Fowler, *Reading Nabokov*, pp. 198–201.

51. It is true that pornography intended for heterosexual males often features lesbian interludes. Freudians would no doubt say such material appeals to a repressed homosexual desire. But Nabokov is not a Freudian.

52. André Maurois, *A la recherche de Marcel Proust* (Paris, 1949; rpt. 1970), p. 220.

53. *The Annotated Lolita*, p. xix.

54. Russian for "fire."

55. Charles Nicol, "Lucid Arrogance" (a review of Nabokov's *Look at the Harlequins!*), *Bookletter*, 25 (November, 1974), 9.

56. Jorge Luis Borges, "Kafka and His Precursors," in *Franz Kafka: A Collection of Criticism*, ed. Leo Hamalian (New York, n.d.), p. 20.

The Art of Persuasion in Nabokov's *Lolita*

Nomi Tamir-Ghez*

The publication of *Lolita* in America in 1958 caused a considerable stir.[1] Most reviews of the novel dealt with the narrow issue of its alleged

*From *Poetics Today*, 1 (1979), 65–83. Reprinted by permission of the journal.

obscenity.[2] Indeed, the novel was published three years earlier in France, since Nabokov could not find an American publisher ready to risk publishing it. After the initial shock subsided, the attention of literary critics was drawn to the text itself, with its frequent literary allusions, multilingual vocabulary, and its network of parodic structures, puzzles, word games, etc.[3] Nevertheless, the novel's morality remained a central issue. What enraged or at least disquieted most readers and critics was the fact that they found themselves unwittingly accepting, even sharing, the feelings of Humbert Humbert, the novel's narrator and protagonist, the "maniac," the "nympholept," the "Shining example of moral leprosy" (in the words of John Ray, Jr., the fictive editor of Humbert's manuscript).[4] Instead of passing moral judgment on this man who violated a deep-rooted sexual and social taboo, they caught themselves identifying with him. Many literary critics have pointed out this strange effect which the novel has on the reader. Miller claims that "*Lolita* [. . .] can be quite simply described as an assault on the reader," who "softened by the power of appeal is, [. . .] ready to forgive all [. . .]"[5] Lionel Trilling, who describes the dynamics of the reader's reaction to the novel, contends that

> [. . .] we find ourselves the more shocked when we realise that, in the course of reading the novel, we have come virtually to condone the violation it presents. [. . .] we have been seduced into conniving in the violation, because we have permitted our fantasies to accept what we know to be revolting.[6]

Booth[7] discusses *Lolita* as an example of a novel in which a "vicious center of consciousness" (i.e., Humbert) with "full and unlimited control of the rhetorical resources" almost makes a case for himself. Appel suggests that the novel actually represents a contest between the author and the reader:

> What is extraordinary about *Lolita* is [. . .] the way in which Nabokov enlists us, against our will, on Humbert's side. [. . .] Humbert has figuratively made the reader his accomplice in both statutory rape and murder.[8]

The purpose of the present paper is: (1) To give a more detailed (though by no means exhaustive) description of the major rhetorical devices which Nabokov uses while practicing his art of persuasion in *Lolita*. In spite of the fact that many critics have felt the strong effect which the novel's rhetoric has on the reader, the specific devices employed to achieve it have not been described. (2) To argue that the narrator does not, in effect, have an unlimited control over the rhetorical resources.

It is Nabokov who controls the rhetorical effects in *Lolita*, and he does it most subtly and skillfully. He allows the narrator's blandishments to affect us just as much as is needed for the novel's total effect. Far from losing hold of the narrator (as Booth's discussion suggests), the author is always there, behind the scene, pulling the strings. He ensures that

Humbert's arguments are not air-tight, and that enough incriminating information leaks out. Nabokov does intend us to identify with the protagonist to a certain degree, to accept him as a human being, while at the same time strongly to condemn his deeds. Throughout the novel, while Humbert does his best to justify himself, the reader is made aware of his rhetoric, and this awareness counteracts any feelings of empathy which might have developed. Only at the end, when he leaves behind all pretense of self-justification and turns instead to self-castigation, does Humbert win over the reader and close the distance between them. While all the efforts of the *narrator* to win over the reader fail, it is the *author* who finally wins us over, using as his strongest weapon the protagonist's own realization of his guilt. Thus, the novel demonstrates how perfectly a skilled author can control his narrative, even when he imposes upon himself the most restrictive rules (i.e., giving an unreliable narrator full control over the whole discourse). In *Lolita* we witness the subtle art of an author playing chess against himself as it were (in *Speak, Memory* Nabokov compares the composition of a chess problem to "the writing of one of those incredible novels where the author, in a fit of lucid madness, has set himself certain unique rules that he observes, certain nightmare obstacles that he surmounts, with the zest of a deity building a live world from the most unlikely ingredients [. . .]"[9]

From all that has been said up to now it should be clear how important it is not to confuse the rhetorical purposes of the narrator with those of the author, nor the devices each of them uses to attain his goal. As will be shown later, the same arguments that are used by Humbert to justify himself, are often used (indirectly) by Nabokov to expose his narrator's guilt. In short, the narrator is but a pawn in the author's general scheme.

I

Before analyzing the specific rhetorical devices used in *Lolita*, a few remarks about the possibilities of rhetorical manipulation in narrative in general are necessary.

Any aspect of the narrative text—not only direct statements of the characters or the narrator—can be manipulated for rhetorical purposes. Hrushovski[10] considers that the literary text can be described by a three-dimensional model: (1) a complex of speech-events; (2) a semantic complex of meanings and references embodying a "world" with people, objects, places, etc.; (3) an aesthetically organized structure, for the organization of which some aspects of (1) and (2)—as well as other devices—are used.

The text is in the first place a complex linguistic structure, which is presented to the reader as a multi-level embedding of speech-events ("énonciations" in the French terminology): The text as a whole represents a discourse of the author, directed at his potential readers. The author presents a narrator or speaker, who in turn presents the characters. As a result, we are usually faced with a basic three-level structure of addressers and addressees, which can be schematically described as follows:[11]

$$A\ [\underline{S\ (c \longleftrightarrow c)\ Ad}]\ R$$

(A = author, S = speaker, c = character, Ad = addressee, R = reader,[ ], ( ) = embedding.)

Only the underlined part represents the verbal material of the text, though the only act of communication taking place in reality is between the two extreme elements of the model: the author, whose intentions are reconstructed by the reader on the basis of material given in the text[12] and the reader himself. The rest is part of the fictional world, which means that it consists of *imitations* of speech-acts, which have no performative force in the real world.[13]

The narrator may be just a "voice," an almost transparent and hardly felt subject of the speech-events (in which case I prefer to call him "speaker" or "subject of enunciation"). But he may also be a well-identified person, who is an active agent of the fictional world. This is the case of the so-called "first person narration."[14] In personal narratives such as *Lolita*, where the narrator tells us about himself, the identity of the different subjects of enunciation may be represented as follows:

$$A \neq (S = c)$$

(the author is different from the speaker, who is identical with the main character).[15]

Often, when the text presents us with a well-identified narrator, there is also an explicit addressee (or "narratee") who is the immediate target of the speaker's speech-act. This fictional addressee should not be confused with the reader, just as the author should not be confused with the speaker of the literary discourse.[16] This principle holds true even when the narratee is referred to as "my dear reader" and the like, since he is always part of the fictional world, and is often endowed with qualities which suit the rhetorical purposes of the speaker and/or author. The addressee, just like the narrator, can be only implied by the text, or can be a fully realized persona, with a profession, a name and other identifying qualities. How the addressee can be manipulated for rhetorical purposes will be shown later.

Every subject of enunciation in the above mentioned hierarchical model of speech-events governs the speech-event(s) embedded in his own (and reported by him), and can manipulate them directly or indirectly and drive home certain values and attitudes. The subject of the embedded speech normally does not have access to the higher level discourse (it can "infiltrate" the higher speech in the form of the so-called "free indirect speech," but it cannot *use* it for its own rhetorical purposes). The author, being the highest frame of all the other speech-instances, the one in which all the others are embedded, is the highest authority and the one responsible for the whole verbal structure and its total message.

There are three main strategies for manipulating others' speech: (1) *Selection*—a narrator cannot report everything which might have been said by all the characters of the fictional world (the narration being necessarily limited in scope). He therefore has to select material which is reported either directly (as direct speech or quotation) or indirectly. The quoted or reported speech is then at the mercy of the higher-level speaker, who can decide whom, and how much, to quote. (2) *Interpretation*—the higher subject of enunciation can always add his own commentary to the speech quoted, thus attributing to it false intentions and meanings, changing emphasis or inserting it in the wrong context. (3) *Alteration*—or misrepresentation—of others' speech, which happens when the narrator is extremely "unreliable." This can occur even when the embedded speech-event is in the form of a direct speech or a document such as a letter or a diary. Humbert resorts to this maneuver more than once. For example, that is how he "quotes" a hotel manager who was trying to persuade him that the hotel beds were big enough: " 'One crowded night we had three ladies and a child like yours sleep together. I believe one of the ladies was a disguised man (my static)' " (120). Obviously, this method is effective only if the reader is somehow informed that the quoted speech was actually misquoted (here by the insertion of "my static"), otherwise he accepts it at face value, according to the convention that whatever is in quotation marks is a direct and accurate quote.

Similar procedures can be applied to the "world" which the speech-events embody: the different speakers can omit relevant information about characters, events, atmosphere, ideas, etc., and they can distort, misinterpret or misrepresent them. Their freedom to do so depends, though, on their respective location in the speech-hierarchy. It is only the author who can *create* the fictive world and do so in a way which is most suitable for his rhetorical purposes. All other speakers are limited to the reality of the fictive world, and their statements about it can typically be verified by checking them against other statements in the same work which refer to this "internal field of reference" (to use Hrushovski's terminology).[17]

The organization of the text and of each of the speech-events can be turned into a most powerful rhetorical device. The order in which information is disclosed—by the author and/or by the fictive speakers—is most crucial for the general effect of any narrative. The sequential unfolding of information can be manipulated in a variety of ways, such as delayed communication of favorable (or unfavorable) facts, disclosure of charged materials at strategic points, etc.[18] Moreover, the material can be organized in such a way as subtly to imply a network of negative and positive analogies between characters, events, actions.

Again, it is ultimately the author who is responsible for the choice of speakers, for the details of the fictional world, and for the overall organization of the text, and if he is successful, they are all used to convey *his* message.

II

In order to create the desired delicate balance between the reader's feelings of identification with and rejection of Humbert, Nabokov makes some initial decisions of over-all strategy which have crucial consequences for the rhetorical structure of the novel. Since Humbert has so much working against him (the reader knows from the outset that he is a criminal and a murderer, though the specifics of the crimes are not yet disclosed), the author's first moves are aimed at investing him with some special advantages to offset the negative balance: (1) *Choice of point of view* from which the narrative is told—Nabokov decided to unfold the story from the criminal's point of view. We can easily imagine how different the book would have been had it been narrated from the perspective of an uninvolved witness, or (so much the worse for Humbert) from Lolita's point of view. When we are given a glimpse into Lolita's feelings (always through a Humbertian filter, and mainly towards the end of the novel), we get an idea what such a story would have been like:

> In her washed-out gray eyes (. . .) our poor romance was for a moment reflected, pondered upon, and dismissed like a dull party, like a rainy picnic to which only the dullest bores had come, like a humdrum exercise, like a bit of dry mud caking her childhood (274).
>
> [. . .] I was to her not a boy friend, not a glamour man, not a pal, not even a person at all, but just two eyes and a foot of engorged brawn—to mention only mentionable matters (285).

Notice that due to the fact that they are introduced from Humbert's point of view even such paragraphs that point quite strongly at his guilt still make the reader sympathize, in the first place, with *him*: The context is always Humbert's emotional world, and in this context what is communicated to us is *his* pain when realizing how meaningless he was for Lolita. (2) *Choice of voice*—not only is the narrative told from Humbert's point of view, but he is the one who tells it, in his own words, using his own rhetoric (the novel could be told from his point of view, but by an impersonal narrator, for example).[19] Hence it is a personal (or "first-person") narration, and as such one of the best devices to induce the reader's identification with the hero (or anti-hero, if you wish). It is not surprising that personal narration with an inside-view of the narrator's emotional world is used in many modern narratives (e.g., Mailer's *An American Dream*) which portray criminal or otherwise immoral or reprehensible behavior, and where the author wishes the reader to sympathize (at least partially or temporarily) with the hero. (3) *Choice of character*—in order further to secure our empathy for the criminal-speaker, Nabokov presents us with an intelligent, well-educated, middle-class man, with good manners and a sharp tongue—a man with whom the average reader can easily identify. Moreover, he is a sophisticated rhetorician, who is able to present his case in a most skillful manner (whence Booth's complaint about "the reader's inability to dissociate himself from a vicious center of consciousness presented to him with all of the seductive self-justification of skillful rhetoric."[20] (4) *A decision to give Humbert full control over the discourse.* In many personal narratives the author introduces some independent speech-events in the form of letters, diaries, or reliable quotations of characters other than the main narrator. This enables the reader to check, verify and put the narrator's speech into perspective. Thus, for example, Faulkner's *The Sound and the Fury* is comprised of three independent personal speech-events (or "monologues"), and one impersonal section, which helps us to further check off the subjective interpretation of events of the three other sections. In *Lolita* Nabokov refrains from using this device. All we have to rely on (with the exception of the tongue-in-cheek "Preface" by John Ray, Jr. and a few quotations of Lolita's) is Humbert's continuous discourse.

Before proceeding to describe the rhetorical devices used by Humbert once he is given formal control over the discourse, it should be emphasized once again that his control is only apparent, that everything he does and says is ultimately manipulated by the author.

III

The text of *Lolita* is supposedly written by Humbert as a defense-speech which he intends to read during his trial. This is the realistic motivation for the highly argumentative and rhetorical style which he uses. My discussion will necessarily be limited only to the major devices which Humbert resorts to. I will start with a description of the general strategies used by the narrator to unfold his story, I will then discuss direct arguments of self-justification, and finally I will point to some of the more subtle and indirect rhetorical devices.

As mentioned above, the entire narrative is composed of Humbert's continuous discourse. All other speech-events are embedded in his and are therefore at his mercy. He takes advantage of this by exercising his privilege of *selection*. Thus, one of the major strategies he employs for self-justification is simply not to allow his potential accuser, Lolita, to voice her complaints. There are very few direct quotations of her speech in the novel, and not many indirect presentations or summaries of it either. Her direct speech is conspicuously absent especially through the crucial chapters 1–29 of Part II which describe the relationship between Humbert and Lolita during their "cohabitation." Typically, when Humbert recounts a heated argument between them during that period—an occasion on which Lolita apparently dared remonstrate with him—he omits most of her accusations with the pretext that "she said unprintable things" (207). What he does allow, though, is reported in indirect speech, to which he adds a description that makes her look almost comic: "She said she loathed me. She made monstrous faces at me, inflating her cheeks and producing a diabolic plopping sound" (207).

Not only is Lolita's voice almost silenced, her point of view, the way she sees the situation and feels about it, is rarely mentioned and can be only surmised by the reader. Again, the realistic justification is quite simple: since it is Humbert who tells the story, it seems natural that he should emphasize his own emotions. The result is that throughout most of the novel the reader is absorbed in Humbert's feelings of fear, desire, suffering, etc., and tends to forget Lolita's side of the story.

What seems like an innocent preoccupation with himself is soon revealed to be a deliberate suppression of important information on the part of the narrator. For many long pages, while trying to build up his defense and prove to his "judges" that, in his words, "I did everything in my power to give my Lolita a really good time" (165), there is no mention of Lolita's feelings, or even of facts that could suggest how she felt. But, as argued above, the author does not wish the reader to be completely taken in by Humbert. Constantly striving to create the desired balance, Nabokov makes his narrator disclose some of the suppressed information, and in strategically foregrounded points. These are, for example, the concluding sentences of the first part of the novel, describing the night after Humbert first makes love to Lolita, after their first "quarrel," and after she finds out that her mother is dead:

> At the hotel we had separate rooms, but in the middle of the night she came sobbing into mine, and we made it up very gently. You see, she had absolutely nowhere else to go (144).

Later on, half-disguised by the catalogue of items which precedes it, the truth of her suffering again emerges for a short moment, only to disappear again in Humbert's flow of rhetoric:

> [. . .] our long journey [. . .] in retrospect, was no more to us than a collection of dog-eared maps, ruined books, old tires, and her sobs in the night—every night, every night—the moment I feigned sleep (178).

Evidently she cries every night, and he has known it for quite some time, but mentions it here for the first (and only) time.

Such revealing passages are, however, rare. Only at the end of the story, in one of the last chapters of the book (Ch. 32) is the truth fully admitted, the crime against the lonely, helpless and desperate child fully acknowledged.[21] Which brings us to the general question of the distribution of information in the novel and its motivation.

The fictive preface of Dr. John Ray, Jr. informs the reader that Humbert wrote his narrative in prison, while awaiting his trial. This means that when Humbert begins writing the story, he already knows its end, and everything leading to it. Moreover, Humbert as narrator (the "narrating I") has learned a few things about himself that as an "experiencing I" he did not yet realize:[22] mainly the fact that he was, and still is, truly in love with Lolita. Still, he (and the author) chooses to unfold events in their chronological order, limiting himself (and the reader) most of the time to his past perspective and knowledge.[23]

Humbert's expressed motivation for choosing his past perspective as a principle of disclosure and distribution of information is his devotion to "retrospective verisimilitude" (73). "I am only a conscientious recorder" he announces innocently (74). The question is what are the rhetorical advantages and disadvantages of this choice both for the narrator and for the author.

Telling his story in chronological order and limiting himself to his past perspective enable Humbert to take advantage of the characteristics of two distinct types of personal narration—the *diary* and the *memoir*.[24] The main characteristic of the diary is the minimal distance between the narrator's "epic situation" (i.e., the situation of telling the story) and the events described. As result, the narrator's experiences are conveyed most vividly, with the immediacy of an experience just gone through. Humbert uses this technique to dramatize the past, to evoke in great detail past events described. As a result, the narrator's experiences are conveyed most The more scenic and dramatized the narration, the more closely is the reader brought into contact with the material, identifies with it and accepts it as human and "understandable."

However, since the story is, after all, a memoir, written some years after the initial events took place, Humbert can allow himself to intervene from time to time from the vantage point of his "reformed" and remorseful narrating self. Thus he can remind us at a delicate point—i.e., when describing how he was waiting in the hotel-lobby for Lolita to fall asleep after administering to her a dose of sleeping pills—that he now regrets it all (125).

Humbert pays dearly, though, for the advantages gained. Most of the time the reader is confronted with the cruel, cynical, unfeeling, egotistic self of his past, obsessed with the nymphet in Lolita and totally disregarding her feelings ("it was always my habit and method to ignore Lolita's states of mind while comforting my own base self," [289] as he himself admits at the end of the novel). On the whole, unfolding the story from the point of view of the experiencing self is more damaging for

Humbert than advantageous. So much so, that one might wonder how come a clever rhetoretician like Humbert did not realize these consequences of his choice. Had he started the story with some of the later expressions of true love for Lolita ("how much I love my Lolita, *this* Lolita, pale and polluted, and big with another's child," [280]), had he taken upon himself the full blame from the outset ("Unless it can be proven to me—to me as I am now, today, [. . .]—that in the infinite run it does it does not matter a jot that a North American girl-child named Dolores Haze had been deprived of her childhood by a maniac, unless this can be proven (and if it can, then life is a joke), I see nothing for the treatment of my misery [. . .]," [285])—he would have had the reader's sympathy on his side all along. But that is precisely what Nabokov wants to prevent.

It is Nabokov, of course, who makes Humbert choose the less advantageous way. While the chosen narrative perspective, as far as the *narrator* is concerned, works both to his advantage and to his disadvantage, in the hands of the *author* it is an ideal tool for properly balancing the reader's reaction to Humbert.

Nabokov has also an aesthetic motivation for preferring this narrative perspective, namely to create his own version of a suspense-story and to play with the reader's expectations. In *Lolita* we know from the beginning that Humbert is imprisoned for having committed a crime, probably murder. We do not know the exact nature of the crime, and if it is murder—who was the victim. This question is a source of great suspense in the novel, especially since the narrator (who is a true representative of the author's intentions in this respect) constantly "teases" the reader and leads him to form false hypotheses. Thus, in contrast to the conventional "whodonit," here the central question is rather "what-was-done" and "who-was-done-in." Humbert could have been arrested for rape of a minor, or for transporting a minor across state lines (the Mann Act). If the crime was murder, there are a few possible victims. The first is Charlotte, Lolita's mother: after a number of hints that something terrible will happen to her ("a bad accident is to happen soon," [81]), and dreams about her death ("Her mother is messily but instantly and permanently annihilated," [55]), he actually plans to kill her, and keeps the reader on edge for a few pages before admitting that "I just could not make myself do it" (89). Another candidate is Lolita herself, whom he could have murdered out of anger, fear or, at the end, jealousy and revenge (although the preface informs us that "Mrs. 'Richard F. Schiller' died in childbed" [6] we discover only at the end of the novel that this is Lolita's marital name). He misleads us to think of such a possibility when he quotes a song about Carmen (he often calls Lolita "Carmen"): "And the gun I killed you with, O my Carmen, The gun I am holding now." (64), and again at the end, when he goes to meet Lolita (now Mrs. Schiller) for the last time, his gun in his pocket (" 'Husband at home?' I croaked, fist in pocket. I could not kill *her*, of course, as some have thought," [272]).

Lolita's husband is another possible victim ("I rehearsed Mr. Richard F. Schiller's violent death," [269]). However, the real victim—as we find out only in chapter 35—is Quilty, the debauched playwright and Humbert's double.[26]

IV

Typically, Humbert's discourse (with the exception of the last chapters) is a mixture of self-accusation and self-justification. He often calls himself "maniac," "hound," and other derogatory names, but he usually gives the impression that he is half-jesting, that the self-accusation is only lip-service, part of his rhetorical schemes. He is evidently trying the best he can to "explain" himself to his judges and to prove that he is not really guilty of any crime. There are numerous overt statements to that effect in the novel (e.g., "I insist upon proving that I am not, and never was, and never could be, a brutal scoundrel," [133]). They are easy to detect and require no special comment. I would like to mention only a few arguments of self-justification which Humbert resorts to quite often when overtly defending himself.

The first argument which Humbert employs as a justification of his crime is a psychological one:[27] childhood fixation, the cause of which is an unconsummated childhood love for a young girl during a summer vacation in a resort hotel on the beach. The girl died shortly afterwards:

> [. . .] there might have been no Lolita at all had I not loved, one summer, a certain initial girl-child. In a princedom by the sea (11);
>
> All I want to stress is that my discovery of her [Lolita] was a fatal consequence of that "princedom by the sea" in my tortured past (42, cf., also, 17, 41).

With the passage of time the need to redeem the past, to "break the spell," to close the circle, turns into a disease, almost madness (Humbert was actually hospitalized a few times in mental institutions). Hence the term "nympholepsy" which Humbert uses to refer to his "condition," suggesting a mental disorder ("lepsy" = seizure, as in "epilepsy.")[28] Moreover, using this term he implies that this is a known and recognized disease, and that he is not the only case (e.g., "nympholepts," [19]). But a sick man cannot be considered responsible for his actions, and Humbert does his best to emphasize this argument.

Another line of self-justification, very different from the above-mentioned one, rests on very detailed and learned accounts, spread throughout the book, of cases which supposedly prove that moral rules and taboos have only relative value, since they differ from country to country and from period to period:

> Marriage and cohabitation before puberty are still not uncommon in certain East Indian provinces. Lepcha old men of eighty copulate with girls of eight, and nobody minds. After all, Dante fell madly in love with his Beatrice when she was nine [. . .]. And when Petrarch fell madly in love with his Laureen, she was a fair-haired nymphet of twelve [. . .] (21).

According to this line of reasoning, Humbert is neither a sick pervert nor a criminal ("I have but followed nature," as he claims elsewhere [137]). He is only an unfortunate victim of an arbitrary social convention: "I found myself maturing amid a civilization which allows a man of twenty-five to court a girl of sixteen but not a girl of twelve" (20). The argument conceals a misleading analogy, though: he is not twenty-five, but probably about thirty-five, and he does not *court* Lolita, but forces her into a relationship which she detests.

Blaming Lolita for the past is another convenient excuse. Humbert tries very hard to prove that despite the uncontrollable urge to satisfy his sexual needs, and despite the fact that after her mother's death Lolita was completely at his mercy, "I was firmly resolved to pursue my policy of sparing her purity by operating only in the stealth of the night, only upon a completely anesthetized little nude" (126). It was Lolita who seduced him, he claims, and he was not even her first lover (see 134–137). He depicts himself as a naive lover, confused and nervous ("What a comic, clumsy, wavering Prince Charming I was!" [111]), while she is a corrupt, experienced, vulgar little girl, who knows no shame. Humbert might be faithfully reporting the situation when he says that "not a trace of modesty did I perceive in this beautiful hardly formed young girl, whom modern co-education, juvenile mores, the campfire racket and so forth had utterly and hopelessly depraved" (135). We also have no reason to disbelieve him when he claims that he was not the one who deflowered Lolita. He would have liked us to think that these are the strongest accusations against him, that this is the worst he could possibly do to her. The point is that the above arguments have little to do with his culpability. They serve only to divert the reader's attention from Humbert's real crimes.[29] He himself knows (and admits) that her earlier sexual experiences were but part of a common, "tough kid" game: "While eager to impress me with the world of tough kids, she was not quite prepared for certain discrepancies between a kid's life and mine. Pride alone prevented her from giving up" (136).

Yet another strategy Humbert uses for exonerating himself is claiming that Lolita is a "nymphet." Being a nymphet, she is not, according to his learned theories, a normal child anyway, but a demon disguised as a child. Listen to this "scientific" lecture-for-beginners on nymphets, nympholepts and nympholepsy—notice the charm of the poetic language and the rhetoric it hides:

> Between the age of nine and fourteen there occur maidens who, to certain *bewitched travelers*, twice or many times older than they, reveal *their true nature which is not human, but nymphic (that is demonic)*. [. . .] You have to be an *artist* and a *madman*, a creature of infinite melancholy, with a bubble of hot poison in your loins and a super-voluptuous flame permanently aglow in your subtle spine [. . .], in order to discern at once, by ineffable signs [. . .] the little deadly demon among the wholesome children" (18–19, my emphasis).

Thus, while seemingly describing objective facts, Humbert transforms the pervert into a "betwitched traveler" haunted by the deadly nymphet. Notice the plural ("travelers") and the second person ("you")—he is not alone in the plight! It is his special sensitivity ("you have to be an artist and a madman") which makes him vulnerable to the magical power of the "demons." After making love to Lolita for the first time Humbert describes her body as "the body of some immortal daemon disguised as a child" (141), and one of the many (often contradictory) reasons he gives for writing the story is the need "to fix once and for all the perilous magic of nymphets" (136). You see, it is they who are dangerous, not he. He treats Lolita accordingly, as a bewitching, adorable nymphet—but not as the human, lonely child she really is.

As can be seen from the examples quoted here, and from many others in the novel, Humbert's overt rhetoric is seen through without too much difficulty. The indirect devices he uses are much more difficult to detect, and therefore easier to succumb to.

V

In standard language the speech situation is consistent and the first and second person refer uniquely. In Banfield's words: "For every expression (E), there is a unique referent of *I* (the speaker) and a unique referent of *you* (the addressee)."[30] In other words, the speaker and the addressee remain the same throughout a given speech-unit. Most narratives respect this rule and present a consistent speech situation. Not so in *Lolita*. Humbert sometimes addresses his words to a jury or to a judge, and sometimes to a reader. He thereby implies the co-existence of two different and inconsistent speech-situations: that of a defendent in court (who is also his own defense lawyer), with the jury as audience (Ad1), and that of an author in prison, writing a manuscript to be published as a book and read by readers (Ad2). The real reader (us as readers-R) is encouraged to visualize at times the first situation, at other times the second, according to details mentioned by the speaker which imply the one or the other. Compare, for example, the two following groups of utterances:

I. "Ladies and gentlemen of the jury, exhibit number one is [. . .]" (11); "I am going to pass around in a minute some [. . .] picture-postcards"

(11); "Exhibit number two is a pocket diary [. . .]" (12); "Ladies and gentlemen of the jury, I wept" (105).

II. "I want my learned readers to participate in the scene [. . .]" (59); "However, I shall not bore my learned readers with a detailed account" (135); "[. . .] the reader (ah, if I could visualize him as a blond-bearded scholar with rosy lips sucking *la pomme de sa canne* as he quaffs my manuscript!)" (228).

The incongruity of the implied speech-situations becomes especially evident when Humbert changes addressees in the middle of recounting one scene (see 59 and 63). This incongruity receives a somewhat forced explanation at the end of the novel, when Humbert explains that he first meant this memoir to be his defense speech at his trial, but later decided that the facts should not be made known as long as Lolita lives, and that the document should instead be published as a book after her death (310). However, this fails to account for the fact that the apostrophe to the reader appears for the first time very early in the novel, and that the jury is still addressed towards the end. The truth is that Humbert needs both addressees for building up his defense, and he shrewdly plays the one (the reader) against the other.

The main strategy employed in the discourse addressed to Ad1 is reasoning. Using some of the arguments mentioned above, as well as many others, Humbert tries to prove to the "ladies and gentlemen of the jury" that he is actually innocent of any crime (e.g. "Ladies and gentlemen of the jury, the majority of sex offenders [. . .] are innocuous, inadequate, passive, timid strangers who merely ask the community to allow them to pursue their practically harmless, so-called aberrant behavior, [. . .] without the police and society cracking down upon them. We are not sex fiends! We do not rape as good soldiers do" [89–90]). Slowly, his tone changes when he addresses them and turns into sarcasm, directed mainly at the women among them: "Gentlewomen of the jury! Bear with me! Allow me to take just a tiny bit of your precious time!" (125). Eventually, it turns into an implicit accusation of the jury, suggesting that they have no right to judge him, that they represent conventionality, and are therefore unable to understand the "artist" and "madman": "Frigid gentlewomen of the jury! [. . .] I am going to tell you something very strange [. . .]" (134). Of course, by ridiculing Ad1, Humbert subtly courts Ad2—the reader—suggesting that *he* is neither frigid (or impotent) nor conventional in his way of thinking, and therefore able to understand.

This attack on the jury is intensified when Humbert addresses it with what at first seems to be a peculiar adjective: "Oh, *winged* gentlemen of the jury [. . .]" (127. Cf., 232). On the one hand, Humbert might be implying that he actually addresses his defense not to the jury of flesh and blood, but to a higher authority ("I thought I would use these notes in toto in my trial, to save not my head, but my soul," [310] he states at the end of the novel. My emphasis). On the other hand, if we turn to Edgar Allen Poe's poem "Annabel Lee," we shall discover that this adjective cleverly conceals an accusation against the jury. Poe's poem plays an important role in *Lolita*.[31] Humbert's childhood love story is a re-enactment of the love described in the poem:

> She was a child and I was a child
>   in this kingdom by the sea.
> But we loved with a love that was more than love—
>   I and my Annabel Lee—
> With a love that the *winged seraphs* of Heavens
>   Coveted her and me.
> (my emphasis)

It is the jealousy of the "winged seraphs" which brings about the death of both Poe's and Humbert's Annabel, and when Humbert opens the story of his childhood love he echoes Poe's lines: "Ladies and gentlemen of the jury, exhibit number one is what the seraphs, the misinformed, simple, *noble-winged* seraphs, envied" (11, my emphasis). Referring to the jurors as "winged gentlemen" means, therefore, accusing them of being envious (and maybe also simple, and misinformed) of his love for Lolita.

The strategy towards Ad2 is different: "the reader" is addressed mostly as a friend and equal, and he is called upon to participate in the events and emphathize with the speaker ("I want my learned reader to participate in the scene [. . .]" [59]). As Humbert's attitude toward Ad1 becomes more critical and cynical, his tone when addressing Ad2 becomes gradually warmer and warmer. The increased number of adjectives and exclamations such as "my Reader" (76), "O, Reader, my Reader!" (205) can testify to that. Moreover, the capital "R" used here and on other occasions is intended to create the impression that the unknown addressee is actually a familiar person, whose given name is simply "Reader." Eventually, the reader is addressed as "comrade" (169) and "Bruder" (= "brother," 264)—echoing the famous lines of Baudelaire's *Les fleurs du mal* and implying a shared guilt ("Hypocrite lecteur,—mon semblable,—mon frère").

An interesting device used for manipulating Ad2 ("Reader"), and through him R (the actual reader) is what Bakhtin[32] calls "the internal polemic"—a discourse which is aware of another (often antagonistic) discourse, and reacts to it either by replying to it or by anticipating it. Humbert's speech-acts are often a reaction to an assumed or anticipated comment of his addressee. But the supposed reaction of the addressee, which can be reconstructed from Humbert's words, is not the reader's most likely reaction, but rather what Humbert would have wished it to be. What actually happens is that Humbert tries to dictate an attitude to the reader, by formulating his attitude for him. Here is an example: the relations between Humbert and Lolita have reached the stage where she (hoping to free herself of him) takes advantage of his lust to extort money from him. Clearly, it is he who prostituted her in the first place, paying her from the beginning a weekly allowance "under condition she fulfilled her basic obligations" (185), and demanding to be sexually compensated for fulfilling any of her wishes. Now he complains about the "drop in Lolita's morals," and asks the reader not to laugh at him: "O Reader! Laugh not, as you imagine me, on the very rack of joy, noisily emitting dimes and quarters [. . .]" (186). But does the reader really feel like laughing? The situation is more tragic than comic (tragic mainly when considered from Lolita's point of view). Using the "internal polemic" technique, Humbert tries to force a certain position on the reader, and to make him consider the situation from his, rather than Lolita's, perspective.

The same technique is used in the novel's most delicate situation, which requires Humbert's most powerful rhetoric—the first time he makes love to Lolita. He gives her sleeping pills, and waits for her to fall asleep. They are both in bed, but he is afraid that she is not yet fast asleep and delays his planned action. Describing these moments he addresses the reader as follows: "Please, reader: no matter your exasperation with the tenderhearted, morbidly sensitive, infinitely circumspect hero of my book, do not skip these essential pages!" (131). Not only does Humbert ascribe here to the reader a rather positive judgement of himself (tenderhearted, sensitive, etc.), but he actually implies that the reader is impatient to see the deed done, and would have liked Humbert to be more resolute in the execution of his design to rape the twelve-year-old girl.

The duality of the addressee finds its counterpart in a duality of the speaker himself. As previously mentioned, there is a narratively inevitable duality of the protagonist, who is both the "narrating I" of the present and the "experiencing I" of the past. Furthermore, while according to the norms of standard language, a speaker refers to himself using the first person pronoun, Humbert often does so in the third person, thus suggesting a split between the "I" and the "not I":[33] "there must have been times, if I know my Humbert—when [. . .]" (72); "So Humbert the Cubus schemed and dreamed" (73); "Oh miserly Hamburg! Was he not a very Enchanted Hunter as he deliberated with himself [. . .]" (111), and so on.

This duality, or "split," in the personality of the speaker is further underlined by Humbert's utilization of his favorite figure of speech: the synecdoche. Trying to create the impression that it was not he, but the "other" in him, who stealthily fondled Lolita, who plotted the crime, he often resorts to statements such as the following (with my emphasis): "*my glance* slithered over the kneeling child . . . the *vacuum of my soul* managed to suck in every detail of her bright beauty" (41); "Humbert the Hoarse put *his arm* around her" (50); "*My hand* swept over her agile giggling legs" (57) "*My knuckles* lay against the child's blue jeans" (53); "*my tentacles* moved towards her" (132). The split is between body and mind, and the body is presented as acting on its own, against the inclinations of the soul, or, as he himself summarizes it: "While my body knew what it craved for, my mind rejected my body's every plea" (20).

VII

In spite of the fact that the author hands the narrative over to Humbert, in spite of the fact that everything is seen through Humbertian eyes, in spite of Humbert's cajolery and argumentation, his cruelty towards Lolita, the harm done her, cannot be smoothed over. The reader need not be "most skillful and mature"[34] to realize that Lolita complies out of fear and despair. Enough details indicating her condition are spread throughout the story. We are told that she has nowhere else to go (144), that she cries every night (178), that Humbert terrorizes her in different ways to keep her submissive (150–153). He isolates her from other children, bribes her with money, which he later steals from her (186), and with promises which he later retracts (171). He imposes his sexual demands upon her even when she is sick and feverish (200), and resorts to force when necessary ("[. . .] thrusting my fatherly fingers deep into Lo's hair from behind, and then gently but firmly clasping them around the nape of her neck, I would lead my reluctant pet to our small home for a quick connection before dinner," [166]).

That Lolita does not enjoy the whole thing (to put it mildly), is clear, and Humbert himself admits it at quite an early stage:

> She had entered my world, umber and black Humberland, with rash curiosity. She surveyed it with a shrug of amused distaste; and it seemed to me now that she was ready to turn away from it with something akin to plain repulsion (168).

All this taken into account, it is hard to agree with Trilling that the novel (i.e., Nabokov) brings us "to condone the violation it presents"[35] The reader is made to see the violation all along and must condemn it, especially at the end, when Humbert explains the full damage he has inflicted upon Lolita ("oh, my poor, bruised child," [286]).

Paradoxically, the fullest disclosure of Humbert's guilt triggers the reader's strongest feelings of sympathy for him (though *not* for his deeds!). It is his self-castigation, his readiness to face and admit his guilt, and his suffering at the realization of the truth, that make us accept him. At the end of the narrative he at last gives up the cynicism underlying his rhetoric, and his tone becomes more sincere. For the first time he is now able to transcend his self-centered passions and think of Lolita as a human being:

> What I heard was but the melody of children at play, [. . .] and then I knew that the hopelessly poignant thing was not Lolita's absence from my side, but the absence of her voice from that concord (310).

Moreover, only at the end does he (and therefore the reader) understand that he actually loves Lolita, not the nymphet in her. When he first meets her and announces that "I knew I had fallen in love with Lolita forever" his love is actually directed at "the eternal Lolita as reflected in my blood" (67). The thought which often haunts him during their trip is that "around 1950 I would have to get rid somehow of a difficult adolescent whose magic nymphage had evaporated" (176). But after confronting the grown-up, pregnant Lolita, "hopelessly worn at seventeen" (279), he understands himself and his love: "[. . .] I looked and looked at her, and knew as clearly as I know that I am to die, that I loved her more than anything I had ever seen or imagined on earth, or hoped for anything else" (279).

Seen that way for the first time—without his jesting pose, suffering for the pain he had inflicted on the girl, and realizing that his love transcends his passion—Humbert at last wins us over, as the author intends him to.

Notes

1. An earlier version of this paper was presented at the Conference on Culture and Communication, Temple University, Philadelphia, March, 1977, and appears in *The Structural Analysis of Narrative Texts: Conference Papers*, ed. Andrej Kodjak, Michael J. Connolly, and Krystyna Pomorska (Slavica Publishers, Inc.: N.Y.U. Slavic Papers II, 1980).

2. For a bibliography of these early reviews see Jackson R. Bryer, "Vladimir Nabokov's Critical Reputation in English: A Note and a Checklist," *Wisconsin Studies in Contemporary Literature*, VIII (1967), pp. 335–340. The bibliography is reprinted in *Nabokov: The Man and His Work*, ed. L. S. Dembo (University of Wisconsin Press, 1967).

3. See especially Carl R. Proffer, *Keys to Lolita* (Bloomington: Indiana University Press, 1968) and Appel's *The Annotated Lolita* (see note 4 below).

4. Vladimir Nabokov, *The Annotated Lolita*, ed. Alfred Appel, Jr. (McGraw-Hill, 1970), p. 7. All subsequent references to *Lolita* are to this edition.

5. Norman Miller, *The Self-Conscious Narrator-Protagonist in American Fiction Since World War II* (Unpublished dissertation, University of Wisconsin, 1972), pp. 188, 198.

6. Lionel Trilling, "The Last Lover—Vladimir Nabokov's 'Lolita'," *Encounter*, XI, 4 (1958), p. 14.

7. Wayne C. Booth, *The Rhetoric of Fiction* (University of Chicago Press, 1961), p. 390.

8. Alfred Appel, Jr., "*Lolita*: The Springboard of Parody," *Wisconsin Studies in Contemporary Literature*, VIII (1967), p. 224. The essay is reprinted in *Nabokov: The Man and His Work.*

9. Quoted by Appel in *The Annotated Lolita*, xl.

10. Benjamin Hrushovski, "A Three-Dimensional Model of Semiotic Objects," Paper presented at the International Conference on the Semiotics of Art, Ann Arbor, Michigan, May 1978.

11. An earlier version of this scheme, which took into account only the speech-situation

of personal (first person) narratives, was presented in Nomi Tamir, "Personal Narrative and Its Linguistic Foundations," *PTL*, I (1976), p. 423. That early version did not yet locate the addressee in the speech-situation. The scheme suggested here was developed and formalized in collaboration with Benjamin Hrushovski. It is presented and discussed at length in our article, "Speech and Position in Literature: A General Model," *Poetics Today* (forthcoming).

12. Cf. Mikhail Bakhtin, "Discourse Typology in Prose," in *Readings in Russian Poetics* (MIT Press, 1971), p. 179.

13. Cf. Richard Ohmann, "Speech Acts and the Definition of Literature," *Philosophy and Rhetoric*, IV (1971), pp. 1–19.

14. Or "personal narration," see Tamir, "Personal Narrative and Its Linguistic Foundations."

15. By "identical" I mean simply that the speaker and the main character appear as one and the same person in the fictional world.

16. See Gerald Prince, "Notes Towards a Categorization of Fictional 'Narratees'," *Genre*, IV (1971), pp. 100–106 and "Introduction à l'étude du narrataire," *Poétique*, XIV (1973), pp. 178–196.

17. See *Segmentation and Motivation in the Text Continuum of Literary Prose: The First Episode of "War and Peace," Papers on Poetics and Semiotics*, V (The Porter Institute for Poetics and Semiotics: Tel Aviv University).

18. This aspect was developed theoretically and demonstrated in detail by M. Perry (see especially his research on Bialik, Mendele, Faulkner). For a recent publication devoted to this subject see Meir Sternberg, *Expositional Modes & Temporal Ordering in Fiction* (Johns Hopkins University Press: 1978).

19. On the distinction between voice and focalization see Gérard Genette, *Figures III* (Seuil, 1972), p. 203 and Tamir, "Personal Narrative and Its Linguistic Foundations."

20. Booth, p. 390.

21. One of the "twists" of the novel is that Humbert's crime against Lolita is neither rape (she complies) nor defloration (she was not a virgin), but having destroyed her childhood, her life and her spirit.

22. On the distinction between the "erzählendes Ich" and the "erlebendes Ich" see Leo Spitzer, "Zum Stil Marcel Proust," in L. Spitzer, *Stilstudien 2* (N. Hueber, 1928).

23. This is a different case from the one discussed above. Here we are dealing with temporarily withheld information, with realistic justification, while before we discussed important information which was suppressed in spite of the fact that it was already known to the experiencing self.

24. For a discussion of these (and other) types of personal narrative see Bertil Romberg, *Studies in the Narrative Technique of the First Person Novel* (Almquist & Wiksell, 1962), especially III, 3.

25. Cf. Trilling, p. 14.

26. Cf. Janet K. Gezari, "Roman et problème chez Nabokov," *Poétique*, XVII (1974), pp. 104–107.

27. In *Lolita* Nabokov parodies (among many other things) psychologists and psychotherapy.

28. Cf. Appel's annotation, p. 339.

29. See also footnote 21 above.

30. Ann Banfield, "Narrative Style and the Grammar of Direct and Indirect Speech," *Foundations of Language*, X (1973), p. 20.

31. See Appel's comments, p. 330.

32. "Discourse Typology in Prose."

33. Cf. Daniel Laferrière, "The Subject and Discrepant Use of the Category of Person,"

Paper presented at the First Congress of the International Association for Semiotic Studies, Milan, June 1974.

34. Booth, p. 390.

35. Trilling, p. 14.

Gaming in the Lexical Playfields of Nabokov's *Pale Fire*

Carl Eichelberger*

Give me the creative reader; this is a tale for him.[1]

Vladimir Nabokov's *Pale Fire* demands not only a creative reader, but a reader willing to participate in a series of involuted and complex games woven into the novel's texture. The spirit of play, in the various senses discussed by Johan Huizinga in *Homo Ludens: A Study of the Play Element In Culture*, pervades every thread of *Pale Fire*'s fictional fabric; however, this is not to suggest that Nabokov's phosphorescent masterpiece is to be read in a purely capricious spirit. In the wake of two world wars, his exile across three continents, and the decay of modernist fictional practice, Nabokov's radical achievement in *Pale Fire* is nothing less than a novelistic "amusement park," creating a world of "limited perfection" for the observant reader's delectation.[2] Previous critics have discussed the use of games in *Pale Fire*, but my attempt here is to examine how the trans-individual nature of games reflects Nabokov's stance toward linguistic referentiality, and in turn, toward the reader's involvement with the text. Language can be viewed as a game with culturally conditioned, shifting rules; an inspection of Nabokov's use of games as a formal ordering principle in *Pale Fire* demonstrates how Nabokov subverts both conventional notions of language and realistic notions of character to reveal new fictional possibilities, and engages the reader in the aesthetic problems fiction writing presents to the author.

In Nabokov's career, as in human development, *homo ludens* ("man the player") precedes *homo significans* ("signifying man"). One of Nabokov's first major literary projects was his translation of Lewis Carroll's *Alice In Wonderland* into Russian during his émigré existence in Berlin.[3] Originally published in 1923 under the pseudonym "V. Sirin" three years before his first novel, *Mashen'ka*, *Anya V Stranye Chudes* contains some fine examples of Nabokov's passion for precision, punning, parody, and play. An instance of Nabokov's linguistic dexterity can be seen in his translation of the Mock Turtle into the Russian *Chepupakha*, an ingenious conflation of *cherepakha* ("tortoise") and *chepukha*

*This article appears here for the first time by permission of the author.

("nonsense"). However, this dexterity is not without its sinister side: Nabokov occasionally indulges in playful punning where Carroll's English is normal. For example, Carroll's first chapter, "Down The Rabbit-Hole" in the original, emerges as "Nyrok v krolich'yu norku." Literally, this reads "A Dive into the Rabbit-Hole," but the words chosen for "dive" and "hole" are also designations in Russian for two other animals: *nyrok* is a type of diving duck (its Latin generic name, *Nyroca*, is based on its Russian common name) and *norka*, a diminutive form of *nora*, "hole," also means "mink."[4] In this witty translation, Alice's Wonderland is populated by an entire menagerie before she even departs from her everyday world. This example illustrates merely one instance of Nabokov's unique linguistic manipulation and distortion to create new, heterodox worlds. At about the same time *Anya V Stranye Chudes* was published, Nabokov began composing the first crossword puzzles, *krestoslovitsï*, for the Berlin daily émigré paper *Rul'* (*SM*, 283). Nabokov's fusion of pattern and play through the creation of intricate puns and *krestoslovitsï* indicates the extent to which *Pale Fire*'s creator merges *homo ludens* with *homo significans*.

Nabokov has stated that "I'm not interested in games as such. Games mean the participation of other persons; I'm interested in the lone performance—chess problems, for example, which I compose in glacial solitude."[5] Speaking of *Lolita*, Nabokov declared, "She was like the composition of a beautiful puzzle—its composition and its solution at the same time, since one is a mirror view of the other, depending on the way you look" (*SO*, 20). The threads of *Pale Fire*'s fabric which are wound of play are no longer interesting from Nabokov's perspective since his role in the creative act has been completed, but they become rites of passage for the reader to gain access to the process of literary creation. To enter the "lexical playfields" of *Pale Fire* (*PF*, 184), it is useful to keep the phrases "glacial solitude" and "mirror view" in mind.

Pale Fire is composed in four sections: foreword, Shade's poem, commentary, and index. Except for John Shade's unfinished poem, the other sections fall under the narrative rulership of Charles Kinbote, who may or may not be the exiled king of a distant land, Zembla. Kinbote's foreword begins by supplying basic biographical data about John Francis Shade, the poet of "Pale Fire," and the text assumes the authority of a critical edition. Textual authority, however, is thrown into doubt on the very first page as Kinbote precludes the reader's judgment by calling canto 2 of "Pale Fire" your favorite" (*PF*, 7). This process of initiating what Gérard Genette calls a "narrating instance," that is, the interjection of the artistic text into the ordinary text, begins to define the boundaries of the lexical playfields in terms of "two protagonists: the narrator and his audience, real or implied."[6] By modulating the reader's expectations of textual authority with Kinbote's subjective interjections, Nabokov devises a narrational strategy which complements his linguistic manipulation to reveal heterodox realities and forms, in the words of Shade's poem,

> Just this: not text, but texture; not the dream
> But topsy-turvical coincidence,
> Not flimsy nonsense, but a web of sense. (*PF*, 44: ll. 808–10)

A "web of sense" can be discerned from the play activities in Kinbote's foreword and the patterns they form which uncover thematic content. Kinbote's verbal play manifests itself primarily in circular and reflexive, or agonistic and oscillatory patterns, embodying "glacial solitude" and "mirror views," respectively. The central image of circularity in the foreword is "that carrousel inside and outside my head" (*PF*, 18). Huizinga persuasively argues that circularity is intertwined with the notion of a magician circumscribing and defining a space within which a sacred ritual is to take place, but "there is no distinction whatever between marking out a space for a sacred purpose and marking it out for purposes of sheer play" (*HL*, 20). Kinbote attempts to break out of his circumscribed solitude by playing ping-pong, an agonistic, competitive form of play used by Kinbote to seduce males by defeating them: in this way, ping-pong becomes a distorted "mirror view" and a comic literalization of Freud's term, "narcissism."[7] In the oscillations between these two patterns, Kinbote rides, through linguistic distortion and artistic interjection, his own hobby-horse onto the playfields where the most obvious and extended example of the collapse of the agonistic pattern into the circular occurs in his attempted appropriation of Shade's poem.

Kinbote's mercurial flutterings between these two play patterns become evident too in his confrontation with the head of his department, Dr. Nattochdag (*PF*, 16). The apparent oscillation of this image pattern—Nattochdag meaning "night and day" in Danish—is subsumed by circularity through the phrase "his swivel chair," and the fact that night and day form a natural cycle. But when Kinbote refers to Nattochdag as Netochka, an *agon* is reestablished in linguistic terms which reveals Kinbote's simultaneous sexual desire and frustration regarding Nattochdag. In Russian *netochka* may be a feminine diminutive of *netto*, meaning "net," linking a necessary fixture of Kinbote's ping-pong table with a primary tool used in Nabokov's other special interest, entomology. However, this sort of Kinbotean speculative reading is marvelously undercut when confronted with the possibility that *netochka* may be a feminization of the phrase *net ochko*, meaning "no point" in reference to a game or sport. As we shall see, then, with regard to Kinbote's use of Shade's Word Golf game, Kinbote's attempt to escape his solitude fails in all cases, and the relation he believes he has established leads to "no point."

The Nabokovian "game of worlds" ("PF," l. 819) rests upon the reader's ability to participate in games ranging from the strictly agonistic to the strictly aleatory.[8] Ability to comprehend the novel's structure results from the perception, on the reader's part, that Kinbote's aleatory textual intrusions form part of the pattern of agonistic appropriation.[9] In other words, the reader must subject the games of the text to his or her "combinational turn of mind" (*PF*, 8).

Shade's combinational turn of mind fuses processes of perception and memory in his extended meditation on mortality. Moreover, Shade's poem emphasizes the schism between language as a culturally conditioned system of codes, on the one hand, and subjective perception of natural phenomena, on the other. The opening of Shade's poem demonstrates the ability to exist in simultaneous, parallel worlds through the "mirror view" like Carroll's Alice:

> I was the shadow of the waxwing slain
> By the false azure in the windowpane;
> I was the smudge of ashen fluff—and I
> Lived on, flew on, in the reflected sky. (*PF*, 23: ll. 1–4)

The "false perception" which causes destruction in one world becomes the "true perception" in the parallel world, allowing transcendence in one Phoenix-like, continuous motion.[10] This continuous motion can be represented by a combination of Kinbote's two primary play patterns, the circular and the oscillatory, into a "lemniscate," the mathematical symbol for infinity (*PF*, 26: l. 137).[11] Understanding of the mathematical combinations in *Pale Fire* dispels the widely held critical notion that the "game of worlds" is between Shade and Kinbote, leading to debates about whether Shade creates Kinbote or Kinbote creates Shade, and enforces the view that the clash is between Nabokov and the reader.[12] As Robert Alter suggests, the lemniscate "neatly diagrams the circular reflective relation of Commentary to Poem and Poem to Commentary," but Alter, along with Andrew Field, Page Stegner, and other prominent Nabokovians, assumes a realistic, Jamesian notion of "character" and does not apply the lemniscate as a way of understanding the interrelationship of Kinbote to Shade and vice versa.[13] Kinbote glosses Shade's "lemniscate" as a "unicursal bicircular quartic" (*PF*, 98); the intertwining of fictional qualities which constitute Shade and Kinbote is revealed in the word "unicursal," meaning "having coordinates expressible rationally through a single parameter."[14] Shade and Kinbote together move from Appalachia to Zembla (alphabetically, from *A* to *Z*), suggesting that the topology of the lemniscate has been distorted by the "mirror view," projecting a Mobius strip with only one surface into space, making the "whole involuted, boggling thing one beautiful straight line" (*PF*, 185). Through radical manipulation of Jamesian notions of "point of view" and "character," Nabokov creates a magic world, projecting from a single source of light a spectrum of fictional colors in kaleidoscopic fashion into *Pale Fire*'s house of mirrors.[15]

Of course, mathematical symbols and patterns are specific ways of encoding and decoding information. Shade's poem makes use of other systems of patterning as well:

> Reading from left to right in winter's code:
> A dot, an arrow pointing back; repeat:
> Dot, arrow pointing back. . . . A pheasant's feet! (*PF*, 23: ll. 22–24)

Before the revelation of the pattern as the tracks of a pheasant, the pattern, "Dot, arrow" is analogous to the "dit-dah" of International Morse Code, signifying the letter *A*. This pattern generates a series of games connected with linear, mathematical, and alphabetic sequentiality, but patterns are frequently disrupted by the intervention of aleatory events or "topsy-turvical coincidence."

Origins, ends, and mysteries are all part of these alphabetic games. Sybil Shade (along with her hissing sibilant initials), née Irondell or Swallow, is allergic to all foods which begin with the letter *A*: "artichokes, avocado pears, African acorns" (*PF*, 163). The Goldsworth residence, which Kinbote moves into, is a paradigm of linear, sequential order: Mrs. Goldsworth's intellectual interests range "from Amber to Zen" and the Goldsworth children are named in alphabetic sequence, but the order moves in reverse: "Alphina (9), Betty (10), Candida (12), and Dee (14)" (*PF*, 60). Even Kinbote's parents are agents of this combinational order: A (Alfin) + B (Blenda = C (Charles) X (Xavier). The skaters of Shade's poem move across the mirror surface "From Exe (X) to Wye (Y) on days of special frost" (*PF*, 36: l. 490). Shade's daughter, Hazel, commits suicide by plunging through the mirror surface of Omega Lake, paralleling the opening of Shade's poem, ending in one world, but flying on in a world of reflections: mirror play and combinational fate in a single image.

The single game which best combines mirror play and combinational possibilities, particularly for Nabokov's fictional purposes, is chess: "Chess is the perfect mirror game, with pieces drawn up confronting each other as in a looking-glass; moreover, castles, knights, and bishops have their twins as well as their opposite numbers."[16] Allusions to chess are slyly placed throughout *Pale Fire* and are used as the primary organizing principle in *The Defense.*[17] Nabokov's description of his method of composing chess problems reveals clues to his method of composing fiction and to the ways his fictional strategies affect the reading experience:

> Deceit, to the point of diabolism, and originality, verging upon the grotesque, were my notions of strategy; and although in matters of construction I tried to conform, whenever possible, to classical rules, such as economy of force, unity, weeding out of loose ends, I was always ready to sacrifice purity of form to the exigencies of fantastic content, causing form to bulge and burst like a sponge-bag containing a small furious devil. . . . It should be understood that competition in chess problems is

> not really between White and Black but between the composer and the hypothetical solver (just as in a first-rate work of fiction the real clash is not between the characters but between the author and the world), so that the great part of a problem's value is due to the number of "tries"—delusive opening moves, false scents, specious lines of play, astutely and lovingly prepared to lead the would-be solver astray. (*SM*, 289–90)

One particular wordplay combines the deception of a chess game with the alphabetic, combinational word game. Shade, in a Socratic dialogue with Kinbote, states that "There are rules in chess problems: interdiction of dual solutions, for instance" (*PF*, 161). Kinbote's description of the Zemblan king's situation during the first months of the rebellion as "being the only black piece in what a composer of chess problems might term a king-in-the-corner waiter of the *solus rex* type" uncovers another level of understanding character in a nonrealistic way (*PF*, 85). With this material as background, the three lakes, "Omega, Ozero, and Zero," do *not* succumb to the interdiction of dual solutions (*PF*, 66–67). Alter reads these lakes as "running us backwards from the ultimate end in the Greek alphabet to the point before beginnings in mathematical notation, with the Russian word for lake, *ozero*, in the middle. Ozero is also a double zero, 00, which, if the circles are tangent, is another version of a lemniscate."[18] This certainly is a plausible reading on one level, but if the double zeroes of *ozero* are *not* tangent, and a hyphen is inserted, the chess notation for castling on the king's side is created (0–0) and this affirms Mary McCarthy's reading: "The king's escape from the castle is doubtless castling."[19]

In one sense, then, the figures casting shadows through the glimmer of *Pale Fire* are chess pieces manipulated by the masterful hand of Nabokov across the black and white board of typography. Kinbote, in his role of the exiled Zemblan king, signs a plan of the Onhava Palace he has drawn for Shade with a black chess-king crown (*PF*, 77). Shade's "jerky shuffle" (*PF*, 8) suggests the eccentric movements of a knight. In this reading, the lone line " 'And now what shall I do? My knight is pinned' " contains a genuine foreshadowing of Shade's death (*PF*, 40: l. 661). Shade's murderer, Gradus, is literally a "poisoned pawn" due to his erratic, uncongenial diet and his manipulation by the powers controlling the Zemblan political structure (*PF*, 197). Nabokov's Magus-like machinations clearly reveal "the splotch of some master thumb"; even though the strings of Nabokov's puppet show are conspicuously displayed, a sense of wonder and exuberance with the intricacies of verbal conjuration reigns supreme (*PF*, 185).[20]

This ludic innovation in the multifaceted surface of *Pale Fire* creates many different effects. Some effects are distinctly comic literalizations of play activities: Shade's "clockwork toy" becomes risibly transformed into Kinbote's gardener/paramour, "Balthasar, prince of loam," and Gradus is described as a "clockwork man." The soldiers in the Zemblan king's court are playing lansquenet in Kinbote's commentary: lansquenet is not only a type of card game, but also "a German mercenary foot soldier of the sixteenth and seventeenth centuries."[21] This literalization of the solecism "playing with each other" emphasizes the play "in relation to the erotic," focusing Kinbote's voyeurism and homosexuality in a ludic, multileveled manner (*HL*, 43).

Of the many games contained between the covers of *Pale Fire*, none has generated as much critical discussion as the anagrammatic Word Golf. If Shade and Kinbote are accorded equal significance as narrative functions, as I have argued earlier, then the lexical transformations required by Word Golf become analogous to the textual levels which must be traversed by the reader and the Word Golf becomes what André Gide called a *mise en abyme* (discussed also by Alter) for the clash between author and world. The *mise en abyme* is a term from heraldry and signifies the inclusion of a smaller coat of arms inside a full sized coat of arms; the literary application of this term is evoked in Gide's *Journal* of 1893:

> In a work of art I rather like to find transposed, on the scale of the characters, the very subject of that work. Nothing throws a clearer light upon it or more surely establishes the proportions of the whole. Thus, in certain paintings of Memling or Quentin Metzys a small convex and dark mirror reflects the interior of the room, in which the scene of the painting is taking place. Likewise, in Velázquez's painting of the *Meninas* (but somewhat differently). Finally, in literature, in the play scene in *Hamlet*, and elsewhere in many other plays. In *Wilhelm Meister* the scenes of the puppets or the celebration at the castle. In *The Fall of the House of Usher* the story that is read to Roderick, etc.[22]

The textual "reality"—a word always in quotation marks when Nabokov uses it—of *Pale Fire* is contained in the palindromic and sequential nature of Word Golf, and Nabokov's definition of reality is as elusive as a working interpretation of *Pale Fire*: "Reality is a very subjective affair. I can only define it as a kind of gradual accumulation of information; and as specialization. . . . You can get nearer and nearer, so to speak, to reality; but you never get near enough because reality is an infinite succession of steps, levels of perception, false bottoms, and hence unquenchable, unattainable" (*SO*, 10–11).

As a Shadean pastime, Word Golf takes on a rule-governed, end-oriented, logical set of qualities: the progression from one word to another with the same number of letters, each transformation a word in itself.[23] However, in Kinbote's index, Word Golf becomes an eternally recursive process:

> *Word golf*, *S's* predilection for it, *819*; see Lass.
> *Lass*, see Mass.

Mass, *Mars*, *Mare*, see Male.
Male, see Word golf. (*PF*, 224, 220)

In this cyclical, reflexive Word Golf game, instead of revealing significant information about Shade, Kinbote's playfulness in telling "the primary story risks the appearance of the fragment of itself that it has pretended to conceal" through the *mise en abyme*.[24] In other words, Kinbote's homosexual proclivities are revealed in this apparatus which magically transforms all lasses and mares into males, and instead of revealing Shade, Kinbote reveals himself. Therefore, there is more than a slight irony in Dillard's critical interpretation of *Pale Fire* offered in a three move Word Golf game.[25] "Inversion" was Freud's term regarding male homosexuality as well as a term extensively employed by critics to discuss the reflexive novel's propensity to turn back on itself. By literalizing this trope, Nabokov reinforces a level of meaning which recalls Kinbote's inability to break out of what Nabokov calls in *Speak, Memory* "the vicious circle of time." While Word Golf is of course another of Nabokov's mirror games, it appears more accurate, then, to view it as an extended metaphor for linguistic and semantic shifts occurring over time and altering shared perceptions of that elusive entity, "reality," which are defined by language.

The levels of the text which the reader must apprehend and proceed from are persistently subverted through structural and linguistic disruption. Since each level becomes an intermediary step in the understanding of *Pale Fire*, and the final level can never be reached due to these disruptions and the novel's insistent reflexivism, Nabokov's *Pale Fire* is consistent with his definition of reality, however different Nabokov's "realism" is from the "realism" associated with Balzac, Turgenev, or James. Nabokov's readers, particularly those who are familiar with these "realistic" authors, must negotiate their ways perilously through the world of *Pale Fire* just as Carroll's Alice must wend her way through Wonderland. This "game of worlds" begins in the "lexical playfields" where notions of correspondences between language and reality begin and end.

Notes

1. Vladimir Nabokov, *Nikolai Gogol* (New York: New Directions, 1944), p. 140.

2. Vladimir Nabokov, *Pale Fire* (New York: Berkley Paperback, 1962), p. 7; Johan Huizinga, *Homo Ludens: A Study of the Play Element in Culture* (Boston: Beacon Press, 1955), p. 10; hereafter cited as *PF* and *HL*, respectively; line numbers of "Pale Fire" follow a colon.

3. Vladimir Nabokov, *Speak Memory: An Autobiography Revisited* (New York: Putnam's, 1966), p. 283; hereafter cited as *SM*.

4. Lewis Carroll, *Alice in Wonderland*, translated into Russian by "V. Sirin," illustrated

by S. Zalshupin, (rpt. Dover Publications, 1976), p. 2. For fuller and complementary discussion of Nabokov's art as a translator of Lewis Carroll, see Simon Karlinsky, "Anya in Wonderland: Nabokov's Russified Lewis Carroll," *TriQuarterly*, 17 (Winter 1970), 310–15; and Beverly Lyon Clark, "Nabokov's Assault on Wonderland," in *Nabokov's Fifth Arc*, ed. J. E. Rivers and Charles Nicol (Austin: Univ. of Texas Press, 1982), pp. 63–74.

5. Vladimir Nabokov, *Strong Opinions* (New York: McGraw-Hill, 1973), p. 117; hereafter cited as *SO*.

6. Gérard Genette, *Narrative Discourse: An Essay in Method*, trans. Jane E. Lewin (Ithaca: Cornell Univ. Press, 1980), p. 31.

7. In response to a question concerning Freud asked him by Alfred Appel, Jr., Nabokov replied "Oh, I am not up to discussing again that figure of fun. He is not worthy of more attention than I have granted him in my novels and in *Speak, Memory*. Let the credulous and the vulgar believe that all mental woes can be cured by a daily application of old Greek myths to their private parts. I really do not care" (*SO*, 66).

8. A superb article on this dimension of Nabokov's art and his demands upon the reader is David Walker, " 'The Viewer and the View': Chance and Choice in *Pale Fire*," *Studies in American Fiction*, 4 (1976), 203–21. In his *Partial Magic: The Novel as a Self-Conscious Genre* (Berkeley: Univ. of California Press, 1975), Robert Alter's chapter on Nabokov, entitled "Nabokov's Game of Worlds," shares many of the concerns of the present essay.

9. Cf. Edward Said's *Beginnings: Intention and Method* (Baltimore: Johns Hopkins Univ. Press, 1975), pp. 230–31 for a more detailed discussion of this phenomenon.

10. A Kinbotean footnote: the phoenix image is more appropriate for D. H. Lawrence than it is for Nabokov, the scholar and entomologist, whose primary image of artistic transcendence is the butterfly. The two are conflated beautifully in Kinbote's foreword: "As a rule, Shade destroyed drafts the moment he ceased to need them: well do I recall seeing him from my porch, on a brilliant morning, burning a whole stack of them in the pale fire of the incinerator before which he stood with bent head like an official mourner among the wind-borne black butterflies of that backyard auto-da-fe" (*PF*, 9).

11. See Alter's discussion of the lemniscate in *Partial Magic*, pp. 189–90.

12. The former position was initially taken by Andrew Field in *Nabokov: His Life in Art* (Boston: Little, Brown, 1967), p. 300: "The primary author—even without Nabokov's acknowledgment that Kinbote really does not know what is going on in Shade's poem—must be John Shade." The latter (and decidedly more heterodox position, particularly in terms of critical compatriots) is expressed by Page Stegner's rather weak *Escape into Aesthetics: The Art of Vladimir Nabokov* (New York: Dial Press, 1966), p. 129: "Moreover, it is even possible, perhaps probable, that Gradus and Shade are as much figments of Kinbote's imagination as Charles the Beloved and the far-distant land of Zembla."

This entire debate is rebutted and sufficiently dispelled in R. H. W. Dillard's outstanding overview of Nabokov's oeuvre, "Not Text, But Texture: The Novels of Vladimir Nabokov," in *The Sounder Few: Essays from the Hollins Critic*, ed. R. H. W. Dillard, George Garrett, and John Rees Moore (Athens: Univ. of Georgia Press, 1971), p. 162: "I fear that the entire question blurs the centrally important fact that Nabokov created both Shade and Kinbote, that they are both equally 'real,' and that they are both elements of a remarkably balanced and meaningful novel which is concerned with the nature of art and its relation to fact and truth."

13. Alter, p. 189.

14. *Webster's Third New International Dictionary of the English Language*, Vol. III (Springfield: G. & C. Merriam Co., 1966), p. 2498. Author's italics.

15. Nabokov's relationship to the realistic tradition in Modernism, particularly to Henry James, is discussed in Ellen Pifer, *Nabokov and the Novel* (Cambridge: Harvard Univ. Press, 1980), pp. 119–31. The anti- or nonrealistic dimension of characters in *Pale Fire* is described in Robert S. Ryf, "Character and Imagination in the Experimental Novel," *Modern Fiction Studies*, 20 (1974), 317–27. *Pale Fire* is analyzed briefly on pp. 324–26.

16. Mary McCarthy, "A Bolt from the Blue" in *The Writing on the Wall and Other Literary Essays* (New York: Harcourt, Brace & World, 1970), p. 22.

17. Mark Lilly's essay, "Nabokov: Homo Ludens," in *Vladimir Nabokov: A Tribute*, ed. Peter Quennell (New York: William Morrow & Co., 1980), contains a fine discussion of the role of chess in *The Defense* on pp. 92–95.

18. Alter, pp. 194–95.

19. McCarthy, p. 22.

20. See Alfred Appel, Jr.'s Intro., *The Annotated Lolita* (New York: McGraw-Hill, 1970), esp. pp. xxxi–xxxii.

21. *Webster's New World Dictionary of the American Language* (New York: World Publishing Co., 1962), p. 821.

22. *The Journals of André Gide*, trans. Justin O'Brien. Vol. I (New York: Knopf, 1947), pp. 29–30.

23. See McCarthy, p. 24.

24. Jean Ricardou, "The Story within the Story," trans. Joseph Kastner, *James Joyce Quarterly*, 18 (1981), 332.

25. See Dillard, pp. 249–50.

The Gift: Nabokov's Portrait of the Artist

Roger B. Salomon*

(I wonder, Van, *why* you are doing your best to transform our poetical and unique past into a dirty farce? . . .)

Nabokov, *Ada*

Like Joyce's *A Portrait of the Artist as a Young Man*, *The Gift* is about a young, exiled writer discovering by trial and error a rhetoric relevant to the nature of the contemporary world in which he (unwillingly) finds himself and to his situation and spiritual needs within such a world. Nabokov's own "portrait of the artist" is that work of his which most completely explores the rhetorical options open to this exiled artist from the aesthetic perspective of the exploration successfully resolved. In his foreword to the 1963 translation, Nabokov himself notes that the "heroine" of *The Gift* is "Russian Literature" and goes on to describe Fyodor Godunov-Cherdyntsev's "literary progress." From chapter to chapter, according to Nabokov, he moves from being a writer of lyric poetry (a Georgian literature of nostalgic memory) to epic biography (a "surge toward Pushkin," as Nabokov puts it), to an ironic realism modeled on Gogol, to, finally, the composition of *The Gift*.[1] The incorporative form of the resulting book turns the previous experiments themselves into subject matter under the inclusive gaze of what Fyodor comes to define as "one complete and free eye, which can simultaneously see in all directions" (*G*, 322).

*This essay appears here for the first time by permission of the author.

In this and other ways, Nabokov emphasizes the crucial drama of "seeing" in the novel. Fyodor's quest for an adequate style—an interior quest involving "verbal adventures" (*G*, 151) which parody the authentic feats of his quintessentially heroic father—at least allows him to discover and define his own mock-heroic role as son, protagonist, and author and the form appropriate to the expression of that role. Like his father before him but now under vastly different circumstances, Fyodor remains committed to visionary experience. *The Gift* explores the various kinds of seeing (the "gifts") still open to him—especially the continued possibility of a perspective that will be in some way transformational. Nabokov's protagonists are fundamentally exiles from authenticity; like those of Joyce, it is their particular ironic destiny, nevertheless, to remain committed to the tasks of the hero. Nabokov's self-conscious fictions, in turn, are the enabling context of his theme—its environment, so to speak—not the theme itself. In other words, it is less accurate to say that Nabokov's work is a metafictional, reflexively "about" art and the artist, than it is say that the role of art and the nature of the artist's qualities are functional to a value system which continues to embrace most of the traditional concerns of the hero and whose delineation remains his major theme.[2]

Fyodor's situation at the beginning of the novel simply makes explicit and literal what *Invitation to a Beheading* presents in symbolic terms: the protagonist hopelessly split between the lost child's world of his memory and imagination—"the hothouse paradise of the past" (*G*, 92)—and the gross, vulgar, ugly Berlin of the 1920s where he lives in sordid meanness as a foreigner, a Berlin whose description, according to Nabokov, was colored in part by the later "rise of a nauseous dictatorship" (*G*, foreword, [p. 10]). An early description of Fyodor in his rented room may be taken as representative:

> For some time he stood by the window. In the curds-and-whey sky opaline pits now and then formed where the blind sun circulated, and, in response, on the gray convex roof of the van, the slender shadows of linden branches hastened headlong toward substantiation, but dissolved without having materialized. The house directly across the way was half enclosed in scaffolding, while the sound part of its brick facade was overgrown with window-invading ivy. At the far end of the path that cut through its front yard he could make out the black sign of a coal cellar. Taken by itself, all this was a view, just as the room was itself a separate entity; but now a middleman had appeared, and now that view became the view from this room and no other. The gift of sight which it now had received did not improve it. It would be hard, he mused, to transform the wallpaper (pale yellow, with bluish tulips) into a distant steppe. The desert of the desk would have to be tilled for a long time before it could sprout its first rhymes. And much cigarette ash would have to fall under the armchair and into its fold before it would become suitable for traveling. (*G*, 19–20).

For this young, homesick exile in "gray" Berlin, the gift of transformational sight is largely missing. Not only is his environment itself totally opaque (the "blind sun" circulating, the linden shadows promising "substantiation" but dissolving "without having materialized," the "coal cellar" at the end of it all); but subjective seeing—the crucial view of the "middleman"—proves also to be very difficult. Nevertheless, it remains his essential task: his father has actually walked the "distant steppe" and desert; his son must attempt something of the same thing with desk and wallpaper. Like all of Nabokov's exile protagonists, Fyodor takes his form (his personal "style," his fundamental moral, spiritual, and emotional commitments) from a previous avatar which is now no longer real, possibly an illusion to begin with (the protagonist in *The Defense* is bluntly called "Luzhin"), certainly a fiction of mind in the present. His actual substance in the contemporary world is grossly, comically dissynchronous with the "dream" role that obsessively continues to shape his being. With form in place but substance gone, attenuated, or changed, Fyodor is a parodic figure, becomes aware of himself as parody, and gropes toward appropriate self-expression in a parodic art.[3]

Fyodor's initial literary stance, however, is not parody but a nostalgic lyricism dealing directly with memories of childhood. In the first chapter of *The Gift*, he has just published a slender volume opening with a poem called "The Lost Ball," whose title and substance obviously set the theme of the entire collection. A child's ball has slipped away in a darkened room, is found momentarily by probing under furniture, then irrevocably lost when it "promptly goes under / The impregnable sofa" (*G*, 22). The act of memory does little to disturb the impregnable sofa and, indeed, largely testifies to its own vulnerability. After referring to a pretty passage in another of these poems about getting up on a winter morning to a hot stove and "the silence of snow, / Pink-shaded azure, / And immaculate whiteness," Fyodor notes sharply:

> It is strange how a memory will grow into a wax figure, how the cherub grows suspiciously prettier as its frame darkens with age—strange, strange are the mishaps of memory. I emigrated several years ago; this foreign land has by now lost its aura of abroadness just as my own ceased to be geographic habit. The Year Seven. The wandering ghost of an empire immediately adopted this system of reckoning, akin to the one formerly introduced by the ardent French citizen in honor of newborn liberty. But the years roll on, and honor is no consolation; recollections either melt away, or else acquire a deathly gloss, so that instead of marvelous apparitions we are left with a fan of picture postcards. Nothing can help me, no poetry no stereoscope. . . . (*G*, 29).

Memory apparently offers us the unpalatable alternatives of either absolute losses or the sterility of its picturesque distortions. Besides, nostalgic memory, at least, is too easy; the minor lyricist can scarcely be the heroic artist. "Because I have an innate distrust of what I feel easy to express, no sentimental wanderer will ever be allowed to land on the rock of my unfriendly prose," writes Sebastian Knight, another artist seeking a role appropriate, in this case, to the very implications of his name.[4] As the above passage from *The Gift* suggests, the young Fyodor alternates between lyric identification with his poetry and considerable objectivity, even to composing mentally the critical review ("We have before us a thin volume entitled *Poems*" [*G*, 21]) which, in fact, his stillborn book never gets. A distancing third person "he" alternates with the more subjective "I" from the beginning of the first chapter and represents the narrative point of view toward which the novel increasingly moves, though only to enhance, not destroy, the delicate antiphony between passionate commitment and ironic commentary.

In various ingenious forms, *The Gift* offers us what is essentially internal *dialogue*, and this dialogue, in turn, constitutes the most important formal expression of the fundamental duality of the parodic or mock-heroic self: its life in two "time zones" (Fyodor dates his present experience from the "Year Seven"); its split into ideal hero and clownish ghost; its self-consciousness (direct or through surrogate voice) of its own duality, one avatar mocking the other, the irony generated by disparity.[5] We have already noted, for example, Fyodor's denigration of memory. At other moments, however, he affirms its enduring power; somehow it will determine the shape of the future or, rather, it *is* the future. As Van Veen, Nabokov's philosopher of time, puts it: "Time is but memory in the making."[6] In another passage, Fyodor imagines an eventual return to Russia:

> Perhaps one day, on foreign-made soles with heels long since worn down, feeling myself a ghost despite the idiotic substantiality of the insulators, I shall again come out of that station and without visible companions walk along the footpath that accompanies the highway the ten or so versts to Leshimo. . . . The day will probably be on the grayish side. . . . When I reach the sites where I grew up and see this and that—or else, because of fires, rebuilding, lumbering operations or the negligence of nature, see neither this nor that (but still make out something infinitely and unwaveringly faithful to me, if only because my eyes are, in the long run, made of the same stuff as the grayness, the clarity, the dampness of those sites), then, after all the excitement, I shall experience a certain satiation of suffering—perhaps on the mountain pass to a kind of happiness which it is too early for me to know (I know only that when I reach it, it will be with pen in hand). But there is one thing, I shall definitely not find there awaiting me—the thing which, indeed, made the whole business of exile worth cultivating: my childhood and the fruits of my childhood. Its fruits—here they are, today, already ripe; while my childhood itself has disappeared into a distance even more remote than that of our Russian North. (*G*, 37–38)

The grayness here is not that of Berlin but rather of its own symbolic double, the grayness of another mode of time and seeing, mysterious, not banal. Or "perhaps" (to use Fyodor's significant qualifier) Russian gray is the gray of imaginative seeing. The lost ball of childhood will not be found, yet the experience of the past will be encountered again in the future. Or, *must* be found in some willed, obsessive pursuit? Here as elsewhere the Nabokov protagonist is, as much as anything, a Quixote of time. Fyodor suggests that the artist's role ("pen in hand") can at least absorb the paradoxes of memory and imagination and, in so doing, furnish "a kind of" visionary experience—"childish" ardency and integrity of belief and commitment in some later context. The supreme model here of ecstatic possibility is his father (invoked again by references to steppes and mountain passes), and we must now examine Fyodor's treatment of that figure to define more precisely those heroic values which the ideal self of the protagonist affirms. What kind of authentic hero does he mimic? This parodic model will, of course, partially determine the nature of the parody.

In Nabokov's fiction the reader questing for answers himself runs into paradox. The authentic hero can *only* be encountered, if at all, in the fictions of the inauthentic son. Like Stephen Dedalus, Fyodor creates the prototypal father whom he comically imitates. The elder Godunov-Cherdynstev never exists in the present ("Year Seven") time of the novel at all. He has been missing since an expedition to Asia undertaken just before the Revolution, and even his son, whose life is embellished by dreams of his return, is terrified by the thought of the possible "arrival of a live father" (*G*, 100). Reality would only make palpable the gap between style and fate and lead finally to anticlimax. Of his own father's relatively meager role in the revolutionary events of 1917–18 and his assassination by a "sinister ruffian" in 1922, Nabokov has written: "History seems to have been anxious of depriving him of a full opportunity to reveal his great gifts of statesmanship in a Russian republic of the Western type."[7] Certainly Fyodor's father belongs (and must remain) in mythic time. Fyodor remembers at one point an old fairy tale of his father's which began: "The only son of a great khan, having lost his way during a hunt," and he goes on to comment parenthetically: "thus begin the best fairy tales and thus end the best lives" (*G*, 146).

Fyodor realizes that minor lyrics will not do in rendering the heroic fairy tale of his father; they are too easy and sterile in their nostalgia, too limited in their subjectivity. He turns, therefore, to an obvious alternative, the epic narrative of Pushkin, a writer with whom he closely associates his father. Reading the work of the heroic artist, he simultaneously does research on the heroic parent; the two figures fuse together: "Pushkin entered his blood. With Pushkin's voice merged the voice of his father" or, as he describes this imaginative process elsewhere:

"Indefatigably, in ecstasy, he was really preparing his work now . . . [he] collected material, read until dawn, studied maps, wrote letters and met with the necessary people. From Pushkin's prose he had passed to his life, so that in the beginning the rhythm of Pushkin's era commingled with the rhythm of his father's life" (*G*, 110). Even Fyodor's grandfather (at one point, a Mississippi gambler, Texas cattle breeder, and duellist) and great-grandfather ("a hero of the Napoleonic War" [*G*, 111]) are caught up finally in the collective portrait.

What Fyodor creates, in effect, is an extraordinarily complete and detailed composite of the nineteenth-century hero as soldier, statesman, adventurer, romantic artist, explorer, and scientist—a composite which precisely defines the nexus of Fyodor's own emotional and imaginative commitments, his moral values, and his spiritual goals. The elder Godunov-Cherdyntsev's life represents both the culmination of this heroic period and its last phase before the arrival of what Nabokov has called elsewhere "our disastrous century."[8] Fyodor's parent is, in effect, the ideal Victorian: the scientist who is traveler, discoverer, encyclopedic and definitive writer (his colleagues call him significantly "the conquistador of Russian entomology" [*G*, 114]); above all, the severe, resolute example of masculine force and power:

> His captures, his observations, the sound of his voice in scientific words, all this, I think, I will preserve. But that is still so little. With the same relative permanence I would like to retain what it was, perhaps, that I loved most of all about him: his live masculinity, inflexibility and independence, the chill and the warmth of his personality, his power over everything that he undertook. As if playing a game, as if wishing in passing to imprint his force on everything, he would pick out here and there something from a field outside entomology and thus he left his mark upon almost all branches of natural science: there is only one plant described by him out of all those he collected, but that one is a spectacular species of birch; one bird—a most fabulous pheasant; one bat—but the biggest one in the world. And in all parts of nature our name echoes a countless number of times, for other naturalists gave his name either to a spider, or to a rhododendron, or to a mountain ridge—the latter, by the way, made him angry: "To ascertain and preserve the ancient native name of a pass," he wrote, "is always both more scientific and more noble than to saddle it with the name of a good acquaintance." (*G*, 124–25)

Authentic nobility—in the most serious and profound sense of that word—is what Fyodor is talking about. This nobility manifests itself in two different clusters of virtues, which can be labeled loosely as "aristocratic" and "romantic" without insisting necessarily on absolute distinctions between categories. The aristocratic qualities I have suggested already and, in any case, can be quickly summarized: bravery, independence, absolute commitment to a code of honor, freedom from the pragmatic attitudes and perspective of the bourgeois world, aloofness, severity, resolution, familiarity with power and leadership, noblesse oblige, above all, a certain style. Fyodor remembers how much he liked "that special easy knack [his father] showed in dealing with a horse, a dog, a gun, a bird, or a peasant boy with a two-inch splinter in his back" (*G*, 125).

Even more significant, however, is his father's ecstatic, visionary romanticism. Power in his hands goes beyond its masculine and aristocratic implications to include vitalistic energy, imagination, the will to measure spaces, God's act of creating the world in its naming: "he was happy in that incompletely named world in which at every step he named the nameless" (*G*, 131). Significantly, Fyodor's father is a lonely, mysterious, visionary quester moving toward "perfect peace, silence, transparency" in the high mountains (*G*, 134), the pursuer of beauty at the very extremities of human experience, the perfect exemplar of what Fyodor calls "knowledge–amplified love" (*G*, 144). Behind the nineteenth-century forebears of his father already noted, is Marco Polo, the prototype of the visionary explorer, who has seen miracles in the same deserts through which the elder Godunov-Cherdyntsev later progresses. Appropriately, a picture of "Marco Polo leaving Venice" hangs in his father's office (*G*, 127). In the Year Seven of present time, the Journey to the East, if not forgotten completely, can only be parodied. Sebastian Knight, for example, goes with a futurist poet on "a Marcopolian journey" through Russia, a trip which involves renting halls and giving poetical performances.[9] And much later in Nabokov's career, Van Veen as a young man puts on performances in the guise of a character aptly called "Mascodagama."

Fyodor's biography in its own way is, of course, also a performance, and he himself finally becomes aware of the limitations of such "secondary" imitation. As the author of *The Gift*, however, he turns these limitations into a crucial dimension of its subject matter. The style of these biographical notes, for example, suggests that what we are reading is as much Fyodor's imaginative projection as any "true" record of his father's expeditions. The visionary role constantly threatens to shift from the object of the biography to its narrator. His father's traverse of the high country is continually punctuated by the phrase "I see" or "this is the way I see it" or, more revealingly, "I can conjure up." At other times, Fyodor will shift to the first-person plural ("our caravan moved east") or a union of first and third ("he and I would take Elwes' Swallowtail" [*G*, 128–34]).

We are made aware, moreover, that Fyodor can never long escape his exile world; like Stephen Dedalus's environment, it constitutes a perpetual mockery of his reveries. After one ecstatic passage, for example, invoking an imaginary transit of the desert of Lob with his father, during which they heard in the sandstorms the same "whisper of spirits" reported by Marco Polo, Fyodor abruptly switches to a description of himself in the act (and failure) of performance:

> All this lingered bewitchingly, full of color and air, with lively movement in the foreground and a convincing backdrop; then, like smoke from a breeze, it shifted and dispersed—and Fyodor saw again the dead and impossible tulips of his wallpaper, the crumbling mount of cigarette butts in the ashtray, and the lamp's reflection in the black windowpane. He threw open the window. The written-up sheets of paper on his desk started: one folded over, another glided onto the floor. The room immediately turned damp and cold. Down below, an automobile went slowly along the dark empty street—and, strangely enough, this very slowness reminded Fyodor of a host of petty, unpleasant things—the day just past, the missed lesson—and when he thought that next morning he would have to phone the deceived old man, his heart was oppressed by an abominable despondency. But once the window was closed again, already feeling the void between his bunched fingers, he turned to the patiently waiting lamp, to the scattered first drafts, to the still-warm pen which now quietly slipped back into his fingers (explaining the void and filling it) and returned at once to that world which was as natural to him as snow to the white hare or water to Ophelia. (*G.* 136–37)

Still seeking a direct and simple response to loss (a response, that is, in which the heroic past is invoked into being by the art form which was its most perfect expression—thus the past not really lost), the earlier Fyodor attempts literally to become "one" with his father. He offers the ardors of desire and the powers of imagination and language as an authentic method of reaching perfect transparency and hearing immortal whispers. The putative author of *The Gift*, on the other hand, now writing his *own* biography in a composite style appropriate to the circumstances, conceives of his persona as two people (the son/father separate from the lonely son), living in two irreconcilable worlds, each with its inexorable claims, each even with a rhetoric expressive of those claims. From such a dual perspective, the strength and intensity of Fyodor's commitment to visionary experience in no way actually transforms or even mitigates the rigors of mean and sordid Berlin. Conversely, however, the banal climate limits or denies only the absolute end of questing, not its value and necessity as a moral and spiritual imperative. In becoming self-conscious of its own absurdity, the heroic code of values paradoxically survives the dissolution of its circumstances. The fundamental action of *The Gift* involves Fyodor's gradual discovery that he is, in fact; the mock-hero of what will be, at best, his own mock-heroic narrative.

One important dimension of Fyodor's discovery is his growing awareness of the instability of language and imagination as authentic instruments of power and truth. Already in writing poetry he had become aware of this problem. Commenting on his various experiments with poetic language, he notes: "as soon as I had embarked on what I thought to be creation, on what should have been the expression, the living connection between my divine excitement and my human world, everything expired in a fatal gust of words, whereas I continued to rotate epithets and adjust rhymes without noticing the split, the debasement, and the betrayal . . ." (*G*, 165). Later, while working on his father's biography and speculating on the where and how of his death, forcing himself toward truth and oneness ("he would . . . I *know*, have [done so and so]"), Fyodor suddenly breaks off:

> But sometimes I get the impression that all this is a rubbishy rumor, a tired legend, that it has been created out of those same suspicious granules of approximate knowledge that I use myself when my dreams muddle through regions known to me only by hearsay or out of books, so that the first knowledgeable person who has really seen at the time the places referred to will refuse to recognize them, will make fun of the exoticism of my thoughts, the hills of my sorrow, the precipices of my imagination, and will find in my conjectures just as many topographical errors as he will anachronisms. So much the better. Once the rumor of my father's death is a fiction, must it not then be conceded that his very journey out of Asia is merely attached in the shape of a tail to this fiction. . . . (*G*, 149)

"So much the better," perhaps, in this case, where the instability of rumor and tired legend invites the possibility that his father may be still alive. But Fyodor has opened Pandora's Box. If one Asian journey is a fiction, how about the others?

He abandons his project when he becomes aware that the verbal creation of proximate worlds can not literally be offered as a simple substitute for or copy of reality itself, that, in effect, he has become a *naive* parodist of his father's life and career. As Fyodor explains to his mother in a letter:

> You know, when I read his or Grum's books and I hear their entrancing rhythm, when I study the position of the words that can neither be replaced nor rearranged, it seems to me a sacrilege to take all this and dilute it with myself. If you like I'll admit it: I myself am a mere seeker of verbal adventures, and forgive me if I refuse to hunt down my fancies on my father's own collecting ground. I have realized, you see, the impossibility of having the imagery of his travels germinate without contaminating them with a kind of secondary poetization which keeps departing further and further from that real poetry with which the live experience of these receptive, knowledgeable and chaste naturalists endowed their research. (*G*, 151)

She responds by telling him of her conviction " that some day you shall yet write this book" (*G*, 151). And, in a sense, she is correct, although Fyodor will write it from the perspective of the self-conscious parodist whose protagonist is now himself as mock hero, himself the verbal adventurer trying to *play* some version of the father, and whose style of "secondary poetization" achieves, in this new context, its own legitimation. The heroic or "Pushkin" period of Fyodor's life ends when he moves his lodgings, a move to which Nabokov gives a literary direction: "The distance from the old residence to the new was about the same as, somewhere in Russia, that from Pushkin Avenue to Gogol Street" (*G*, 157). In other words, Fyodor travels steadily from lyric to epic to a more direct encounter with ironic realism.

The straight fairy tale, at least, will not do. In a slightly later novel, *The Real Life of Sebastian Knight* (1941), the narrator (V.) is also a potential biographer (in this case, of a famous brother) and also directed initially to create or recreate an authentic romantic hero. His adviser is a nostalgic old governess, who lives wholly in the events of the past, and who urges him to "write that book, that beautiful book . . . make it a fairy-tale with Sebastian for prince. The enchanted prince. . . ." But V. senses the implications of this advice in the very looks of the governess: "I glanced at her misty old eyes, at the dead lustre of her false teeth. . . ."[10] Andrew Field has pointed out the tension in Nabokov's early poetry between the pull of childhood, couched in the mode of Georgian elegy, and a determination to live and write in a present context. One poem is reminiscent of Stevens's "Sad Strains of a Gay Waltz":

> some lady who writes
> or ha'penny bard
> will bewail the disappearance of former dances;
> but for me, I'll tell you frankly,
> there is no special delight
> in a rude and unwashed
> marquis dancing a minuet.[11]

The mock-heroic genre, let me emphasize, is a strategy for personal and literary survival. Nowhere is this more obvious than in the work of Nabokov. As it did for Joyce and Stevens before him, such a strategy requires that Nabokov come to terms with romanticism and realism, acknowledging these perspectives, finally, in a complex art that includes the claims of both. Having explored the present possibilities of heroic romanticism, it is scarcely surprising that *The Gift* next brings literary realism under scrutiny.

On the face of it, however, Fyodor's next biographical venture, a treatment of the great realist critic Chernyshevski, seems anomalous. It puzzled and disturbed Fyodor's publisher, and he rejected it; so did Nabokov's own publisher, with a complete edition of *The Gift* not appearing until 1952 (as Nabokov reports in his foreword to the Putnam edition). The fat, dirty, coarse, inept, comic Chernyshevski has apparently little in common with Fyodor's sublime father; nor could his literary theory, with its strong emphasis on empiricism, common sense, and social concerns, be expected to have significance for the romantic artist. In fiction as in life, Fyodor's (or Nabokov's) portrait of Chernyshevski seems an act of gratuitous satire, an aggression against a hero of Russian liberalism at a time when the liberals were already under heavy attack from external enemies.

But Fyodor's biography is, in fact, a complex exercise in ironic perspective; a perspective he has clearly in mind from the beginning. As he explains to Zina, his girl friend and patient auditor: "I want to keep everything as it were on the very brink of parody. You know those idiotic '*biographies romancées*' where Byron is coolly slipped a dream extracted from one of his own poems? And there must be on the other hand an abyss of seriousness, and I must make my way along this narrow ridge between my own truth and a caricature of it" (*G*, 212). Given the anticlimax (the collapse into *roman*) of the earlier Fyodor's own attempt at heroic biography—scarcely "idiotic," to be sure, but nevertheless a failure of aesthetic control, a failure of the artist-hero even in his own "act"—it is appropriate that he turn to the possibilities of parody as a deliberate, self-conscious method of bringing visionary experience and reality into a controlled, comprehensive balance. Fyodor's metaphor of the ridge-walker *between* describes the same categorical duality, the same perspective "between" two truths and inclusive of both that is characteristic in general of mock-heroic. And it is understandable that the claims of reality might be more readily acknowledged in an historically important figure with whom one has no personal, intellectual, or nostalgic connection.

But Fyodor is not essentially concerned with the easy irony of demolishing the romantic legend of the chief spokesman of realism. His task, rather, is the more difficult, subtle, and significant one (obviously too subtle for many of Fyodor and Nabokov's critics!) of finding heroic possibility in Chernyshevski's obsessions, comic absurdities, and various misadventures. Fyodor makes clear that he will continue to pursue his own truth—now, however, exploring its embodiment in another mode, an ironic art squarely concerned with the gap between human conceptualizations of reality and the actual opacity of reality to imagination and desire. His version of Chernyshevski's career emphasizes at once aspects of reality darker than the partisans of realism would acknowledge and dimensions of idealism which they chose to ignore or deny. The resultant portrait of a "mad," grotesque visionary observed by an apparently "saner" narrator-artist culminates Fyodor's preparatory biographical studies of others (his next protagonist will be himself as young lyricist and biographer) and has wide implications for Nabokov's own career.[12]

Fyodor's treatment of Chernyshevski turns materialism on its ear as a form of idealism and yet accepts the banal emptiness of reality itself, an emptiness which, as Erich Heller long ago pointed out, tends to constitute the hidden agenda of the great realists. Incongruity (the explicit models here are Gogol and Flaubert) is the key to Fyodor's portrait, the fundamental incongruity of concrete horrors everywhere in tangled juxtaposition with idealistic commitments. Fyodor, for example, alludes to one passage from Chernyshevski's diary which describes him as rushing into a tenement house to relieve himself (he enjoys pastry, then suffers heartburn and vomiting). While there, he is interrupted by a startled young woman, and Fyodor comments: "The heavy creak of the door, its loose, rusty hook, the stink, the icy cold—all this is dreadful . . . and yet the queer fellow is quite prepared to debate with himself about true purity, noting with satisfaction that 'I didn't even try to discover whether she was goodlooking' " (*G*, 239). The episode, in small, is a metaphor of Chernyshevski's entire experience.

On the one hand, his ardor, dedication ("this indefatigable man" [*G*, 276]), and the quest for "true purity" (that phrase so evocative in Nabokov of the child hero) endow Chernyshevski with a dimension of nobility. Compared with their political contemporaries, Fyodor notes, "such uncompromising radicals as Chernyshevski, with all their ludicrous and ghastly blunders, were, no matter how you looked at it, real heroes in their struggle with the governmental order of things (which was even more noxious and more vulgar than was their own fatuity in the realm of literary criticism) . . . Other oppositionists . . . who risked less, were by the same token worth less than these iron squabblers" (*G*, 215). For Fyodor, Chernyshevski's idealism exists beyond the mockery of its concrete circumstances and in sharp distinction to other human alternatives. It exists, indeed, even as a vivid refutation of Chernyshevski's own materialism. Fyodor notes the many times in which the philosopher's life itself had refuted his axiom that "the tangible object acts much more strongly than the abstract concept of it" (*G*, 273). In another important passage, Fyodor directly attacks Chernyshevski's materialistic ethics:

> the idea that calculation is the foundation of every action (or heroic accomplishment) leads to absurdity: in itself calculation can be heroic! Anything which comes into the focus of human thinking is spiritualized. Thus the "calculation" of the materialists was ennobled; thus, for those in the know, matter turns into a incorporeal play of mysterious forces. Chernyshevski's ethical structures are in their own way an attempt to construct the same old "perpetual motion" machine, where matter moves other matter. We would very much like this to revolve: egoism-altruism-egoism-altruism . . . but the wheel stops from friction. What to do? Live, read, think. What to do? Work at one's own development in order to achieve the aim of life, which is happiness. What to do? (But Chernyshevski's own fate changed the businesslike question to an ironic exclamation.) (*G*, 294)

On the other hand, Fyodor's irony is not limited to making us aware that Chernyshevski's social oblivion and terrible Siberian exile make nonsense of any egoism-altruism machine. If his fate mocks materialism, it constitutes equally the mockery of his heroics. Beyond even Chernyshevski's personal clownishness, is his existence in a farcical world. "It is amazing," Fyodor observes, "how everything bitter and heroic which life manufactured for Chernyshevski was invariably accompanied by a flavoring of vile farce" (*G*, 296). On this point, Fyodor is particularly insistent and expansive:

> such was the fate of Chernyshevski that everything turned against him: no matter what subject he touched there would come to light—insidiously, and with the most taunting inevitability—something that was completely opposed to his conception of it. He, for instance, was for synthesis, for the force of attraction, for the living link (reading a novel he would kiss the page where the author appealed to the reader) and what was the answer he got? Disintegration, solitude, estrangement. He preached soundness and common sense in everything—and as if in response to someone's mocking summons, his destiny was cluttered with blockheads, crackbrains and madmen. For everything he was returned "a negative hundredfold," in Stranholyubski's happy phrase, for everything he was backkicked by his own dialectic, for everything the gods had their revenge on him. (*G*, 229)

In a world where mockery is the voice of destiny, mockery, in turn, must become part of the artist's voice as guarantor of its authenticity—an authenticity which, as I have already noted elsewhere, paradoxically achieves its final, full authority only in self-conscious awareness of its own ultimate inauthenticity. For Nabokov mockery is the true message of realism and one that must be accepted even by those who despise realism. It is mockery that draws down the greatest wrath of Fyodor's imaginary reviewers. According to one, "excessive zeal, and even kindness, in the process of exposing evil is always more understandable and forgivable than the least mockery—no matter how witty it may be—of that which public opinion feels to be objectively good" (*G*, 317). Or again: "he makes fun, not only of his hero: he also makes fun of his reader." Even satire would represent a clear and understandable position: "It would at least be a point of view, and reading the book the reader would make a constant adjustment for the author's partisan approach, in that way arriving at the truth. But the pity is that with Mr. Godunov-Cherdynstev there is nothing to adjust to and the point of view is 'everywhere and nowhere' " (*G*, 318). Here, with some help from behind the scenes, our critic does, indeed, get to the essential point: Nabokov's irony is inclusive, not exclusive, a mode of affirming contradictory truths, not arriving at *the* truth.

Even parody must be always self-conscious of itself as a parodic *style*. As another (more sympathetic) imaginary critic tells Fyodor, "you sometimes bring up parody to such a degree of naturalness that it actually becomes a genuine serious thought, but on *this* level it suddenly falters, lapsing into a mannerism that is yours and not a parody of a mannerism, although it is precisely the kind of thing you are ridiculing . . ." (*G*, 351). In other words, a totality of perspective must be aware of and mock even its own totality as a particular kind of perspective or "mannerism." In all this, Nabokov seeks to define a humanism that includes mockery and places art (the modern road to heroic freedom and adventure) at the center of human experience as opposed to realistic, utilitarian, moralistic humanisms which subtlely or grossly denigrate art and thus the possibility of heroic values. Mockery, in short, is precisely the enabling device which makes life and art possible, not a mordant weapon operating at their expense.

With the completion of his biography of Chernyshevski, Fyodor has largely come into his only inheritance, his only possible "gifts" in the face of obvious loss. Not the least of these gifts is his love affair with Zina Mertz (the "real hub" of the Gogol chapter, according to Nabokov [*G*, foreword, 10]). Sexual passion, of course, looms large in Nabokov's later work, but even in *The Gift*, where sex is not mentioned and the relationship seldom dwelt on, Zina is both the focus and central manifestation of Fyodor's desire. Human love, characteristically, both mocks and invokes the spiritual love which it imitates, whose shade or shadow it is. Of his encounter, for example, on the street with another young girl who "contained a particle of that fascination, both special and vague," found in Zina, Fyodor notes that

> he felt for a moment the impact of a hopeless desire, whose whole charm and richness was in its unquenchability. Oh trite demon of cheap thrills, do not tempt me with the catchword "my type." Not that, not that, but something beyond that. Definition is always finite, but I keep straining for the faraway; I search beyond the barricades (of words, of senses, of the world) for infinity, where all, all the lines meet. (*G*, 341)

The passage characteristically moves between the objective "he" and a passionate, lyric, questing "I" that seeks, forever hopelessly, to break out of its prison through the sheer strength of desire.

Not surprisingly, late in the novel, Fyodor experiences the return of his father's presence, now in a more modest pastoral mode. He enjoys summer walks in the Grunewald forest ("a primeval paradise within two miles from Agamemnonstrasse" [*G*, 345]),

> And as often happened on these woodland days, especially when he glimpsed familiar butterflies, Fyodor imagined his father's isolation in other forests—gigantic, infinitely distant, in comparison with which this one was but brushwood, a tree stump, rubbish. And yet he experienced something akin to that Asiatic freedom spreading wide on the maps, to the spirit of his father's peregrinations—and here it was most difficult of all to believe that despite the freedom, despite the greenery and the happy, sunshot dark shade, his father was nonetheless dead. (*G*, 347)

This is, of course, an aesthetic "act" like any of his others. He invites the reader's participation ("Give me your hand, dear reader, and let's go into the forest together" [*G*, 343]); he sustains the act by careful discipline ("He avoided looking closely [at girl sun-bathers] for fear of switching from Pan to Punch" [*G*, 347]); and he experiences the final breakdown of the act in the full face of reality, the usual anticlimax:

> He descended to the sandy shore of the lake and here in the roar of voices the charmed fabric which he himself had so carefully spun completely fell to pieces, and he saw with revulsion the crumpled, twisted, deformed by life's nor'easter, more or less naked or more or less clothed—the latter were the more terrible—bodies of bathers (petty bourgeois, idle workers) stirring on the dirty-gray sand. (*G*, 348)

A description of this lower-class German chamber of horrors continues for two long, detailed paragraphs, culminating in a reference to an all-pervasive smell, "an unforgettable smell, the smell of dust, of sweat, or aquatic slime, or unclean underwear, of aired and dried poverty, the smell of dried, smoked, potted souls a penny a piece" (*G*, 348). This is the world and its ordinary inhabitants in which the heroic soul must somehow attempt survival and affirmation—the world of Stephen Dedalus's bogwater, reeking cow pies, and cold tea, of Wallace Steven's own gray particulars, not to mention the coarse and vulgar Spain where Don Quixote tries to live out his dreams.

But the experience of the Grunewald, at least in the hands of the later Fyodor (a literary treatment of what even originally was fundamentally an "aesthetic" adventure), involves a genuine totality of perspective (Pan *and* Punch). The shadow or spirit of his father's questing ("something akin to" it) still retains its positive and all-important role as the entire focus of his moral and spiritual commitments and clearly distinguishes him from the "smoked, potted souls" on the beach. It distinguishes Fyodor also from another young romantic exile whose suicide in the Grunewald is described early in the book. This person, involved with two others in a relationship that turns from friendship into a muddled love triangle, believes that only death will restore "an ideal and flawless circle" (*G*, 57). Fyodor, however, accepts life (reluctantly) as a muddle and feels death to be a horror; his own saving ground incorporates these "realities" into a more comprehensive spatial perspective. Fyodor, finally, like his creator, attains to a parody romanticism which mocks (that is, secularizes) transcendental Power, while still affirming in its own fashion the energized word and the continued possibility of questing for that word. Reality forever "imprisons," but it does not prevent imaginative apprehension. As Wallace Stevens describes both possibilities and limits in "An Ordinary Evening in New Haven": "A great town hanging pendent in a shade, / An enormous nation happy in a style, / Everything as unreal as real can be, / In the inexquisite eye."[13] For Fyodor even fate itself seems to play or at least sanction the game. He tells Zina later in the novel that "the most enchanting things in nature and art are based on deception" (*G*, 376), and suggests to her that he will build the plot of his next work (*The Gift*) around this theme. Appropriately enough, in enhancing such a theme fully, he will move from romantic lyric and epic toward literary pastiche. Even the realistic structure and concrete detail of *The Gift*—as Fyodor calls it, "a good, thick old-fashioned novel" (*G*, 16)—is obviously, by such very reference, turned into self-conscious imitation.

Fyodor or Nabokov, let me stress again, engages in parody not for metafictional ends, but as a means of continuing "the spirit of his father's peregrinations" toward an ideal consummation of ecstasy and love, the only proper goal of the heroic soul. "Ecstasy" and "love" are, indeed, Nabokov's terms, used in *Speak, Memory* to describe the "timeless" pursuit of butterflies, one of his own methods for achieving "something akin to" the Power of the past. "The highest enjoyment of timelessness . . . ," he writes, "is when I stand among rare butterflies and their food plants. This is ecstasy, and behind the ecstasy is something else, which is hard to explain. It is like a momentary vacuum into which rushes all that I love."[14] Nabokov's parodies, likewise, are only another method of setting protagonists and author free within the confines of their prison to find at least "shimmers" of spiritual truth. He systematically exploits the style toward which Fyodor must painfully grope in *The Gift*. Many of the more popular and banal literary genres—the detective or "mystery" story, the confessional, the exposé or investigative biography (the search for the truth about someone)—are already naive parodies of romantic/heroic narrative and become, in Nabokov's hands, perfect vehicles for descriptions of the romantic quest in a banal world.

The focus remains always on the "act" (action, performance) of questing, on whatever spiritual intimations that process itself may furnish. Ends remain illusory, anticlimactic, fatal, even utilitarian. Ecstasy, love, creative "naming" (all those apparent ends associated within the prototypal butterfly hunt) are finally *human* qualities, expansions of the self, emotional and imaginative aggrandizement, rather than dimensions of the absolute. To say as much is to limit whatever claims are made for these qualities, not to denigrate them or make their pursuit less crucial. Nabokov, for example, writes of his mother, who enjoyed searching for mushrooms on the grounds of their country estate, that "her delight was in the quest, and this quest had its rules"—set, of course, by herself.[15] The family, to be sure, ate the mushrooms for dinner, but this is almost beside the point, scarcely the real concern of mother and son. In *The Gift*, Fyodor, his father, even Chernyshevski have most in common the heroic quality of their seeking, their act of pursuit as hunters, not what, if anything, they find. But Fyodor alone becomes the ironist, and in the ironic history of his own quest, he finally discovers an adequate vehicle for his heroic theme. It is a lesson which Nabokov had already learned, and it is the crucial lesson of his literary career.

Notes

1. *The Gift*, trans. Michael Scammell (New York: Putnam, 1963), foreword, [p. 10]; hereafter cited in the text as *G*.

2. Concerned himself with refuting metafictional readings, Robert Merrill admirably sums up the dominant thesis of Nabokov studies: "He has been labeled a metafictionist, a parafictionist, a fabulator, a pattern maker, and an artificer. . . . The writers with whom he is most often associated are Beckett, Borges, and John Barth; repeatedly we are assured that Nabokov, like his fellow illusionists, 'dismisses mimesis and identification with the hero distainfully as mythology,' and that his subject is either the conflict 'between different concepts of art' or nothing less than 'form itself' " (*Modern Fiction Studies*, 25 [1979], 439–40). Merrill's own quotations are representative views from various books and articles on Nabokov.

3. Discussions of Nabokov's parody are popular with his critics (not to mention Nabokov himself), but these discussions tend to emphasize the critical and deconstructive dimensions of parody or its quality of reflexivity, artifice, game. I am more concerned with the mechanics of ironic affirmation, with parody as a device for continuity and preservation. Paradoxically, this kind of parody enables the writer to span the unbridgeable rift between past and present. For good, representative discussions of Nabokov's parody see Alfred Appel, Jr., "*Lolita*: The Springboard of Parody," in *Nabokov: The Man and His Work*, ed. L. S. Dembo (Madison: Univ. of Wisconsin Press, 1967), pp. 106–43, and Dabney Stuart, *Nabokov: The Dimensions of Parody* (Baton Rouge: Louisiana State Press, 1978).

4. *The Real Life of Sebastian Knight* (New York: New Directions, 1979), p. 27.

5. In my recent work, I have been attempting to extend the concept of mock-heroic beyond its too narrow identification with a type of predominantly eighteenth-century satiric literature. Rather, I use the term "mock-heroic" here and elsewhere to describe a form of ironic narrative which ambivalently both affirms heroic values and mocks those same values, a narrative form extending from Cervantes to Byron, Joyce, W. C. Williams, Wallace Stevens, and others. See my articles "Mock-heroes and Mock-Heroic Narrative: Byron's *Don Juan* in the Context of Cervantes," *Studies in the Literary Imagination*, 9 (Spring 1976), 69–86 and "The Mock-Heroics of Desire: Some Stoic Personae in the Work of William Carlos Williams," in *The Stoic Strain in American Literature*, ed. Duane MacMillan (Toronto: Univ. of Toronto Press, 1979), pp. 97–112.

6. *Ada or Ardor: A Family Chronicle* (New York: McGraw-Hill, 1969), p. 595.

7. *Speak, Memory* (New York: Putnam, 1966), p. 176.

8. From a poem in his collection *Drops of Paint*, quoted in Andrew Field, *Nabokov: His Life in Art* (Boston: Little, Brown, 1976), p. 71. Field traces Nabokov's own "Georgian" phase at some length. Nabokov has argued (in the Foreword to *The Gift*, [p. 9]) that Fyodor's experience should not be construed as his, and this is true enough on the literal level. As my comments everywhere suggest, however, I view Fyodor's quest for an adequate form, both its dynamics and its outcome, as essentially Nabokov's own.

9. *The Real Life of Sebastian Knight*, p. 29.

10. Ibid., p. 23.

11. "A University Poem," quoted in *Nabokov*, p. 83.

12. I am not arguing that Nabokov, like Fyodor, *discovers* this formula in *The Gift*. He had, of course, used it already in such novels as *The Defense* (1930). My point, rather, is that Fyodor's analytic quest for this formula, his growing awareness of its significance and its certain equivalence to the earlier straight heroics and nostalgia—all are the concern of *The Gift*; Fyodor's quest, in other words, becomes Nabokov's own self-conscious subject. As Nabokov's first major book, the culmination of his writing in Russian, *The Gift* is his most complete and explicit description of the development of his mock-heroic art. Like most major work, it both summarizes past achievement and marks out new directions, thus a beginning as much as an end.

13. *The Collected Poems of Wallace Stevens* (New York: Knopf, 1964), p. 468.

14. *Speak, Memory*, p. 134.

15. Ibid., p. 43.

The Ambidextrous Universe of Nabokov's *Look at the Harlequins!*

D. Barton Johnson*

"Space is a swarming in the eyes; and time, A singing in the ears." These lines are a part of John Shade's meditation on death and the hereafter in his poem "Pale Fire" in Nabokov's novel of the same name.[1] They also bespeak Nabokov's interest in questions of space and time in relation to man's fate. As we shall see, these particular lines were to have a curious future. Some two years after the appearance of *Pale Fire*, Martin Gardner, perhaps best known as the long time mathematical games editor of the *Scientific American*, published a volume entitled *The Ambidextrous Universe: Left, Right and the Fall of Parity.*[2] The book is a popular account of one of the major scientific breakthroughs of our time—the physicists' overthrow of parity, a scientific event which is shown to be "intimately connected with left and right and the nature of mirror reversals" (9). In his discussion of space and time Gardner compares these dimensions to the two lenses in a pair of glasses without which we could see nothing. The external world is not directly perceivable and can be apprehended only through these lenses which, however, shape and color all of our perceptions (144). It is in this context that Gardner aptly quotes the above lines from "Pale Fire" which he jokingly attributes to John Francis Shade. Only the imaginary poet (and not Nabokov) is cited in the index.

Nabokov was apparently bemused by Gardner's reification of his invented poet and retaliated in his 1969 *Ada*.[3] In the "Texture of Time" section in which Van ruminates on the mysteries of space and time, he links space with the senses of sight, touch, and kinesthesis; time, on the other hand, is more closely associated with hearing. Van then quotes the line "Space is a swarming in the eyes, and Time a singing in the ears," attributing it to "John Shade, a modern poet, as quoted by an invented philosopher ('Martin Gardiner') in *The Ambidextrous Universe*, page 165" (542).

When Nabokov's last novel, *Look at the Harlequins!*, appeared in 1974 no mention was made of either John Shade's lines or of Martin Gardner. To Nabokov readers not familiar with Gardner's book it might have appeared that the humorous exchange had come to an end. To one knowing Gardner's book, however, it is clear that the exchange not only was not over but had entered another, more serious dimension in that Nabokov's last novel has obvious (albeit tacit) affinities with the central thesis of Gardner's *Ambidextrous Universe.* The final episode in the exchange came with the 1979 revision of Gardner's volume, now newly resubtitled *Mirror Asymmetry and Time-Reversed Worlds.* So apparent are these affinities that Gardner discusses Nabokov's *Look at the Harle-*

*This essay appears here for the first time by permission of the author.

quins! in a new section in which he asserts that "questions about the symmetries of space and time are so essential to the plot that I like to think that the book was influenced by Nabokov's reading of the first edition of this book" (271). In what follows we shall examine the interrelations of the two books and show how Nabokov adopted a cosmology implicit in Gardner's *Ambidextrous Universe* and adapted it to conform to one of the conceptual models that underlie a number of his major fictions.

Look at the Harlequins![4] is the autobiography of Vadim Vadimovich N., an eminent Anglo-Russian writer born in 1899. The autobiography, composed in the years following the seventy-five-year-old author's miraculous recovery from a mysterious and massive paralytic stroke, is a highly selective one focusing upon three "characters" in the writer's long life: his wives, his books, and his Dementia (85). Although it is the four wives and, to a lesser degree, his books that provide the narrative framework, it is the third character, Dementia, that is VV's true mistress and Muse. One reading of the memoir strongly suggests that VV's account of his wives and books is in large part the product of his Dementia. We shall see, however, that even the narrator's dementia may not be entirely what it seems.

Vadim Vadimovich's Dementia is a many splendored thing. VV, who spends his childhood being passed among rich relatives thanks to the tangled marital lives of his putative parents, suffers sieges of insanity throughout his life. Even as a child of seven or eight he harbors "the secrets of a confined madman" (8), something he becomes at least seven times. Nor is his lunacy confined to those intervals of hospitalization. At other times he intermittently is afflicted by *kegelkugel* headaches, neuralgia, and confusion about his surroundings. VV describes his early illness as "a certain insidious and relentless connection with other states of being which were not exactly 'previous' or 'future' but definitely out of bounds, mortally speaking" (7). The nature of these "aching links" with the unknown becomes more evident only during VV's final seizure. This haunting sense of other states of being is manifested in various ways. One of these is termed the "numerical nimbus" by Moody, a London psychiatrist (Moody = mood = joy = Freud) who briefly treats VV. The "numerical numbus" attacks are sometimes occasioned by a faint ray of light falling upon the sleeper which awakens him into a state of madness. Along this narrow beam descends a row of bright dots "with dreadful meaningful intervals between them" (16). These intervals must be measured and calculated so that their secret message is revealed. Successful decipherment will allow the dreamer to escape a horrible death and flee into a region resembling landscape vignettes (a brook, a bosquet) like those surrounding an initial Gothic B commencing a chapter in a frightening old book for children. It seems obscurely important that in this region "the brook and the boughs and the beauty of the Beyond all began with the initial of Being" (16).

The foregoing symptoms are not those considered the most grave by the narrator. Vadim Vadimovich is most tormented by what would seem to be an inconsequential quirk—his inability to mentally transpose left and right. So distraught is he by this apparently trivial inability that he feels honor bound to confess it to each of his four brides-to-be. The compulsion seems all the stranger in that it does not extend to the revelation of seemingly much more serious aspects of his dementia. The narrator's preoccupation with his left/right aberration is obscurely linked with another oddity which, while not openly associated with the former, proves to be closely connected with it. Each of VV's four confessions is preceded by scenes in which the autobiographer becomes autovoyeur standing nude before a mirror while taking physiological and psychological stock before committing himself to each new relationship.[5] Typical of these narcissistic exercises is the first in which "a warning spasm" shoots through VV's "flayed consciousness" as he gazes at the reflected "symmetrical mass of animal attributes, the elephant proboscis, the twin sea urchins" (31). Two things are to be noted about the mirror scenes. One, overt, is the emphasis on bilateral symmetry; the other, tacit, is the mirror's property of reversing left and right—a capability that mocks the narrator's own mental inability to visualize this mundane act.

Vadim Vadimovich's confessions to his prospective brides, although they range in time from 1922 to 1970 and are set in varied formats, display a remarkable uniformity. As Vadim and his first bride-to-be, Iris, lie on the Côte d'Azure beach he asks her to visualize the two hundred pace tree-lined lane running from the village post office to the garden gate of her villa. As they walk (in imagination) they see a vineyard on the right and a church graveyard on the left. Arriving at the villa, Iris suddenly recalls that she has forgotten to buy stamps. At this point in the scenario Vadim asks Iris, with eyes closed, to imagine herself turning on her heel "so that 'right' instantly becomes 'left' " with the vineyard now on her left and the churchyard on the right (41). Iris visualizes the left-right reorientation as easily as she would make the about-face in life. Vadim, however, cannot. Some "atrocious obstacle" prevents him from mentally transforming one direction into its opposite. As he says, "I am crushed, I am carrying the whole world on my back in the process of trying to visualize my turning round and making myself see in terms of 'right' what I saw in terms of 'left' and vice versa" (42). For VV, any given stretch of the universe is either permanently right-handed or left-handed and any attempt to mentally reverse the two brings him to the brink of madness. Iris pragmatically suggests that they should simply forget what seems to her "a stupid philosophical riddle—on the lines of what does 'right' and 'left' *mean* in our absence, when nobody is looking, in pure space, and what, anyway, is space . . ." (42).

Since the narrator's left/right quirk is wholly one of visual imagination and does not have immediate physical consequences, his preoccupation with it would seem to be warranted only in that he believes it to be a forewarning of the so-called Dementia paralytica that finally strikes him down. This fear becomes reality soon after the seventy-one-year-old VV arrives in Switzerland with his last love. In order to ease the awkwardness of his ritual premarital confession he hits upon the expedient of asking her to read an early chapter of his just completed *Ardis* manuscript in which the hero describes his (and VV's) "tussles with the Specter of Space and the myth of Cardinal Points" (321). While "you" reads, VV takes his preprandial stroll down a lane ending at a parapet from which he gazes at the setting sun. As he turns to retrace his steps that which has happened so often in thought becomes a reality: "I could not turn. To make that movement would mean rolling the world around on its axis and that was as impossible as travelling back from the present moment to the previous one" (236). VV collapses into a paralyzed trance from which he gradually emerges with a new understanding of certain questions of his existence.

We now come to the question of why VV's madness takes such a strange form—the mental inability to transpose left and right. In addition to the bizarre symptoms already outlined VV has yet another oddity—one that would seem to be much more fundamental than those sketched above. Throughout his long life the narrator is haunted by the feeling that he and his works are but pale shadows, inferior variants of another vastly more gifted Anglo-Russian writer and his works. VV's madness, misdiagnosed as dementia paralytica, is obviously demetia praecox, now better known as schizophrenia. *LATH* is the fanciful "autobiography" of the narrator's mad half. Glimmers from his sane half occasionally filter into the narrator's mind giving him inklings of his other self—the self which is the original of which VV is the paler, flawed copy. The identity of the original (who never appears in the narrative) is more or less of an open secret. He is, of course, another Nabokov figure whom we shall refer to as "Vladimir Vladimirovich" (in quotes) as opposed to the narrator, Vadim Vadimovich. VV's strange inability to mentally transpose left and right is symptomatic of his inability to evert himself into his "other," that is, to integrate the halves of his split personality and to merge his delusional world with its "real" world counterpart.

There is reason to suppose, however, that there is yet another dimension to VV's duality. The deranged narrator is on several occasions badly shaken by intrusions into his delusional world of bits of evidence that things are not as they seem. These encounters lead him to reflect on his troubled sense of identity. It is not by chance that these musings on his identity are often cast in terms of "another world." It is possible and plausible to assume on one level that VV is schizoid and has created a fantasy world within the real world. On another level, however, it is possible to suppose that there are two worlds and the narrator, perhaps during his extended periods of insanity, is in the wrong one.[6] In other words, the duality exists on the level of worlds, as well as in VV's mind. Let us examine the evidence for such an interpretation.

On one warm wet Paris night as VV walks to a meeting with the Russian bookseller Oksman, he is especially oppressed by his recurrent feeling of duality. He senses that his life is "an inferior variant of another man's life, somewhere on this or another earth"—a life which the narrator is condemned to impersonate (89). During his talk with Oksman he is further shaken by the bookseller's reminiscences about VV's father at a time when the father was, according to VV, long dead. Also distressing is that Oksman (and several other characters) confuse VV's novels, such as *Tamara* and *Camera Lucida*, with those of another writer, the author of *Mary* and *Camera Obskura*. Later that night the emotional pressure of these "coincidences" brings VV near the point of breakdown. Most traumatic, VV says, is that these events seem to "establish a sudden connection with another world, so soon after my imagining with especial dread that I might be permanently impersonating somebody living as a real being beyond the constellation of my tears and asterisks—*that* was unendurable, *that* dared not happen!" (96–97). The "other world" motif is echoed in other passages. The sight of a woman's bare back "recalled something from a parallel world . . ." (74). Many years later, VV is tormented by the suspicion that *Ardis*, his most private book, "might be an unconscious imitation of another's unearthly art . . ." (234). The most significant of these "other world" references occurs near and at the end of VV's narrative as he describes his awakening from his three-week-long coma. His first concern is establishing his identity: "my family name began with an N and bore an odious resemblance to the surname or pseudonum of a presumably notorious (Notorov? No) Bulgarian, or Babylonian, or maybe, Betelgeusian writer with whom scatter-brained *émigrés* from some other galaxy constantly confused me" (248–49). Suddenly his name flashes into his mind. To be noted here is the *B* which echoes the "enchanted region" of brooks, bosquets, and the Beyond—all guarded by the Gothic *B* in VV's "numerical nimbus" nightmares (16). This region of the Beyond would seem to be associated with the other world sensed and now perhaps glimpsed by the narrator. During his trance VV's speeding mind has seemingly experienced that which lies beyond death. As he says: "Problems of identity have been, if not settled, at least set. Artistic insights have been granted. I was allowed to take my palette with me to the very remote reaches of dim and dubious being" (239). The very last lines of VV's story reassert the two world theme. As the convalescing author drifts off to sleep, thoughts of the tea with rum which had earlier been promised hypnogogically float through his mind—"Ceylon and Jamaica, the sibling islands. . . ."

The frequency and contextual positioning of these "other world" references may plausibly lead to an interpretation that posits the existence of two worlds—nonidentical twin worlds with parallel individuals. There may really be two VVs—one of whom has somehow fallen into the other world where he becomes his "other's" shadow.

The most obvious point at which Nabokov's *LATH* and Gardner's *Ambidextrous Universe* intersect is in their shared preoccupation with left and right as fundamental categories. Gardner's book is an examination of one of the most basic of all natural laws—the conservation of parity. This law holds that the universe and the laws that govern it display a fundamental, invariable mirror symmetry with no preference for either right or left (176).[7] The universe is, in Gardner's felicitous phrase, "ambidextrous" and his book is, *inter alia*, a fascinating survey of the myriad ways in which symmetry permeates the universe at all levels: animals and plants, art and illusion, astronomy, chemistry and physics. The starting point and guiding metaphor is, however, mirror imagery—a subject long dear to Nabokov and of immediate import in *LATH*. Even at the most superficial level we need point only to VV's recurrent mirror fetish prior to his ritual left/right confessions and his mirror image initials.

Gardner's discussion of left and right shows these concepts to be more elusive than they might seem at first blush. Consider the following questions. What would happen if the entire universe were instantly transposed so that left became right and vice versa? (146–47). Put in another way—if the cosmos were completely empty (observerless) save for a single human hand, would it be possible to determine whether the hand is the left or the right? (141). These questions are closely akin to that of "what does 'right' and 'left' *mean* in our absence, when nobody is looking, in pure space" (42), raised by Iris in response to VV's confession of his inability to mentally transpose left and right. As Gardner notes, Iris dismisses the question as "a stupid philosophical riddle" (217). We shall, however, see that the riddle is far from stupid and that it opens the door to a much larger issue that is critical to our understanding of Nabokov's novel.

The above paradoxes dealing with consequences of instant total reversability and with the hand in empty space are respectively drawn from Leibniz and Kant by Gardner and are utilized by Nabokov in both *Ada* and *LATH*.[8] Of the greatest moment for our argument is that they are introduced in the course of Gardner's explanation of the fourth dimension, or more precisely, any spatial dimension higher than three. Gardner demonstrates that in each spatial dimension certain operations that are manifestly impossible in that dimension are easily performed in the next higher dimension. Consider, for example, that in two dimensional space the mirror image figures ⅃ and L are not superimposable even though they are identical in every respect apart from handedness, that is, they are enantiomorphs. If, however, the two figures are allowed the advantage of a third dimension, depth, then one may be picked up and turned over, that is, moved through 3-space, and be superimposed on the other. Their left/right asymmetry disappears in the next higher dimension. By projection, the same applies to 3-dimensional enantiomorphic solids with regard to 4-space, and so on *ad infinitum*. Unfortunately it is impossible or nearly so for 3-space beings to visualize objects in 4-space just as it would be impossible for 2-space beings to imagine the superposition of the above-mentioned ⅃ and L since it entails a higher dimension.[9] The left/right reversal of mirror imagery exists on every dimensional level and the enantiomorphs of each level become identical and superimposable only on successively higher levels.

The idea of the fourth dimension is beloved by science fiction writers. One of the first writers to base a science fiction story on the idea of the left/right reversal of an asymmetrical object by moving it through 4-space was H. G. Wells, a particular favorite of Nabokov.[10] In "The Plattner Story," a tale which is no less permeated by the left/right opposition than *LATH*, the hero, a young chemist, inadvertently blows himself into the fourth dimension where he spends nine days before a second explosion returns him to ordinary 3-space with the difference that the left and right sides of his body are reversed and he writes a mirror image script with his left hand.[11] During his sojourn in 4-space Plattner discovers that he is living in a dark "Other World" inhabited by the souls of those who formerly lived on earth.

Wells's fictional use of the right/left mirror image idea in the context of another world has strong resonance with the use of this theme in Nabokov's novel. There can be no doubt of Nabokov's awareness of the story since Gardner specifically discusses it (148). Although Nabokov makes no specific mention of "The Plattner Story," there are a number of references to Wells' work in *LATH*. In reply to Iris' "I adore Wells, don't you," VV affirms Wells as "the greatest romancer and magician of our time," but rejects his "sociological stuff." Both of the lovers are much moved by a shared detail in Wells' 1913 novel, *The Passionate Friends* (22).[12] Iris also makes passing reference to the minor Wells' character Mr. Snooks (22) and is chillingly entranced by the early science fiction tale *The Island of Dr. Moreau* (88).[13]

The interrelations between the cosmology of Nabokov's *LATH* and Gardner's "ambidextrous universe" are not limited to those outlined above. Gardner's far-ranging survey touches upon the foregoing matters as preliminary to his main topic—the fall of parity and closely related ideas in theoretical physics. Strangely enough some of these recent advances seem to parallel earlier, often fanciful, speculations such as Wells' and to argue at least the theoretical possibility of twin worlds. In the late 1950s physicists determined that virtually every subatomic particle had an antiparticle twin (192). It is now thought that an antiparticle may be a mirror image reflection of a particle opposed to its twin counterpart only in electrical charge which distinction in turn signals some type of asymmetric spatial structure in the particle itself (197). In other words, a particle and its antiparticle differ from each other only in terms of "handedness"—left versus right—as a mirror reverses the image it reflects. These mirror image particles, just like their counterparts, can, in principle, combine to form anti-atoms and antimolecules—in short, antimatter, which, apart from its opposite handedness displays the exact structure of its counterpart in "our" world. Antiworlds and even antigalaxies populated by antipeople are perfectly possible in principle and are hypothetically related to their counterparts on our world in terms of left/right mirror imagery.

Let us now return to the world of *LATH*. We have noted the book's use of the left/right opposition as a metaphor for VV's apparent schizophrenia, his sense of being an impoverished nonidentical twin of another, more gifted Anglo-Russian writer. On several of the occasions that the nonidentical twin is mentioned (nonidentical because left and right are interchanged), it is suggested that he lives in another world, possibly even another galaxy. It seems probable that as well as borrowing the left/right opposition from Gardner, Nabokov also borrowed a cosmology for *LATH*. Vadim Vadimovich N., an antiperson corresponding to "Vladimir Vladimirovich N.," lives on an antiworld that literally mirrors, in a distorted fashion, the other VV's world. VV, perhaps due to his peculiar madness, has intimations of his counterposed twin and his world. The fictional universe of *LATH* and its narrator is a twinned antiworld opposed to Nabokov's world just as the fictional universe of *Ada*, Anti-Terra, is opposed to the mythical Terra, that is, our world. Terra is mentally accessible to anti-Terrans only in states of madness just as VV is most susceptible to his feeling of the other world and his other self in periods of severe mental distress. Also to be considered is the possibility that VV, like Wells' Plattner, has somehow fallen into the "wrong" world by accident but retains only distressing memory traces of his own world.

Although the exact nature of the physical relationship between VV's two worlds is not critical to an understanding of *LATH*, it is worth pointing out that they are not necessarily remote from one another. As we have observed, the resolution of the problem of the left/right reversal of asymmetric objects lies in the fourth dimension which subsumes the three spatial dimensions of the ordinary world. Thus one of VV's worlds may be contained within the other just as the world of plane, 2-space geometry is contained within that of solid, 3-space geometry. Further, Gardner points out that it has been (half seriously) proposed by physicists that reversed mirror image worlds might coexist in the same segment of space-time. Although the physicists' two worlds could not interact, it is, Gardner says, conceivable that they could interpenetrate each other somewhat like a pair of checker players playing one game on the black squares while a second pair simultaneously plays another game on the red squares (259). This sort of imagery is also evoked by the interlaced black and white diamond pattern of the harlequin costume and depicted on the dust cover of Nabokov's novel. This pattern neatly symbolizes the intra-adjacent worlds of Vadim Vadimovich and "Vladimir Vladimirovich." In any case the "other," fourth dimensional world may be identified with that "other state of Being" that VV senses in his madness and into which he dreams of escaping (7, 16).[14]

The pervasive left/right opposition that characterizes *LATH* is an analogue of the two opposed worlds implicit in the novel's cosmology. Not only is the hero haunted by the idea of a mirror image double but so is his entire world. We shall see that symmetric left/right imagery provides a framework for a number of other incidents and themes in the book as well as those fundamental ones just discussed. These minor left/right symmetries seem to observe the pattern described by VV as he awakes from his final seizure of dementia paralytica. At first physical sensation returns in a pattern of left/right symmetry; then within the left and right panels of imagination, and, finally, further images occur within each of the panels (242–43)—symmetries within symmetries within symmetries.

First among the left/right symmetries that afford *LATH* its formal structure, we have the names (and initials) of its characters. Most central, of course, is the opposition of the antiworld's Vadim Vadimovich to the real world's "Vladimir Vladimirovich." Nor is it by chance that within each of the opposed twin universes the names of each of the protagonists are, in turn, doubled, that is, Vadim, son of Vadim; Vladimir, son of Vladimir. Within the fictional antiworld the name of Vadim's real father also offers a doubling, albeit a partial one, Nikifor Nikodimovich. Also of note is that the V of Vadim Vadimovich can be viewed as a slightly skewed, truncated derivative of the N of the father's names much as Russian aristocrats gave their bastard children truncated family names based on their own. Compare Nabokov's *Pnin* and VV's *Dr. Olga Repnin.*

The narrator's six Russian and six English novels are, as we have noted, distorted reflections of Nabokov's own Russian and English books. It is thematically appropriate that as VV undertakes his last self-evaluation in his mirror before deciding to join his life to that of his last love, he looks "into another, far deeper mirror," where he sees and contemplates first his Russian and then his English oeuvre. The two symmetrical sets are explicitly described in terms of two worlds (228–29). It will be recalled that this transition between languages and literary worlds resulted in an extended period of madness for the writer coincident with his arrival in "the new world," a journey that physically duplicated his linguistic migration from Russian to English.[15]

There are still other odd examples of handedness in connection with VV's writing. In his early pocket diaries he notices that among his accounts of events "factual or more or less fictional" he sees that "dreams and other distortions of 'reality' " are written in a special left-handed slant (19–20). Another curious detail surfaces in VV's account of his first English language novel, *See under Real.* The conception of the book first comes to him as he lies in bed. It is not by chance that his first English novel appears to him under his right cheek "as a varicolored procession with a head and a tail, winding in a generally westerly direction. . ." (123). There is, then, a correlation of Russian with left and English with right, an appropriate simulation of VV's life and career and, secondarily, of the translation process to which each of his works is eventually subjected.

All four of VV's premarital confessions of his left/right spatial aberration are described in circumstantial detail in terms of short walks from one landmark to another and back.[16] It is curious that either directly or inferentially each of these meticulously described walks proceeds in an east/west direction (or its reverse) but never north/south or in an indeterminate, unspecified direction. All of VV's journeys starting from his youthful escape from Russia are marked by this left/right bi-directionality. Thus the East/West opposition is yet another analogue of the left/right opposition that structures the worlds of *LATH*.

The incest theme also has obvious congruity with the left/right symmetry of the narrative. The narrator, his wife Iris, her brother Ivor Black, and Wladimir Blagidze all appear to be the children of the master spy, Count Starov. The incest theme is sounded once again in the episode with Bel, the narrator's daughter. Here a particularly marked left/right symmetry develops which seems to be reflected in both of the novel's worlds. It would seem to be beyond coincidence that Bel and VV's ultimate love, "you," are both born on the same day. "You" is regarded as the intrusion of "Reality" into the writer's dualized existence (226, 250). This situation yields a remarkably elegant equation bridging the novel's twin worlds: Bel is to "you" as Vadim Vadimovich is to "Vladimir Vladimirovich." Another such equation involves the narrator's pen name: V. Irisin : Vadim Vadimovich :: V. Sirin : "Vladimir Vladimirovich." On the most abstract level it would not seem inappropriate to see incest as a metaphor for the interaction of VV's Russian and English works.

The ambidextrous universe model in which one world is a flawed mirror image of another world in a higher dimension has been used by Nabokov in a number of his fictions, albeit not in the exact configuration suggested by Martin Gardner's book. One of the earliest uses of the cosmology was in *Invitation to a Beheading* written in 1934. Cincinnatus, the artist protagonist, awaiting execution in a totalitarian dystopia, has inklings of another world, a utopia peopled by beings like himself. These two worlds are symbolized in the novel by the Russian words *tut* ("here") and *tam* ("there") which form the conceptual antipodes of the book. Cincinnatus fears his approaching death but dimly senses that it marks not the end of life but the point of transition between the worlds—translation from a false world to a real one. This theme is further developed in Nabokov's *Bend Sinister* from the early 1940s. Philosopher Adam Krug, the victim of a nightmarish revolutionary state founded on the principle of equality of individual consciousness, comes to sense the existence of a higher consciousness on another world that shapes both him and his world. Ultimately, Krug is spared first through the insight afforded by seeming madness and then, just before he is shot, by translation into the world of infinite consciousness, the world of his author sitting at his typewriter. As the novel's title implies, Krug's world is a "left-handed" one imperfectly counterpoised to that of his creator. *Ada*, the work that occupied Nabokov throughout much of the 1960s, is explicitly formulated in terms of a world and an antiworld, Terra and Anti-Terra. The events of the novel take place on Anti-Terra (or Demonia) where the hero, Van, devotes his professional life to the exploration of the existence of Terra, a distorted mirror image of his own antiworld.[17] Here again, madness and death are the transition zones between the two worlds.

Nabokov's last novel, *Look at the Harlequins!*, is the culmination of his development of the ambidextrous universe theme which we have seen to provide the underlying cosmology for a number of his major works. The events of these novels all take place on antiworlds. Their plots hinge upon the strivings of the antiworld hero to apprehend the parallel real world of his creator. In each case gleams and glimmers of the real world are uniquely afforded to the antiworld hero in dreams and/or madness, although full realization comes only at death, the transition point between the two worlds. There is, however, another source of evidence of the existence of the "real" world that is available to Nabokov's antiworld protagonists and to his readers. This is the elaborate and intricate set of patterns and clues that are implanted in the text(ure) of the fictional antiworld. It is the growing awareness of these allusions and patterns that often leads the hero (and the reader) to divine the existence of the other, "real" world with its resident author.

In each of his twin world novels Nabokov provides the hero (and the reader) with some fundamental opposition, a bi-polar metaphor that demarcates each of the paired worlds. In *Invitation to a Beheading*, it is the *tut/tam* ("here/there") opposition. In *Bend Sinister*, it is the contrast of the linear and the curved, specifically the swastika versus the circle. In *Ada*, the opposition is explicit: Anti-Terra versus Terra. In *Look at the Harlequins!* Nabokov has drawn upon the fundamental left/right opposition of Martin Gardner's *Ambidextrous Universe* to supply the emblematic structure for his fictional cosmology.

Notes

1. Vladimir Nabokov, *Pale Fire* (New York: Putnam, 1962), p. 40.

2. New York: Basic Books, 1964. Page number citations show that this is the edition utilized by Nabokov. We shall also have occasion to cite the new "Second revised, updated edition": *The Ambidextrous Universe: Mirror Asymmetry and Time-Reversed Worlds* (New York: Scribner, 1979). Unless otherwise specified, citations are to the new edition.

3. Vladimir Nabokov, *Ada or Ardor: A Family Chronicle* (New York: McGraw-Hill, 1969).

4. New York: McGraw-Hill, 1974. I shall follow Nabokov's and his narrator's convention of referring to the book by its punning acronym *LATH*. The lath, bat, or wand are fixed attributes of the commedia dell'arte figure of the harlequin; see H. Grabes, *Fictitious Biographies: Vladimir Nabokov's English Novels* (The Hague: Mouton, 1977), pp. 123–25. Since the surname of the narrator is intentionally obscure I shall refer to him by the initials of his first name and patronymic, that is, VV. VV's last love is known only as "you" and we have followed this same usage.

5. These scenes are as follows: Iris—p. 31. Louise—p. 174. "You"—p. 227. The parallel scene for VV's second wife, Annette, exists in nascent state on p. 88.

6. Compare the situation of Cincinnatus in Nabokov's *Invitation to a Beheading* (Harmondsworth: Penguin, 1963) who senses that he is trapped in the wrong world (p. 78).

7. The law of conservation of parity was thought to be absolute until 1957 when it was shown that in weak interactions at the subatomic particle level there is indeed a slight preference for right-handedness although at the macrolevel the law continues to hold. See Gardner, chapter 20.

8. Kant's "hand in empty space" is used by Nabokov on p. 373 of *Ada*. As I have noted, Iris' formulation—as well as the central conceptual structure of *LATH*—derives from the questions posed by Leibniz and Kant.

9. The art of computer graphics is now beginning to create visual models of what were formerly abstract mathematical constructs. For a survey, see Kenneth Engel, "Shadows of the Fourth Dimension," *Science*, 80, No. 5 (July–August 1980), 68–73.

10. Nabokov, who was not known for the generosity of his critical judgments, once described Wells as a "writer for whom I have the deepest admiration." In a 1970 interview with Alfred Appel, he singled out the science fiction "romances": *The Time Machine*, *The Invisible Man*, *The Country of the Blind*, *The War of the Worlds*, and *The First Men on the Moon* (in Vladimir Nabokov, *Strong Opinions* [New York: McGraw-Hill, 1973], p. 175). "The Plattner Story," discussed below, may be found in H. G. Wells' *Tale of the Unexpected* (London: Collins, 1970). In addition to Wells, Nabokov shares another favorite author with Martin Gardner. Cf. Nabokov's 1923 translation *Anya v stranye chudes* (*Alice in Wonderland*), recently reissued (New York: Dover, 1976), and Martin Gardner's *The Annotated Alice* (New York: Clarkson N. Potter, 1960).

11. VV's meeting with the bookseller Oksman triggers particularly severe distress about the narrator's otherworldly double. After this meeting he returns home and records the encounter in an undescribed cipher (p. 97). It would be thematically appropriate if that cipher were a mirror image one such as that used by Leonardo da Vinci in his notebooks; see *The Literary Works of Leonardo Da Vinci*, comp. and ed. Jean Paul Richter, 3rd ed. (New York: Praeger, 1970).

12. Given Nabokov's (and VV's) distaste for Wells' "sociological" literature, their affection for *The Passionate Friends* is curious for the book, especially in its latter part, is a feminist tract. Perhaps Nabokov's fondness for it is due to its earlier part which describes the developing romance of Steven and Mary on an idyllic English country estate not unlike that of the Nabokov family near St. Petersburg and on which Nabokov had his first romance. The power of the book over Nabokov's imagination is attested by his response to a *Times Literary Supplement* query on the most underrated books of the last seventy-five years. Nabokov cited Wells' *The Passionate Friends* as "my most prized example of the unjustly ignored masterpiece" and describes how at age fourteen or fifteen he went through all of Wells' fiction in his father's library. His claim that he never reread *The Passionate Friends* finds some support in the fact that he slightly misquotes a favorite line that he uses in *LATH* and cities again his *TLS* response made some sixty years after his reported reading of the book; see *TLS*, January 21, 1977, p. 6 and a corrected version in the issue of January 28, 1977, p. 106.

13. *The Island of Dr. Moreau* (1896) is brought to VV's mind by his reference to the bookseller Oksman (Oxman) for his name evokes the half-man, half-beast creatures fashioned

by Wells' mad vivisectionist. No "ox-man" appears in the Wells' story, however. Mr. Snooks is to be found in the satirical story "Miss Winchelsea's Heart," in *Twelve Stories and a Dream* (London: Macmillan, 1903; New York: Scribner, 1905). The school teacher/heroine who rejects Mr. Snook's proposal out of snobbery over his name gets her just deserts when he marries her friend and changes his name back to its elegant ancestral form "Sevenoaks."

14. So far as I know Nabokov has never explicitly mentioned the fourth dimension in his work. The concept was, however, extremely popular among Russian intellectual, artistic, and spiritualist circles during the early years of the century. The origin of this interest may be traced to the works of an American mathematician, Charles Howard Hinton, who is briefly discussed by Gardner (pp. 223–25). Gardner quotes a passage from *A Picture of Our Universe* in which Hinton discussed mirror-image positive and negative electric charges and the fourth dimension. In the course of illustrating a point Hinton urges the reader to conceive of our world as if "there were to be for each man somewhere a counterman, a presentment of himself, a real counterfeit, outwardly fashioned like himself, but with his right hand opposite his original's left hand. Exactly like the image of the man in the mirror" (p. 225). Hinton's *The Fourth Dimension* (New York: J. Lane, 1904) and other of his works appeared in Russia ca. 1915 but their contents had earlier been popularized by P.D. Ouspensky in his *Chetvertoe izmerenie, Opyt izsledovaniia oblasti neizmerimago* (The Fourth Dimension: An Attempt to Investigate the Region of the Unmeasurable) (St. Petersburg, 1909) and *Tertium Organum, Klyuch k zagadkam mira* (*Tertium Organum: A Key to the Mysteries of the World*) (St. Petersburg, 1911). For a survey of the importance of these ideas to Russian avant-garde art circles, see Charlotte Douglas, "Views from the New World. A. Kruchenykh and K. Malevich: Theory and Painting," *Russian Literature TriQuarterly*, 12 (1975), 353–70. I am indebted to Douglas for much of the above information.

15. Nabokov has used mirror imagery as an emblem of the two linguistic worlds of his own literary career. Note in the Russian and English versions of his autobiography the "rainbow words" ВЁЕ ПСКЗ and KZSPYGV, which chromesthetically spell out the primary and secondary mirror image rainbows that respectively symbolize Nabokov's Russian and English works. See in this connection my "Synesthesia, Polychromatism, and Nabokov," *Russian Language TriQuarterly*, 3 (Spring 1972), 378–97. Mirror imagery (with its inherent left/right inversion) is also used by Nabokov as a metaphor for the translation process. See, for example, the cover design of Nabokov's own translation (New York: Phaedra, 1967) of his English *Lolita* whereon the Cyrillic title word is printed in spectral colors once from left to right and then once again in inverted letters, from right to left.

16. The four "confession" scenes are as follows: Iris—Part I, chapter 7; Annette—II, 7; Louise—IV, 4 and "you"—VI, 2.

17. For an interesting exploration of the science fiction aspects of *Ada* see Roy Arthur Swanson, "Nabokov's *Ada* as Science Fiction," *Science-Fiction Studies*, 2, No. 1 (March 1975), 76–88. In this same issue, Charles Nicol, in a brief review of Bobbie Ann Mason's *Nabokov's Garden: A Guide to "Ada"* (Ann Arbor: Aridis Inc., 1974), vigorously concurs with Mason's argument that "Anti-Terra exists only in Van's imagination" (p. 91). Nicol then extends this assertion specifically to *Invitation to a Beheading* and *Bend Sinister* and adds that with the possible exception of the short story "Lance" all of Nabokov's "other worlds" are solipsistic. Such an interpretation can be made of *Look at the Harlequins!* and I have done so in my earlier, unpublished article "Inverted Reality in Nabokov's *Look at the Harlequins!*" I am now persuaded, however, that there is much to be said for a nonsolipsistic "two worlds" interpretation of the novel based upon a study of the implications of the information given in Martin Gardner's *The Ambidextrous Universe* and upon H. G. Wells references in *LATH*. For "antiworld" readings of the three books mentioned by Nicol, see my "The Alpha and Omega of Nabokov's Prison-House of Language: Alphabetic Iconicism in *Invitation to a Beheading*," *Russian Literature*, 6 (1978), 347–64 and "Spatial Modeling and Deixis: Nabokov's *Invitation to a Beheading*" *Poetics Today*, 3 (Winter 1982), 81–98; "The Scrabble Game in *Ada* or Taking Nabokov Clitorally," *Journal of Modern Literature*, 9 (May 1982),

291–303; and, forthcoming, "Don't Touch My Circles: The Two Worlds of Nabokov's *Bend Sinister.*" On the other hand, I would concur with Professor Nicol's thesis as it pertains to *The Eye, Despair, Solus Rex*, and *Pale Fire*. For supporting evidence on the latter, see my "The Index of Refraction in Nabokov's *Pale Fire*," *RLT*, 16 (1982), 33–49. In sum, I think it may be said that each of the novels of Nabokov's mature years adheres to one of two basic models: a schizophrenic model in which the alternative world is obviously delusional, and a twin-world model with the features I have outlined.

Nabokov and the Art of Exile

Ellen Pifer*

Like countless other Russians of the middle and upper class, Vladimir Nabokov was forced to leave his native country during the Bolshevik Revolution. Over twenty years later, again like countless other Russian émigrés and intellectuals, he fled Europe as Hitler came to power. Unlike so many of his compatriots, however, Nabokov was able, in the most extraordinary way, to turn two decades of isolation and rootlessness into an artistic advantage. While living as an émigré writer in Berlin during the 1920s and 1930s, Nabokov deliberately cultivated the condition of exile. He began by rejecting émigré life as a possible subject for his second novel, *King, Queen, Knave* (the Russian *Korol', dama, valet*, published in 1928). Nabokov was frankly dissatisfied with the cast of émigré characters he had assembled in his first novel *Mary* (*Mashen'ka*, 1926). They were, he said, "so transparent to the eye of the era that one could easily make out the [social] labels behind them." Thus, for his second novel, *King, Queen, Knave*, Nabokov deliberately chose "a set of exclusively German characters," although he claimed he "spoke no German, had no German friends, had not read a single German novel either in the original, or in translation." In art as well as nature, Nabokov said, such a "glaring disadvantage may turn out to be a subtle protective device."[1] From what dangers, we may ask, did the young writer find it necessary to protect his fiction?

The danger, in Nabokov's view, lies in the very nature of the novel and its inordinate capacity as a literary genre to promote general ideas and social "labels" or types. We are easily drawn, unconscious and uncritical, into the web of a novel's expansive world. An immediate and unchallenged identification springs up between the reader and the fictional characters, who are embedded in the conflicts and circumstances of everyday life. Existence may be ultimately mysterious to us; but the daily, concrete living out of our existence becomes so familiar in its repetition that it ends by appearing inevitable and even predictable most of the time. The novel, containing more of life in its everyday, repetitive aspect than any other literary form, has an analogous power to present its world

*This essay appears here for the first time by permission of the author.

as familiar and inevitable. Promoting this illusion, novels also tend to promote the most generally accepted ideas that circulate among members of a particular historical and social era. As Mary McCarthy has said, novels are obliged to "carry the news." We "expect a novel to be true, not only true to itself, like a poem, or a statue, but true to actual life. We not only make believe we believe a novel, but we do substantially believe it, as being continuous with real life. . . ."[2] For McCarthy, the terms "actual" and "real life" suggest life in its collective sense; obliged to "carry the news," the novel disseminates social information to the members of a community.

Despite the potentially shattering force of current events on his own life as an exile, Nabokov was not interested in promoting social or historical formulations in his fiction. As already mentioned, in his second novel, *King, Queen, Knave*, he sought to detach himself as an artist from the émigré's natural preoccupation with social-historical conditions. Although he returned, in subsequent novels, to the setting of Russian émigré circles, he did not forget what the "pure invention" of his second novel had taught him.[3] In *The Gift* (originally *Dar*, published serially during 1937–38), Nabokov's eighth novel and his finest work in Russian, the main character—himself a young Russian émigré writer—confronts the necessity for cultivating a form of that "inner disentanglement" already discovered by his author ten years earlier.[4] In one particular episode of *The Gift*, Nabokov specifically demonstrates how dangerous to the writer's vision is the psychic baggage of labels and stereotypes we unconsciously assume as members of collective society.

In this episode, Fyodor Godunov-Cherdyntsev, the young writer, is seated on a Berlin streetcar, depressed by the prospect of another dull trip across the city, to give yet another foreign language lesson to an untalented student. (Giving private lessons is the means by which Fyodor ekes out a meager living in this foreign city.) As the tram passes through "the familiar, hopelessly ugly streets" of Berlin, Fyodor eyes his fellow passengers with a dislike fattening into "vague, evil, heavy hatred." The Russian émigré's recognizable feelings of isolation and hostility distort Fyodor's perceptions of the German citizens around him, ultimately draining them of all humanity:

> [Fyodor's] reason knew that they could also include genuine, completely human individuals with unselfish passions, pure sorrows, even with memories shining through life, but for some reasons he got the impression that all these cold, slippery eyes, looking at him as if he were carrying an illegal treasure . . . belonged only to malicious hags and crooked hucksters. The Russian conviction that the German is in small numbers vulgar and in large numbers—unbearably vulgar was, he knew, a conviction unworthy of an artist; but nonetheless he was seized with a trembling, and only the gloomy conductor . . . seemed outwardly, if not a human being, then at least a poor relation to a human being.[5]

Soon a "lean man in a short coat with a fox-fur collar" sits down across from Fyodor, bumping the young man with the corner of his brief-case as he settles down in the seat. The trivial jostle transforms Fyodor's irritation "into a kind of pure fury," so that he instantly concentrates on the man opposite him "all his sinful hatred" (which the author, in parentheses, compassionately identifies as hatred "for this poor, pitiful, expiring nation"). In the passenger's physical features and gestures, Fyodor discerns only the repulsive characteristics of the "typical" German:

> [He] knew precisely why he hated him: for that low forehead, for those pale eyes . . . for a love of fences, rows, mediocrity; for the cult of the office; for . . . figures, money; for the lavatory humor and crude laughter; for the fatness of the backsides of both sexes, even if the rest of the subject is not fat; for the lack of fastidiousness . . . for the weakness for dirty little tricks . . . for someone else's live cat, pierced through with wire . . . and the wire cleverly twisted at one end; for cruelty in everything, self-satisfied, taken for granted; for the unexpected, rapturous helpfulness with which five passersby help you to pick up some dropped farthings; for. . . . Thus he threaded the points of his biased indictment. . . . (93–94)

As Fyodor's fury mounts, so does the rhetorical fervor of this passage. His own emotions begin to reflect the sadistic malice he ascribes to the entire German nation; the cruelty and inhumanity which Fyodor attributes to "them" is revealed as an element of his own xenophobic perception. Fyodor's mental abuse of a whole nation is itself a cruel and "self-satisfied" indulgence. The empty rhetoric of Fyodor's mounting emotion is soon punctured, however, by the reality of specific detail. The "typical" German seated opposite Fyodor takes "a copy of Vasiliev's newspaper from his pocket" and coughs with the "Russian intonation" of a fellow émigré! Fyodor is wise enough to recognize in this abstract defeat a personal victory: "That's wonderful, thought Fyodor, almost smiling with delight. How clever, how gracefully sly and essentially good life is!" He heartily applauds the vital resistance of life, and human beings, to generalizations. He now begins to peruse the man's features once again—this time discovering, with a keen sense of self-irony, "the compatriotic softness" of Russian eyes and the obviously Russian cut of the traveler's mustache. Fyodor's thoughts are "cheered by this unexpected respite" from a gloomy and hostile state of mind (94). Like most of Fyodor's experience in *The Gift*, this moment on the tram marks an essential stage in his development as a writer, because the exercise of Fyodor's literary "gift" will require that he forsake conventional forms of perception, which are "unworthy of an artist."

Like Fyodor's encounter on the Berlin streetcar, Nabokov's experience of exile contradicts conventional expectations. His lifelong nostalgia for his native country and language did not cause Nabokov to bewail his considerable losses. With wry humor, he liked to characterize the private fortune and numerous estates which his family was forced to abandon in Russia as their "unreal estate." With startlingly little evidence of regret, Nabokov transformed social misfortune into artistic advantage; to repeat his own words, he turned the "glaring disadvantage" of exile into a "subtle protective device." Of the sixteen novels Nabokov completed after writing his first one, none may be said to be "transparent to the eye of the era." Not only did Nabokov abandon social labels and formulations in his literary practice, he ultimately rejected his contemporaries' obsession with social-historical process—the tendency of generations of novelists, and Western intellectuals in general, to perceive in that process the very force and form of human fate.

Refuting the "accepted notion of a 'modern world' continuously floating around us," Nabokov regarded such historical postulations as belonging "to the same type of abstraction as, say, the 'quaternary period' of paleontology." He contrasted these abstract historical classifications with the private reality of the artist: "What I feel to be the real modern world is the world the artist creates . . . which becomes a new *mir* ["world" in Russian] by the very act of his shedding, as it were, the age he lives in."[6] Nabokov's account of the artist, "shedding" the age he lives in like a reptile emerging from a dead skin, does not imply withdrawal from the world but a renewed form of confrontation with it. The artist conceives reality afresh only after he has deliberately separated himself from the apparent world formulated everyday by the pressing interests of society. A novelist who aims, in Mary McCarthy's words, "to carry the news" of this world winds up, in Nabokov's view, dragging the carapace of social-historical formulations along with him.

By contrast, Nabokov identified himself as "the type of artist who is always in exile even though he may never have left the ancestral hall or the paternal parish."[7] It was his particular destiny, however, to leave both. When the émigré circles in Paris and Berlin were shattered by a new set of political crises, Nabokov removed himself and his family once again, this time to the United States. After the remarkable feat of launching a second literary career—now as an American novelist writing in English—Nabokov published *Lolita*. Not long after its rather scandalous reception, *Lolita* brought him both notoriety and sudden financial independence. Nabokov's response was to give up his teaching post at Cornell and set sail for Europe. Significantly, he did *not* regard this departure for Europe as a return to the past, or home, but as yet another phase of exile, this one self-imposed. By this time the United States had become, in Nabokov's own words, his "adopted country"; he remained a loyal American citizen and taxpayer for the rest of his life. He left the United States, nonetheless, and took up residence in Montreux, Switzerland, from 1959 until his death in 1977. These were, in his own words, years of "rosy exile." To those unaware of Nabokov's motives for cultivating exile, it may seem paradoxical that during these years in Switzerland, he repeatedly expressed his affection for America. Odd as it may seem, Nabokov had a deep sense of commitment to the "adopted country" he had abandoned and yet continued to call home. In Switzerland, in 1964, he told an interviewer:

> I am an American writer, born in Russia and educated in England where I studied French literature, before spending fifteen years in Germany. I came to America in 1940 and decided to become an American citizen, and make America my home. It so happened that I was immediately exposed to the very best in America, to its rich intellectual life and to its easygoing, good-natured atmosphere. I immersed myself in its great libraries and its Grand Canyon. I worked in the laboratories of its zoological museums. I acquired more friends than I ever had in Europe. My books—old books and new ones—found some admirable readers. I became stout as Cortez—mainly because I quit smoking and started to munch molasses candy instead, with the result that my weight went up from my usual 140 to a monumental and cheerful 200. In consequence, I am one-third American—good American flesh keeping me warm and safe.[8]

Thousands of miles from America, gazing at the summits of Swiss mountains and at Lake Geneva below, Nabokov declares it is *America* keeping him "warm and safe." Statements like these prompt us, once more, to ask how and why he could say this—having been separated yet again from the country he called home. How and why could he find "rosy" that condition of isolation and estrangement which so many expatriates have found intolerable? For the answers to such questions, we must again consider the nature of Nabokov's enterprise as a novelist. We must consider his absolute commitment to art and to rendering reality in his own particular way.

For the artist, he said, "isolation means liberty and discovery."[9] It was not isolation from human beings that Nabokov welcomed, however, but estrangement from the exorbitant demands made on one's attention by the current affairs of social life.[10] What we, as members of a society, credit as "reality," Nabokov came to regard as mere "average reality." It is, he said, "only the reality of general ideas, conventional forms of humdrummery, current editorials."[11] As Nabokov's use of the term "average" suggests here, collective reality is always a compromise. What we share or have *in common* as members of a group or nation is, of necessity, the most familiar and least interesting aspect of what he called "true reality." True reality is not, in Nabokov's view, what human beings agree on but what is most unusual and original in their perception: "The only real, authentic worlds are those that seem unusual."[12] Moreover, the closer we get to the nature of an individual's perception—or to the nature of nature, the universe and time—the stranger and more unusual "reality" will seem. "You can get nearer and nearer . . . to reality," said Nabokov, "but you never get near enough because reality is an infinite succession of steps, levels of perception, false bottoms, and hence unquenchable, unattainable. You can know more and more about one thing but you can never know everything about one thing: it's hopeless. So that we live surrounded by more or less ghostly objects. . . ."[13] Reality, then, is something for which human beings have an insatiable longing—a metaphysical thirst which is, in Nabokov's words, ultimately "unquenchable."

Not coincidentally, Nabokov used the same word—"unquenchable"—nine years later, when describing the oddly prophetic dreams of exile he had as a child. He related how, "during trips with my family to Western Europe, I imagined, in bedtime reveries, what it would be like to become an exile who longed for a remote, sad, and . . . unquenchable Russia under the eucalipti of exotic resorts. Lenin and his police nicely arranged *that* fantasy."[14] Even as a boy of ten, Nabokov found the suggestion of exile, brought on by a vacation beyond the borders of Russia, to be a fruitful or "rosy" state of consciousness. As he says in his autobiography, *Speak, Memory*, "homesickness has been with me a sensuous and particular matter."[15] To be displaced from one's habitual surroundings, estranged from the familiar, is to be brought into a more intense and evocative relationship with that environment. "Home" becomes that remote but essential reality which one's imagination and memory struggle, "unquenchably," to discover and repossess at a distance. For Nabokov, then, the condition of exile—of existing at the furthest reaches from one's "home" or origins—is the quintessential condition of human beings on this planet. Each of us, patriot or expatriate, lives irretrievably estranged from the mysterious origins of our existence. We may struggle to know and possess our unquenchable and elusive "true reality"; but we can never, metaphysically speaking, arrive home. As Van Veen says in *Ada*, we are all "visitors and investigators in a strange universe, indeed, indeed."[16] In *Ada*, *King, Queen, and Knave*, and nearly all of his other novels, Nabokov examines the inherently uncomfortable, precarious, and at the same time creative relationship of human beings to ultimate reality. By exiling himself, a second time, from the security of a deceptively familiar social environment, Nabokov nurtured that sense of essential estrangement which underscores our existence and provides the focus for "reality" in his fiction.

Comparing his twenty years of self-imposed exile in Switzerland to the twenty years he spent as an émigré in Europe, Nabokov said: "I think I am trying to develop, in this rosy exile, the same fertile nostalgia in regard to America, my new country, as I evolved for Russia, my old one, in the first post-revolution years of West-European expatriation."[17] To us, exile may still seem an unfortunate accident of history; but for Nabokov it came to represent both an ontological condition and an artistic necessity. Ultimately he refused to assign any historical date whatsoever to his lifelong experience as an exile. My "happy expatriation," he said, "began practically on the day of my birth."[18]

Notes

1. Foreword, *King, Queen, Knave*, trans. Dmitri Nabokov and Vladimir Nabokov (New York: McGraw-Hill, 1968), pp. vii–viii; hereafter cited in the text.

2. "The Fact in Fiction," *Partisan Review*, 27 (1960), 438–58; rpt. in *The Humanist in the Bathtub* (New York: New American Library, 1964), pp. 183, 186.

3. In Nabokov's words, "the fairytale freedom inherent in [treating] an unknown milieu answered my dream of pure invention" (Foreword, *King, Queen, Knave*, p. viii).

4. Ibid., p. viii.

5. *The Gift*, trans. Michael Scammell and Vladimir Nabokov (New York: Putnam's, 1963), pp. 92–93; hereafter cited in the text. In the following quotation from this English translation, the Russian word translated as "fury" is *"bešenstvo,"* a noun which connotes, in medical terminology, the disease of rabies and which in ordinary usage signifies a state of frenzy (*Dar* [New York: Chekhove Publishing House, 1952], p. 93).

6. Interview by Martin Esslin, *The New York Times Book Review*, May 12, 1968; rpt. in Vladimir Nabokov, *Strong Opinions* (New York: McGraw-Hill, 1973), p. 112.

7. Interview by Nicholas Garnham, *The Listener*, 80 (October 10, 1968), 463–64; rpt. in *Strong Opinions*, p. 117.

8. Interview by Alvin Toffler, *Playboy*, 11 (January 1964), 35–41, 44–45; rpt. in *Strong Opinions*, pp. 26–27.

9. Interview by Philip Oakes, *The London Sunday Times*, June 22, 1969; rpt. in *Strong Opinions*, p. 139.

10. A virtual consensus has developed nonetheless among critics of Nabokov's fiction, including those who are favorably disposed as well as those who are negative. Most of them agree that Nabokov is either indifferent or downright hostile to his fellow man—preferring the sublimities of art to the vulgarities of human life. For a brief summary of this critical opinion, see my article, "On Human Freedom and Inhuman Art: Nabokov," *Slavic and East European Journal*, 22 (1978), 52–63; a more extensive treatment of the subject appears in my book, *Nabokov and the Novel* (Cambridge: Harvard Univ. Press, 1980).

11. Interview by Nicholas Garnham, p. 118.

12. Ibid.

13. Interview by Peter Duval Smith and Christopher Burstall, *The Listener*, 68 (November 22, 1962), 856–58; rpt. in *Strong Opinions*, p. 11.

14. Interview by Alden Whitman, *The New York Times*, April 23, 1971, p. 16; rpt. in *Strong Opinions*, p. 178.

15. *Speak, Memory: An Autobiography Revisited* (New York: Putnam's, 1966), p. 250.

16. *Ada or Ardor: A Family Chronicle* (New York: McGraw-Hill, 1969), p. 107.

17. Interview by Jane Howard, *Life* magazine, November 20, 1964, pp. 61–68; rpt. in *Strong Opinions*, p. 49.

18. Published letter to John Leonard, editor, *New York Times Book Review*, November 7, 1971; rpt. in *Strong Opinions*, p. 218.

An Annotated Bibliography of Nabokov Criticism

Beverly Lyon Clark*

This discussion of some of the best and most innovative criticism on Nabokov will, I hope, help to initiate novices and provoke further consideration on the part of those most familiar with Nabokov criticism. It complements the introduction and the essays in the present volume by giving a detailed account of what other critics have said.

I have tried to include the best conceived criticism, but I have also aimed for diversity. The annotations appear in the order in which the criticism was first published. Quotations are from the first published version, except where otherwise indicated.

Trilling, Lionel. "The Last Lover: Vladimir Nabokov's 'Lolita.' " *Encounter*, 11 (October 1958), 9–19. Rev. and rpt. in *Speaking of Literature and Society*, ed. Diana Trilling. New York: Harcourt Brace Jovanovich, 1980, pp. 322–42.

Trilling's influential early essay begins by detailing *Lolita*'s publishing history and then discusses censorship and pornography. Trilling stresses that *Lolita* is not pornographic in the legal sense—"is not shocking in the way that books which circulate in secret are usually said to be shocking" (10)—but is shocking nonetheless.

It shocks because it describes the love of a middle-aged man for a twelve-year-old girl. It shocks because, "[w]ithin the range of possible heterosexual conduct, this is one of the few prohibitions which still seem to us to be confirmed by nature itself" (13)—unlike female virginity or marital fidelity. It shocks further because, "in the course of reading the novel, we have come virtually to condone the violation it presents" (14).

Why would Nabokov wish to shock us? Not to explore the psychology of deviance. Not to subvert morality. Not primarily, Trilling decides, to satirize American life. But instead to write about love—"not about sex, but about love" (15).

Trilling means in particular the passion-love elucidated by Denis de Rougement, a love that "had nothing to do with marriage and could not possibly exist in marriage" (15), a love whose power was measured by the scandal it ignited. How can the modern novelist portray such love, generate such scandal? Not through adultery, any more. But perhaps through violating taboos regarding young girls. Hence *Lolita*: "although it strikes all the most approved modern postures and attitudes, it is concerned to restore a foredone mode of feeling" (18).

Yet Nabokov's portrayal of Humbert's love is not altogether straight-

*This essay was written specifically for this volume and appears here by permission of the author.

forward, Trilling notes. There are hints of irony, hints not of a tragic Humbert but of an antiheroic one. And what Trilling finally stresses is Nabokov's ambiguity of tone, his "ability to arouse uneasiness, to throw the reader off balance, to require him to change his stance and shift his position and move on" (19). Such mobility may in fact make the book American, may make it remarkably able "to represent certain aspects of American life" (19). (And the European Humbert's pursuit of an American girl is not just "the history of his love-affair with an American girl-child" but also "the history of his love-affair with America" [11].)

Ambiguity, passion, morality, irony, America—Trilling has touched most of the strings that later critics sound. And he acclaimed *Lolita* before many recognized its genius. One may quibble with details. Since passion here is less mutual than in earlier literature, does *Lolita* perhaps diverge from tradition? Is Lolita not only the "cruel mistress" but also cruelly mastered? But Trilling's early analysis is seminal and compelling.

McCarthy, Mary. "A Bolt from the Blue." *New Republic*, 146 (June 4, 1962), 21–27. Rev. and rpt. as "Vladimir Nabokov's 'Pale Fire'." *Encounter*, 19 (October 1962), 71–84. Rpt. as "A Bolt from the Blue." In *The Writing on the Wall and Other Literary Essays*. New York: Harcourt, Brace and World, 1970, pp. 15–34. My references are to the *Encounter* essay.

Like Trilling's article, McCarthy's enthusiastic review of *Pale Fire* laid the foundation for subsequent criticism. (Unlike Trilling, though, she did not care for *Lolita*: she almost seems to be compensating here for negative comments that she sent to her former husband Edmund Wilson and that he forwarded to Nabokov in 1954.) The second version of her review includes substantial additions; McCarthy has discovered Nabokov's title, for example, in a passage in *Timon of Athens*, a passage that Kinbote misquotes.

McCarthy traces the levels of *Pale Fire*, the planes of reality: the New Wye world of Shade and Kinbote; the Zembla of King Charles (alias Kinbote); the New Wye reality again, according to which Zembla is just a fantasy. And Kinbote is in fact Botkin, who is fleetingly referred to as a Russian professor. (Perhaps he is. But McCarthy's interpretation does not quite account for all the details: I would argue that there are teasing connections between Kinbote and Botkin, as there are among many elements of the story, but their identity remains merely a possibility.) A final level is the reader's reality outside the book. Yet each level has given way to the next so that this one may not be final either, the book becoming an "infinite perspective regression, . . . a book of mirrors" (72).

McCarthy discusses the multiple mirrors in the book, the relationship between Zembla and New Wye, commentary and poem. Kinbote's insistence on Zembla, for instance, may seem crazy, but he senses a true connection with Shade's poem: "On the plane of everyday sanity, he errs. But on the plane of poetry and magic, he is speaking the simple truth, for Zembla is Semblance, Appearance, the mirror-realm, the Looking Glass of Alice" (72).

McCarthy's pursuit of mirrors and reflections leads her on a "cryptogrammic paper chase" (to borrow a phrase from *Lolita*): she skims from literary allusions to colors to chess to astrology, from Nature's shams and freaks to wordplay and etymology, from stones and lakes to anal canals, from mythology to theft to butterflies. The function of these reflections? "The repetitions, reflections, misprints, and quirks of Nature are taken as signs of the presence of a pattern, the stamp or watermark of a god or an intelligence" (78). They point ultimately to love and loss and pity. And possibly to eternity, but "[i]n the game of signalling back and forth with mirrors, which may be man's relation with the cosmos, there is perhaps no before or after, first or second, only distance—separation—and across it, the agitated flashing of the semaphore" (84). McCarthy concludes by finding *Pale Fire* "a creation of perfect beauty, symmetry, strangeness, originality, and moral truth, . . . one of the very great works of art of this century" (84).

Her comments are often astute, in this early evaluation of *Pale Fire*. Sometimes she may overread, becoming a little too Kinbotian in pursuing connections, but her exuberance is akin to Nabokov's, a fitting tribute to him.

Robbe-Grillet, Alain. "Note sur la notion d'itinéraire dans *Lolita*." *L'Arc*, 24 (1964), 37–38.

In this brief article, little known among English-speaking critics, Robbe-Grillet (whom Nabokov has called "the best French writer") anticipates much later criticism of *Lolita*. He notes that Humbert's palliative for the loss of happiness is travel. And he anticipates George Steiner's argument that Nabokov's extraterritoriality is "profoundly of our time" (*TriQuarterly*, 17 (1970), 127): Robbe-Grillet notes that nowadays we are all emigrants, all exiles.

Humbert's emigration, his wandering, is not only physical but also mental, governed by "le cercle, le double, la solitude, la répétition" (37). Even his early travels with Lolita are effectively solitary, for she remains immersed in her comic books, immune to his interests. And the later shadowing Quilty is Humbert's double, a feature of Humbert's mental itinerary, for in retracing his own steps Humbert finds echoes of himself, objects that "se multiplient à l'infini" (38).

Some critics consider *Lolita* a satire, specifically of American life. But Robbe-Grillet finds more kinship with Antonioni, Dostoevski, and Kleist (not a family tree that Nabokov would acknowledge, especially not Dostoevski). Robbe-Grillet also acknowledges that in an interview with a prying journalist Nabokov has disclaimed a personal penchant for nymphets, claiming that he might just as well have written about a bicycle and a parrot. But the book's compelling and labyrinthine passion (could a parrot have such passion for a bicycle?) constitutes part of its reality, part of its greatness.

Wilson, Edmund. "The Strange Case of Pushkin and Nabokov." *New York Review of Books*, July 15, 1965, pp. 3–6. Rev. and rpt. in *A Window on Russia: For the Use of Foreign Readers*. New York: Farrar, Straus and Giroux, 1972, pp. 209–37.

Wilson's attack on Nabokov's monumental translation of Pushkin's *Eugene Onegin* marks the ebbing of his friendship with Nabokov. Wilson finds the translation flat-footed, in "a bald and awkward language which has nothing in common with Pushkin or with the usual writing of Nabokov" (3). He finds only two traits common to Nabokov's other writing: "Aside from this desire both to suffer and make suffer—so important an element in his fiction—the only characteristic Nabokov trait that one recognizes in this uneven and sometimes banal translation is the addiction to rare and unfamiliar words, which, in view of his declared intention to stick so close to the text that his version may be used as a trot, are entirely inappropriate here" (3). Wilson chastizes Nabokov for using archaic words, making grammatical mistakes, using a clumsy style. He examines other translations, specifically comparing four different versions of one stanza (including his own), and he finds, for instance, that Walter Arndt's translation "is likely to give the reader a better idea of what the poem sounds like in Russian than Nabokov's so tortured version" (4).

Wilson finds the extensive commentary flawed as well: he berates Nabokov for inconsistency in transliterating, for insensitivity to English prosody, and for misinterpretation. The textual apparatus suffers "from the same faults as Nabokov's translation—that is, mainly from a lack of common sense—something that is not detrimental to the fantastic fiction he writes, of which it is, in fact, an essential element, but which in an erudite work of this kind is a serious disadvantage" (4). Nabokov has moments of brilliance, but his scholarship is heavy-handed. And even when Wilson announces that he is turning to positive comments—and notes how thoroughly Nabokov has explored Pushkin's sources—he devotes most of his energy to arguing that Pushkin knew more English than Nabokov gives him credit for. Wilson admires Nabokov's criticism of Pushkin's Russian predecessors, but devotes more energy to complaining of Nabokov's judgments—his "compulsion to give unnecessary information" and "his instinct to take digs at great reputations" (6). With slightly fewer qualifications Wilson appreciates Nabokov's sensitivity to poetry (the translation to the contrary) and Nabokov's discussion of historical context. Wilson concludes by seeing the translation as a dramatization of the tension between Nabokov's Russian and English sides: despite Nabokov's quirkiness, "his sense of beauty and his literary proficiency, his energy which seems never to tire, have made him a cultural live wire which vibrates between us and that Russian past which still provides for the Russian present a vitality that can sometimes inspire it and redeem it from mediocrity" (6).

Nabokov responded to his critics, especially Wilson, in *Encounter* (February 1966, rpt. in *Strong Opinions*). He counters "practically every item of criticism" in Wilson's essay, which is so uniformly wrong that "one wonder[s] if, perhaps, it had not been woven that way on purpose to be turned into something pertinent and coherent when reflected in a looking glass" (*Strong Opinions*, p. 247). Nabokov uses "rare and unfamiliar words"? Perhaps he wants to convey rare and unfamiliar things. And so on, down Wilson's list.

In a 1971 afterword Wilson responds to Nabokov's response and appraises Nabokov's other work, with greatest emphasis on what he dislikes: Wilson characteristically praises Nabokov's English, only to cluck at errors and to suggest disparagingly that Nabokov may have assumed that publishers would have corrected them. (Perhaps Wilson counted on publishers to correct his own error—repeated when he reprinted the essay—in his discussion of the "principle [sic] problems" of Russian.) Wilson has also silently omitted some hotly contested points from his earlier essay.

Acerbity aside, much of Wilson's discomfort seems to stem from Nabokov's espousal of literalism. Nabokov's translation may not be poetic and readable—but he did not intend it to be. He wanted to capture nuances of meaning, not to create his own poem (though we may well question whether one can avoid creating one's own poem). Nabokov may not always have chosen the best words—but Wilson's comments are even less trustworthy. And Wilson fails to appreciate the scholarship of Nabokov's commentary—a somewhat eccentric scholarship, as in Nabokov's book on Gogol, but powerful and enlightening nonetheless.

Appel, Alfred, Jr., ed. and introd. *The Annotated Lolita.* By Vladimir Nabokov. New York: McGraw-Hill, 1970. Portions of Appel's commentary previously appeared in the *New Republic* (1967), *Wisconsin Studies in Contemporary Literature* (1967), the *Denver Quarterly* (1968), and *TriQuarterly* (1970). The second printing (paperback) contains corrections and additions.

Designed to illumine the text for college students, *The Annotated Lolita* contains astute criticism of the novel. In his introduction Appel examines involution, or self-conscious reminders of a work's fictionality. Nabokov achieves involution through parody, coincidence (such as the recurring 342 in *Lolita*), patterning (including puns, anagrams, spoonerisms, chess, and butterfly motifs), the work-within-the-work (such as Quilty's *Enchanted Hunters*), theatrical effects and metaphors, and generally the authorial voice. Appel also traces themes, including improvisations on such autobiographical themes as exile. And he places *Lolita* in biographical and cultural contexts, finding, for instance, that Nabokov "has, along with Nathanael West, defined with absolute authority the inevitable mode, the dominant dark tonalities—if not the contents—of the American comic novel" (xlix). In particular, *Lolita* is a parody, "a burlesque of the confessional mode, the literary diary, the Romantic novel that chronicles the effects of a debilitating love, the *Doppelgänger* tale, and, in parts, a Duncan Hines tour of America conducted by a guide with a black imagination . . ." (liii). Yet Nabokov moves beyond parody, uniting it with pathos, making Quilty "both a parody of the Double as a convention of modern fiction, and a Double who formulates the horror in Humbert's life" (liv).

Appel focuses on Nabokov's parodic games—not because they are the most important level of the novel, but because they have received insufficient attention. Later critics sometimes cite Appel as an exponent of aesthetic gameplaying, but he recognizes the book's humanity as well, the extent to which "Nabokov is able to have it both ways, involving the reader on the one hand in a deeply moving yet outrageously comic story, rich in verisimilitude, and on the other engaging him in a game made possible by the interlacings of verbal figurations which undermine the novel's realistic base and distance the reader from its dappled surface, which then assumes the aspect of a gameboard" (lx). Appel certainly celebrates the gameplaying, the traps for the unwary reader, yet Nabokov is humanistic as well: "his triumph in art is but a heightened emblem of all of our own efforts to confront, order, and structure the chaos of life, and to endure, if not master, the demons within and around us" (lvii).

Appel's notes to the text are more analytic than notes to texts usually are. They are impressively thorough and perceptive, as when he remarks that "*Lolita* is so deeply moving a novel because of our sharp awareness of the great tension sustained between H. H.'s mute despair and his compensatory jollity" (371). Or when he suggests, in a discussion of pornography, that "more than one voyeuristic reader has unconsciously wished that Quilty had been the narrator, his unseen movie the novel. But the novel's 'habit of metamorphosis' is consistent, for the erotica which seemed to be there and turned out not to be was in fact present all along, most modestly; and it is Nabokov's final joke on the subject, achieved at the expense of the very common reader" (429). Appel even offers Nabokov's comments on some of the notes: Nabokov stresses that he, "half-painter, half-naturalist, finds the use of symbols hateful because it substitutes a dead general idea for a live specific impression. . . . I think your students, your readers, should be taught to *see* things, to discriminate between visual shades as the author does, and not to lump them under such arbitrary labels as 'red' (using it, moreover, as a sexual symbol, though actually the dominant shades in males are mauve—to bright blue, in certain monkeys)" (362). Occasionally Appel becomes playful, not strictly the annotator who spells everything out for the student, as in his gloss for Humbert's discarded pseudonym, Lambert Lambert: "No literary allusions intended" (437). Appel recognizes that he plays Kinbote to Nabokov's Shade, but he does so without falling into Kinbote's traps, or only into traps that turn out not to be traps: "At first wince (to quote H. H.), such minutiae may seem no better than Kinbotisms, but they are calmly offered as an example of the precise manner in which Nabokov's memory speaks to him and, as well, to suggest how he does indeed stock his 'imaginary garden with real toads' " (409).

Lubin, Peter. "Kickshaws and Motley." *TriQuarterly*, 17 (1970), 187–208. Rpt. in *Nabokov: Criticism, Reminiscences, Translations and Tributes*. Ed. Alfred Appel, Jr., and Charles Newman. A Clarion Book. New York: Simon and Schuster, 1970, pp. 187–208.

Lubin offers Nabokov a romping, ramping tribute, "dim inklings, slim synecdoche (Schenectady for New York)" (188). He touches on Nabokov's autoplagiarism, the migration of characters and phrases among books. And he scrutinizes the precision of Nabokov's language, his presumed obscurities, his neologisms, his borrowings from other languages.

Lubin also discusses tmesis, the insertion of an extra word in the middle of a compound word—or, as he extends the figure, in the middle of a phrase. In some instances, as in "safety gold pin" (*Ada*), "[a] semantic petticoat is slipped on between the naked noun and its clothing epithet" (194–95). In another, "the Arctic no longer vicious Circle" (*Ada*), we see a geographical-figurative duck-rabbit. Lubin also asks why Nabokov interrupts his phrases. Is he harking back to the looseness of Russian word order? Or is he echoing what he delights in on a large scale: interrupting the plot with red herrings, surprising us when we discover whom Humbert has indeed murdered?

More daring is Lubin's parody, affectionate parody, of an interview. Lubin's Nabokov says, as Nabokov's Nabokov in effect has, "I pass the metaphysical buck. I bypass the museum of general ideas (which is to your left as you stroll down University Avenue). . . . The stale truths of Mediterranean profundits leave me cold. And the fact that the title of my last Russian novel, transliterated, is DAR, and the title of my latest English novel is ADA, has no political implications whatsoever" (198). (In an addendum to the *TriQuarterly* volume, later reprinted in *Strong Opinions*, Nabokov finds Lubin's interview "a little more exquisitely iridized than my own replies would have been," but Lubin's "multicolored inklings" are "absolutely dazzling.") Lubin has the erudition and flair to sustain his spirited tribute to "Shakespeare's current avatar" (203). He sustains it so well that other critics, like Jane Grayson, have started citing Nabokov lubens (the disease is contagious).

Moynahan, Julian. *Vladimir Nabokov*. Univ. of Minnesota Pamphlets on American Writers, No. 96. Minneapolis: Univ. of Minnesota Press, 1971. Rpt. as "Vladimir Nabokov." In *American Writers: A Collection of Literary Biographies*. Ed. Leonard Unger. Vol. III. New York: Scribner's, 1974, pp. 244–66.

Like Proust, Moynahan argues in his opening pages, Nabokov is an artist of nostalgia, drawing from the past "rich material for an art of memory which illuminates the whole range of time through which the artist has lived" (5). Both seek to define human consciousness and to glimpse eternal truths.

After sketching the biography, Moynahan examines Nabokov's autobiography, a creative work in its own right, a work whose themes and images echo those of the fiction. Consciousness seeking patterns that hint at transcendence, imprisonment pierced by the windows of imagery, faith in marriage—these themes recur as Nabokov "creates over a period of more than forty years a body of work in fiction which is like no other writer's anywhere in our part of the twentieth century" (16).

Nabokov's novels do not directly imitate life but "are imitations of imitations of life" (16), for he parodies such traditional prose forms as the biography, the ghost story, the metaphysical fantasy, and the scholarly commentary. Nabokov's parodies stem not from frivolity or aggression but from the recognition that each narrative type implies a perspective—and Nabokov's parody and crossbreeding open the forms to new perspectives. Moynahan briefly examines the deployment of narrative forms in *King, Queen, Knave*, *The Eye*, *The Defense*, *Invitation to a Beheading*, and *Bend Sinister*.

He reserves four books for more careful examination. Two of these, *Laughter in the Dark (Kamera Obskura)* and *Lolita*, are "melodramas of audacious metaphysical crime centering upon the theme of the 'nymphet' " (25). *Laughter in the Dark* focuses on visual themes of art connoisseurship and blindness, caricature and filmmaking. Nabokov is sympathetic to Albinus' longings but "understands, as Albinus does not, that the beguiling images and forms beckoning in the murk of human reality are for seeing and not for possessing—an insight available to the true artist though not to the connoisseur with his checkbook and collections" (30–31).

Humbert of *Lolita*, on the other hand, is more conscious of his responsibility. And he consciously plays roles: Dante, Proust, Poe, Faustus. The novel is in the tradition of the quest for the American dream, America here being "Europe's dream of itself according to the romantic error that past time is retrievable" (35). At the same time, *Lolita* breaks with tradition, inaugurates black comedy, having "killed fictional naturalism, already moribund, with one merciful blow" (31).

In his discussion of *The Gift*, Moynahan explicates the Russian background. He argues that the novel aims "to locate and consolidate the great tradition of Russian writing" and also "to expose an anti-tradition incarnate in social critics of the Chernyshevskian school whom Nabokov insists on seeing not only as the promulgators of a sound tradition of reformism and social concern but also as responsible for their own and others' bad writing . . ." (39). This book, "Nabokov's happiest," may also free him "from his Russian past, narrowly and nostalgically considered, by earning a free entry into the vital dialogue of Russian art over the centuries" (40).

Like *The Gift*, *Pale Fire* plays with art and artifice, yet it transmutes artistic devices "into something like the total dream and artifice of eternity" (40–41). Moynahan's claim that Charles Kinbote is V. Botkin, fresh from a mental hospital, may be a trifle suspect, as is his claim that *Pale Fire*, more than Nabokov's other novels, "shows a humane and tender sympathy for its imprisoned characters and seems to promise a final fulfillment of their immortal longings—if not now, sometime; if not here, then elsewhere" (45). Yet Moynahan perceptively notes the kinship, despite seeming disparity, between Shade and Kinbote, between Shade's poem and Kinbote's commentary: "The highest goal of scholarship, which is to recapture the life out of which the masterpiece emerged, to capture the life of the poem as well, is served, however lefthandedly, by Kinbote's scandalously unprofessional commentary on 'Pale Fire' " (43).

Moynahan's judicious monograph is an excellent brief introduction to Nabokov's work.

Bader, Julia. *Crystal Land: Artifice in Nabokov's English Novels.* Berkeley: Univ. of California Press, 1972.

Bader focuses on artists and artistry in her perceptive study of Nabokov's English novels. She stresses that she is not seeking allegorical equations, but rather "each character and plot is a study in the permutations of perception, sensibility, and imagination brought into contact with love, insanity, perversion, and death" (5).

In *The Real Life of Sebastian Knight*, Bader argues, Sebastian lives in his brother's recreation of his life. And both live in Nabokov's artistry, becoming "no more than reflections of the artistic preoccupation with different motifs" (15). The novel thus contains multiple mirroring, including reflections in Sebastian's novels and in V.'s dream. And all ultimately mirror the artistic process, the search for meaning.

Similarly, Bader finds in *Pale Fire* an "emotional-stylistic exploration of the artist's imagination" (31). Unfortunately, Bader falls prey to the then-popular distraction of trying to find the real author in the book: is Kinbote a creature of Shade's imagination, or vice versa? Bader opts for Shade as the central consciousness. True, Nabokov continues to play his game of mirrors here, piercing the realistic surface with rays of connection. But, as more recent critics argue, why cannot the reader accept all the characters as existing on the New Wye plane of reality, at the same time that they are all Nabokov's creatures? All are indeed "figments of the omniscient author's imagination" (40)—not just figments of Shade's.

In *Lolita* Bader recognizes "the compelling presence of the realistic foreground" (58), but through it glimpses the theme of artistry. The "real perversion," she contends, is not Humbert's nympholepsy but the book's "artistic originality" (66), which transcends the traditional. And perhaps the killing of Quilty dramatizes "Humbert's ritualistic killing of pseudo-art, which has defiled his own passionately loved art object" (76–77). In any case, the book lacks a stable "reality," despite momentary glimmers of "realism," and essentially "illuminates the undercurrents, both playful and agonizing, of the literary process" (81).

An even more "realistic" surface appears in *Pnin*, whose central character "is one of Nabokov's most 'alive' and touching creations" (83). Pnin is "part of an artistic design, but also reflect[s] the unfathomable deviations of life" (86)—he succeeds, for instance, in escaping the narrator at the end.

Bend Sinister too has a "realistic" surface, depicting "the integrity of a humane man confronted with mindless tyranny," yet it also "presents the image of the author manipulating a dreamer in the midst of a nightmare" (95). The author shapes the book (witness frequent hints that the work is still in process), and his stand-in Krug shapes what he can, "remain[ing] superior to the forces of totalitarianism, and retain[ing] his awareness of a brighter, gentler, more passionate mode of being" (114). Bader finds hints of this brighter mode in moths, puddles, and literary references, especially references to *Hamlet*.

In *Ada*, the last work Bader examines, Van "creates a fantasy world of passion where [his and Ada's] feelings for each other are mirrored onto imagined landscapes" (123). "Reality" becomes a matter of perception. Mirrors of the creative process include allusions, artist figures, repeated scenes, similar characters. Nabokov constructs mosaics of detail, fleeting and fragile moments "whose very discontinuities underline the mystery of human consciousness and the struggle to present this mystery" (140).

Bader's argument works best for Nabokov's most self-conscious works, like *Ada*—when, for example, she concludes that themes like love, perversion, death, and obsession are metaphors for art. Bader stresses that in such works Nabokov does not escape into aesthetics but presents his own version of reality, "a version of brilliantly and boldly inventive iridescence which mirrors the pain and rapture of perception" (160). Bader's lens for examining Nabokov's fiction may blind her to other elements—she finds artistry everywhere. Yet her work illumines a side of Nabokov acclaimed by critics since Khodasevich in 1937.

Bruss, Elizabeth W. "Vladimir Nabokov: Illusions of Reality and the Reality of Illusions." In *Autobiographical Acts: The Changing Situation of a Literary Genre*. Baltimore: Johns Hopkins Univ. Press, 1976, pp. 127–62.

As both an artist and a scientist, Nabokov recognizes that "[f]acts are never 'bare': they are the trajectory of the questions with which one began and the needs which initiated the inquiry" (128). Bruss shows how "Nabokov confronts the fictions in autobiography" (128), both in his autobiographical burlesque *Lolita* and in his "real" autobiography *Speak, Memory*.

Humbert of *Lolita*, Bruss notes, shifts from genre to genre: confession, case study, memoir, novel, among others. And he himself cannot be pigeonholed either. Yet his primary fault is that he is "a literalist of the imagination, willfully clinging to what he knows to be limited perspectives and evanescent realities" (131)—especially to his creation of Lolita out of Dolores. He attempts "to copulate with his own dreams and to murder his own nightmares in his vengeful guilt and disappointment" (134). Unlike Humbert, Nabokov himself is attentive to others in *Speak, Memory*, and he does not dwell on the most dramatic intimate events, the killing of his father, the courting of his wife. He becomes "a transparency rather than an image, a means of access to experience rather than an actor" (139).

Moreover, Nabokov celebrates "the consciousness of illusion" (135). His autobiography does not have "an a priori shape, an identity fixed forever by a process of religious conversion or historical necessity or even the 'laws' of association"; instead, it derives from "a creative act, involving imagery and careful counterpoise to bring out the design which otherwise might be undetectable" (137). Thematic repetition allows a temporary fixing of evanescent details in art. Unlike Humbert, too eager to prove the truth and therefore missing it (though indirectly revealing it), Nabokov attends to the implications of perception and memory and recognizes the inevitable unreality of the autobiographical act.

Humbert's warping of experience includes his attempt to quote other characters—contrary to Nabokov's practice in his autobiography. Humbert likewise warps time and space, trying to create a two-dimensional world, trying to solipsize Lolita (without recognizing how circumscribed his own world is), trying to annihilate time. (And in attempting to make sense of Humbert's faulty time scheme, Bruss flirts with the possibility that Humbert simply imagined killing Quilty, a metaphor for destroying himself.) Nabokov, though, conscious and responsible, is receptive to coincidence in *Speak, Memory* as well as to traditional configurations of time and space. He recognizes "the conventionality of all measurements" and can "treat any moment as if it were the present and all places—even the far-off shores of Russia—as if they were here" (148). Central to Nabokov's art is consciousness, which "transforms the past, as a new level of perception makes a new configuration accessible" (152). Nabokov's perceptions do not, however, become shrilly insistent. He simply shows what he does, unlike Humbert, who tries to reify images of himself. And Nabokov respects his audience, unlike Humbert, who tries to tyrannize. Nabokov's perceptive reader can nevertheless, with the help of Nabokov's index, itself an aesthetic object, trace the filiations among, say, pavilions, stained glass, jewels, butterflies.

Comparing Nabokov and Humbert may inevitably lead one to denigrate Humbert. Bruss may be right to mistrust protean Humbert's final declaration of humanity, his guilt and sorrow over his treatment of Lolita. But she ultimately reduces Humbert to a fraud, minimizing his vitality and his conflicting impulses, some humane. Still, her analysis of *Speak, Memory* is sensitive. And she examines a work too often ignored, as if critics dismissed it as bare fact, not a work of art.

Grayson, Jane. *Nabokov Translated: A Comparison of Nabokov's Russian and English Prose*. Oxford: Oxford Univ. Press, 1977.

In this excellent, painstaking study, Grayson examines Nabokov's translations, primarily those of his Russian work into English. He always at least supervised the translations: they always bear his imprint.

The novels that Nabokov revised most—*Laughter in the Dark (Camera Obscura)*, *Despair (Otchayanie)*, *The Eye (Soglyadatai)*, and *King, Queen, Knave (Korol', dama, valet)*—share "a consistent cold detachment" (26), the characters remaining creatures of the author. Nabokov's revisions tend to increase the detachment, to tighten structure and heighten verbal effects: "Nabokov dresses up his characters in bright costumes, teaches them to project their voices, he burnishes the set until it glitters; he then takes his reader, sits him in the upper balcony and hands him a pair of opera glasses—the reader has become a spectator" (114). Grayson demonstrates all these effects with extensive catalogs of modifications in structure, characterization, and style.

Nabokov revised other works less extensively. These works, including *Mary (Mashen'ka)*, *The Gift (Dar)*, and *Lolita* (translated into Russian), generally rely less on pattern and plot and more on emotional involvement with the hero. Thus Nabokov increased the artifice in his translations only when such an increase was thematically appropriate. Similarly Nabokov made only minor revisions in translating short stories and drama and also, at times, when reissuing a work in the same language (for example, when converting *New Yorker* short stories into *Pnin*).

Nabokov extensively reworked chapters of his autobiography—from

English (or French) to English to Russian to English. Although some additions reflect greater recall of details, some changes (such as those that tighten structure) reflect a more literary motive. As in some of his other translations, Nabokov lengthens the perspective, but here such distancing leads not only to greater detachment but also to greater understanding and nostalgia. Nabokov's practice, in translating himself, thus differs from the literal translation he eventually espoused when translating others. Sometimes he modifies the cultural reference, as when he substitutes an allusion to Shakespeare for an allusion to Pushkin. Often he sacrifices sense to sound, more eager to preserve a formal effect than a precise meaning.

Grayson concludes with comments on Nabokov's style. His English, she argues, has improved over time, yet still he seeks the esoteric, "deliberately retain[ing] certain russicisms and select[ing] unusual vocabulary in order to impart an originality and individuality to his style," making it impossible "to draw any clear distinction between what is 'foreign' or 'non-standard' and what is original and calculated to enrich the scope of the English language" (190). And perhaps being a "foreigner" gives Nabokov a fresh perspective on the language: "He sees patterns of sound and potential meanings in words which the native speaker, his perception dulled through familiarity, would simply pass over. He deviates more readily from set modes of expression and conventional registers of style, inventing new and arresting word combinations, employing high-flown, recherché vocabulary alongside the most mundane colloquialisms. The results are not always successful—some of Nabokov's English writing is uneven, some is mannered and contrived—but at its best this 'foreignness,' this fresh off-centre vision, can make for that 'strangeness', that *ostranenie* which, as a fictitious Nabokov has acknowledged in interview, is central to all true artistic perception" (216).

Grayson's scholarship is sound and, although she suggests some intriguing conclusions about Nabokov's style, her work is perhaps most useful as a reference for scholars examining Nabokov's revisions. One drawback is that she frequently invites the reader to admire the difference between Russian and English versions—without translating the Russian. Thus the book is most valuable to the scholar who knows Russian. But it is valuable to others nonetheless.

Merrill, Robert. "Nabokov and Fictional Artifice." *Modern Fiction Studies*, 25 (1979), 439–62.

Merrill counters the view that Nabokov's works are primarily about art by suggesting that such a view obscures their richness. He argues that slightly more than half of Nabokov's novels focus on the fates of characters—are "represented actions"—and thus artifice and authorial intrusions are subordinate. Nabokov may not always identify or sympathize with his characters, yet in most of his Russian novels the characters are the center of interest—as also in *Lolita*.

Merrill acknowledges the verbal patterns in *Lolita*, the trail left by Quilty, but points out that Humbert claims responsibility for them. We need not look outside the novel for the source of these patterns—we need not consider them evidence of an intrusive authorial voice. In fact, we can locate the novel's distinction not in artifice but in character: in "the creation of one of modern fiction's most interesting and complex characters" (451).

Pale Fire, on the other hand, is more artificial. But Merrill laments that too much criticism of it has been devoted to annotating details and tracing patterns, too little to explicating meaning. What is its meaning? Character here is less important than in *Lolita*, and we must find the focus of the novel elsewhere: in Shade's and Kinbote's efforts to cope with mortality, with the extinction of thought and feeling, through art and love. Both attempt to overcome mortality, but both inevitably fail: "art is the most precious human product, yet art makes nothing happen. Let us fight the utter degradation, ridicule, and horror of death, but let us not suppose that this fight will be 'won' in the sense that Shade and Kinbote suggest" (461–62). Though the struggle can never be won, the book's meaning nevertheless inheres in this struggle. And thus we oversimplify even as metafictional a book as *Pale Fire* if we consider it merely metafiction.

Pifer, Ellen. *Nabokov and the Novel.* Cambridge: Harvard Univ. Press, 1980. Portions of this book originally appeared in the *Slavic and East European Journal* (1978) and *Modern Fiction Studies* (1979).

In contrast to critics like Bader, who find Nabokov's central theme in art, Pifer finds it in consciousness. She eloquently combats the assumption that Nabokov preferred artifice to humanity; while not denying his artistry, she focuses on Nabokov's humanism and commitment to moral truth. She examines Nabokov's most "artificial" works, and also those that have received less critical attention.

Pifer starts with a discussion of literary characters, countering charges that Nabokov is manipulative. She reminds us that all characters are constructs, though some authors are more covert than others. And plausibility depends on consonance with "the author's vision of reality and . . . the logic of his method in rendering this reality" (10). If we remember that we always "represent the world to ourselves" by means of constructs, we can understand why "[a]rt is, for Nabokov, a means of grappling with the nature of reality, not a retreat from it" (13).

In *King, Queen, Knave*, as in other novels, Nabokov does not "approximat[e] our general notions of reality" (23) but rather examines the operations of consciousness in perceiving the world: the differences in characters' perceptions, not the gross similarities. And therein lies their autonomy: "By demonstrating that each man's world—that privately created construct—is more 'subjective' than we commonly think, Nabokov, the alleged literary despot, affords his 'galley slaves' a potential freedom that is inaccessible to the characters of formal realism" (32). A character like Dreyer attains some measure of autonomy and consciousness, especially in contrast with bestial, mechanical Martha and Franz.

Like Dreyer, Cincinnatus of *Invitation to a Beheading* has more consciousness than those around him, a "gnostical turpitude" that the totalitarian state finds inimical. Comparisons with Tolstoy and Solzhenitsyn illumine how Nabokov's artifice can nonetheless be traditionally humanistic, how artifice allows Nabokov to locate "the triumphs of human consciousness outside, or beyond, the temporal sphere of historical reality—where tyranny, brute force, and 'better guns' will always have a field day" (67).

Bend Sinister similarly portrays how totalitarianism attempts to crush the individual. Where Cincinnatus is in danger of granting too much reality to his sham environment, though, Krug does not sufficiently recognize the threat.

Pifer then turns to Nabokov's toying with doubles. Much as Hermann of *Despair* is not a true artist, despite his pretentions, he has not found a true double in Felix. Doubles are never real: characters who see sameness do violence to the individual. Unwilling to condone murder, Pifer also condemns Humbert of *Lolita*, refusing "to obscure the moral and psychological issues with which Humbert himself has to grapple" (108). Pifer denies Quilty any symbolic status as Humbert's double. (I would argue that he has some.) She is right, though, not to reduce either Shade or Kinbote of *Pale Fire* to a double, as earlier critics like Bader have attempted. Yet Pifer is unwilling to acknowledge links between the two characters, or between poem and commentary, unwilling to "perpetrate the law of averages, obscuring the nature of each character's unique reality" (117).

For Nabokov, then, reality, is unique—and he rebels against the traditional realism of the novel, much as the first novelists rebelled against their forebears. Like the first novelists he seeks to be true to individual experience—not to the conventional and familiar.

Pifer digresses from her main theme in her discussion of *Ada*, where the moral yardstick she has used no longer applies. For in *Ada*, Nabokov's most self-conscious novel, "the middle range of human experience [is] largely obliterated" (134), and the godlike Van and Ada are superhuman, at times inhuman. Van's art and ardor are devastating to human life. And although Pifer suggests that its devastation pales in comparison with that on our own Terra, she has trouble accommodating *Ada* to Nabokov's commitment to moral truth, to the beneficent influence of consciousness.

Pifer concludes her superb study by stressing Nabokov's commitment to moral as well as aesthetic principles. He revered kindness: "Only in the realm of art did he advocate dictatorship" (162). And art itself must be free from external constraints: "Only in unique, independent, and essentially nonutilitarian forms, then, does art embody the true nature of man, who may not justifiably be subverted to serve any individual or collective will" (169).

Peterson, Dale E. "Nabokov's *Invitation*: Literature as Execution." *PMLA*, 96 (1981), 824–36.

Countering the early critics who isolate Nabokov on lexical playfields, Peterson joins recent critics, like Bruss and Pifer, who find Nabokov moral. In *Invitation to a Beheading*, "Nabokov's most autonomous, self-enclosed fictional world," Peterson sees "an honest solution to the problem of perpetuating a humanist and ethical literature once we have seen through the convention of nineteenth-century narrative realism" (825).

Too often critics have reduced *Invitation* to allegory, whether political or artistic. But Nabokov's work resists allegory, trapping the reader into tangled complicity, such that "Nabokov's writing makes us feel the terror of being subject to arbitrary revisions and reruns inside an announced plan of execution" (827). The jailer Rodion is not the only one peering through the peephole, aching to tear Cincinnatus apart: "Both the reading of novels and the analysis of character are acts of cannibalism at a metaphoric level; the ultimate aim of the activity is to suck the final marrow of meaning from the perfectly exposed innards of a perfectly executed figure" (831).

Cincinnatus tries to resist an entrapment that "is simultaneously political, philosophical, marital—and, of course, ineluctably fictional" (828). Society tries to entrap him by labeling him, making him transparent, but he remains opaque. Why is the opaque Cincinnatus so long captive to "this pathetically patched, outmoded society" (829)? Because he seeks tangible pleasures and literal escape, and he reads reality into his plot, like an unwary reader, "a captive of his own trust in semblances and verisimilitude" (832). Even his writing can trap him—it can objectify not only his yearning for freedom but also his sense of imprisonment.

What then do we make of Cincinnatus' escape at the end? Or of the escape of one Cincinnatus, the other falling victim to the executioner? Instead of providing a neat ending, Nabokov startles us, inciting us to think about liberation and about vitality, which "shimmers with the aura of a multivariable dimensionality that is impossible to catch in the commonplace mirrors of daylight realism" (833).

Nabokov would agree with advocates of moral fiction that art should not oversimplify, but he would disagree about method. Since art is not identical with reality, nor a substitute, he would "spoil the illusion of lifelike narrative so that the reader would become conscious of the true chasm between lived experience and imaginative activity" (834). Moral fiction thus reminds us of the unreality of art, and true humanity may inhere in eluding narrative imprisonment, as Cincinnatus does. Peterson himself succeeds in capturing Cincinnatus for us, momentarily, and then freeing him, his memory resonating in our consciousness.

Index